Memoirs of the Notorious

STEPHEN BURROUGHS

of New Hampshire

With a preface by

ROBERT FROST

LINCOLN MAC VEAGH

THE DIAL PRESS

NEW YORK · MCMXXIV

PRINTED IN U. S. A.

VAIL-BALLOU PRESS, INC.
BINGHAMTON AND NEW YORK

PREFACE

By Robert Frost

Pelham, Massachusetts, may never have produced anything else; it had a large part in producing the *Memoirs of the Notorious Stephen Burroughs*—this good book; or at least in starting the author on the criminal career of which it is a record. I like setting up the claim for Pelham, because I once lived there or thereabouts. But it is the kind of town I should have wanted to magnify anyway, whether I had lived in it or not, just one high old street along a ridge, not much to begin with and every year beautifully less. The railroads have worked modern magic against it from away off in the valleys and the woods have pressed in upon it till now there is nothing left but the church where Burroughs preached his unsanctified sermons, a few houses (among them, possibly, the one where he preached the funeral sermon that began his undoing), and here and there a good mowing field of about the size of a tea-tray in the sky.

I was back there the other day looking for Burroughs, and I saw three great ghosts instead of one, Burroughs, the rogue, Glazier Wheeler, the coiner, and Daniel Shays, the rebel, a shining company. Such places always have all their great men at once, as if they were neither born nor self-made, but created each other. I suppose I saw the three as they must have gotten together to talk subversion of an evening at the Leanders'. Poor old Shays! He was so scared by his own rebellion that once he started running away from it, he never stopped till he got to Sandgate, Vermont,—if you can imagine how far out of the world that is—at any rate it was then outside of the United States. Burroughs should have told us more about his Pelham friends, and especially about Glazier Wheeler, who on his serious side was concerned with the transmutation of metals and may have been a necromancer.

[v]

PREFACE

I was anxious to ask Burroughs if he wouldn't agree with me that his own chief distinction was hypocrisy. Many will be satisfied to see in him just another specimen of the knowing rascal. I choose to take it that he is here raised up again as an example to us of the naïve hypocrite.

We assume that by virtue of being bad we are at least safe from being hypocrites. But are we any such thing? We bad people I should say had appearances to keep up no less dangerously than the good. The good must at all costs seem good; that is the weakness of their position. But the bad must seem amiable and engaging. They must often have to pass for large-hearted when it is nothing but a strain on the heart that makes the heart secretly sick. That is one curse that is laid on them; and another is that in every out-and-out clash with the righteous they must try to make themselves out more right than the righteous. You can see what that would lead to. No, I am afraid hypocrisy is as increasing to evil as it is diminishing to good.

I was not a church-goer at the time when Burroughs was preaching in Pelham, and there may have been circumstances in aggravation that he does not set down, but, let him tell it, I see little in the story to count against him. If the sermons were sound and the preacher able, it couldn't have mattered much that they were stolen and he not ordained. Technically, he was an impostor. and I suppose I am too inclined to be lenient with irregularity in both school and church. But I remember that Melchizedek was not a Levite and men have taught in colleges with no degree beyond a bachelor's. And take Burroughs' first serious lapse in attempting to pass counterfeit money in Springfield. Crime couldn't be made more excusable. Just one little dollar at a drugstore in the interests of scientific experiment and to save the tears of a lovely lady. I suspect he was not frank with us about what brought him sneaking back to Pelham after he was driven out with pitchforks. The friendship of the Leanders, was it? And equally that of Mr. and Mrs. Leander? And not at all the poetic young dream of easy money? The sweet hypocrite, we must never let him drop.

And couldn't he write, couldn't he state things? In his lifetime, he made the only two revolts from Puritanism anyone has yet thought

PREFACE

of, one backwards into Paganism and the other, let us say, sideways into the Catholic Church. In making the first, he put the case for Paganism almost as well as Milton puts it in the mouth of the sorcerer Comus: "We that are of purer fire." How well he argues against holding anyone locked up in a jail in a free country, and in favor of free coining in a free country!

I should like to have heard his reasons for winding up in the Catholic Church. I can conceive of their being honest. Probably he was tired of his uncharted freedom out of jail and wanted to be moral and a Puritan again as when a child, but this time under a cover where he couldn't be made fun of by the intellectuals. The course might commend itself to the modern Puritan (what there is left of the modern Puritan).

Let me tell the reader where he must put this book if he will please me and why there. On the same shelf with Benjamin Franklin and Jonathan Edwards (grandfather of Aaron Burr). Franklin will be a reminder of what we have been as a young nation in some respects, Edwards in others. Burroughs comes in reassuringly when there is question of our not unprincipled wickedness, whether we have had enough of it for salt. The world knows we are criminal enough. We commit our share of blind and inarticulate murder, for instance. But sophisticated wickedness, the kind that knows its grounds and can twinkle, could we be expected to have produced so fine a flower in a pioneer state? The answer is that we had it and had it early in Stephen Burroughs (not to mention Aaron Burr). It is not just a recent publisher's importation from Europe.

Could anything recent be more teasing to our proper prejudices than the way Burroughs mixed the ingredients when he ran off on his travels? He went not like a fool with no thought for the future and nothing to his name but the horse between his legs. He took with him a pocketful of sermons stolen from his father, in one fell act combining prudence, a respect for religion (as property) and a respect for his father (as a preacher). *He* knew how to put the reverse on a ball so that when it was going it was also coming. It argues a sophisticated taste in the society around him that he should have found friends such as the Leanders to enjoy his jokes with him.

[vii]

PREFACE

A book that I for one should be sorry to have missed. I have to thank my friend W. R. Brown for bringing it to my attention.

South Shaftsbury, Vermont
1924

PUBLISHER'S FOREWORD

This amazing record of boyhood pranks, mature adventure, and crime, written with an engaging frankness not surpassed by Casanova himself, prince of philosophic rascals, is here reprinted from the Albany edition of 1811. That edition was published while the author was still alive and is the earliest which has come into my hands. Its text and notes are here reproduced. Changes have been made in the somewhat unusual grammar, spelling, and punctuation, only when necessary to make the meaning clear to the modern reader. The Appendix with its statement, "Burroughs resides at present" etc., is retained. But since I have found some later remarks in regard to Burroughs' closing years which appear to me to shed some light upon his character, and consequently upon the actions of which he gives an account in the *Memoirs*, I here subjoin them.

FROM THE AMHERST EDITION OF 1858

Much that has been said and published regarding the later years of Burroughs' life and the fortunes of his family is purely fictitious, or so much travestied as scarcely to be recognized by the side of the simple truth. It was long believed by many that he became a Roman Catholic priest and was immediately raised to a high dignity in that church, where he accumulated great wealth by the perquisites of his office, by pardoning sins and granting indulgences. Nothing is farther from the truth. He did indeed become a Catholic; but instead of holding a high position, he spent his days as a humble penitent, seeking forgiveness for the multiplied offenses of a long life of sin.

Respecting his career after the time at which his Memoir closes, not much is known that can be called authentic. That his career was full of incident we cannot doubt; for a temperament so energetic, to say nothing of passions and propensities so active as his, could not endure thirty or forty years of tame, common-place existence. It is to be re-

[ix]

gretted that he did not continue his autobiography, so Franklin-like in its simplicity and truthfulness, down to the three score years and ten which he not only attained but passed beyond. But with the exception of a few well-authenticated facts, the last half of his life is shrouded in a darkness which the biographer cannot hope to penetrate. These facts we now present to the reader.

From the period at which his Memoir closes, down to the spring of 1799, he lived with his father at Hanover, N. H., in great harmony, and had the chief management of his farm and business in general. The parents seem to have taken great satisfaction and comfort in their son and his children, and expressed that satisfaction in letters to friends as well as by a course of kind parental treatment of him. In one of the father's letters he says: "During the time that he has resided with me (which is about two years and a half) he has conducted to my good acceptance. As an evidence of confidence in him, I have committed to his care the whole management of my temporal affairs, and have hitherto been well satisfied as to the wisdom, propriety and economy of his management; as also with the dutiful and affectionate temper with which he has attended to and treated his parents."

But this pleasant state of things was not of many years' duration. They commenced building a large house, and, like many others who undertake to build, they did not count the cost, and became embarrassed. This led to uneasiness and mutual crimination, and finally to open rupture and separation. The sorrowing father was compelled by a sense of duty to retract the approval quoted above, and abandon the hope that his son would ever experience a true, reliable, and permanent reformation. Burroughs went to Canada, and settled at Shipton, where he commenced business as a manufacturer of, and dealer in, counterfeit money. There being then no law in Canada to forbid the counterfeiting of the United States currency, either paper or metallic, he carried on his nefarious business with entire impunity, and on a large scale, and by means of his agents kept a constant current of spurious money flowing into "the States."

At some time, we know not when, and by means we know not what, he was led to repent sincerely of his evil ways, and to abandon not only them but the place where he had practiced them, and the associates with whom he had been connected. He removed to a small Canadian town called Three Rivers, and there passed the remainder of his days in quiet and usefulness. He engaged successfully in school-teaching, and there are several graduates of American colleges whose preparatory studies were pursued under his tuition. He lived to a good old age, and died, it is believed, a peaceful death.

A gentleman who visited him when he was about seventy years old says: "He seemed altogether absorbed in his studies and in the contemplation of his speedy departure to a better life; but never serious, certainly not sad, and not often grave or solemn, but more commonly playful and always cheerful. But he never, save once, in the remotest allusion, referred to his former course of life. In one of our first interviews, when conversation took rather a sombre direction with reference to my own broken health at the time, he said he thought I need not be discouraged. He did not expect to live out half his days when he was at my age, but was now nearly seventy. I inquired if his health was feeble at that period of life. 'No,' said he, 'but every one then said I should be hanged before I was forty!'

"I was often at his rooms, and derived much satisfaction, and no little advantage, from his conversation. He had an extensive library of choice books, seemed to be a busy student, and much employed in writing. His room was hung round with copies or originals of the masterpieces of some of the distinguished painters of Christian life and suffering, and everything about him indicated very convincingly the genuineness of his repentance and reformation. Few men possessed such extraordinary powers of conversation. His manners were courteous and dignified, without being distant or affected, and he possessed the happy faculty of communicating vast stores of knowledge, which his extensive reading and long and varied experience of life had accumulated, without any apparent consciousness of his being the instructor, or yourself the pupil. I left him with sincere regret, and with unaffected admiration of his strongly diversified talents, and most extraordinary conversion from a life of sin and crime to one of penitence and devotion."

Since the *Memoirs of Stephen Burroughs* was first brought to my attention by Mr. Robert Frost (who more likely than he to pitch upon this remarkable product of New England?), I have consulted many

[xi]

FOREWORD

readers but have found none in whom the name of Stephen Burroughs evoked even the ghost of a memory. Yet the *Memoirs* was once an immensely popular book, to judge from the number of editions published in the first half of the last century. That it was deservedly popular and will be popular again. and occupy a secure if modest place in our literature, I have no doubt. As a document bearing on the cultural conditions in this country at the end of the 18th century it is obviously of first-rate importance; it is a most entertaining narrative of adventure; but more important for its enduring fame, it is the complete self-revelation of a character. what Carlyle would have called a Book, fixing in indelible lines a portrait of the individual, Burroughs, and the type of the Eternal Scamp.

L. MacV.

New York, May, 1924.

MEMOIRS

OF THE NOTORIOUS

STEPHEN BURROUGHS

OF NEW HAMPSHIRE

The following is a Letter from the Author to a Friend,[1] who had requested a Narrative of his Life.

Washington, 25th July, 1794.

DEAR SIR,

THE uninterrupted attention of your politeness to my welfare since my arrival in this country, is a sufficient inducement for me to attend to any request which you shall barely intimate. You mentioned yesterday, whilst I was enjoying the agreeable society of your family, that a relation of my adventures would be highly gratifying at some convenient time, when opportunity would serve. You say, that what had come to your knowledge previous to any acquaintance with me, but more especially what has occurred since my residence in this place, has filled you with an almost irresistible anxiety to be made acquainted with the more minute circumstances of a life which has been filled with so many curious anecdotes and unheard of occurrences. I fear the relation will poorly answer your expectations. My life, it is true, has been one continued course of tumult, revolution and vexation; and such as it is, I will give to you in detail, (in this method, rather than verbally, it being more convenient to peruse it at your leisure, than to listen to the dull tale of egotisms which I must make use of in a verbal relation). When you become tired with reading, you will be under no necessity of holding the book in your hand from the feelings of delicacy, but can lay it by at leisure. This liberty you could not so conveniently take with a dull relater of a more dull narrative. You say my character, to you, is an enigma; that I possess an uncommon share of sensibility, and at the same time, maintain an equality of mind which is uncommon, particularly in the midst of those occurrences which are calculated to wound the feelings. I have learned fortitude in the school of adversity. In draining the cup of bitterness to its dregs, I have been taught to despise the occurrences of misfortune. This one thing I fully believe, that our happiness is in our power more than is generally thought; or at least, we have the ability of preventing that misery which is so common to unfortunate situations. No state or condition in life, but from which we may (if we exercise that reason which the God of Nature has given

---

[1] The *Memoirs* are written in the form of a long letter addressed to this gentleman.

[1]

us) draw comfort and happiness. We are too apt to be governed by the opinion of others, and if they think our circumstances unhappy, to consider them so ourselves, and of course, make them so. The state of the mind is the only criterion of happiness or misery. The Cynic Diogenes was more happy than the Conqueror Alexander, and the Philosopher Socrates more happy than either. They all had, undoubtedly, passions and feelings alike, which, not properly regulated, would have rendered them equally unhappy. Yet, whenever reason stood at helm, the vessel was brought into the haven of peace.

[2]

CHAPTER I

"Full well I know you; deep, too deep engrav'd
On memory's tablet your rude horrors live."

IN relating the facts of my life to you, I shall endeavor to give as simple an account of them as I am able, without coloring or darkening any circumstances; although the relation of many matters will give me a degree and kind of pain, which only they who feel can describe. I have often lamented my neglect of keeping minutes of the occurrences of my life, from time to time, when they were fresh in my memory, and alive to my feelings; the disadvantage of which I now feel, when I come to run over in my mind the chain which has connected the events together. Many circumstances are entirely lost, and many more so obscurely remembered, that I shall not even attempt to give them a place in this account. Not to trouble you with any more prefatory remarks, I will proceed to the relation.

I am the only son of a clergyman, living in Hanover, in the state of New Hampshire; and, were any to expect merit from their parentage, I might justly look for that merit. But I am so far a republican, that I consider a man's merit to rest entirely with himself, without any regard to family, blood, or connection. My father being a Presbyterian by principle, I was educated in all the rigor of that order, which illy suited my volatile, impatient temper of mind; this being the case, my first entrance on the stage of life, was by no means the most agreeable. My thirst for amusement was insatiable, and as in my situation, the only dependence for that gratification was entirely within myself, I sought it in pestering others, especially those who were my superiors in age, and in making them appear in a ludicrous situation, so as to raise the laugh at their expense, and partake of the general diversion, which such a matter created. My success in those undertakings was so great, that I became the terror of the people where I lived, and all were very unanimous in declaring, that Stephen Burroughs was the worst boy in town; and those who could get him

[3]

whipt were most worthy of esteem. Their attempts to bring on my back a flagellation were often very successful. for my heedless temper seldom studied for a retreat, when I was fairly in danger; however. the repeated application of this birchen medicine never cured my pursuit of fun. A neighbor of my father, an old man, had a fine yard of watermelons, which had been purloined by somebody for three or four succeeding nights; the old man, being of a hasty, petulant disposition, was determined to watch his watermelons. with a club, and severely beat the thief. One night he took his stand in a convenient place for watching, unknown to any one. Accident made me acquainted with the old man's situation, and suspecting his intention, I went to a son of his, a young man of about twenty, and told him I saw a man in the watermelon yard, whom I suspected to be the thief, and advised him to go cautiously to the yard, and peradventure he might catch him. Accordingly the young man went; but no sooner had he got into the yard, than the old man. supposing this to be the thief, rushed from his hiding place, and attacked his son with his club, and severely handled the poor fellow before he found out his mistake: the son, supposing the thief was beating him, bawled out to his father, who he expected was at the house, "Murder! father! father! murder! murder!" This scene of merriment I enjoyed to the full, but soon paid for it through the nose. The plot being discovered, and the agent who set this machine in motion clearly detected, complaint was made, and I tasted of the same food I had so ingeniously cooked for the old man's son. I should hardly mention the insipid anecdotes of my childish years, were it not for the purpose of showing how those small occurrences had a decided influence in giving a tone to the character which I sustain at this time, and in directing the operations of my after life. So much do the greatest events depend upon circumstances so minute, that they often pass unobserved, and consequently, wrong causes are attributed to the effects which take place. Being passionately fond of information. I embraced all opportunities for reading, which my desultory life would admit, and unfortunately many novels fell in my way, of that kind, which had a direct tendency to blow the fire of my temper into a tenfold rage. The character of Guy, Earl of Warwick, was my favorite. I felt an enthusiastic ardor to tread the stage on which he had so fortunately exhibited. I often

[4]

viewed myself at the head of armies, rushing with impetuosity into the thickest of embattled foes, and bearing down all who dared to oppose me. Reading and dwelling so much on those romantic scenes, at that early period of life, when judgment was weak, was attended with very pernicious consequences in the operations of my after conduct. Nothing gives the mind of childhood a more unfavorable bias, than a representation of those unnatural characters exhibited in novels and romances. It has a direct tendency to lead the mind from the plain simple path of nature, into the airy regions of fancy; and when the mind is once habituated to calculate on the romantic system, error and irregularity are the common consequences. Likewise, when a man is long habituated to think erroneously, we can hardly expect that he will be able to root out the first unfavorable sentiments of his education. I will candidly confess, that I too strongly feel the truth of this doctrine, even to this day. Permit me here to digress a moment from the narrative, and offer a remark on education for your consideration. The motives of the most sincere friendship to you and your family induce me to do it. I have been in the habit of educating youth for seven years, constantly; in the course of my business, I have endeavored to study the operations of the human heart, that I might be able to afford that instruction which would be salutary; and in this, I find one truth clearly established, viz. a child will endeavor to be, what you make him think mankind in general are. His first ambition is to be like his parents; he soon finds that his neighbors, the inhabitants of the country, nay, the world of mankind, are to be his associates for life, and to whom it is necessary for him to recommend himself, in order to enjoy the benefit of their society, without alloy; he therefore endeavors to assimulate himself to the character which he supposes mankind generally possess. This motive, I believe, has an operation more or less on every man. If these remarks are just, which I think no observing man will deny, how evident is this truth, that a child, in forming his own character. will be essentially directed by that idea which you instil into his mind respecting mankind? Give him an idea, that the inhabitants of the world esteem virtue, integrity, mildness, and modesty, and that the contrary are obnoxious to them, he will be most likely to pursue that course unremittingly. Perhaps an objection may arise in your mind, to the truth

[5]

of this observation, and you will say, it often happens that those, who are the most strict in cultivating principles of integrity in the minds of their children, are disappointed in their endeavors to make the children virtuous. In answer to this objection, I will observe, that our actions are as strong a language, and perhaps stronger, than our words; and as the observations of children are extremely keen, they discover at once, whether our words and our actions speak the same language; and when they find them interfering, they immediately conclude, that deception is the object of the parent, and not sincerity, that he utters words that he does not believe himself, and puts on a false appearance to answer some sinister end; a view of which insensibly leads the child into the practice of dissimulation. The ambition in children of becoming like their superiors, rightly directed, is of the utmost importance, in forming them such as they ought to be. To grant a child your approbation, when doing, or desiring to do right, is a reward which he will ever seek after, when he thinks it within his reach; therefore, to keep that reward uniformly within his power, is a matter of importance; and not, by indulging a petulant disposition, destroy or render doubtful his expectations of obtaining what he merits. Here you establish the first principles of justice in his mind, upon which he will practice, when he becomes an active member of society. As the child advances to a riper state, and becomes what is generally termed a youth, he feels the strength of his disposition for assimilating his character to the feelings of mankind increase, and he will adopt such measures as his judgment then dictates; hence, to inform his judgment, is the only way to make him capable of conducting well; to restrain him, by dictatorial dogmas, from the paths of error, will answer but a temporary purpose; until he learns by the lessons of reason, or by the more feeling effects of prudence, he never will be in a capacity to act his part in life with propriety. We must expect to find many errors in the calculations of youthful years, and those errors ought to be pruned by the most careful hand, lest the harshness of the pruning should appear to the subject the cruel stroke of an enemy, rather than the gentle touch of a friend. To censure the faults of youth beyond what they ought to bear, is generally attended with fatal consequences. It destroys the object of their pursuit, viz. approbation; they revolt at the injustice, which they sensibly

[6]

CASE OF A YOUTH NAMED DODGE

feel; therefore, inflicting unjust punishment is generally attended with fatal consequences in the system of education. It destroys the principles of equity in the youthful breast, and substitutes in their room, the despotic principles of tyranny. This cause strongly operates in society. Hence, my Lord Hale, with great pertinency and humanity says, "better ten guilty escape, than one innocent person suffer." I have often seen instances where the ambition of youth to do well, has been destroyed, by censuring their faults with too much severity; one of which I will mention. I once taught a school in a town of Massachusetts, by the name of Charlton. Having a school consisting of eighty members, I divided them, according to my usual custom, into two classes. My school, at this time, was entirely regulated according to my mind, and in the most obedient order, greatly to the satisfaction of the parents of the children, who frequented the school. Application was made to me at this time, by a clergyman in the vicinity, for the admission of his son into the school. With great difficulty I persuaded the committee, who had the direction of admitting members, to admit him. My desire for his admission sprang from the same cause which the committee's aversion did. The youth was fifteen years of age, and had been expelled from all the schools in the country, consequently, whatever Dodge, the name of this youth, was concerned in, must, in the opinion of people, be adopted from a wrong motive. Convinced from my own feelings under similar circumstances, that a different line of conduct towards him, from what had been observed, would produce a different effect, I was desirous of trying the experiment. Accordingly, when he came to my school, I intimated to him, that he must take the lead of one of the classes, which composed the school; and that I expected from his exertions and example, his class would make a very respectable appearance. I endeavored to convince him, that this appointment was not from design, but from a real esteem of his merit, by showing him many little distinctions. His conduct, for about twelve or fourteen days, was equal to my most sanguine expectations; but returning from dinner one day, I found the school in an uproar at the conduct of Dodge, who, in my absence, had gone into the upper loft of the house, and had most scandalously insulted some young women, who were at the back side of the schoolhouse. Complaint was made of this, with all the exag-

[7]

gerations which are apt to attend the transgression of such a character. Dodge himself was present at the time, and discovered that mortification in his countenance, which made me feel sensibly affected for him. I treated the report as though I could not believe that Dodge had conducted in such a manner as to render it possible, that the thing should be as represented; that some mistake must have existed, and refused to pay any further attention to it. It would have been to you, sir, a matter of curiosity, to have observed the workings of the countenance of Dodge under this trial; and when he found that my confidence in him was yet unshaken, so contrary to his fears, I was really afraid he would have fainted. This had the desired effect. Never had I one in my school who conducted better afterwards, during his whole continuance with me, which was about a year.

I would not wish to be understood that a relaxation of discipline is ever to be admitted; on the contrary, the most uniform course of this administration should be attended to, without the least deviation. Our commands, in the first place, ought to be reasonable, humane, and parental, calculated to promote, not only the good of the subject of our government, but likewise embracing for their object, the benefit of the whole community. When the commands are once given, never ought we to suffer a breach of them under any circumstances whatever. By such a practice we make good subjects, good legislators, and good executors. By these means we habituate our youth to submit to good and wholesome laws, without being in danger of that restless turbulent disposition, which so frequently distracts the government of a Commonwealth. We likewise make them good legislators, by giving them constant examples, in our mode of governing them, of justice, humanity, and parental kindness; and when those principles are once established in the human breast, the governing object of such characters will be, to enact and establish such laws as will distribute and support the genuine and real principles of their education. They, likewise, will make men, who, in their executive capacity, will promote the highest good of society, by uniformly adhering to an undeviating course of executing laws to which they are appointed. But I return from this digression to the narrative.

[8]

CHAPTER II

BEING possessed with the most romantic ideas of military prowess, I longed for an opportunity of signalizing myself in that department, and consequently, embraced the first opportunity of entering into the military line. At this time a regiment of the continental forces, commanded by Col. Hazen, were marching through the country where I lived, and I, at the age of fourteen, enlisted into an artillery company attending the regiment, as a private soldier. This circumstance soon coming to the knowledge of my father, he applied to the officer under whom I had enlisted, and obtained my discharge. Chagrined and disappointed at this unexpected repulse, I concluded that all my prospects for fame were at an end, knowing of no other opportunity by which I could, probably, introduce myself into the military department. The regiment were on a march, which took them about six weeks, and returned through Hanover again, on their way to headquarters. While they lay encamped in this town, about five miles from my father's house, I began to consider the probability of joining them again; thinking that should I neglect this opportunity, all my future prospects in life were at an end. After revolving this subject some time in my mind, I came to a resolution to elope from my father, about the time the regiment were to march, and go off with them. Report said they were to march on Monday morning, therefore, that was the time fixed in my mind to leave my father's house. On the Sunday preceding the time of their march, my father was absent, on a change with a neighboring minister, and so produced a favorable opportunity for the execution of my plan. On some pretended cause, I tarried from church that day, in order to have an opportunity of making those arrangements which I thought necessary to equip myself for a soldier. Accordingly, I took a bed blanket and

[9]

tied it full of clothes and provisions, not knowing that I should ever be provided with either by the public. My provision consisting of bread and cheese, that being the only kind which was ready cooked, would best answer my purpose. All this baggage, together with an old musket, belonging to my father, powder-horn filled with powder, and thirty balls, I laid by in a convenient place until the important moment should arrive. About the dawn of day, on Monday morning, I placed myself under the enormous load, contained in the blanket, after being accoutred with powder-horn and musket. and pursued my way with great energy to the camp, where I arrived a little after sunrise. My appearance in camp, in this ludicrous plight, was an object of universal curiosity and amusement. Sweating under an enormous load of bread and cheese, brandishing the old family musket of my father's, accoutred with a due quantity of powder in a horn, by my side, and a sufficiency of ball in my pocket to kill thirty men, if rightly directed, I made the appearance of more than Quixotic bravery. Surely the knight of La Mancha, had he seen me in my present plight, would have dismounted from the most redoubtable Rozinante, and would have yielded to me the palm of chivalry, as the most accomplished knight on the sod.

These first dawnings of resolution and perseverance, which were manifested in this ridiculous essay, I found were pleasing to the officer, under whom I had formerly enlisted; to whom I again applied for admission into his company, but previously declared, that I would not again enlist with him, unless he would engage not to discharge me if my father should pursue me. The regiment did not march till near the middle of the day, much to my disappointment, and I received the disagreeable intelligence that my father had arrived in camp previous to their march.

The resolution of my officer, who was a man of feeling, was not proof against the solicitations of my father. He again discharged me, and my father took me home. As the obstacles to my joining the army increased, my resolution to surmount them gained strength, and my anxiety for this purpose had risen to such a degree, that I determined to elope the first minute I was from under my father's eye, and follow the regiment. All that day and night I was guarded with the utmost attention. About ten o'clock the next morning I was sent on an errand to the next neighbor's, about the distance of ten rods. When I had gotten that distance, I ran with all my might, and never stopped until I had run twenty-eight miles from home, where I overtook the regiment. There I enlisted with another officer, determined not to be dismissed again by my former misplaced confidence. I had not been here long before my father, with two other men, came full tilt after me. Being somewhat doubtful whether I should again be discharged, I determined to make my own safety by flight, but the men who were with my father, observing my operations, pursued and overtook me after some little difficulty. However, the officer under whom I had enlisted absolutely refused to discharge me, unless I gave my consent. Accordingly, my father made application to me, for my approbation in the matter. This was a new scene; to view my parent before me a supplicant, beseeching me to return with him; stating to my view, the situation of a disconsolate mother, the most affectionate of parents; the yearnings of his own feelings of compassion towards me, and the unhappy situation to which they should all be reduced, should I still persist in my desperate resolution of leaving them; this was a situation too affecting for me to bear. A flood of contending passions rushed on my mind. To return from the first attempt for military fame, before I had fairly set out, after forming such strong resolutions to the contrary, appeared to me pusillanimous and foolish. On the other hand, to break through all the ties of nature, compassion and benevolence, was what my soul sickened at viewing. One moment I was determined on going, at the next I was for returning. No permanent resolution could I form till the next morning, when the revallee being beaten, all the feelings of military ardor were again rekindled, and I was determined to march. My father finding my resolution fixed, took a most solemn and affecting leave. This scene I cannot reflect upon without feeling the weakness of a woman.

The night following, when the hurry of contending passions had subsided, and I had full leisure for taking a retrospective view of those very singular transactions, they filled my mind with the severest compunctions. To view my parent returning to a disconsolate family, laden with sorrow, whilst I had been deaf to all the calls of nature

[11]

and compassion, were circumstances which filled me with the keenest sensation of distress; and the night following I was not able to close my eyes to sleep, such were the agitations of my mind.

There I determined to return to my father, notwithstanding all the mortifying circumstances which would attend such a procedure. Early the next morning, a clergyman, by the name of Olcott. came to me, to persuade me to return to my father. This he found no difficult matter to do. I told him frankly I was willing: but when he made application to my officer for a discharge, he was flatly refused. We marched from thence to headquarters, at West Point, without meeting with any occurrences worth relating.

When the regiment had arrived on the North River. they were constantly alarmed by the enemy. and had a number of skirmishes with them. At such times I was always kept back with the baggage, and never suffered to go into action, notwithstanding all my entreaty. I fully believe, had I been indulged in my romantic disposition, I should have rushed foolishly into that danger, from which I never should have returned. These repulses brought about that mortification and disappointment which cured me of my military ardor. Filled with resentment and chagrin, I suddenly left the army and returned home to my father. Soon after my return, my father wrote the following letter to General Washington for my discharge, and sent it by the hand of the honorable Bezaleel Woodward, Esq. who was then on his way to Congress, from the state of New Hampshire.

"Hanover, N. Hampshire, Dec. 24, 1779.
"MUCH HONORED SIR,

"These wait on your excellency to inform, that while Col. Hazen's regiment remained at Coos, Lieut. Crowley, an officer of the train, meeting with my son. a young lad of the age of fourteen years, persuaded him to enlist into his company; with some difficulty I obtained his release from that enlistment. But the young lad having had his mind inflamed by many fair promises and airy encouragements, with unappeasable desires to join the service, afterwards eloped from me, and enlisted under Capt. Lloyd, on the regiment's return from these parts to headquarters. But finding his expectations disappointed, he left the army soon after its arrival at headquarters, and

[12]

is now at home with me. As a sovereign God has not long since deprived me of four children, and has left me but two to survive their death; and as this son is a lad so much under the age that is commonly deemed necessary to constitute a soldier fit for the service, and as I had ever designed him for a public education, your excellency will please to indulge my request, that he may be discharged from the service. Though I have the cause of America sincerely at heart, and ever have, and trust ever shall exert myself to the utmost of my ability in its behalf; yet your excellency will not wonder at any degree of reluctance in me, against my son's engaging in the service under my present circumstances. Your excellency will please to signify your pleasure by the bearer, and due obedience shall be rendered to your commands with cheerfulness. With daily prayers, that the God of armies will be your shield and friend, and honor your excellency as an instrument of complete salvation and deliverance to the United States of America, I am your excellency's

"Most obedient humble servant,

"EDEN BURROUGHS.

"His Excellency GEORGE WASHINGTON. ESQ.

"P. S. During the time my son was in the army, he never passed muster, nor drew any bounty or clothing."

[13]

CHAPTER III

"Scenes of my youth! pale sorrow flings
A shade o'er all your beauties now;
And robs the moments of their wings,
That scatter pleasures as they flow."

SOON after this my father placed me at school under the tuition
of the late Joseph Huntington, D.D., whose fame for an instructor was very noted throughout all the New England States;
where I continued one year, and was then removed to Dartmouth College, of which I became a member.

Whilst I was with Doctor Huntington, many of those boyish pranks
which students are apt to practice, in order to give themselves the
tone of wits, were performed by me to the no small diversion of myself and the other students, and to the great hindrance of my pursuit
in literary acquirements. This was the hour of folly. From the effect of this age flowed a continued stream of crude, undigested whims,
which kept the school and myself in a constant uproar. I became
an inmate in the family of my preceptor, which consisted of the
Doctor, Mrs. Huntington, two sons by a former wife, nearly my own
age, and a number of small children, how many I do not recollect.
The Doctor himself was a character whose parallel is not commonly
found. A man of very considerable oratorical abilities, which consisted more in smooth figures, and ingenious declamation, than in close
metaphysical reasoning. A mind by no means tied down to established modes and forms, but internally despising them; possessing an
unbounded ambition; fond of flattery. A temper, when undisturbed,
philanthropic, but disappointment and chagrin changed it into the
boisterous rage of a northwest whirlwind. Mrs. Huntington, a character truly amiable. Joseph, second son to the Doctor, after his own
name, about one year younger than myself. This youth was truly
the son of his father. The fire of his ambition was great; his resolution was equal to his ambition; and his eccentricity was equal to both;
with a strong mind, equal to his father, he despised the shackles of

education, broke through all the little obstacles of vulgar prejudice, and pursued those paths to which the fire of genius, and the want of judgment at that time directed him. The rest of the family had nothing uncommon in their characters which distinguished them from mankind in general.

Being full of vivacity, Joseph and I were almost perpetually prosecuting some scene of amusement or diversion. Some of those pastimes were graduated upon a scale of innocence, and some, I am sorry to say, embraced for their object the vexation and detriment of the neighbors. Our chief force was aimed at a neighbor, commonly known by the name of Tiger, on account of his morose misanthropic disposition. One night we repaired to his house and took logs from his woodpile, about two feet in length, and piled them up against his door, until they reached the top, laying them in such a manner as to incline into the house. After arranging matters in this order, we made a noise as if attempting to get into the old man's garden, sufficiently loud for him to hear; immediately upon this the old man crept softly to the door, and opening it suddenly, down came the logs so rapidly as to knock him to the floor, and cover him over. The noise which this made alarmed the family universally, with an idea that they felt the shock of an earthquake, and that the last judgment had arrived, which set some a-screaming and some a-praying, and for a long time these ideas so wholly occupied the minds of the family, that the old man could not get any assistance from the load of timber, under which he was buried. Immediately upon his being freed from his confinement, he put on some clothes and repaired to Doctor Huntington's, in order to enter a complaint against Joseph and myself, whom he suspected of being the agents in this disagreeable scene; and the reason of his suspicion was founded in this, viz. but a few days before, Joseph and I were caught by him, picking some early apples off a tree in his garden; a complaint of which was made, and we obliged to pay three shillings. But as we were seen to go to bed that night and found in bed when he came with this last complaint, and no evidence that we had left our bed, it was concluded that his suspicions wanted proof, and there this matter ended.

Soon after this, we contrived another plan to disturb the old man's quiet. Joseph went to him, and with a woeful countenance professed

[15]

his sorrow for his having given him trouble, and in order to evince his sorrow, told him he had to inform of an intention of some of the scholars to rob his apple trees that night, and advised him to watch, that he might detect them; and if he should, they would have to pay him a considerable sum of money. This bait the old man eagerly swallowed, and took his stand accordingly for watching.

The other part of this contrivance I was to act myself, as being the best fitted for it, on account of my superior agility. Accordingly, about ten at night, I crept along close to the garden fence till I came, as though by accident, near to the old man, at which I turned and ran, and he after me. Being able abundantly to outrun him, I kept but a very small distance before him, pretending to run with all my might, in order to raise his expectations of being able to overtake me; when coming to the edge of a ditch, which contained about three feet depth of mud and filth, I clapped down on my hands and knees before the old man, and he stumbled over me plump into the ditch; but catching hold of the skirt of my coat, tore it off and carried it into the ditch with him. This was a clue which served the next day to unravel the plot in part, as it related to me; and when complaint was made to our Preceptor, he acquitted us entirely, as not having done anything unlawful, nor having attempted it according to the proof.

This was a scene of great diversion to the Doctor. The woeful countenance which Tiger made about falling into the ditch, together with my strutting about without a skirt to my coat, altogether made so ludicrous an appearance, that notwithstanding all the exertion of the Doctor, he could not suppress the rising inclination to laugh, but would, once in a while, burst forth in spite of himself. Not long after this I had intelligence of the death of an only brother by a letter from my father to the Doctor, a copy of the answer to which is as follows:

"Coventry, (Conn.) 20th Nov. 1780.
"REV. AND VERY DEAR SIR,

"In your great affliction I am afflicted; and the sight of your letter, with the melancholy tidings, made a very deep impression upon my heart. I have several times tasted of the bitter cup; may we learn to live wholly on God. If our houses are not so with him as we naturally wish, and do not grow and flourish agreeably to our fond

[16]

hopes; yet there is an everlasting covenant, ordered in all things, and sure; let this be all our salvation, and all our desire. Dear sir, I condole with you and Mrs. Burroughs in this furnace of affliction, and our prayers for each other, I doubt not, are mutual. With regard to Stephen, he behaves well, and makes good progress in his learning; seems well contented: we take the same care of him as of our own children, as to everything he stands in need of. I am glad to see that he takes serious notice of the death of his dear brother. I have done, and shall do, all in my power that, with the blessing of God, he may make a good improvement of it, and be a spiritual gainer by so great a loss. You know how, dear sir, to leave your now only son with God, as well as all your other concerns, for time and eternity. While Stephen is with me, be assured that I will be as kind and faithful a parent to him as I am capable. But alas! what are friends, children, or any of the dying enjoyments of this transitory world! had you not a better portion, you would be very unhappy; but you can say with the Prophet, "although the fig tree shall not blossom ———."

"May Mrs. Huntington's sincere love and sympathetic condolence, together with mine, be acceptable to Mr. Burroughs and his lady. I have the honor to be, my dear sir, with great respect,

"Your most obedient, humble servant.

"JOSEPH HUNTINGTON.

"REV. MR. BURROUGHS."

As it is a custom generally through the state of Connecticut to keep Saturday evenings as the commencement of holy time, and consequently, to consider Sunday as expiring with the beginning of the succeeding evening, the relation of the following circumstance will not be so much wondered at.

One Sunday, after sunset, a number of the Doctor's students had assembled in the street, and were somewhat noisy about a pastime by which they were amusing themselves. This noisy merriment appeared to the Doctor to be mistimed, when exhibited in the street, at so great a proximity with the Sunday; and therefore, he wished us to desist from pursuing our sport in the street, and attend to it in the dooryard; telling us we might do anything in the yard, if we would not make any noise in the street. We accordingly all came into his yard, and began our amusement again; but soon stopped by an idea being suggested

[17]

of the great liberty which the Doctor had granted us. of doing any-thing in his yard. His office of necessity stood within the limits of the yard; therefore, it was proposed, and immediately agreed, to upset this building.

Dr. Huntington rising very early the next morning, according to his usual custom, saw the destruction of his little house. On making inquiry of the scholars, they all denied that they knew how the house came to be overset, until he came to me, and said, "Burroughs, do you know how the little house was turned over?" "Yes, sir." "Well, who turned it over?" "We, who were at play, last evening, in the yard." "How came you to turn it over?" "You said, sir, we might do any-thing in the yard." The Doctor said no more; went down; procured some hands; and replaced the necessary on its former foundation. Not long after this, the Doctor wrote the following letter to my father.

"Coventry, (Conn.) March 8th, 1781.
"Reverend and dear sir,

"You and your lady will please to accept our best regards: no doubt the welfare of your only son lies near both your hearts: he is well; has a fine genius, makes swift advances in the classics. There is in him such an exuberance of life and spirits, as requires uncommon vigilance and care in the oversight and direction of his ways, in this early period of life, which however, I trust may in future time make him so much the more active and useful in the service of God and his country. I hope he will pass a good examination at the next commencement, if you choose he should enter College. At his own earnest request, he boards about a mile and a half from my house, with a young man a little older than he; I have thought proper to dispense with the dis-tance of way, in consideration that the family and whole vicinity are attached to religion, virtue, and good order, more than any other neigh-borhood in this place, and more, almost, than ever I knew anywhere in the world. Mr. Wright lives next door to him: he and all the neigh-bors have a great respect for you, and unite in every friendly effort for the best interest of your son. I often tell him, however, that he may return and board with me whenever he is willing; meanwhile, I take the same care of all his wants as though he was in my own house.

"Such are the times with us, sir, that the support of those ministers

[18]

who live by the penny, without farms, is one half curtailed, even among parishes that do the best for them, and if such times continue, I must give my sons their education at home. I hope, however, in the good providence of God, they will live to have the benefit of Dartmouth College.

"What we can do for your son in the family, is left wholly to your generosity; and indeed, was my income as in years past, the whole expense I should look upon not worthy of any account. Rest assured, sir, that the best interest of your son is daily consulted, to the utmost of my ability, and I hope and trust that his parents and his country will rejoice in his honor and usefulness in days to come.

"I am, dear sir, with great affection and respect,

"Your most obedient humble servant,

"JOSEPH HUNTINGTON.

"REV. MR. BURROUGHS."

Sometime after this, boarding about a mile and a half from the Doctor's, with another lad nearly of my own age, we took an old horse that ran in the road, and mounted him, as we were going to school, without saddle or bridle, and rode him through the street full tilt. This circumstance becoming known, the owner of the horse applied to a justice of the peace and obtained a warrant for us, and being taken, were brought before him and fined, together with the cost, fifteen dollars; the owner having summoned twenty witnesses to prove one fact. Soon after this I returned to my father, and brought the following letter from the Doctor to him.

"Coventry, (Conn.) Sept. 5th, 1781.

"REVEREND SIR,

"On examination, I trust you will find your son well accomplished to perform the exercises of a freshman at college; with constant study I think he is able to do it better than freshmen in general did at Yale College in my day. I have done everything in my power for his education and his morals, and am exceedingly grieved to acquaint you, that one affair has happened since I last wrote to you, which must be uncomfortable to his parents, as indeed it has been to me.

"Stephen was so unguarded, about the middle of June last, as to take

[19]

and use a horse several times, and that even in a cruel manner, without the knowledge of the owner, who lived not in my parish, but in the vicinity, near the borders of it: the owner of the horse happens to be one of the most inhuman, cruel, revengeful, spiteful monsters that ever disgraced humanity; and as soon as he found out the matter, he was wholly bent on vengeance and the utmost cruelty. I took and pastured the horse eight weeks, and repaired all damage more than sevenfold; I also offered the man two crowns if he would settle the matter without a lawsuit, and took every other step I could think of to save expense and prevent a public noise; but all in vain. The monster knew that the law in such a case is extremely severe, awarding threefold damages and all costs, and nothing could glut his infernal malice till he had drawn your son before authority. And, for threefold damages and costs, obtained judgment against him for about fifteen dollars; for the payment of which, two of my neighbors, Mr. Porter and Mr. Hawkins, gave their security, and your son returned to his study as before. The affair gave me unspeakable distress of mind, and even kept me awake several nights. The authority could do nothing in the case but what they did; the law is plain. The monster that prosecuted summoned a a great cloud of evidences on purpose, I suppose, to gratify his malice in augmenting the cost. Our people, sir, have all the highest respect and veneration for you, and are ready to interpose and do all they can to save you trouble, and with one voice cry out upon the wretch that has been so cruel to you and your son.

"It is highly necessary, sir, that you should make us a visit as soon as may be after commencement. I am in fear you will think somewhat hard of me, that I did not retain Stephen in my own house; when I see you, I will give you the fullest satisfaction in that matter. Had he been willing to have lived with me the whole time, I should have rejoiced at it, notwithstanding the extreme difficulty of my keeping any boarders in these times. I hope God will dispose and improve him in some important and honorable station in life, as he has certainly an excellent genius; though he is as yet in the vanity of youth.

"I mourn that I cannot wait on you, as I intended, and the other worthy gentlemen of the board.

"May our kindest regards be acceptable to Mr. Burroughs and lady; may all New Covenant blessings be your portion, and that of your re-

[20]

maining children: after all our trouble may we meet in everlasting rest.

"My kind love to all my friends and acquaintance in your parts. I remain, Rev. and dear Sir, with the firmest attachments, and most cordial affection, your faithful friend, and most obedient humble servant,

"JOSEPH HUNTINGTON.

"Rev. Mr. BURROUGHS."

Inasmuch as you are now on the subject of Dr. Huntington and his correspondence with my father, I will here insert two other letters written by him some years after; one, when I was in great adversity, and the other, at a time of apparent prosperity.

"Coventry, (Conn.) 26th Jan. 1783.

"REV. AND VERY DEAR SIR,

"Your late epistle came safe to hand; and while I was affected with pleasure in your kind remembrance of me, I was impressed with much sympathy and grief in the case of your dear and only son. The ways of divine Providence are a great deep; what God does we 'know not now, but shall know hereafter.' St. Austin, when a youth, was very vain, vicious, wild, and ungovernable: his pious mother, Monica, was continually in prayers and tears for him: an eminent Divine, one day, told her, that so many prayers would never be lost. You well know what God did for St. Austin, and what a blessing he was to the Church, and to the world. Let us submit, pray, hope and wait.

"We are in good health; have no news more, perhaps, than what you have been acquainted with: the work of God has been considerable among us, and yet continues; the effusion of the divine Spirit with you has been more copious; Oh! may it be on all the world, 'as rivers in the wilderness, and as floods on the dry ground!'

"I beg that my most cordial regards, with Mrs. Huntington's, may be acceptable to Mr. Burroughs and his lady.

"Remaining as ever, dear sir,

"With great respect,

"Your most obedient humble servant,

"JOSEPH HUNTINGTON.

"Rev. Mr. BURROUGHS."

[21]

"Coventry, (Conn.) 23d Oct. 1784.

"REV. and VERY DEAR SIR,

"Could you know the tender feelings of my heart toward you and your family, it would give me comfort; my friendship is warm as ever, while I lament the separation made among your people, and mourn that we could not worship together, when I last waited on you at Hanover. But as my prayers have been answered with regard to your son, so I believe they will be with respect to your people: you have now great comfort in the former, you will, I hope, soon have in the latter; and the whole people shall unite and rejoice in your light, as in days past.

"Mrs. Huntington unites with me in love and respect to Mr. Burroughs, his lady and son. God Almighty. grant you every New Covenant blessing. I have the honor to be, dear sir, with much respect,

"Your most obedient, humble serv't,

"JOSEPH HUNTINGTON.

"Rev. Mr. BURROUGHS."

CHAPTER IV

"In life's gray morn, what vivid hues
Adorn the animating views,
By flattering fancy drawn?
But storms with gloomy aspect rise,
To cloud the azure of the skies;
Now mists obscure the dawn."

A T commencement, 1781, I was presented, examined, and ad- *College!*
mitted a member of Dartmouth College. Here I had a new
situation before me, and another part to act; not possessing
all the advantages to act it with éclat. The reports of my many wild *wildness?*
eccentricities had come before me, magnified in a tenfold degree, and
I found all were waiting with open mouths to see an explosion. Those,
who were fond of such scenes of diversion, were disappointed at my
neglect in exhibiting some specimens of fun, which I had determined
to lay by entirely. Others, who were of a different cast, lowered upon
me with a threatening brow, indicative of their intention to check my
wildness in its first appearance.

Here, I found my situation very different and disagreeable; on the
one hand, I was excited, invited and flattered to gratify those who were
fond of amusement; on the other, I was watched, with the scruti-
nizing eye of jealousy, for misconduct, and a readiness to censure in me
what would be thought innocent in others, to humble and check that
growing propensity to disorder, as was alleged. My father was careful to have me take a room with one Jacob Wood, A. M., who, of all
others, was best calculated to humble and mortify any, whom he entertained a suspicion against, as differing from his own principle or
practice. A man of small stature, and yet greater mental abilities;
rigid and enthusiastic in his notions of religion, which consisted in a
sour, morose, misanthropic line of conduct towards all who were not
of his party. To be an inmate with such a character, you will readily
conceive, no way comported with a disposition like mine; and con-

[23]

sequently, we never enjoyed that union and harmony of feelings in our intercourse as roommates, which was necessary for the perfect enjoyment of social life. Possessing a mind very unstable, he was often out of humor, at his want of success, in making me submissive and humble to his caprice; and being desirous of my sharing a part of his chagrin, he assailed my ears with a perpetual stream of petulant criminations. He sought opportunities to mortify me before company, by representing me as a person inattentive to matters of religion, and consequently, wanting every virtue. This mode of procedure, I could not tamely dispense with; my invention was the only means of resort for retaliation.

One night, while he was paying his devoirs to a young lady, word was brought him, that in a fit of the epilepsy, I was about expiring, and wished for him to perform the last kind office of a friend, to pray with, and for me. This was a business he always attended with great promptitude: his Dulcinea being equally possessed with the laudable ambition of proselyting, agreed to accompany him to the room. But when they came there, they found it empty of every living thing, and not even the appearance of any person's being there that night; for the truth was, I had, the day preceding, obtained leave of absence, and was gone to my father's. This was readily understood as a pun upon his sacerdotal character, than which, nothing could have wounded him more. His character, in that respect, he wished to have considered as sacred; and to trifle with that, that was striking at the very root of all his sanctimonious self-importance. He suspected me to be the author of this mortifying scene, and was unwearied in his endeavors to gain some evidence of the fact; but all his exertions were ineffectual. Notwithstanding all these singularities and eccentricities, I believe him to be a man of an honest heart, led to practice those ridiculous plans by a misguided zeal for religion.

About this time, the Indians had made inroads upon some of the frontier settlements, and destroyed them. It was feared they would make a descent upon Hanover, and burn Dartmouth College, with the buildings in its vicinity; and consequently, the minds of the people were full of fear, and easily aroused by an alarm of any kind. One evening, being in company with a number of others, we proposed and

[24]

agreed, to make a visit to a yard of watermelons, belonging to a man in the vicinity, who kept them for sale, and help ourselves to some of them. We accordingly put our plan in execution; and went as far as the river, half a mile out of town, in order to eat them more securely. After we had finished our repast, every one took his own way, in order to get to his room unperceived. I came directly into town, by the most obvious rout, in company with one Paine. When we had gotten to the green, around which the buildings stand, we discovered some person walking before my door, suspecting, as I supposed, my absence from my room; which being against the laws of College, at that time of night, would give him an opportunity, if he made the desired discovery, to involve me in difficulty.

All these circumstances were very apparent to me, and therefore, I wished to avoid being known to him, as well as to avoid the discovery of the watermelons. We therefore turned off another course, than directly to the College, and rolled our gowns close together, and tucked them up on our backs, so as to make the appearance of men with packs on their backs. This man, Higgins by name, seeing us by this time, came on towards us; we quickened our pace—he pursued us with equal speed—we ran—he ran after us, and hallooed with all his might. I was now sensible, that an alarm would be made among the inhabitants, and of course, some immediate and decisive measures must be taken to prevent a discovery, or a suspicion of the watermelon business falling on me; I therefore, turned a short corner, where my pursuer lost sight of me, and ran directly back to the College, and got into my room undiscovered.

Fortunately, my roommate was not at his lodgings this night. I heard an enquiry in the rooms adjoining respecting the noise; I went into one of them, and found they were about starting after Higgins, to learn the difficulty. We accordingly all started together, and after running about one hundred rods, came up to him, who was still hallooing for help. On enquiry, he told us that he had discovered two men, carrying packs on their backs, lurking about the town, whom he supposed to be spies from the Indians, and that they had fled on discovering him. The town was alarmed, the militia turned out; the boats up and down the river were stopped; the woods were scoured,

[25]

but nothing found, nothing discovered; all night, the fruitless search was continued.[1]

About the dawn of day, the people returned, weary and fatigued, into town, and assembled for mutual consultation. Some thought one thing, some another. Some thought the whole difficulty began in nothing, and ended in the same. Some thought it a trick of the scholars to make themselves diversion. At the suggestion of this idea, one Capt. Storrs observed, that he saw Burroughs and Paine pass by his house, about six minutes before he heard the outcry. The name of Burroughs cast a suspicious appearance upon the business; they all turned their eyes on me, as the author of this alarm and uproar. I cited those who ran from the College with me, on the first of the outcry, to vouch for my innocence; they readily did it. All were satisfied, on my account, except my good friend Mr. Wood. He rolled the eye of jealousy over the business—he was dissatisfied. He took Paine to a private room in the College, and there, by a reiterated course of flattery, threatening, terrors, and soothings, he obtained the mighty secret, as it related to me. I was immediately informed of the business, by a person whom I had placed in a room adjoining, to overhear whatever should be the result of this conference.

It was now about sunrise. I immediately went to the owner of the watermelons, and told him, that passing his yard last evening, after he was in bed, I had taken twelve of his watermelons, knowing he kept them for sale, and came to let him know it, and pay for them. After counting his watermelons, and finding twelve taken, according to my account, he took the pay, and gave me his receipt. I now returned to my room, ready to meet the heavy blow I saw was preparing against me.

By this time it had taken air, that I was the author of last night's alarm. Every countenance was turned upon me in an oblique direction. They had all heard that theft was combined in the business; they had all determined I must fall under this blow; therefore, they were waiting for the awful moment of my being summoned before the authority of College. Ten o'clock, the all tremendous hour, arrived! I ap-

[1] This is too high colored. There was indeed an alarm, and the writer of this note was one of the pursuers; but the fright did not continue all night, nor did the militia generally turn out.

THE COOLNESS OF A STOIC

peared; a number had gathered, which crowded the room. After the charge was read against me, Mr. Ripley, one of the Tutors, addressed me in a speech of half an hour's length, stating the enormous crime I had been guilty of, the course of iniquity I must have led through life, to be detected in such an atrocious high-handed breach of law, at the age of sixteen; the disgrace I had brought on my family connections, and the seminary of which I was a member; that my expulsion, which would undoubtedly succeed, would be but only a prelude to my punishment by the civil law; that ruin and disgrace were the only effects, which would fall on my devoted head.

This rant I heard with the coolness of a stoic. After he had talked himself out of breath, I had liberty to answer. I mentioned the hardness of my case, in being accused, condemned and executed without any proof, or even being heard in my own defence. That I did not know what evidence they could produce of my being guilty of the crime laid to my charge, but whatever it was, I hoped to be sufficiently able to overturn its validity, and clearly establish my innocence. At least, the humane language of candor taught us to hold every man innocent till he was proved guilty. True it was, I had taken watermelons from Mr. Smith the night preceding, but had early that morning informed him of the fact, and paid for them. This information was like a thunder-clap to some of the spectators. All their hopes of seeing ruin fall heavy on my head were now quashed in the twinkling of an eye. Mr. Smith, the owner of the watermelons, having been sent for, testified to all the facts which I had stated; and of course, here the business ended.

My father consented for my removal from the room where I had lived. I accordingly changed my lodgings, to my no small satisfaction. During the succeeding vacation, my father, attentive to his wonted humanity, took a classmate of mine, by the name of Coffin, home to his house, whose pecuniary circumstances were difficult, and gave him his board and tuition, gratis. He likewise supplied Coffin with provisions for his subsistence for the next winter, on condition of his paying for them afterwards, at a time he himself had fixed, as being most convenient. The time being elapsed, I asked Coffin for the money, according to his promise, in behalf of my father, in order to answer some small engagements which I was under for the payment of money.

[27]

He paid but little attention to my request; I repeated it a number of times afterwards, but without effect. At length Coffin told me plainly, he had no intention of paying the debt; stating the difference between his and my father's circumstances; that my father was better able to do without it than he was to pay it. I remonstrated in warm terms on the unreasonableness of his conduct. This brought about a violent resentment on his side, which he never failed to show when he had an opportunity. He united himself under the banner of my friend Wood, in order to increase their strength by union. Mr. Ripley, the Tutor, was likewise disaffected, not only by the chagrin of being found to be a false preacher, when he was on the subject of the watermelons, but likewise on account of a violent antipathy and resentment against my father, owing to their disagreeing in sentiment with regard to the management of certain religious matters; and therefore was determined, according to the good old rule, "to visit the iniquities of the fathers on the children." He, uniting his force with those above mentioned, formed a powerful triumvirate against me.[2]

About this time the President of the College left here, intending a tour to Europe. The Tutors now became the only executive authority of the College. My friend Ripley was the second in standing, and consequently a great degree of influence fell into his hands. This influence he was careful to exercise on every occasion. On a certain day of the week, when my class were called upon to declaim, I did not attend; the reason of my absence was owing to this circumstance. I had sent my shoes to the shoemaker, and contrary to my expectation, they had not yet returned, and I had not shoes decent for my appearance abroad. Mr. Ripley sent for me to appear, and perform my part of the exercises of the day; the excuse, which existed, I sent him, but the messenger returned with positive orders for me to attend. I attended with such shoes as I had, mounted the stage, and declaimed. I made my obeisance, and retired. He called to me, and publicly reprimanded me for appearing in such habiliment. At a certain time

[2] It is justly due to the memory of Professor Ripley, to acquit his character of such an unmerited aspersion. I do not accuse the author of falsehood. He undoubtedly considered this gentleman as his enemy; but it is believed that nothing could be more erroneous. Mr. Ripley labored with young Burroughs, as a tender father with his child, to dissuade him from his vicious courses; but, unfortunately, the latter considered all his exertions as the effect only of personal prejudice.

he made a request to my class to assist him in a certain piece of business, which he was desirous of performing one afternoon. I turned out to assist him. We were detained till ten o'clock at night. The next morning I was absent from recitation. He sent for me—I came— he again reprimanded me for being deficient in my classic lesson, though he knew the cause was my performing service for him at his request. Finding matters thus disagreeably situated, I determined to quit that ground which I could not maintain with any probability of success. I accordingly left College, and went to my father's.

CHAPTER V

"And thus my days in one sad tenor run,
And end in sorrow, as they first begun."

TO remain an inactive member of society was far from my desire; various plans were proposed by my father for my entering into business, or at least, preparing myself for it, but none appeared so eligible as going to sea; therefore, it was determined for me to bend my course that way. My father fitted me out with a horse, saddle, bridle, and about twenty dollars in money, and let me loose upon the broad theater of the world, to act my part according to my abilities. The want of experience and a natural hasty temper, prone to inconsiderate actions, augured no very favorable prospects before me.

I had been a member of the seminary of Dartmouth College sufficiently long, to be filled with that sort of learning which gave me an exalted idea of my own importance, and which was of no manner of use, in my pursuits through life. This may appear strange, that I should spend three years in gaining that, which was good for nothing. However strange it may seem to you, sir, yet it is a fact. One year, I was studying to prepare myself for admittance into that seminary, where I spent two in learning nothing, or that which amounted to the same in the end.

Perhaps you may think I entertain an opinion of this College as being, in point of usefulness, much below the other Universities on the continent; but this is not the case. It is a melancholy consideration, that our youth should spend so much time in acquiring that knowledge, which is of no use to themselves or to the community, of which they are members. To acquire an accurate knowledge of the dead languages, seven years is a short time; and after this is effected, to what does it amount? Does it give bread to the persons possessing it, or does it serve to enlighten, enrich, or render more happy any part of the community? I contend, that the person who has learned to make a shoe, *what we learn useful? worthwhile?*

does more good to society, than he who has spent seven years in acquiring a knowledge of the dead languages. If this position is founded in truth, then this consequence will follow, that more than one half of the time spent at the Universities, according to their present establishment on this continent, is thrown away; and that the position is founded in fact, I will endeavor to prove.[1]

The happiness of ourselves, together with the good of society, is the governing pursuit of every valuable member of the community; therefore, whatever conduces to this end, is the only object worthy of attention. The good of society may be comprised in these three points, viz. 1st, To obtain what is necessary to supply the calls of nature, by the least painful measures. 2d, Rules for the regulation of mankind, in their relative situation, which, in their operation, will tend to harmonize the conduct of the whole towards individuals. 3d, A supply of food for the mental part of creation: for the mental part requires a certain supply, in order to render us sensibly happy, as well as the corporeal. Mankind, in their present state of existence, find it necessary to submit to the pain of labor, in order to protect themselves from the cries of hunger and thirst, from the inclemency of the climates and seasons, and from the unjust encroachments upon their industrious acquisitions and natural rights. These are the first objects which mankind find themselves under the necessity of attending to; hence, we find the most savage and barbarous nations occupied in these pursuits. Nations that have made no improvements in useful knowledge, are subject to the greatest degree of pain, in supplying the simple calls of nature. The precarious effects of the chase are the most general supplies to the calls of hunger with them, and as that is a resource of so doubtful a nature, those people often suffer the pain of hunger unsatisfied; therefore, no wonder we find the inventor of the plow immortalized and deified, because the good which he had done to mankind was so essentially felt and known. They then saw the uncertainty of a support changed into a certainty; that they now were able to provide for themselves and families, and consequently, the different sexes could enter into that connection, which contributed greatly to increase the

[1] It is not strange the author should reason in this manner. He was expelled from College in the second quarter of his second year; and it is a fact, he studied but very little while he was a member.

[31]

happiness of society, without the danger of seeing their tender offspring perish miserably for the want of sustenance. This object occupies the feelings of mankind now, as it has done heretofore. They find the same necessity for a support for themselves and offspring; and consequently, those acquirements, which serve to render men able to procure a support, in an easy and certain way, are now the most essential to the good of society. That learning the dead languages has no direct or indirect tendency to this acquirement is a truth so obvious, that more need not be said on the subject; therefore, with regard to the usefulness of this species of knowledge, in the first and most essential pursuit of mankind, we find that it is not founded in fact.

The second most important object, for the good of society, is those rules for the regulation of mankind in their relative situation, which, in their operation, will tend to harmonize the conduct of mankind towards each other. Legislation is a subject, perhaps, of all others, the most difficult to bring to perfection, so as to have a thorough understanding of its nature and operation. It has been the study of the greatest men in all ages, since society has been formed; and yet, much is to be learned on this subject.

To understand the operations of the human heart, so as to adopt rules for the regulation of man in his conduct towards his fellow members of society, in such a manner as to render those rules easy and acceptable to all, and under which all will enjoy the blessings of society uninterrupted, is an object of such magnitude and importance, that every breast possessing the principles of philanthropy, must be fired with ardor in the investigation. As far as mankind deviate from such a government, so far they are politically unhappy, and in as great a degree as they approximate to this golden age, not of poetic fiction, but of reality, so far they approach towards real political perfection. What a perversion of the talents and time of our youth, whom we intend for public employments! to keep them tied down to the study of the uninteresting and unessential branches of the Latin, Greek, and Hebrew languages, the greater part of their continuance at the University, to the utter neglect of political knowledge! I am bold to affirm, that not one to twenty of those who are dubbed with the title of A. B. or A. M. understand that constitution or

[32]

form of government under which they live. Will not the mind of sensibility cry out with the orator, on another occasion: "O, the times! O, the manners!"?

The last object of attention, though not less interesting, is a supply of food for the mental part of creation. The mind of man is made capable of greater enjoyment than what barely relates to the senses. The systems of morality and philosophy are what I mean to be understood as food for the mind, or mental part of creation. When the mind of man becomes disengaged from the primary objects of nature's call, it then mounts to things of greater magnitude than what barely relate to itself; it views creation, the works of providence, and the end to which all these things point. The doctrine of right and wrong, or in other words, virtue and vice, is a subject which supplies food for the mind, or which gives the highest polish to the happiness which it enjoys. When we view the curious order of nature, and see that all things are governed by fixed and unalterable laws, which once discovered, lead to a knowledge of future events and useful improvements; that the parent of nature has carefully and curiously provided for all his children, even to the minutest insect, we cannot but be filled with that delight at viewing the fitness of things, which no other subject can create. I will contend, that more satisfaction is enjoyed in viewing the operation of nature on a single kernel of wheat, after it is committed to the ground, and there is more usefulness in that contemplation, than in the study of the dead languages through life. Can a knowledge of these languages help a person in the investigation of ethics, philosophy, or mortality?

I am aware it will be said, that to read the scriptures in the original tongues will enable a person to understand them much better, than to be able to read the translations only; and therefore, it is necessary that all who intend the study of divinity as their pursuit, should be acquainted with these languages. Happy would it have been for mankind had these effects followed: but, the truth is far otherwise. We find the Christian world broken into parties and factions by those very characters who have been enabled to read the scriptures in the original; and much greater disagreement has happened in the interpretation, than what has been among those who can read the transla-

[33]

tions only; and even in this enlightened age, when so many are favored with this great privilege, we do not find a more general agreement respecting the doctrines of scripture.

I appeal to your own observations, whether I have not stated matters of fact, as they exist, without miscoloring or exaggeration, in respect to the study of the dead languages. Then the greater part of the time spent at Universities amounts to nothing, or what is worse. It habituates the mind to a system of error, and puts it upon the pursuit of wrong objects, and of course it becomes difficult to break those chains of habit which education has forged.

Look around on mankind; do we see any of those luminaries, who have been granted to the world as Heaven's richest boon, from among our collegiate characters? On the contrary, a Washington, a Franklin, a Rittenhouse, have shone resplendent, without the borrowed rays of a College. We are prone to form a wrong estimate of education, perhaps, more than of any other object of our attention. When a youth has spent four years at a University, and has gone the common round of establishing a character for ability, by stealing watermelons, robbing hen-roosts, geese-houses, etc. and playing tricks upon the inhabitants' cows and horses, and can speak a number of sentences which others do not understand, his fond mother looks at him with a pleasing significance, and tells her inquisitive neighbors, that her son has got to be a man of science, and in order to establish her doctrine recounts all the manœuvres he has practiced at College, in order to get a hen out of the roost. The father thinks these are marks of greatness of mind and depth of knowledge, and from these evidences, forms the most pleasing expectations of his son's future greatness. These anecdotes are recounted by the neighbors to their families, through a long course of succeeding winter evenings' amusements. They drink deeply at this fountain of entertainment. When they hear of the foolish pranks of scholars, they are exhilarated at the recital; they dwell upon them with pleasure, and behold the performers with admiration. Whereas, let it be said, that such or such persons have outstripped their fellows in depth of thought, or perspicuity of reasoning and invention, the tale becomes lifeless, and is soon forgotten.

Our youth, possessing the ambition of becoming famous, strike out into that road which the unaccountable prejudices of mankind have marked for them. They wish to start into notice, and will most assuredly adopt such measures, as they see have brought others forward into public esteem. I believe, sir, you will be heartily tired with my digressions, before I get through my tedious narration; but I ask for that exercise of patience, towards my weakness, which I know your generosity will grant. My feelings are so warmly interested in the ideas which some of my observations communicate, that I cannot suppress them, without doing great violence to my mind. But to return to the narrative.

I left my father's house, about the 20th of November, at the age of seventeen, and directed my course for Newburyport, a small seaport town in the state of Massachusetts, where they fitted out many small vessels for privateering. After I had travelled the chief of the day, I entered into the woods about sunset. Being unacquainted with the way, I was not aware of riding more than a mile or two, at farthest, before I should come to inhabitants; but to my surprise, I continued my course till it became quite dark, without discovering any traces of human beings, except the road I was travelling. It began to snow violently, and the night was extremely dark. I suddenly found myself against a team and wagon, containing a family moving into the country. After enquiring the distance through to inhabitants, and the nature of the road, I found I had got the greatest part of the night's work before me. I accordingly quickened my pace, and waded through the snow, which by this time had become pretty deep, with all the exertion in my power. My horse, which had not been refreshed since I left home, now became fatigued; alighting, I drove him before me, till I became weary with travelling myself; and then mounted again. I pursued such measures alternately, till about twelve at night, when I espied a light, at a little distance before me.

A person, who has been in a similar situation, will readily conceive the nature of my feelings at this time. The sight of this illumination, through a small cranny of an old log hut, was attended with those effusions of pleasure, which the miser never feels when hoarding up his treasures. Entering the building from which the light proceeded, I found it a hut, made in that rude state, which did not admit of the polish of art. Logs cut from the forest were laid on the top of each other, to the height of eight feet, when a roof was added, the rafters

[35]

snowing)
found
inn

of the same materials, covered with the barks of trees. This building was about twenty feet square; a large fire being built in the midst, the family lay around it on the ground. The whole group presented a subject fit for the pencil of Hogarth. Inquiring how far it was to a public inn, I was informed, that one was kept there. Necessity constrained me to accept those accommodations, for the want of better.

Some refreshment for my horse being obtained, I was conducted to a bed kept for travellers, as the best piece of furniture in the house. Nature was too much fatigued to hold a parley with inconveniences. I soon fell into a profound sleep, which continued, I suppose, about two hours, when I awoke. By the complaints which my bones uttered, I was jealous my bed was not made of down. I arose, called for my horse, and after travelling five miles farther, over a bad road, I came to a tavern, where accommodations were to be had for man and horse. I enjoyed myself in this situation much better, since my other entertainment had been so disagreeable. I stayed at this house until noon; when I found myself refreshed with food and sleep, I again pursued my journey. The next day, I arrived at a town called Londonderry, where the father of a classmate of mine lived, on whom I called, and to my great satisfaction, found the son at his father's. I told them my intention of going to sea, and the reason why I had left College. They tried to persuade me to relinquish my purpose, but when they found me fixed, the old gentleman wrote to some of his acquaintances in Newburyport, to befriend me in my pursuit.

Intending to sell my horse, saddle and bridle, and with the avails to prepare myself for sea, I here found the market for horses so low, that a sale for him would not be easily obtained, without great loss; I therefore concluded to send my horse back to my father. I arrived at Newburyport and delivered my letter of introduction to Capt. McHurd, to whom it was addressed. This man kept a house for boarders and lodgers; I accordingly put up with him. Not finding any privateers going to sea soon, I concluded to go in a packet, which had a letter of marque, to France. Having no doctor engaged, I undertook to act in that capacity; and after obtaining the assistance, advice and direction of an old practitioner in physic, together with marks set

[36]

on each parcel of medicine, I thought myself tolerably well qualified to perform the office of a physician on board the ship. We did not sail till the first day of January, 1783. When I lost sight of America, I cannot say but what my feelings were more disagreeably affected than I expected. Those attachments which we form in childhood, to places, to persons and things, are pretty strong, I believe, in the minds of all; and none can give them up without a struggle.

Soon after we had lost sight of land, I began to grow intolerably sea-sick, which continued without intermission for four days. This is a species of sickness, though not dangerous, yet as disagreeable to bear as the most violent disorder to which the human constitution is subject. This served, in a great measure, to cool my ardor for spending my days on the salt water. On the fifth day I began to feel more at ease; the motion of the vessel was not so irksome; my appetite began to recover, which before was quite gone. We made the island of Sable, lying in 45° north latitude, where we went on shore. This island is a dreary barren place, about thirty miles in length. Some wild horses and hogs were placed on this spot, for the support of seamen who might be cast away. Accidents of this kind being very common here, on account of the shoals extending from its shores at a great distance into the sea. Here was likewise a small hut, a porridge pot, and fire-wood, flint and tinder box. Here, the sailors recounted many circumstances of the marvellous, representing this as the abode of spirits, hobgoblins, etc. They affirmed with much positive assurance, that many families had attempted living here, induced by great rewards from government, but all their attempts were in vain, owing to sights and noises, which had disturbed them. It was said that this island, in time of an easterly storm, would shake with great violence, which I was rather induced to believe, because a natural reason can be assigned for this phenomenon. Leaving this place, we proceeded on our voyage, till the eighth day of our departure, when, about 10 o'clock in the morning, the man at the masthead cried out, a sail! a sail was discovered ahead; we hove to, in order to see which way she was going. We soon found her making from us with all her force. We put about and made sail after her, till about sunset. We found her a merchant's brig from New York, bound to

London, with pearl-ash, commanded by one Pratt. After we had manned our prize, we pursued our route, without any material occurrence, till the twenty-third.

About 11 o'clock in the morning, we espied a sail astern, which we soon saw was in pursuit of us; we made all the sail we could, to run from her and found she carried to it (a sea term for not taking in sail) through some pretty severe squalls. We lost sight of her about sunset: we made an island on the coast of France, pronounced in the French language, Graw—how they spell it, I do not recollect. We came to under this island, and fired for a pilot. One soon came off to us: about 1 o'clock at night, we got under way again. This pilot was the first person I ever saw wearing wooden shoes; his dress and appearance were miserable; the use of the knife and fork was unknown to him. He was invited into the cabin, and victuals set before him; he felt himself in such an awkward situation, that, instead of eating, he filled his pockets with hard bread, and went on deck. This is the situation of the peasantry, though not in quite so deplorable a condition, through France, so far as I had opportunity of observing. About 10 o'clock the next morning, we made Bellisle, and soon after, saw a sail standing for us, right ahead. We thought her the same that pursued us the day preceding; she proved to be the same. She was a Lugger, carrying 12 six pounders, and was chasing a brig mounting 6 guns. We soon passed the brig, and speaking with her, found her from Boston, bound to Nantz. We entreated her to put about with us, and look at the Lugger, which, by this time, was hove to, waiting for us. All our entreaties were in vain; she ran in under the fort of Bellisle. We carried 18 guns, but unfortunately, ten of them were wood, so that little advantage could be expected from them. We hauled up our courses, put up our boarding netting, cleared our decks, lit our matches, and made all ready for action. We had on board twenty-one men besides the prisoners. The thirteen stripes of the United States were flying; but the Lugger, as yet, showed no colors. We came so near as to hail—she answered in French—and after understanding we came from America and were bound to Nantz, she offered us a pilot, and when we told them we had a pilot already on board, she affected not to understand, but made towards us with a pretended design of accommodating us with a pilot. Not more than

Lugger?

[38]

ten men were to be seen on her deck. By this time, she was sufficiently near to discover those on board by their countenances. Mr. Severe, our first mate, knew the commander of the Lugger to be a man from the isle of Jersey, having been taken by him the preceding year. The mate vociferated like a stentor, "give them a gun! give them a gun!" We fired, but so strongly prepossessed were the gunners, that the Lugger was a Frenchman, that they pointed over her, and did her no damage. She ported her helm, and fell astern as much as half a mile, expecting that we fought with 18 guns. We kept on our course—seeing this, she made all the sail possible after us, hung out the English colors, and her deck became instantly filled with men. She first came up on our windward board, but now altered her intention, and came round on our lee-side. We began to fire stern chases at them, and they returned our salute with bow chases. While Mr. Severe was elevating the gun at our bow he received a swivel ball, which carried away his right cheek, went through and broke his right arm, and two of his ribs. We caught him up, and carried him into the cockpit, where I dressed his wounds, and at the desire of one, Bootman, a passenger, left Mr. Severe in his care, and returned on deck. Our ship was thinly manned, and the help of every hand was felt. A chest of loaded small arms stood on the quarter deck, where I took my station. The Lugger, by this time, was grappled to our ship, and attempted sword in hand to cut away our boarding nettings. Every man was ordered to his boarding pike, and for ten minutes, the conflict was truly sharp, but the issue was in our favor. They retreated on board their own vessel, the guns were their next resort. With cannon and small arms they poured in upon us a shower of balls, and we endeavored to pay them in like kind, to the full amount of our receipt, so that a balance should be left in our favor, and not against us. The captain and myself had fired nearly all the small arms which were loaded. The commander of the Lugger kept bellowing from his quarter deck, that if we did not strike, he would give us no quarter. I took a blunderbuss, which remained loaded, and taking aim very leisurely, at the mouth of his trumpet, let fly. I believe this did his business; at least, I heard no more of this bravado. Twice more did they attempt to cut away our boarding nettings, but, to as little effect as at first. We by this time, had disabled their fore-top-mast, and carried

[39]

away their gib-boom. They cut from us, and made all the sail possible towards the Penmarks, which were hidden and dangerous rocks, lying under water, where they expected we should not follow them. In this conjecture they were right. We arrived the same day in the river Loire, and came to an anchor at a town called Penbeef, thirty miles below the city of Nantz. The next day I went up to the city, and took lodgings at one madame M. Harty's, a house of general resort for the Americans. To undertake a particular description of the places through which I went, will be less interesting than the accounts of travellers of more observation; being too young, at that time, to make those remarks, which would serve to throw any light upon your previous knowledge of those places, by the information of other authors.

Soon after my arrival, I had an advantageous offer of going as Doctor's second mate in a ship bound to the East Indies. I accepted of the offer, and was preparing to go; but the ship. which lay at Penrine, ten miles below Penbeef, had order suddenly to sail, and so left me behind.

We received our dividend of the prize money, which was 42 guineas each. Being possessed with so much money, and some time on hand, I determined to take a short excursion through the country, in order to see what of France my finances would admit. I accordingly set out, with two more Americans, for Angers, from thence to Brest, from there to L'Orient, and then back to Nantz. I was absent on this excursion about three weeks, if I remember right. As nothing more occurred than what happens to travellers generally, I shall not take up your time in giving you the uninteresting detail.

When I returned to our ship, I found some alterations had taken place in my absence, which proved a source of the utmost mortification to me afterwards. The prize brig had been bought by the Captain, and fitted out for Lisbon; on board of which went the first mate as commander, and one Kenne was engaged to succeed him in our ship. The third mate supposed this, by the right of succession, belonged to him, and accordingly, desired me to write to the Captain, who was at Nantz, in his behalf. I did according to his desire. which I was induced to do by the drunken irregular conduct of Kenne, who had disgusted the whole crew, he having proved a worthless wretch. This

[40]

act of mine was the cause of a mortal enmity towards me, which he was but too successful in showing. When the Captain came on board, I found his feelings were cooled towards me. However, no open breach as yet took place. We sailed for America sometime in April, and being becalmed off the western isles, we went on shore at St. Michaels; when we came on shore, we saw a great concourse of people about half a mile distant. Our curiosity led us to see what was the occasion of this assemblage: when we came to the spot we found a Negro bound to a cannon, and a man standing by with a stake in his hand, sharpened at one end. The people were Portuguese, and consequently, we could not understand their language, nor learn the occasion of what we saw, only from conjecture. The Negro appeared to be in great distress, with fearful apprehensions. The dreadful operation of empaling soon began, which consisted in driving the stake through his body, from one end to the other, till it came out a little above his shoulders. The agonies, which he manifested by writhings and hideous yells, had such an effect on my mind, that I almost fainted. The wind breezing up, we soon returned on board, to my great satisfaction. I could not, for a number of days, get the scene of this horrid action out of my mind; and even now, sir, my blood recoils with horror at the recollection! What strange infatuation! That man, who is placed in this state of dependence, instead of granting that help which the voice of nature calls for, should exert his power to make a fellow creature more miserable than if left to the savage beast of prey!

We sailed from hence, and I soon began to perceive that Kenne was intriguing against me, by holding conferences often with Jack, the cabin boy. One day it was said, that wine had been clandestinely handed out of the cabin to two men, who appeared to be drunk. I was ordered, in a very peremptory manner, to leave the cabin, and remove my chest into the forepeak. I moved according to order, but you can scarce conceive the emotions of my mind on the occasion. No reasons were offered for this order.

The conduct of the Captain before, had been of such a nature as to gain my warmest esteem. I felt those emotions of friendship for him which would have carried me almost any length to serve him.

To receive this treatment from him, and, as I supposed, by the influence of a low, dirty scoundrel, added a poignancy to the sting of disappoint-

[41]

ment, which is more easily conceived by a mind of sensibility than language can describe. For the Captain to suppose it possible, that I could be actuated by so base a motive, as to hand his wine clandestinely to any of the crew, was a sacrilegious profanation of the feelings of my heart.

All intercourse between the Captain and myself was at an end. I often had visits from Kenne, who, in the most arrogant, insulting manner, triumphed over me; and it was well for him that I was sick with the smallpox at this time. About the time I was recovering from this disorder, I found by the noise, that a number of the crew was drunk on deck. The Captain came down into the forepeak, and clapped me into irons; being in a great passion, he accused me of breaking open a box of wine and giving it to the men, in order to revenge the affront of being turned out of the cabin. I endeavored to expostulate, but in the room of being heard, I received a brutal kick on my head. All this did not wean my affection from the Captain. I considered him a dupe to the low intrigues of those wretches who were unworthy his notice.

We arrived at Newburyport, where I left the ship, and put up at a boarding house. Here I remained three days, about entering on board of a sloop bound to the West Indies. I had removed all my things out of the ship, and had no further communication with any one belonging to her. I intended a further investigation of the treatment I had received. While I was contemplating these circumstances, I was arrested in the street, and carried before a justice of the peace, and there found to my surprise, the cabin boy, Kenne, and an Irishman, who testified that one Bradley, who had before run away, and could not be found, told them that I gave him wine out of the cabin: that afterwards, I broke open a chest of wine, and handed him the bottles; and likewise broke open a bale of silk, and hid one piece of it; all which was done through a revengeful disposition. Something worth observing took place on their side, viz. Kenne and the cabin boy were those, who made the discovery of the wine box being broken open; of the silk bale being broken, and the place in which the piece of silk was hid; it being where no man would have mistrusted, who did not know beforehand: it was concealed in a cask, once in my use. Kenne was the man who informed the Captain, that the wine was gone out of the

[42]

cabin; and as he was half drunk the greater part of the time, from his first coming on board till we arrived, I never doubted in my own mind, what became of the wine. And as for Bradley's telling the story, which they related, I knew it was false, unless it was done by a pre-concerted plan. However, I was committed to jail, where I lay some time, how long I do not remember, and was then turned out in a manner as unaccountable.[2]

By this time all my money and clothes were gone I know not where; I never saw them more. The assistance of my friend Ripley was not wanting to embellish this scene, who was in Newburyport at this time. My situation did not afford me the opportunity of calling those to a legal account, who had confined me, contrary to law, and dismissed me in such a clandestine manner. I returned to my father's, sunken and discouraged; the world appeared a gloomy chaos; the sun arose to cast a sickly glimmer on surrounding objects; the flowers of the field insulted my feelings with their gaiety and splendor; the frolicksome lamb, the playful kitten, and the antic colt, were beheld with those painful emotions, which are beyond description. Shall all nature, said I, smile with joy; shall the brute creation break out into irregular transports, by the overflowings of pleasing sensations, whilst I am shut out from even the dim rays of hope? The comparison between my situation, and that of the rest of intelligent nature, was so much against me, that I could not bear the ideas which this brought into view, without groaning with pain, under the pressure of the load.

Those who had before pursued me, with their unabating enmity, proclaimed their triumph. I found a censorious world little desirous of inquiring into circumstances. It was sufficient for them to have such facts, as served to raise a slanderous report; and they felt easy, without giving themselves the trouble of inquiring into the causes, why those facts existed, and the circumstances attending them.

[2] The writer of this saw the author at Newburyport, at this period. The Captain, after reading the memoirs, told the writer, that Burroughs had given a much more correct history of the voyage to and from France, than he was capable of doing him-self; and that he was pretty well convinced Kenne was the rogue.

CHAPTER VI

"Descend, bland Pity, from thy native sky,
 Come with thy moving plaint and melting eye."

AFTER I had remained at my father's house about one year,
without attending to any kind of business, I concluded, from
what reason I was capable of exercising, that it ill became me,
as a man, to remain thus inattentive and useless. I determined to
enter into business of some kind; and as a school was the only employment which immediately offered, I entered into that calling. At a
town called Haverhill, thirty miles from Hanover, I engaged to teach
an English school for four months. No sooner was I seated in the business here, than I found my friend Ripley busy in his endeavors to throw
me out of employment. He came to Haverhill, and in that plausible
manner, of which he was master, stated the evil consequences of continuing me in that business; the base examples I should set before
the children who attended my school; and although I did very well
now, yet, notwithstanding my subtilty to conceal my disposition, I
should, ere long, do something that would make them repent of their
credulity, and expose myself to their universal censure. His representation had but too much effect on the people. He was a clergyman, and
consequently must speak the truth. They were afraid—they kept their
children chiefly at home, for fear of some terrible explosion. which had
been foretold by their spiritual leader. With indignation I quitted them
and the school.

I then took a school in a town called Orford, eighteen miles below
Haverhill, and twelve miles from Hanover. Fortunately for me, I
had kept this school long enough to get established, before Mr. Ripley
knew where I was, and of course, his efforts for my overthrow here
were ineffectual. I continued this school until the expiration of the
time agreed for. to the universal satisfaction of all concerned. I
began this school in November, and ended with the month
of February. The usual time for schooling, in all the towns

[44]

MISADVENTURE WITH A HUSBAND

through the eastern states, is only in the winter, some few populous towns excepted.

Whilst I taught this school, I became acquainted with a woman, who was supposed to be a widow, possessing those amiable qualifications calculated to attract the attention of every admirer of the fair part of creation. I paid strict attention to gain her affections, and flattered myself I had in a measure succeeded. After the school was ended, I returned to my father's. I had not been long with my father, before I had a visit from Joseph Huntington, who was a member of Dartmouth College. He came in a sleigh, and brought a classmate. who was of that peculiar turn of mind, as to be a butt for the ridicule of all the wits in College; and it was certain, he would be lead into all the scrapes then in vogue. Huntington proposed to me to take a ride that evening in his sleigh, telling me at the same time, he had brought A—— with him to steal a beehive. For the diversion of drawing A—— into a ludicrous situation, I immediately consented to be one of the party. We accordingly all got into the sleigh, and drove away about two miles, when, coming near where bees were kept, we sent A—— after them, who was ever prompt to do what he was set about by any one. He soon returned with a hive to the sleigh, when we drove off with great speed to the College, where I found a number assembled, ready to partake of the repast which the honey afforded. All were regaled with this delicious morsel but myself, having an insuperable antipathy to honey, which wholly incapacitates me from ever making use of it.

I am now, sir, at a place in my narrative which has caused me pain in relating, because I view my conduct entirely wrong, and my mode of reasoning upon such subjects, at that age, quite ridiculous. For some unaccountable reason or other, youth are carried away with false notions of right and wrong. I know, for instance, that Huntington possessed those principles of integrity, that no consideration would have induced him to deprive another, by stealth, of any species of property, except fruit, bees, pigs, and poultry. And why it is considered by youth generally, that depriving another of those articles is less criminal, than stealing any other kind of property, I cannot tell; but it is a fact, that almost all do esteem this so; and robbing others of those articles is thought to be only the playful wantonness

[45]

of thoughtless inexperience. I will ask you, sir, whether our treatment of those things does not give too much reason to convince youth, that we view them in that light ourselves.

We parted at 11 o'clock that evening, and I returned home. The man who lost the bees, suspected the scholars as the authors of this depredation, and accordingly, went to the governors to enter his complaint. Search was made, and by the inattention of A——, a discovery was effected. It was found, likewise, in the discovery, that I was of the party. This was a fine bone for my friend Ripley to pick. He did not fail to fulfil the office of a clergyman, by setting his face against iniquity. He was determined I should be made a public example. After Huntington and A—— had settled with the owner of the bees, Ripley represented to him the necessity of not making any settlement with me, but prosecute in the law, and there have it terminate. Coffin was ready to back this representation with all his oratory. They succeeded; I was informed into the circumstances; and as another circumstance had now taken place, which co-operated with this, it is necessary I should go back a little in my narrative, and bring forward this event to the present time. The lady, of whom mention has been made, and who was supposed to be a widow, I still addressed on the terms of courtship: matters between us had proceeded to considerable length. I went to visit her one day, after I had left Orford, and coming to a neighbor of hers about six rods distant, I saw a man standing in the door of her house, a stranger, whom I never before saw; and upon inquiring who he was, received information that her husband was alive, and had come home. This intelligence was like heaven's artillery, charged with tenfold vim. The wheels of nature ran backward! The blood curdled in my veins, and I fell almost senseless into a chair! I was aroused from this stupor, by female shrieks! Howlings of bitter lamentation assailed my ears . . . God of nature! what greater scenes of distress are reserved in store? What sharper arrows yet remain in thy quiver?

. . . .

May I hide myself with a mantle of darkness, and retire from the stage of action, into eternal obscurity.

[46]

CHAPTER VII

"Fir'd is the muse? And let the muse be fir'd,
Who not inflam'd, when what he speaks, he feels?"

WEARY with life, I returned to my father's, made some small arrangements, and left the country. One pistareen was all the ready cash I had on hand, and the suddenness with which I departed, deprived me of a chance to raise more. Travelling on leisurely, I had time for reflection. What, said I, again an outcast among mankind? Where am I going? What can I do with myself in this world, where I meet with nothing but disappointment and chagrin? True it is, I am an outcast, but who cares for that? If I will not use the means for my own preservation and prosperity, what am I to expect? Is it to be supposed that whining over misfortunes is calculated to make them better? No, by no means. Then arouse, said I, for shame; use such means as you have in your power. The greater embarrassments, the more honor in overcoming them; lay aside the idea of being any longer a child, and become a man. If others endeavor to throw obstacles in the way of your prosperity, show them that you can rise above them.

This dialogue with myself was productive of the most happy effects; I began to look about me, to see what was to be done in my present situation, to what business I could turn my attention.

The practice of Law, which would have been most to my mind, I could not undertake, until I had spent some time in the study, which would be attended with expense far beyond my abilities: therefore, this object must be laid aside. Physic was under the same embarrassments: business of the mercantile line, I could not pursue for want of a capital; and even a school, at this time of the year, was hardly to be obtained.

Business of some kind I must enter into, and that immediately, in order to answer the present calls of nature. And what can that be? said I; have not I enumerated all the callings, which are profitable for

[47]

me to attend to? I might possibly write in an office, or tend in a store, on wages, had I any person to recommend or introduce me into that business. But what can now be done? A stranger—moneyless—and friendless. There is one thing, said contrivance, which you may do; and it will answer your purpose;—preach! Preach? What a pretty fellow am I for a preacher! A pretty character mine, to tickle the ears of a grave audience! Run away from my own home for being connected in robbing a bee house, and for my attention to a married woman; having been through scenes of tumult, during my whole career, since I have exhibited on the active stage of life. Besides all this, what an appearance should I make in my present dress? which consisted of a light grey coat, with silver-plated buttons, green vest, and red velvet breeches. This, said I, is a curious dress for me to offer myself in, as a preacher; and I am by no means able to obtain a different suit.

These objections, truly, are weighty; many difficulties must be surmounted, in order to enter into this business; but as this is the only kind you can attend to, said I to myself, under present circumstances, you can but be destitute of resource, if you make the trial and do not succeed. At any rate, it is best to see what can be done; therefore, in order to obviate the first difficulty, viz. of disagreeable reports following you, it will be necessary to prevent, as much as possible, your being known, where you offer yourself to preach; and in order to prevent that you must change your name. This being done, you must go some distance, where you are not personally known; and the probability is, that you can continue in such business, till some opportunity may offer for your entering into other employment. As for your dress you cannot alter that at present, and therefore, you must make the best of it you can. I do not think it will be an insurmountable obstacle; if you fail in one attempt, mind not to be discouraged, but repeat the trial, until you succeed.

After I had held this parley with myself, I was determined to follow the foregoing plan, according to the best of my abilities. I exchanged my horse for another, much worse, and received three dollars for the difference. This furnished me with money for my immediate expenses in travelling. I pursued my course down Connecticut river about one hundred and fifty miles, judging that by this time, I was far enough from home to remain unknown. I concluded to begin my

[48]

operations. Hearing of a place called Ludlow, not far distant, where they were destitute of a clergyman, I bent my course that way, it being Saturday, and intended to preach the next day, if I proved successful. I arrived about noon, and put up at the house of one Fuller, whom I found to be a leading man in their religious society. I introduced myself to him as a clergyman, and he gave me an invitation to spend the sabbath with them and preach. You will readily conclude that I did not refuse this invitation. The greatest obstacle was now surmounted, as I conceived, viewing myself as fairly introduced into the ministerial function. I retired to rest at the usual time, and after I had composed my mind sufficiently for reflection, I began to consider under what situation my affairs now stood, and what was to be done under present circumstances. I had engaged to preach on the morrow. I had almost forgotten to tell you that my name here was Davis. People had been notified that a sermon would be delivered. This business I never had attempted. It is true, the study of divinity had come under my attention, together with every other subject of common concern, in a cursory manner. I concluded that sermonizing would not be so difficult as the other exercises of public worship. Many disagreeable possibilities arose into view. What, said I, would be my feelings, should I make some egregious blunder in travelling this unbeaten road? I must be exposed to the mortifying consideration of being observed by a whole assembly, in this ridiculous essay to preach, and not be able to carry my attempt into execution; and all those things possibly may happen. Those considerations made so dismal an appearance, that I once concluded to get up, take my horse privately out of the stable and depart, rather than run the risk of the dangers which were before me. But upon more mature reflection, I found the hard hand of necessity compelled me to stay. When I awoke the next morning, my heart beat with anxious palpitation for the issue of the day. I considered this as the most important scene of my life—that in a great measure, my future happiness or wretchedness depended on my conduct through this day. The time for assembling approached! I saw people began to come together. My feelings were all in arms against me, my heart would almost leap into my mouth.

What a strange thing, said I, is man! Why am I thus perturbated with these whimsical feelings? I know my dress is against me, and will cause some speculation; but I cannot help it, and why need I afflict myself with disagreeables before they arrive? I endeavored to calm my feelings by those reflections. I fortified my countenance with all my resolution, and set out with my bible and psalm book under my arm, those being the only insignia of a clergyman about me. When I made my appearance, I found a stare of universal surprise at my gay dress, which suited better the character of a beau than a clergyman. My eyes I could not persuade myself to raise from the ground till I had ascended the pulpit. I was doubtful whether I had the command of my voice, or even whether I had any voice. I sat a few minutes, collecting my resolution for the effort of beginning: I made the attempt—I found my voice at command—my anxiety was hushed in a moment, my perturbation subsided, and I felt all the serenity of a calm summer's morning. I went through the exercises of the forenoon without any difficulty. No monarch, when seated on the throne, had more sensible feelings of prosperity, than what I experienced at this time.

During the intermission, I heard the whisper in swift circulation among the people, concerning my appearance in such a dress. The question was often asked with great emphasis, "Who is he?" but no one was able to give those answers which were satisfactory. A consultation took place among some leading members of the society, relative to hiring me to continue among them as a preacher, as I had intimated to Mr. Fuller that I should be willing to continue among them in that capacity, should such a matter meet with their approbation. I attended on the afternoon's exercises without any singular occurrence. The meeting being dismissed, and the people retired, I was informed by my landlord, that they did not agree to hire me any longer; accordingly, I found my business here at an end.

I was advised by Mr. Fuller, to make application to Mr. Baldwin, minister of Palmer, about twenty miles distant from Ludlow, for information where were vacancies, and for an introduction into those vacancies. I accordingly set out for Palmer on Monday morning, and arrived at Mr. Baldwin's about four o'clock in the afternoon. I introduced myself to him as a clergyman wanting employment. I saw he noticed my dress, but asked no questions. He examined into my edu-

[50]

cation, knowledge of divinity. tenets. etc., and finding all agreeing with his ideas of orthodoxy, he concluded to recommend me to a town called Pelham, eighteen miles distant from Palmer. The next morning I set off for Pelham, with a letter to one Deacon Gray. I arrived, and delivered my letter, and was hired, in consequence of the recommendation of Mr. Baldwin, without any hesitation, for four sabbaths, five dollars a sabbath; boarding, horse-keeping, etc. etc.—I now found myself, in some measure, settled in business. The want of an immediate relief to my temporary inconveniences was now supplied. I found the family into which I had fallen, to be an agreeable, sociable circle, and I was much respected in the family, not only on account of my sacerdotal character, but likewise on account of the ease with which I mixed with them, in all their little social enjoyments.

hired!

CHAPTER VIII

"Companion of the wretched, come,
Fair Hope! and dwell with me awhile;
Thy heav'nly presence gilds the gloom,
While happier scenes in prospect smile."

BEFORE I proceed to the relation of succeeding events, it will be necessary to give a description of the people inhabiting this town, as much will depend on knowing their character, to rightly understand the relation of incidents which will follow.

The town of Pelham was settled with people chiefly from the north of Ireland. They were of course, strict Presbyterians. They valued themselves much on being acquainted with the nice distinctions between orthodox and heterodox principles and practice. They likewise wished to be thought shrewd in their observations on ministers and preaching. A people generally possessing violent passions, which once disturbed, raged, uncontrolled by the dictates of reason; unpolished in their manners, possessing a jealous disposition; and either very friendly or very inimical, not knowing a medium between those two extremes. The first settled minister they had among them was one Abicrombie, from Scotland, a man of handsome abilities, but violent passions, resolute and persevering. Not many years after he was settled among them, a difficulty took place between him and the people, which was carried to considerable length, and ended in his dismission. After Mr. Abicrombie left this people, they made application to one Grayham, who at length settled among them, to their universal satisfaction; being a very handsome speaker, and otherwise possessed with popular talents as a preacher. Mr. Grayham was a man of very delicate feelings, of superior refinement, and inheriting a great desire for that peace which establishes the enjoyments of society.

After preaching a number of years to this people, he found an uneasiness prevailing among them, the chief cause of which was, his practicing upon a system of manners more refined than what was

[52]

prevalent in the place; consequently, they accused him of pride, of attention to the vanities of the world; of leaving the plain path of scripture, and following after the vices of Rome. Mr. Grayham labored to convince them of their mistake; of his wish to live with them upon the most intimate terms of equality; of his ever having it in view to pursue such measures as would, in their operation, conduce to their good and prosperity; and in that pursuit, he had expected his examples and precepts would answer a valuable purpose. His expostulations, remonstrances and entreaties were all given to the wind. The difficulties increased, and the clamor grew louder. The mind of Mr. Grayham was too delicately strung to bear those strokes of misfortune; they insensibly wore upon his constitution, till at last he fell a sacrifice to the tumult, and sought his rest in the grave.

The town of Pelham remained destitute of a minister for a considerable time. They tried a number of candidates, but not finding any with whom they could agree, no one was yet settled. At length, a Mr. Merrill came among them. He was a man possessing the gift of utterance and flow of expression, perhaps equal to any. He was an eccentric genius, and imprudent to the last degree; possessing violent passions—headstrong and impetuous. The plausible part of his character was so captivating, that the town agreed to settle him. He accordingly was installed. His imprudences soon made their appearance. Complaint was made, but they found one now who paid but little attention to their complaining. Both parties began to give way to passion. Their contention increased, and a flame was kindled which set the whole town in an uproar. Mr. Merrill refused to start from that foundation to which his legal contract entitled him; therefore, the other party determined to use extraordinary and violent measures. This attack Mr. Merrill dared not meet; therefore, he suddenly left the town. Matters were in this situation when I came to Pelham. From the information of Mr. Baldwin, and from the communications of my landlord and family, I soon gained a pretty thorough knowledge of the people whom I was amongst; and I endeavored to adapt my conduct to their genius as far as I was capable. I found myself soon able to dress in a habit fitting my calling. I soon found, likewise, that my endeavors to suit the people had not altogether failed. At the expiration of the four Sabbaths, they engaged me to preach

[53]

sixteen more. I began to form an acquaintance in the neighboring towns, and with the neighboring ministers.

This happened to be a time of great mortality among women in child-bed; consequently, I was called to preach many funeral sermons in this and the neighboring towns, many of which were destitute of a clergyman of their own. I always attended this business when I had a call. This circumstance began to raise a wonder in the minds of some, how I could be prepared for preaching so constantly. and on so short notice, being as yet only nineteen years of age. I had, in reality, ten sermons with me, written by my father.

At a certain time, being suddenly called to preach a funeral sermon, I had none of my own written, proper for the occasion. I took one of my father's, and delivered it to a crowded audience. As this sermon was delivered in a private house. it was in the power of any to look into my notes. One, who had wondered at my always being prepared to preach. took this opportunity of looking over my notes, and thought they appeared too old to be lately written. This circumstance was mentioned to a number, who began to grow uneasy with apprehension of my preaching sermons not my own. Mr. Baldwin coming to Pelham about this time, they mentioned the matter to him, that he might make some enquiry into the business. and inform them. He accordingly mentioned the matter to me, in a confidential manner, and desired to see the sermon alluded to. I was sensible the handwriting of my father was so different from my own, that the first view must clearly convince any observer, that this sermon was not written by myself; I therefore thought it the better way to treat the matter ingenuously, and tell him the simple matter of fact.

I told Mr. Baldwin, that the sermon was a manuscript which I had in my possession, together with some others, written by another person, and that the want of time to prepare a discourse had induced me to take this, rather than refuse to preach. Mr. Baldwin made some observations with regard to my situation; of the necessity of a great degree of prudence; and of the impropriety of using other sermons as a general thing. He returned to Palmer, without giving the men any account respecting the matter of their suspicion. Not gaining that intelligence by Mr. Baldwin which was expected, those who were uneasy, spread their suspicions among others, until there became un-

[54]

easiness pretty generally through the town. They proposed a number of ways to obtain that satisfaction, with regard to their suspicion, which would either clear me from the fact of which they were jealous, or else establish them in it. They, at length, agreed to this method, viz. to send one of their number to me, on Sunday morning, previous to my going into the meetinghouse, and desire me to preach from a passage of scripture, which he should give me. I was informed of all these circumstances previous to the time of trial. Their reasoning upon this subject was of this nature, viz. that if I was able on the shortest notice, to preach on any occasion, I should be able likewise to preach on Sunday, from such a passage as should be given me on the morning of the same day; and should I not be able to preach, the evidence would be conclusive against me, that I preached the sermons of others, and not my own.

The Sunday following, I was waited on by Mr. Clark, who desired me to oblige him, by delivering a discourse from the first clause of the 5th verse of the 9th chapter of Joshua; the words were, "old shoes and clouted on their feet." I informed him I would deliver a discourse from that text, and accordingly he left me. I truly felt somewhat blanked, at the nature of the passage I had to discourse upon. However, I was determined to do the best on the subject I was capable. I endeavored to make some arrangements in my mind on the subject. I had not thought long on it, before the matter opened to my mind, in such a manner, as to give me much satisfaction. As your patience would hardly endure the repetition of a tedious sermon, I will not trouble you with it; yet, sir, indulge me in giving you some general outlines of this discourse, as it was founded on a very singular passage, and delivered on a very extraordinary occasion.

CHAPTER IX

"Thus airy pleasure dances in our eyes,
And spreads false images in fair disguise,
To lure our souls; till just within our arms
The vision dies, and all the painted charms
Flee quick away, from the pursuing sight,
Till they are lost in shades, and mingle with the night."

I N handling this discourse, the exordium consisted of a description of the Gibeonites; the duplicity which they practiced upon the Jews; the nature and general tendency of deceit, etc. After I had gone through with the introduction, I divided my discourse into three general heads, viz. to consider in the first place of shoes; secondly, of old shoes; and thirdly, of clouted shoes. In treating of the first general head, viz. shoes, I considered them in a metaphorical sense, as showing our mode of conduct in life. We are all, said I, sojourners in this world but for a season, travelling to another country, to which we shall, ere long, arrive: we must all be shod. in order to enable us to travel the road before us. We find the good man represented as having his "feet shod with the preparation of the gospel of peace." All mankind are in a state of motion; none remain inactive on this stage of probation; all are moving forward with rapidity, and hastening to their final end. Not only the natural world, but likewise the mental, is filled with briars and thorns, stones and rubbish which wound us at every step. when we are not shod to guard us from those injuries we should otherwise receive from those impediments Mankind, finding this to be the case, have immediate recourse to such coverings for their feet, as they imagine will protect them from the injuries to which they are exposed, etc. etc.

In treating the second head, viz. old shoes, I endeavored to show, that they represented those, "who had been hewing to themselves cisterns. broken cisterns, which can hold no water." We find, said I, from the earliest ages of the world. mankind practicing upon that system. They have continued ever since to tread in the steps of their

[56]

predecessors, and to wear the same old shoes. The old shoes represent old sins, which mankind have made use of from old times, down to the present day. And would to God they had been worn until mankind had been ashamed of them. A spirit of jealousy and discord, perhaps, may be accounted as old as any shoes now worn. How soon after the creation do we find this same destructive principle raging in the little family, which then composed the whole human race. Murder was the consequence; revenge and hatred were perpetuated by it. "Now I am possessed with this accursed passion," said Cain, "whoever shall find me, shall slay me." The direful influence of this passion spreads its dismal effects among all mankind, when it once prevails. Solomon, viewing the operation of this principle upon the human heart, says, "Jealousy is more cruel than the grave." It deluges countries, destroys societies, and renders man hateful to man. All civil and religious bodies are destroyed, when once this hateful monster is allowed an entrance. Ministers and people, parents and children, husbands and wives, fall a sacrifice to the influence of "jealousy, that green-eyed monster, which makes the meat it feeds on." Therefore, woe be to that people who cherish the seeds of jealousy, or practice after her counsels, etc. etc. etc.

In considering the last general head, viz. of clouted shoes, I observed, that those, who wore those old shoes, and practiced upon a system of jealousy, were sensible of its odious and hateful nature, and of consequence, ashamed to be seen by God, man, or the devil; nay, they were ashamed to be seen by themselves, therefore, they had recourse to patching and clouting themselves over with false and feigned pretences, to hide their shame and disgrace. This vice has been considered, by all wise men, as the most destructive to human felicity, and the least excusable, and most unreasonable, of any passion incident to the human heart. It is passion, which debases the human character to its lowest ebb, as says a noted author, "Where I see a jealous people, I expect likewise, to see everything base and sordid among them."

Look around, my hearers, and judge for yourselves; whenever you have left this first-born son of hell triumphing in your bosoms, how soon has joy and comfort fled from your hearts? How soon has this doleful monster turned all the sweets of life into wormwood and gall? etc.

[57]

I concluded this discourse by an application of the subject, after the following manner. My hearers, where shall I apply this doctrine? Is it calculated for a people only at some great distance? Can we not bring it home, even to our own doors? Search and see. Try yourselves by the sanctuary, and if there your garments are not washed in innocence, you will find, "Mene, mene, tekel upharsin," written on your walls. Will you suffer this hateful monster to rage among you? Will you wear these old filthy clouted shoes any longer? Will you not rather put on that "charity which endureth all things, which hopeth all things?" Will you not rather be "shod with the preparation of the gospel of peace?" etc. etc. etc.

After this sermon was delivered, I found the people, though somewhat disturbed at my esteeming them jealous, satisfied with regard to my ability in sermonizing, and they afterwards remained quiet on that head. I found it necessary to purchase me a horse, saddle, and bridle, as well as to clothe myself anew entirely, with such apparel as became a clergyman; therefore, I was under the necessity to anticipate my wages to answer these purposes, after I had disposed of my old horse, saddle and bridle to the best advantage.

No person of my acquaintance knew where I was at this time, except Joseph Huntington, whom I had left at Dartmouth College; with him I continued a correspondence by letter; he engaged to make me a visit in September, as he should then be on his way to Coventry, and could take Pelham in his journey. I once saw a person whom I had formerly been acquainted with at Coventry, by the name of Avery; but he did not appear to recognize me, being under a different name, and in a different dress. The first of my seeing him was in the meetinghouse. I made it convenient to fall in with him afterwards. to see if he had any recollection of me. and found he had not.

Not long after this, I saw a young man by the name of Powers, with whom I was acquainted at Dartmouth College. I saw he paid close attention to me, whilst I was preaching, and concluded from a number of circumstances, he knew me. He lived in Greenwich, a town adjoining, and had connections in Pelham. I therefore concluded it to be a matter of consequence to throw myself in his way, and come to an explanation with him. Accordingly, after meeting. I made it convenient for him to speak to me, which he readily did; and he being

[58]

informed into the motives of my conduct, promised not to say anything which should create an uneasiness among the people.

At another time, coming from a town called Colrain, having been on a visit to the clergyman living in that town, I met one Church, with whom I was acquainted at the College; he now being a clergyman, and seeing me in a clerical habit, stared with surprise at me. I frankly told him my situation, and where I was preaching. At the relation of this, his phiz became lengthened, he assumed all the importance attached to his function, and addressed me in a lengthy harrangue, showing the sacredness of the character which I had assumed, and of the great importance of "walking worthy of the vocation wherewith I was called." I pulled off my hat, made him a profound reverence, and rode on.

Soon after I had left this Knight of the Cross, I began to reflect upon the nature of my own conduct, and upon mature consideration, blamed myself much for giving him that information which I had, with regard to my own matters. This information, said I, can do him no manner of good, and it may do me much injury. The secret is now gone from me, and I cannot recall it. I cannot receive any possible good from communicating this matter, and many possible evils may befall me in consequence of it.

I will leave matters in this situation, and go back some way in my narrative, in order to fetch forward a number of matters, necessary to understand many events, which will hereafter be related.

When I first came to Pelham, I formed an acquaintance with a family, which must remain nameless, for reasons which you will under- _the family_ stand by the after relation. The man was possessed of information far above the rest of the inhabitants. His manners and sentiments were equally refined; his wife possessed those amiable accomplishments which made her a paragon of excellence among the rude inhabitants of this town. This couple lived together on such terms, as to do honor to their refinement. The most tender affections marked all their actions, while their parental care had formed a family of the most lovely children. With this family I formed an acquaintance, which was not only intimate, but ardently affectionate. I lived with them on such terms of nearness and confidence, as I never expect to do with any other. All their propensities, feelings, and sentiments were in

[59]

union with my own; so that not a discordant sound was heard among us. In fine, I do not know the act of friendship too romantic or desperate for me to have performed, for this amiable family, had occasion called; my feelings of friendship were so strong towards them, I communicated all the secrets respecting myself to them, without disguising any circumstance. The man told me that measures were in such a train, that he should soon be in possession of an independent fortune. Prompted by the feelings of friendship, he wished me to enjoy a part of the blessing in store for him; he therefore let me into the knowledge of his wealth and greatness. He informed me that one Philips, who was then at work in New Salem, with the noted Glazier Wheeler, a money-maker, known throughout all New England, had the art of transmuting metals, so as to make copper into good silver, which would stand the test of every essay made upon it. This knowledge Philips had agreed to communicate to my friend, who, for distinction sake, I will call Lysander. Said I, if this can be done, at no considerable expense, it is a matter of the utmost consequence; but his working with Glazier Wheeler is an exceptionable circumstance against him, in my opinion; however, he may have his own reasons for it, and those reasons, were they known to me, might be satisfactory. Lysander appeared to entertain the highest confidence in the business. His wife was more doubtful; who, by the bye, was the most penetrating of the two. In order to put the matter out of all doubt, I agreed to attend Lysander on a visit to this wonderful transmuter of metals, and there examine his experiments, until we had reduced the matter to a certainty. The visit was to be made in the night, to prevent any suspicion arising from the circumstance of being at the money-maker Wheeler's. We accordingly, one night, set out on our destination, it being a rout of about twelve miles, and arrived there about 10 o'clock. We made our business known to Philips, who was willing to give us proofs of his skill.

He in the first place, weighed one half ounce of copper, and put it into a crucible, and then put the crucible into the fire; after it remained there a short space of time, he put in a paper, containing something wrapped in it, and immediately the matter in the crucible became turbid, and began to foam and boil with great violence, for about ten minutes, and then settled down into a clear beautiful metal,

[60]

which, when poured off and cooled, was good silver, weighing one half an ounce. It stood the trial by aqua-fortis, and several ways, so that I had no doubt of its being good silver. My only doubt remained as to the contents of the paper, which was put into the crucible. This contained a certain powder, as Philips said, which served to destroy the verdigrease, which the copper absorbed, and the remainder was pure silver. I wished to see the powder—with some seeming reluctance, he showed it me. I saw it was in reality a powder. I wished him to try the experiment again, and to put the powder in open, so as to have it seen after it was in the crucible. He pretended it would not do quite so well this way, but, to gratify our curiosity, consented. The experiment, in all its circumstances, was repeated, excepting his laying a large flat coal over the mouth of the crucible, immediately after the copper was put in. The effect was the same—one half an ounce of good silver was poured out of the crucible.

I again desired him to furnish me with the materials, and let me go through the operation myself, without his coming near the fire. He consented. I weighed the copper, put it in, and proceeded according to his method, which I had seen him perform, till the powder produced the boiling foam in the crucible, when he cried out to me to stir it. I did not recollect seeing him stir it; however, I put an iron rod, about the bigness of a large nail-rod, and about eighteen inches long, into the crucible, and stirred the contents. There was nothing but this iron rod which would answer to stir the metal with. When we emptied the crucible, we found half an ounce of good silver. Once more I begged his indulgence for another experiment; and that he should not be in the room when it was performed. He readily consented. Lysander and myself proceeded together in the experiment, *secundum artem*. When we came to stir the metal, we could find nothing calculated for that purpose, except a short piece of a walking-staff; we therefore made use of that; but saw afterwards, we had burnt off about four inches of that end we had put into the crucible. We poured out the usual quantity of good silver. I was now satisfied beyond all doubt. We returned to Pelham with no small satisfaction. I felt all the confidence in the business which was possible to feel on any subject. I saw, in my own imagination, my fortune certainly made. Not a doubt remained in my mind of becoming the richest

[61]

man on the continent of America. But how fleeting our joys! how vain our expectations! Can you suppose the whole of this an illusion? It was truly so. All the plausible experiments which were performed by Philips and ourselves, were a series of the most consummate duplicity, which was ever performed. We did not make this discovery till sometime afterwards; but I will go forward with the account now, for the reason of its being so closely connected with the incidents already related.

When the first copper was put into the crucible, he put half an ounce of silver in likewise, which was wrapped in the paper, with some powder, which consumed the copper and left the silver. The next operation was after this manner: being prevented from conveying the silver into the crucible, by my request of seeing the powder put in, he therefore secretly put his silver on the forge, and laid a large flat coal over it. At the proper time, he took up the silver and coal together with his tongs, and laying them over the top of the crucible, the silver unperceived fell in. The next deception was performed thus: at the time in which I was ordered to stir the metal in the crucible, an iron rod was the only thing to be found for such a purpose: on the lower end of this rod was fixed the silver, blackened like iron, which being put into the crucible, melted off. The last experiment for supplying us with silver, was performed by making the end of the piece of walking-staff hollow, and placing the silver in the end of it, which being burnt off, left the silver in the crucible. Thus this mighty fabric of wealth was blown away in an instant, like the baseless fabric of a vision. This adroit deceiver obtained property of a number, to the amount of two thousand dollars, and suddenly was missed.

As he will be found on the stage a number of times, in the course of this narrative, it will be necessary to give some more particular description of this singular man. He was about five feet eight inches high, dark complexion, thick set, down look, plausible in conversation, very ingenious in executing mechanical undertakings, and what is more surprising, he had but one arm. He had the entire command of his feelings, so that his countenance or actions never betrayed his inward sensations, persevering in any undertaking, perfidious, subtle, and designing; lost to all feelings of fidelity, either towards the public, as a member of the community, or towards individuals, to whom he had

[62]

more immediately pledged his faith; a rank coward, yet possessing the happiest abilities of imitating courage of any man I ever saw. There was no part of the coining art but what he was master of, and could, with one arm only, execute it to perfection.

Being fully possessed with the idea that our prosperity was certain, we concerted a plan to carry on the business to that amount, as to answer a purpose of magnitude. We therefore concluded to charter a vessel, load her with copper, coal, provision, etc., necessary for the business, and retire to the isle of Sable, where we could pursue our plan uninterrupted. A writing was made and signed by all parties, for our regulation in prosecuting said purpose.

CHAPTER X

"It was a season when the lingering night
Disputes her empire with the rising light;
A rosy blush here paints the doubtful morn,
There glimmering stars the uncertain shades adorn."

AT the time fixed on, Joseph Huntington came to see me at Pelham; I introduced him to my acquaintance, and particularly to Lysander. We opened our schemes of aggrandizement to him, without reserve. He was pleased with our prospects, and in the overflowings of our friendship, we agreed to allow him, as the highest favor possible for us to communicate. to set his hand to our agreement, and so become a partner in our business. In the course of Huntington's remaining with me at Pelham, he made several unguarded mistakes, which reduced me to a very disagreeable situation. He called me by my proper name, a number of times, before the family where I lived. He excused himself by saying, that Burroughs was my nickname at College, and was given in consequence of my looking so much like one of that name. One Sunday morning, as people were going to meeting, I was leaning back in my chair, the pommel resting against the door case. Huntington, seeing the situation in which I was resting, put his staff against the chair and pushed it off the case, and down I fell on the floor. This impudent action, done on Sunday, by my known and intimate friend, had a very disagreeable appearance, and made people look with astonishment at the circumstance; however, I reproved Huntington with some warmth, and he, seeing the nature of his folly, bore it with patience. The Monday following, Huntington was to proceed on to Coventry. I rode with him about twelve miles on his way, and then returned; but previous to my return, an affair took place which gave a new face to the scene of things.

As we were riding by the house of Mr. Forward, minister of Belchertown, he came out of his house, and desired us to call, alleging that Mr. Chapin, a minister from Windsor, was in the house, to whom

[64]

he offered to introduce us. Mr. Chapin was a man well known to me, and I presumed I should be equally well known to him. I excused the matter, alleging that I was in haste, and therefore, could not do myself the pleasure of accepting his invitation. Mr. Forward was pressing for us to alight, and go in; and while this dialogue continued, Mr. Chapin came out of the house, and addressed me by the name of Burroughs. I endeavored to convince him of his mistake, but to no purpose; he insisted in a very peremptory manner, that my name was not Davis, but was bona fide Burroughs. I replied that those insults were not grateful to my feelings, and what I should not bear. "Your humble servant, gentlemen." We then rode on, though repeatedly desired to stop. When Huntington and I were by ourselves, we were merry upon the circumstance of being driven into so short a corner.

After I had parted from Huntington, I was under the necessity of returning back the same road I came, and consequently, must pass again the house of Mr. Forward. Soon after I had gone by the house, I heard somebody calling after me, "Mr. Davis, Mr. Burroughs," but for reasons which you will easily conceive, I did not answer. As I rode on towards Pelham, I endeavored to concert measures of retreat against the storm, which was fast gathering, and would soon burst upon me, if it were not averted. The news would soon come to Pelham, of my real name, character, etc. This would serve to arouse the indignation of that people to its full height. To continue among them any longer, would be out of the question; and to meet the rage of their resentment, after the whole matter of fact should be promulgated, I dared not, neither did I wish it. One Sunday more I was to preach among them, before my time of engagement expired, and for this Sunday, I had already received my pay; but under existing circumstances, it was doubtful in my mind, whether they would insist on my fulfilling my engagement. At all events, I was determined to leave them very suddenly. I accordingly came to my landlord's that evening, put my horse in the barn, and after the family were all retired to rest, I put my things in order, took my horse, and silently left the house. In this situation, I sought Lysander, related the circumstances which I was under, and concluded to lie by with him, till I should see what the event of those things would be.

[65]

The next morning, Mr. Davis was not to be found. My landlord was almost frantic with surprise and grief. The town was alarmed, and suddenly was all in a flame. About 11 o'clock P. M. a man came from Belchertown, with information respecting the character who had been exhibited among them as a preacher. This blew the flame into a tenfold rage. No pen can describe the uproar there was in the town of Pelham. They mounted, hue and cries after me in every direction, with orders to spare not horseflesh. They perambulated the town, and anxiously asked every one for some circumstance, which would lead to a discovery where I was. All this took place whilst I lay snug in the corner, observing their operations. In holding a consultation upon these disagreeable matters, every one was anxious to clear himself of being the dupe to my artifice, as much as possible. "I never liked him," says one. "I always thought there was something suspicious about him," says another. "He ever had a very deceitful look," says a third. In fine, it had come to this, that not one now could discern anything which ever appeared good or commendable about me, except one good old lady, who said, "Well, I hope they will catch him, and bring him back among us, and we will make him a good man, and keep him for our preacher."

You may with propriety ask me, what the people of Pelham expected they could do, should they overtake me in their pursuit? I know the question will naturally arise; but I cannot give you an answer, for I do not know their intentions or expectations. Perhaps they thought, for they were a people very ignorant, that I had broken the laws of the land, to the same amount as I had offended them.

About 12 o'clock, the night following, I took my leave of Lysander, promising to return and see him again, as soon as the tumult was hushed, and concert further measures for our prosecuting our schemes for gaining wealth by transmutation; being obliged so suddenly to leave the country, that we could not ripen our plans for the present. It was not without the most sensible pain I left this amiable family. Journeying on, I had time for reflection. At dead of night—all alone —reflection would have its operation.

A very singular scene have I now passed through, said I, and to what does it amount? Have I acted with propriety as a man, or have I deviated from the path of rectitude? I have had an unheard of,

[66]

difficult, disagreeable part to act: I do not feel entirely satisfied with myself in this business, and yet I do not know how I should have done otherwise, and have made the matter better. The laws of the land I have not broken, in any instance; but my situation has been such, that I have violated that principle of veracity which we implicitly pledge ourselves to maintain towards each other, as a general thing in society; and whether my peculiar circumstances would warrant such a line of procedure, is the question? I know many things may be said in favor of it, as well as against it. How I came into this disagreeable situation, is another matter. I know that the leading cause which produced it, was founded in wrong. My giving countenance to an open breach of the laws of the land, in the case of the bees, was a matter in which I was justly reprehensible; but that matter is now past; the owner of the bees is remunerated to the utmost extent which is provided for by law, and therefore, I must take things as they now are, and under these circumstances, do the best I can. I know the world will blame me, but I wish to justify my conduct to myself let the world think what it may. Indeed, I know they are not capable of judging upon the matter, with any propriety, because they ever will and ever must remain ignorant of the particular causes which brought these events into existence. They understand the matter in the gross, that I have preached under a fictitious name and character, and consequently, have roused many ideas in the minds of the people not founded in fact. Therefore, they concluded from this general view, the whole to be grounded in wrong. The name impostor, is therefore easily fixed to my character. An impostor, we generally conceive, puts on feigned appearances, in order to enrich or aggrandize himself, to the damage of others. That this is not the case with me, in this transaction, I think is clear. That I have aimed at nothing but a bare supply of the necessaries of life, is a fact. That I have never, in one instance, taken advantage of that confidence which the people of Pelham entertained towards me, to injure them and benefit myself, is a truth acknowledged by all. Under these circumstances, whether I ought to bear the name of imposture, according to the common acceptation, is the question?

That I have a good and equitable right to preach, if I choose, and others choose to hear me, is a truth of which I entertain no doubt:

[67]

but whether any circumstance will justify my putting on a false appearance, in order to introduce myself into that business, is the only doubt remaining on my mind. I think it my duty, at least, to steer as clear of this base guise for the future, as my safety will admit.

About 1 o'clock at night, leaving the confines of Pelham, I overtook Powers, the person whom I have before mentioned, likewise coming out of Pelham. He knew me—I asked him where he had been. He was embarrassed about giving me an answer. I mistrusted he had been employed in searching after me; I laid it to his charge. After some hesitation, he owned the fact. I put on a fierce look, and commanded him to stop, in a very peremptory manner; he obeyed. Now, said I, Powers, you see my situation; you are the only person who knows where I am; therefore, I am determined to take measures for my own safety; and for that reason, promise me, with the solemnity of an oath, that you will give no information respecting me. Powers began to expostulate. I added still more terror to my looks, and commanded him to swear to secrecy immediately, if he ever wished for the opportunity. He was terrified. He began to imprecate curses on his head, of the most horrid nature, if he should divulge his having seen me, or knowing which way I had gone. We then fell into familiar chat on various topics; rode on together till we arrived at the place where he left me to go to his father's. I went on without suspicion of danger; but no sooner had I left Powers than he took his way back again with all speed, and informed the people of Pelham of his discovery. It was about the dawn of day when he had returned to Pelham, and gave this important information. The news was like an electric shock. It was communicated through the town with that rapidity which would have done honor to a cause of importance. The people were assembled, and a select number appointed to pursue me.

All these things were unknown to me, whilst I rode on leisurely and securely, thinking of no danger. I had determined to bend my course for Rutland (Mass.), where I expected to find an acquaintance of mine, by the name of Frink, who was doing business in the mercantile line in that town: and if, fortunately, I could obtain business of some other kind, through his means, I determined to drop preaching, which subjected me to so many false appearances, contrary to my inclination. I arrived about 8 o'clock A. M. at Rutland, and found Mr. Frink, according to my expectation, at his shop.

[68]

CHAPTER XI

"No joy, no glory, glitters in thy sight,
But thro' the thin partition of an hour;
I see its sables wove by Destiny,
And that in sorrow buried; this in shame;
While howling Furies ring the doleful knell."

I RELATED to him the scenes through which I had passed; my motives in performing such parts in those scenes, and my present determination. Mr. Frink had no business of his own in which he wished to engage me, but said he would make enquiry among his acquaintance, and see what could be done. In the meantime, he wished me to tarry with him, and make myself easy, until he could have opportunity of making the necessary inquiry. After I had taken some refreshment, and put out my horse, I went into his counting-room, to have some further conversation on the subject of my business. Whilst I was leaning my elbow out at the window, I turned my eyes at the sudden and violent trampling of horses, and saw a large number of people from Pelham after me. Seeing so many, and they riding with such fury, gave me a sudden impulse of fear, and I thought to elude them by flight; therefore, sprang out of my chair, and ran across the shop, in order to go out at the back door; but no sooner had I arrived there, than I was met by one Konkey, who attempted to seize me. This aroused my indignation, and with my walking-staff, I gave him a blow across the right arm, which broke it. Having by this mean made myself a passage, I ran round the end of the shop, which I supposed would be most out of sight; but when I turned the corner, I met, full in the face, two of my deacons. I then turned and ran about twenty rods, down a small hill, and the Pelhamites all after me, hallooing with all their might, "Stop him! stop him!" To be pursued thus, like a thief, an object of universal speculation to the inhabitants of Rutland, gave me very disagreeable sensations, which I was determined not to bear. I therefore stopped, took up a stone,

[69]

and declared that the first who should approach me, I would kill on the spot.

To hear such language, and see such a state of determined defiance, in one whom they had lately reverenced as a clergyman, struck even the people of Pelham with astonishment and fear. They were very credulous in stories of the devil, witches, etc., and now thought the devil had appeared in human shape, ready to destroy them. They all stopped; amazement being pictured on their countenances, except one Hind. This man valued himself much on his courage and dexterity, and in order to show his superior ability, advanced alone, till he came within my reach; when, with a stroke of my stone, I tumbled him to the ground, apparently a lifeless corpse. This was a sufficient corroboration of their first suspicion, and they were now very certain, that the devil had actually taken the liberty to hold a tight dispute with them. A sharp dialogue took place between those men and myself. Seeing a large number of people beginning to collect and come toward me, I moved on about two rods in front of the Pelhamites, and they after me. I told them in the most decided manner, that instant destruction should be their portion, if they attempted to approach any nearer. They believed, and kept their distance, till coming to a barn, which had only one small door, I went in, determined to defend the door, which I expected to be able to do, on account of its advantageous situation. After I had entered the barn, I found there a situation, which pleased me much better, viz. the haymow, there being only one place, by which it was possible to ascend it; therefore, when I was on the top of this haymow, I could keep off any number of men that should attack me. I accordingly seized this stronghold with dispatch, mounted my fortress and carried with me a scythe-snath, as a weapon of defence, to keep off the assailants. When the Pelhamites saw, through the crannies of the barn, where I had taken my station, they ventured to come in, together with a number of the inhabitants.

I found the people, who came into the barn with the Pelhamites, were anxious to learn the reason of this uproar. Deacon M'Mullen, of Pelham, informed them that I was an impostor; I had called my name Davis, when in reality it was Burroughs; had come among them under that character, and grossly deceived them; preaching with them through the summer. It was demanded of him whether this Burroughs

[70]

had, during the time of his preaching among them, preached well, and conducted accordingly? The answer was in the affirmative. "Well," says a bystander, "why need you make any difficulty? he preached well—you paid him well—all parties were satisfied, and why need you now be uneasy? What signifies what he called his name? A name does no good nor hurt, as to the matter of his doctrine; therefore, it will be well for you to make the best use of his preaching; and of course, you will find yourselves rewarded that way, for the money which you have paid him." "But," said the deacon, "we have paid him for one Sunday which he has not preached." "As to that matter," said the bystander. "I think he is wrong, if that be the case. If he has engaged to preach, he ought to fulfil his engagements; but as the Sunday is not yet come, on which he is to preach, I think it a hard interpretation of his conduct, to say he has cheated you out of that sermon, until that time comes, so that you may see whether he will perform his engagements or not." "He certainly has attempted to murder Doctor Hind and Mr. Konkey," said Deacon M'Mullen. He therefore ought to be apprehended, and prosecuted according to the severity of the law." "As to rightly understanding that," replied the other, "I believe a number of circumstances will come into view. At first, you came upon him in a riotous, tumultuous manner, indicating by your conduct, that your intentions towards him were evil, and under this situation, he might well suppose, that to submit tamely to what you were about to do, might be exposing himself to immediate death. And secondly, he took those measures to discover the violence of your intentions, which prudence dictated, under such circumstances, by telling you to keep your distance; and at the same time, declaring his determination, in case you did not do it. Therefore, as self-defence is justifiable, and as it will appear that his conduct was dictated by self-defence, I believe it will be somewhat difficult to make it evident to any impartial jury, that he has transgressed the law, in the instance you mention." "If he has broken the law no other way," said the deacon, "he has done it in threatening to kill a young man last night, by the name of Powers, because he'd not promise to keep it a secret that he had seen him." "If that be the case," said the other, "he certainly is cognizable by the law, when that is proved. But where is this Powers?" "At Pelham," said the deacon. "Then," said the

[71]

other, "it is out of your, or my power, to do anything in this business. It would be subjecting us all to very hard terms, to be liable to be apprehended, on every report of our breaking the peace. If the said Powers, whom you mention, has been threatened with death, and under that threatening, he absolutely fears that his life is in danger from Burroughs, and to all this, will give testimony under oath, before any justice of the peace, it will then be in his power to obtain such security as to render him safe against the threatenings of Burroughs; but for others to undertake a prosecution of this business, upon a vague report, is not only out of the question, but is ridiculous to the last degree."

Deacon M'Mullen being driven from all his strongholds, began to grow uneasy at the approaching termination of that cause upon which he had entered with so much sanguine assurance. However, as his last resort, he adverted again to the pay which I had anticipated for one day's preaching, which I had not yet performed, and said he was very sensible I did not mean to perform, and to my deceiving them under a false name.

"As to obviating the first difficulty, this objection arises," said the bystander, "from whom did Burroughs receive this money which you mention?" "From Deacon Gray, our committee for supplying the pulpit," said Deacon M'Mullen. "Then," said the other, "the business stands thus: Burroughs stands indebted to Deacon Gray for money had and received of him, to the amount of the sum total. On the other hand, Deacon Gray stands indebted to Burroughs for the services which he has rendered, according to their agreement. Now, if Deacon Gray's advances have been greater than his receipts, undoubtedly Burroughs is indebted to Deacon Gray for the balance, and ought to pay him according to contract; but as you have no power to act for Deacon Gray, I do not conceive how you can have any demand, either mediately or immediately, against Burroughs on that account; and if Burroughs should even pay you back the five dollars, which you say, though without any legal evidence, he owes Deacon Gray, yet that would not exonerate Burroughs from the debt, or make him less liable to pay it over again. And as for his deceiving you by a false name, I will tell you how you may settle that matter, in the best way I can think of. I recollect, some years since, when Mr.

[72]

TRUCE AND A LUCKY ESCAPE

Abicrombie was your minister, there was an uneasiness prevailing among his people on account of his intemperance; they therefore chose a committee, of whom I think you. Deacon M'Mullen, was one, to deal with him for this crime. They accordingly came. The old fox understood how to avoid the trap. He had laid in some excellent West India rum, treated the committee with great hospitality, and, in the language of the poet, caused them to 'drink deep at the fountain of pleasure,' till they were unable to leave him through the night, on account of dipping too deep into the sweets, for which they were about to reprove him. Under this situation, they concluded the next morning, as the better way, to make their report to the church, that Mr. Abicrombie had given them christian satisfaction. They did so, and here this matter ended. Now," continued this bystander, "the way that I propose is, for Burroughs to do as Mr. Abicrombie did, and for you to accept it as christian satisfaction from this minister as well as that. Wood keeps an excellent tavern hard by; I propose for all to move up there."

This proposal was finally accepted by all. I therefore came down, and we all went up towards the tavern. I called for drink, according to the orator's advice, to the satisfaction of all, till Hind, whom I had knocked down with the stone, came among them. He foamed with rage and disappointment. A number of them retired into another room to consult on measures to be adopted for their future procedure. I learned that they had entered into a determination to carry me back to Pelham by force of arms. I was doubtful whether people would interfere where they were not immediately interested, so as to prevent this being done. I concluded it best, by all means, to put this project out of the power of the Pelhamites. Being in a room on the second story, I locked myself in. When they came after me, they found my door locked, and immediately determined to break it open. They sent some of their number for an ax. Hearing this, I jumped out of the window, on to the horse-shed, and off that on to the ground, close by those who were after the ax.

Coming so suddenly among them, they had not time to recollect themselves, so as to know what this meant, till I had run the distance of twenty rods, when they started after me; but one of their number much exceeded the rest in swiftness, so that in running sixty rods, he

[73]

was twenty rods before the others. By this time I was out of breath by running, and coming to a high wall, made of small stones, I jumped over it, and sat down behind a tree standing against the wall. I took a stone in my hand as I went over, intending to knock down the foremost man when he came up to me, which I supposed would be easy to do, as I should take him by surprise, and execute my plan before he could defend himself; after this should be performed, I could easily out-run the rest, as I should by this time be rested, and be forward of them. An alder swamp, about half a mile distant. was my object.

When the foremost man came up to the wall, I heard him panting and puffing for breath, and instead of being able to leap over, he ran against it, and threw it down in such a manner as to cover me almost entirely from sight; the stones falling against the tree in such a manner as to do me no injury. The man ran through the breach of the wall, and continued his course about fifteen rods beyond me, and stopped till the others came up, who anxiously inquired what had become of Burroughs? The other replied, that he had run like a deer across the meadow, and gone into the alder swamp.

They concluded it would be in vain to follow me—gave up the chase—went back to the tavern—took a little more satisfaction, and returned to Pelham. After they were gone, I crept out of my hiding place, and returned to Frink's store. My first object of going into business, through his recommendation, was now lost. After this uproar, I did not wish to find employment in Rutland; neither did I suppose Mr. Frink would feel that freedom in recommending me to others.

[74]

CHAPTER XII

"Again the youth his wonted life regain'd;
A transient sparkle in his eye obtain'd;
A rising glow his tender thoughts confess'd,
And the soft motions of his melting breast.
But soon dark gloom the feeble smiles o'erspread;
Like morn's gray hues, the fading splendor's fled;
Returning anguish froze his feeling soul;
Deep sighs burst forth—and tears began to roll."

EARLY the next morning I left Rutland, and travelled on towards Providence, endeavoring again to learn where I could find a vacancy for preaching. On the road I heard of a town called Attleborough, nine miles from Providence, where they were destitute of a preacher, and wanted one. I came to this town, and engaged to preach four Sundays. Here, I called myself by my own name, and engaged only for a short time, expecting I could tarry here that length of time without any disagreeable reports following me. I took lodgings at Mrs. Weld's, widow of the former minister of Attleborough. The family consisted of the old lady and her maiden daughter. They were both agreeable, and of course the whole time I spent here was pleasing. I formed, whilst in this place, many new acquaintances, which heightened the enjoyment of the scene; one in a particular manner, which I cannot think of, even at this day, without feeling the flush of pleasing emotions.

I found the people of Attleborough were desirous to have me continue longer, after the term of my first engagement had expired; but I positively refused to do it, alleging that I was engaged to preach at Danbury, in Connecticut, which in fact was true, having entered into an engagement of that kind with a man belonging there, who had heard me preach in Attleborough.

I had determined in my own mind to take Coventry in my way, as I went to Danbury, and see Joseph Huntington, for this particular purpose, viz. Hearing that a gentleman from Amherst was going to

[75]

Dartmouth College, previous to holding the anniversary commencement, and that he had a design to make such representations to the corporation of said College, against Huntington, for acting a part in the Pelham business, as should deprive him of the degree of A.B. As H——n had passed his examination for this degree, and was approved previous to his leaving the College, it was in his power to obtain his degree at any other College. Therefore, I had a desire to give him information of the evil which was hatching against him, that he might avoid it by applying elsewhere, and obtaining that which his own Alma Mater was about to refuse. I accordingly came to Coventry, and gave him this information. Huntington, accordingly, made immediate application to the College in New Haven, in Connecticut, and obtained his title of A.B.

When these matters came to be known at Dartmouth College, that Huntington had fairly stolen a march upon them, and consequently, warded off the stroke of fulmination which they had laid by in store for him, there was no small stir about the matter; but no help could be obtained, for then he had his diplomatic commission, which could not be recalled, or wrenched out of his hands. They suspected the Doctor as being confederate with his son in this business; and hence, an altercation, warm and recriminating, took place; but their suspicion of the old Doctor's being acquainted or active in this business, was entirely unfounded.

The Doctor had ever designed his son should receive a degree at the College in New Haven as well as at Hanover, and as the commencement at New Haven was previous to that at Hanover, he was very willing his son should take his degree at New Haven in the first place; but was, at that time, totally ignorant of any intention of refusing his son the same degree at Dartmouth College.

The commencement at Dartmouth College having arrived, the Doctor and his son came on. When the reasons of the corporation were offered for not granting his son a degree, the Doctor thought them highly inadequate to answer such a purpose, and remonstrated with warmth on the impropriety of their conduct, but all to no purpose. The Doctor had been enthusiastically pursuing the prosperity of this College, being a member of the corporation himself. These difficulties

[76]

cooled his affections. He soon after resigned his office of trustee, and dropped all further connections with the institution.

When I left Coventry, I was determined to make a visit to Lysander, in Pelham, and see whether he had brought his business of transmuting metals to perfection; and whether he had made the necessary arrangements for prosecuting our intended voyage to the Isle of Sable; and, in fine, to see what aspect the whole business now wore. I accordingly travelled again into the state of Massachusetts, and arrived in Pelham about one o'clock at night, at the house of Lysander.

Those who have felt the glow of friendship, will readily conceive of my feelings, at meeting again in this agreeable family. The contemplation of this object kept me in the highest flow of spirits, during my solitary ride through the greatest part of this gloomy night. My heart expanded with fraternal kindness towards them. My whole soul was tuned to the soft harmony of friendship; and I had formed in my mind a thousand tender expressions, to communicate the overflowing of my feelings towards them. Never did the lover fly with greater rapture to the arms of his mistress, than what I did to the embraces of this beloved family. A thousand soft expressions I had anticipated from them. My heat beat quick with the palpitations of pleasure, and my whole soul was in ecstasy at entering their house. My reception was equal to my most sanguine expectations; and to endeavor to describe this scene, would but show how absolutely incapable language is, to a real representation of those exquisite joys, which flow from a heart of sensibility.

We mutually recapitulated the entertaining occurrences which had taken place, in the time of our absence. We laughed at the strange whims and manœuvres of the Pelhamites; at their chagrin, when returning from Rutland; at their consultations and execrations upon me, for an impostor; and upon the people of Rutland, for not rising up to a man, and fighting the battle of the Lord. After we had ended the first friendly salutation, and that course of information which flows in upon the mind immediately after those salutations, I inquired of Lysander, what were his prospects with regard to transmuting metals, and more particularly of changing copper into silver. At this question, my friend Lysander looked disconcerted and seemed embarrassed

[77]

at giving me an answer. His wife smiled significantly. I saw there was something in the business I did not understand. My anxiety and curiosity were excited. I enquired with solicitation into the meaning of what I saw.

Lysander by this time, saw I was in earnest. He at first entertained an idea that I was treating him in a satirical manner. That I was fully possessed with a knowledge of facts after which I enquired, and consequently, rallied him on a subject too disagreeable to be called into remembrance in this manner. He was now satisfied of the contrary. His countenance fell. The tear glittered in his eye. He said, "Burroughs, we have been deceived! greatly deceived by Philips, that king of villains. Could you have thought, that all the experiments which he tried before us, when we were at Salem, were nothing but the vilest deception? It truly is the case. We were not alone the dupes of his duplicity. He had led as many as thirty men into the same belief, until he had obtained property of us to the amount of two thousand dollars, and then he was suddenly missed. Search was made after him, in every direction, but all to no purpose. He could not be found. Nothing could be heard of him. That elegant mare, that you formerly so much admired, the villain had obtained from me, with one hundred dollars in cash, when he left this country.

"His partner, who was knowing to all his hellish manœuvres to deceive, was equally cheated with the rest of us. Philips, having promised him one half the booty for his assistance, but left him equally destitute with the rest. This man, finding matters in this forlorn situation, revealed all the artful plans which Philips had recourse to, in order to make mankind believe he possessed the secret of changing one metal into another.

"We could not any of us believe, but what Philips had the knowledge he pretended to, so fair were his experiments, until we saw them all unveiled by his partner, who went over them again, showing us, at the same time, how Philips practiced the deception at every experiment."

As I have already given you an account respecting this series of deception, I shall not repeat Lysander's narrative of it any further in this place. I now found those ideas of wealth, which had before so wholly possessed my mind, entirely unfounded. The painted vision

[78]

fled quickly from sight; the airy bubble broke in an instant, and left me in the abyss of poverty.

My hopes in this resource had been sanguine. I had reflected upon the subject till I was as confident of extensive wealth, as of any occurrence which had not taken place. I felt all the enjoyment of the advantages resulting from property. I had formed in my own mind, schemes of conduct through life. How I should make the rich respect me, and the poor adore me. What exquisite pleasure, said I, shall I enjoy in relieving the heart of distress? In distributing bread to the hungry, clothes to the naked, and consolation to the broken-hearted? I had already, in imagination, distributed such benefits through the land, as not to leave a poor person to inhabit his poverty. I beheld myself at the head of a people, distributing joy and gladness. I saw the brow unclouded with care. Hilarity and vivacity were in the countenances of all; an index of peace and quiet within. Hail, happy people! said I, where no want is known to thee, where no anxious care corrodes the breast.

These were, sir, the fond images which I had pictured in my imagination. I was at this time, in a state of real delirium; but it was a delirium of joy; a state of happiness which I believe none can have a just idea of; for I expect none ever allowed their imagination so far to get the start of their judgment; and therefore, when I awoke from my delirium, to a sense of my real situation, and saw that in the room of distributing wealth to others, I had but barely the necessaries of life for myself, and that the supply for those necessaries was on a very precarious footing. I awoke to distress, anguish, mortification, and chagrin. My feelings were shocked beyond description, with this sudden reverse of fortune!

I believe that the disappointment would not have been greater, or more keenly felt, had I in reality been in possession of all the enjoyments which I had so ingeniously pictured to my view, and from that state, had been reduced on a sudden, to poverty as great as what in reality now existed. My friend Lysander and his wife saw the workings of my mind. They had passed through the same scenes themselves. They tried to console my feelings. They discoursed upon the uncertain events of this world like philosophers. They adverted to the disappointments which all meet with daily: to that fortitude

[79]

which we ought to exercise under every trial, so as to rise above disappointment, rather than to have disappointment rise above us. That riches and poverty were nothing but imaginary beings, created by our own fancy, by comparing one situation with another, and thereby giving a name to each; also they adverted to the calls of nature, as being very simple, and easily supplied, if we would rest contented with that supply; and that everything beyond tended to render us uneasy, rather than to contribute to our happiness.

How easy it is for man to give the most salutary advice to his fellow. In reasoning upon a system in theory, many will discover a depth of wisdom beyond our expectations; yet, when they attempt to reduce this advice, founded in theory, into practice, how great the contrast! The feelings of the human heart, the weaknesses of nature, and the errors of judgment, all set themselves in array against us, when we attempt to listen to the dictates of wisdom in our practice.

Happy would it have been for Lysander and family, yea. thrice happy would it have been for me, had we attended in our practice to those lessons of reason: but alas! the mania of wealth had taken strong possession of our minds, and we listened with eagerness to her calls. This soon reduced me to a state of wretchedness far beyond the power of language to describe. But, sir, as your messenger is in waiting, I will end this letter, concluding that the God of night will cast his sable mantle over your mind before you read this chapter: I am as always, etc.

CHAPTER XIII

"I see the circling hunts of noisy men
Burst Law's enclosure, leap the mounds of right,
Pursuing, and pursued, each other's prey;
As wolves, for rapine; as the fox, for wiles;
Till Death, that mighty hunter, earths them all."

IN order to give me some consolation for the disappointment which I had suffered, Lysander told me he had a plan in agitation which would operate nearly as well as we expected the other would have done. "Glazier Wheeler," said he, "is a man who can be depended on for his honesty to those for whom he undertakes to work, and he can make one silver dollar into three counterfeits, which will pass as well as any. And it will be in our power to prosecute our intended expedition to the Isle of Sable upon this scheme, with nearly as great profit as we expected from transmuting metals. We shall not be with the old man a great while, before we shall be able to work at that business as well as he; and should we find it necessary, can hire a number of hands, and drive the business, at this place to a great extent; as we shall be retired from the observations of the world, and can carry on the business without molestation."

My answer to Lysander was to this purport.—"You are sensible that counterfeiting the coin of any country is contrary, not only to the laws of that country, but likewise to the laws of our own minds, having implicitly engaged to observe and protect those laws, when we once take advantage of their efficacy to protect us in the enjoyment of our rights and privileges; therefore, should the business succeed according to our most sanguine wishes, and the coin pass to the end of time as standard silver, yet we should as really violate the simple principles of justice, as though we should be detected in passing coin so base as to serve only a temporary purpose, and die in the hands of an innocent person. The transgression would be as absolute, should it never transpire to the world, or be attended with any personal injury, as though it should be proclaimed to the universe; therefore, this reason alone would be sufficient to deter me from wishing such a thing to take place.

[81]

Another very powerful reason is, the danger we run in prosecuting such a matter, and the ruin which would inevitably follow a detection. Glazier Wheeler, it appears, has followed this business for fifty years constantly; yet he never could bring his art to such perfection as to have his money pass undetected. How often has he been confined, pilloried, cropped and whipped for this business? How many have been involved in the same difficulty, who embarked in this dangerous voyage with him? How then can we expect to share a better fate? And what would be the consequence of a detection? The property which you now possess would be swept away; your children would cry in vain for bread; your reputation, which you now hold so dear, would be lost forever; and you would entail misery and infamy on your posterity. You must then be separated from your companion, from your children, from your friends; confined in jail, a receptacle for the off-scourings of nature; treated with contempt; injured without pity; made the scoff and jeer of fools. This, sir, is a scene for a mind of sensibility."

The wife of Lysander heard this discourse with the utmost attention. Her countenance was a strong index to the feelings of her mind. Her color went and came. She now grew pale with apprehension, and now her cheeks reddened with the flush of desire, to prevent her beloved husband from rushing into dangers so desperate. She remonstrated. She expostulated. She entreated. But all to no purpose. Lysander was fixed, and nothing was able to remove his resolution. He turned to his wife, with a look of that ineffable sweetness which overpowers the mind, and said, "My dear, I wish very much to see you in possession of a coach, which I shall send you in a few months."

"As to the objections which you offer, Mr. Burroughs," said Lysander, "I will endeavor to answer them in such a manner as to give you full satisfaction on that subject. If mankind had no disposition to infringe upon the rights of each other, there would be no need of law; and the whole nature, design and spirit of law is to protect each other from injury; and where no injury is intended, nor in fact done, the whole essence of law is attended to. I know the law speaks in general terms, because it cannot descend to particulars, there being such an infinity, as to put it beyond the power of man to comprehend the whole in a system; therefore, general principles must direct us in

[82]

our interpretation of law. We ought, in our conduct, to act as men possessing reason sufficient to direct us under the various occurrences of life, so as to vary our conduct according as circumstances shall point out, keeping in view, and practicing upon the spirit of law; and when we attend to this, we cannot be said, in reality, to transgress the laws of the land, nor indeed the laws of our own mind, because we in fact do fulfil our compact with society, viz. protect each other from injury.

"From what I have observed, I believe you will readily agree with me, that I am right in prosecuting my present plan, if I can make it evident, that no danger of injury will arise to any one from it, and that by it, many will be made better. Money, of itself, is of no consequence, only as we, by mutual agreement, annex to it a nominal value, as the representation of property. Anything else might answer the same purpose, equally with silver and gold, should mankind only agree to consider it as such, and carry that agreement into execution in their dealings with each other. We find this verified in fact, by those bills of credit which are in circulation through the world. Those bills, simply, are good for nothing; but the moment mankind agree to put a value on them, as representing property, they become of as great consequence as silver and gold, and no one is injured by receiving a small insignificant piece of paper for an hundred bushels of wheat, when mankind stamp that value upon it, by agreeing to receive it for that amount. Therefore, we find the only thing necessary to make a matter valuable, is to induce the world to deem it so; and let that esteem be raised by any means whatever, yet the value is the same, and no one becomes injured by receiving it at the valuation. Hence, we find the world putting an enormous value upon certain stones, which intrinsically are of no use, as for instance, the diamond, the carbuncle, etc. These stones cannot be made use of in any pursuit of life. They will not serve for food, for raiment, or for any instrument of any kind whatever; therefore, of what real use can they be? Their scarcity, and certain peculiarities, have induced mankind to esteem them; and this esteem stamps a value upon them, so that they pass from one to another as the representation of property; hence, the holders of them always have a valuable possession, and probably always will have, which they at any time can exchange for property of more immediate consequence to their support. Had I the art of mak-

[83]

ing diamonds, do you suppose I should transgress the laws of equity in putting that art into practice? except I should fill the world with them, so as to destroy their scarcity, and hence depreciate their value in the hands of others. To put this art into practice, so as to enrich myself, and not destroy that due proportion between representative property and real property, is doing myself a favor, and injuring none. Gold and silver are made use of for convenience, to transact our business of barter and exchange with each other, as the representation of property, it being less cumbersome, and more easy to communicate from one to another, than real property of any kind: hence, when there is a due proportion of representative property, business can be transacted to the greatest advantage, and with the greatest ease. And when the public experience a scarcity or redundancy, they of course suffer an inconveniency: therefore, that person who contributes his mite to keep the balance between these two species of property justly poised, is a blessing to himself, and to the community of which he is a member. That an undue scarcity of cash now prevails, is a truth too obvious for me to attempt to prove. Your own observation will convince you of it. Hence, whoever contributes, really, to increase the quantity of cash, does not only himself, but likewise the community, an essential benefit. And, that this can be done, in the pursuit which I have undertaken, and without endangering the safety of any one, I will convince you by ocular demonstration."

He then presented me with a bag of dollars, which he said were made by Glazier Wheeler. I poured them all out; I examined them with care, as I then thought; I compared them with other dollars, which were good. I could discover no difference.

His arguments now stood all plain before me; they were collected in a line; and what do you think was the consequence? I blush to tell you the truth!—I feel ashamed of my own weakness!—My great want of solid judgment at that time, almost persuades me to hide the relation of this fact. These arguments convinced me, unfounded as they were.

Lysander told me his intentions were to pay strict attention to the business, and did not doubt his finally raising himself and family to a state of the greatest affluence. He had already obtained a sufficiency to answer present purposes. He should soon obtain much more. The business was at a stand, just at present, for want of drugs proper for carrying it forward. He intended to go soon to Springfield, where he should obtain whatever he wanted for such a purpose.

Lysander had not yet passed, or attempted to pass, any of his money. As I expected to leave his house the next night, on my route to Danbury, and to pass through Springfield on my way, he agreed to set out with me, and go his route in my company. His wife had ever felt dissatisfied about this business; being easily alarmed with the least appearance of danger, towards one in whom her happiness was so essentially embraced; but when I drew the dreadful picture of a detection, she grew almost frantic with fear; and when she saw that no entreaties would prevail over his determination, she embraced the first opportunity of conversing with me alone; and besought me in those moving terms, which would have melted a savage, to use my influence to prevent him from prosecuting his present undertaking.

Her grief spoke more powerfully for her, than all the oratory of a Burke. I could not resist her importunity. The language of her countenance and actions were irresistible. When Lysander came into our company, I began the attack in the most vulnerable part of his fortress. I endeavored to set the distress of his wife in its true light before him. I recapitulated his own arguments, which he had before used, in order to induce me "to be contented with a bare competency." I repeated to him emphatically the words of Young, in his "Night Thoughts," viz.

> "Why all this toil, for triumphs of an hour?
> What tho' we wade in wealth, or soar in fame,
> Earth's highest station ends in 'Here he lies.' "

I told him I knew perfectly well his sincere affections for his wife, and his ambition of seeing her become possessed of an equipage, etc. "But believe me, sir, not all the pomp and splendor of riches will repay her for the pain and anxiety she will endure on your account, for the space of one day, when you have absolutely launched into this dangerous ocean; therefore, sir, inasmuch as her happiness is a leading motive in your pursuits in life, you will make a most egregious blunder in your calculations, even provided you are ever so successful in your undertakings."

[85]

The feelings of Lysander were moved. The struggle in his own breast was apparent in his countenance. He sat in silence a while, then burst into a flood of tears, and retired into another room. Not many minutes had elapsed before he returned. His countenance wore a more settled aspect. He mentioned his weakness with some confusion. He said he was ashamed of being seen in tears, especially on such an occasion, not having resolution sufficient to withstand our united attacks. "But," said he, "the business is fixed—the die is cast— I have pledged my faith—I have given my word to procure those articles at Springfield. Not only myself, but more than a dozen others, are now waiting for me to fulfil my engagements. Shall I, of all others, after having agreed in the most solemn manner, to yield my aid in the prosecution of this business, now in open violation of faith, retreat and leave them in suspense?

"I feel the emotions of gratitude towards you, Mr. Burroughs, for the warmth of your feelings in my concerns; but this truth is manifest to me, that the enthusiasm of your feelings, as well as my wife's, does not give you an opportunity of reasoning coolly and candidly upon this subject. Enough has been said. These articles must be obtained; and no entreaties shall deter me from paying attention to it."

What could be done? What more could be said? Lysander's wife I saw was inconsolable. What would you have done, had you been in my situation? Words had now become entirely out of the question, and only one thing remained to be done; and that I determined to do.

I told Lysander I would take his money; go to Springfield; purchase all the articles; and return with them immediately. With some reluctance, he consented; gave me twenty dollars for the business; made out his account of the articles wanted; and directed me to the apothecary's shop, to which I must apply for them. At night, I left them with ten thousand blessings accompanying me.

Riding alone through the dreary night, reflection would make me a visit. The scenes through which I had passed had been so rapid, and filled with the emotions of sensibility, to that degree, as to leave but little room for reflection.

I have now, said I, set out to perform that business, which, two days since, I do not believe the art of man could have persuaded me to. It is a new undertaking; but I believe not attended with danger; for

[86]

the money is executed so well, as to prevent any man from distinguishing it from standard silver; at least, it looks as well to me as any money; and I do not see why I cannot distinguish counterfeit from true money, as well as others.

I think my motive for this undertaking is founded on the principles of uprightness. I think the sentiment of friendship is the uppermost object in this undertaking. Possibly a species of vanity might have some influence on my mind; and that I might wish to show the wife of Lysander how ready I was to undertake such a desperate business to befriend her; though, in reality, the danger consisted chiefly in her own fancy.

What would be the consequence, should one among the ten thousand events, which daily occur, serve to reveal the part, which I am now about to act? What would be the opinion of people concerning me, but of the most disagreeable kind, after having passed the ordeal of Pelham reports, founded on facts, which, to the world at large, would appear very unfavorable? They would undoubtedly form their opinion from ostensible facts, that I was divested of honesty, uprightness and integrity. And even should I declare to the world, that my intentions were not against the good of society, this declaration would fall upon the unbelieving hearts of a multitude, prone to place confidence in an evil report, and difficult in giving credit to that which is favorable.

These circumstances would, moreover, be attended with the following disagreeable events, viz. reports of my misfortunes, or crimes, would spread and probably be attended with that exaggeration, of which reports of that kind generally partake, and reach my friends, connections and enemies; and of all misfortunes, that which gives triumph to an enemy is the most keenly felt. My friends would mourn, my enemies would rejoice.

A view of these disagreeable events, which probably might happen, made a very deep impression on my mind. I was almost ready to faint under the trial, and thought to relinquish my undertaking. But again, said I, should I fail upon this first trial, what a pitiful appearance should I make in my own eyes? I set out on this expedition with an idea that my friendship would carry me any length. I have pledged my friendship for the performance of this business; and shall

[87]

this be said of Burroughs, that in fair weather he was possessed with friendly sentiments, but the moment the prospect became overcast with clouds, his friendship failed? How shall it be known whether I really possess those sentiments of benevolence, of which I have made such a pompous display, otherwise than by standing the trial in time of adversity? If the feelings of Damon and Pythias were graduated upon that scale of cool deliberation, which has appeared in my reasoning upon this subject, those God-like acts of benevolence, towards each other, would never have been recorded of them, which not only made Dionysius stand in mute astonishment, but left a memento to the end of time, to what an amazing height virtuous friendship may arise.

Contemplating upon matters, in this point of view, it gave me pain to think that I had even hesitated about my performing the engagements which I had entered into. I felt a degree of guilt, which I wished to hide from my own view; it produced a mortification which was exceedingly painful; therefore, I determined in my own mind, never again to allow myself to query upon the propriety of my undertaking, but to pursue it with unremitting attention, till it was accomplished.

About 11 o'clock A. M. I arrived at Springfield; made application at the shop where I was directed; told the shopkeeper my demands; and received from him the articles according to the bill. I delivered him his money and departed. Stepping into the printing-office, across the way, to do some business, I was there, in a few minutes, arrested by an officer of justice. The business at the apothecary's had made so little impression on my mind, that I could not conceive what could be the cause of my being arrested, at the time when the officer made me a prisoner. He informed me; and in an instant, the whole view of my desperate situation opened upon me. I was taken before justice Pincheon, who treated the business with a great degree of candor. However, a company of attorneys' clerks, merchants' clerks, etc., being called together by this event, were very active in making observations against me, and hunting for evidence, for fear I should not be committed for trial. After all circumstances had been attended to with care, on both sides of the question, and the justice was about giving his final decision on the business, a part of the beforementioned clerks came into the office, hauling after them a man like the Trojans, when they had found the Greek Sinon vociferating, "Here is a man who knows him! here is a man who knows him!"

When the stranger was introduced, and silence prevailed, justice Pincheon asked what he knew concerning me? The answer was, "that I was the greatest villain in the world; had come to Pelham under a fictitious name; had there preached, when I was unworthy of the business; had endeavored to kill a number of men in Pelham; had cheated them out of their money," etc.

This man you will readily understand, was a Pelhamite. He rode post from Springfield to Pelham, constantly once a week. He felt all the prejudice incident to that people. He gave his testimony in a very categorical manner. It was now determined that I must take up my abode in jail, and there continue till the session of the Supreme Court, when I should take my trial for passing counterfeit money. I was accordingly committed. And now, sir, I believe I have brought your patience to a very severe trial, by the length of my tedious narrative: therefore I will leave the business here till to-morrow; for I feel almost sick myself, with ruminating upon the gloomy scenes through which I soon passed after this.

[89]

CHAPTER XIV

"Love of gain
Strikes like a pestilence, from breast to breast;
Riot, pride, perfidy, blew vapor's breath;
And inhumanity is caught from man."

AS the apothecary was the only witness against me, which could be produced at Court, I entertained warm expectations of being acquitted on my trial.

In the state of Massachusetts, many inconveniences had been experienced from the frequent circulation of counterfeit money; therefore, the governor had offered a reward of twenty-five pounds, L. M., to any person, who should detect another in making or passing counterfeit money, knowing it to be such. Hence, the complainant became interested in the issue on trial, and of course, ought to be excluded from giving his testimony.

The apothecary, it is evident, would be entitled to the reward from government, the moment I became convicted of the crime for which I remained confined. Hence, I felt confident that his testimony could not, according to every principle of justice, and would not, be admitted.

In cases where not more than one dollar is in dispute, this regulation is invariably and sacredly adhered to, viz. that no one shall be admitted a witness in a case, wherein he is mediately, or immediately concerned; and certainly, said I, where character, liberty, and property are all at stake, they will not dare to deviate from this rule of impartiality.

Those who would plead for the propriety of the apothecary's being admitted a witness in this cause, must either deny this general rule, viz. "that a man interested in a cause, ought to be excluded from bearing testimony in that cause," or else the being entitled to twenty-five pounds, in case of my conviction, did not make the apothecary interested in the case.

Immediately after my confinement, a number of speculating geniuses resorted to me, expecting I would turn evidence for the state, and involve many more in the situation to which I was reduced: they therefore were anxious to improve this time of harvest, and enrich themselves from the bounty of government. Hence, they offered me their exertions in my behalf, and moreover, half of the reward which should be received, in case of the conviction of others, from government.

Had these speculators known with what contempt I viewed their conduct, they might have saved themselves some considerable trouble. To speculate in human woe, and barely for the sake of enriching themselves, reduce others to a state of wretchedness and misery, is an object so detestable as to excite horror in every feeling breast. Had their real motive been the good of society, their object would have been laudable; but it was a matter of public notoriety, that Glazier Wheeler had wrought openly for months past in New Salem: but these heroes took no notice of him, until the moment it was known that a reward was to be obtained for prosecuting money-makers to conviction; then all their ardor was in action; and this too, for the benefit of government.

Those who applied to me, found their expectations frustrated; that I had no design to communicate to them any knowledge I possessed concerning others; therefore, they turned their course to different objects; and determined, since I would not further their designs, that I should suffer the effects of popular prejudice.

The printer, in Springfield, inserted a paragraph in his weekly publication, not calculated to fix the most pleasing idea upon the minds of people through the country, viz. That I had been to a clergyman under pretence of coming from a mission among the Indians, and being poorly clothed, had stated to the clergyman, that my clothes had been worn out during my continuance among them. That the clergyman had invited me to preach, and in order to my appearing in character, offered me a suit of clothes; that I had accepted the offer; and in order to prepare myself for the exercises of the next day, had retired into his study, begging the favor of his watch, to know how long I might allow myself to study previous to retiring to rest. That after the clergyman and his family had retired to rest, I had silently left the house; carrying with me at the same time, watch, clothes, etc.

[91]

And leaving this text, written on paper, folded as for a sermon: "You shall seek me early, but shall not find me."

These matters were all calculated to fix an invincible prejudice against me, in the minds of those people by whom I must ultimately be tried; and consequently deprived me of that favor which every person ought to have, upon a matter of such infinite consequence to his prosperity in life. I saw these matters, and what would be the probable event.

I expected application would be made to me, for a discovery of my confederate, or confederates, at the session of the Supreme Court; and therefore, ought to form some system in my own mind, to regulate my conduct upon such an occasion. I ought either to discover the person of whom I received the money, and for whom I had acted in passing it, or else I ought to exonerate him entirely from crimination, or even suspicion; and in order to weigh these matters in the balance of justice, it will naturally arise into view, what is his situation, contrasted with my situation and circumstances? The connections which have existed between us, and our views and expectations under that connection?

True it is, that this act was performed solely for his advantage, not having my own emolument in view, either directly or indirectly; therefore, ought he not to suffer the consequence of this business? Moreover, his character stands as fair in this county, as any man's whatever; and of consequence, he would stand a better chance on trial, in the prejudices of people, than I should. He is likewise a man of property, and can of consequence, make arrangements for assistance, by counsel and friends, which I cannot expect; and even should he be convicted, the exertions of government may be more mild towards him, than they would towards me; for judges are but men, and are subject to like passions and prejudices. with other men; and it is not impossible, but that they may feel the operation of prejudice in a trial respecting me, as well as others, which I daily see are governed by it.

These were the arguments in favor of my making a discovery of the person from whom I had received the money. The arguments on the other side were, that Lysander, it is true, has a character, property, etc., to lose, and which he moreover must lose, in a great measure, should he be subjected to trial. He has a family, a description of which I have already given you, which must share his fortune in the world; therefore his ruin must bring ruin likewise on his family. A wife, possessed of every tender feeling, must suffer more than is possible for a man to suffer, who is calculated by nature, to endure the robust toils of pain and hardship; and as she must suffer with her husband, in feelings, at least, it will be involving two in misery, as great as what I can endure, should I reveal this business respecting Lysander.

It will likewise involve those who are perfectly innocent, in difficulty, as well as the guilty, viz. Lysander's wife and children; therefore, whether will it be better to meet the impending storm alone and unsupported, or else to exculpate myself, by throwing the same burden upon six others, and all of them entirely innocent, excepting one? Moreover, why did I undertake this business, unless it was to hazard the danger myself, which attended this undertaking? I am determined. The arguments are more against me than they are for me, and I must stand the power of this storm, thick and fast gathering over my head.

Happy was it for me, that I was ignorant at that time of the dreadful trials and miseries which I had to encounter, before I was released from a state of confinement; otherwise, my courage must have sunk; my resolution must have failed.

My blood, at this distant period of time, runs cold, at taking a retrospective view of those scenes. Since I have been writing this narrative, necessity has compelled me to have recourse to minutes, which brought those scenes into view, which have been a great tax on my tranquillity. I cannot now close my eyes in sleep, without being called to act these things over again in imagination. I start from sleep often, sweating with agony of mind, under the apprehensions which those images present to my view.[1]

My determination being fixed, I laid my account to conduct accordingly. Many people visited me daily, out of curiosity, to see a character entirely new; the public being fully possessed with the belief, that I had absolutely stolen a watch and suit of clothes from a clergyman,

---

[1] These observations the writer of this note has often heard Burroughs repeat with emotion. How then is it possible he could have again plunged himself headlong, and with his eyes open, into the same gulf of misery!

[93]

and had left him the text before mentioned; and all I could say or do, had no influence to make them believe to the contrary.

Some said this clergyman was Dr. Huntington of Coventry, and some said it was Mr. Trumbull, of North Haven; but those two gentlemen denying any such transaction towards them, said the matter was a fact, but who the clergyman was was unknown. It appeared that the world were determined not to give up any unfavorable idea which had once been broached concerning me, let it be ever so unfounded or improbable. Therefore their ears were open to every breath of slander which was puffed against me. My visitants would often look at me, when relating matters of fact, with an arch significance, declarative of their knowing the bottom of the business, notwithstanding all my plausible declarations. I do believe, if I had set out with warmth, to prove to the world that I was a man, and not a woman, that a great number, from that circumstance, would have been able at once to look through the deception which I was endeavoring to lay them under, and known for certainty that I was, in reality, a woman; so strong was the desire of mankind, at that day, to elude my deceptions, which they thought I was master of, to the utmost degree.

In this situation, you will readily conceive it could hardly be expected that I should run clear of a verdict against me, let the proof be ever so inadequate; for the wisest and most considerate of men will be influenced in their reasonings by those popular clamors, more or less; and they cannot avoid it, so liable is human nature to err in the devious path of life.

The speculators in government bounties had now taken Glazier Wheeler, who was likewise committed for trial. This man you will likely have a curiosity to be made more minutely acquainted with, as he will make somewhat of a figure in this narrative. He was a man tottering under the weight of years, having long since, to all appearance, been a presumptive candidate for the grave. He was a man of small mental abilities, but patient and persevering in any manual pursuit, to admiration. Credulous in the extreme, which subjected him to the duplicity of many who had resorted to him for his work: inoffensive and harmless in his manners, simple in his external appearance, and weak in his observations on men and manners. He had spent all his days in pursuit of the knowledge of counterfeiting silver, so as

[94]

to bear the test of essays. He had always been unfortunate, and always lived poor.

This was the man concerning whom the world had said so much, and who was to take his trial at the same time with me. One other, by the name of Jones, was likewise committed, either for counterfeiting or passing counterfeit money, which I do not recollect. Likewise one by the name of Cook was in confinement, to take his trial for burglary. These were the men who waited for the approach of the court with fearful apprehensions of the event.

Many circumstances had taken place whilst I lay confined here, which served to give me a pretty sanguine dependance on my own abilities. I had written a scrawl of ribaldry, and entitled it "the Hay-Mow Sermon," representing my exploits in Pelham, at Rutland, etc., and delivered this often to those who came to see me as a phenomenon. I found many applauded this as a witty thing, until I finally began to think it so myself. The flattery of those who were willing to alleviate the miseries of my situation, by making me at peace with myself, had such an operation on my mind, that I seriously began to think myself a man of some consequence, and was determined to let this circumstance be fully known at court, when I should have an opportunity of displaying all my abilities in such a conspicuous manner as to create admiration in the minds of all.

This was the state of things when I was called to the bar, and my indictment read. The judges on the bench, at this time, if I remember right, were Messrs. Cushing, Sargent, Sumner and Dana. The attorney-general was Robert Treat Paine, of whom you have heard.

. . . .

In the indictment, I was charged with passing two pieces of base metal, the counterfeit of Spanish milled dollars, knowing them to be such, etc. To the indictment I plead not guilty. I had no counsel at this time, owing to the following reason, viz. When I was first committed to confinement, I expected to be in want of more money than what I had on hand, for expenses in jail, attorney's fees at trial, etc. Therefore, I sold my horse, saddle and bridle, and had a promise of the money in ten days, but to my no small disappointment, have not received my pay to this day: of course, at the time of trial, was entirely destitute of money.

[95]

Being wholly unacquainted with the practice of the gentlemen of the bar at that time, I had embraced the opinion that they never would attend to the application of any, without an advanced fee. This idea I afterwards found to be entirely groundless. Under this apprehension, I applied for no help, having no money to remunerate a counsellor for his assistance. This being the case, I stood alone in the business, which communicated an idea to the gentlemen of the bar, that a confidence in my own abilities induced me to look with indifference on their assistance. This, of consequence, did not serve to ingratiate myself into their favor. This was not all. In my address to the jury I flung out some hard expressions against them, owing to my mistaken idea of their venal practice; all which served to create myself enemies, without the least apparent advantage arising from it.

I have often thought that a retrospective view of a thousand foolish calculations which people make in the days of youthful inexperience, and the thoughtless unmeaning impetuosity, with which they pursue these objects of calculation, would serve greatly to lessen the resentment which the wiser part of mankind often feel towards them.

After I had plead to the indictment, the attorney-general arose and opened the cause to the jury, stating in the course of his observations, that I had been a most abandoned character, leading a life of iniquity from the beginning; that I had been a counterfeiter not only of the coin of the country, but had likewise counterfeited a name, a character, a calling: all which seemed to communicate this idea to the world, that I had given a loose to the practice of every enormity; that my wickedness had at length found me out; and that I should now suffer a punishment due to my long course of crimes.

After he had closed, he proceeded to call on his evidences. When the apothecary came on to the stand, I objected to the court, against his being admitted, being a person interested in the business. After hearing the arguments pro. and con. the bench took the matter under consideration, and determined that his evidence might be taken; giving for reason, that it had before been determined; and that the reward which government had offered, would militate against the conviction of crimes of that nature, rather than promote it, if the complainant should be excluded from giving testimony.

[96]

As soon as this determination of the court was declared, I pretty much gave up the idea of being acquitted. However, I thought it necessary to make the last defence I was able to; therefore, after the witnesses were examined, I began my address to the jury, and in the course of my observations, took notice of the remarks of the attorney-general; that he had, contrary to every principle of law and justice, asserted facts, in open court, apparently with a wicked design, to fix a prejudice in their minds, in order to prevent my trial being impartial, not even attempting to produce evidence to support the base assertions which he had made.

I continued still further: I am astonished, said I, to see all justice and virtue fled from the bench. That those characters whom we are taught to revere, on account of their eminent station, should so far debase their own importance, as to remain in silence, when the most flagrant violations of all rules of order are perpetrated before them in open court: therefore, gentlemen of the jury, I turn to you as the only support, which now may be depended on, for the enjoyment of our just rights and privileges.

And now, sir, what do you think of this rant? I know what you will say, viz. that it was the ebullition of a mad, hair-brained fellow. My feelings, it is true, were wounded by the observations of the attorney-general, and I verily expected to punish all those whom I thought to blame in the business; but how weak was my reasoning upon such a subject! How mad the part which I acted! I soon found to my cost, that in the room of punishing others, I was irritating that power in whose grasp I was embraced.

I continued my remarks to the jury, upon the evidence which had been exhibited against me, with as much argument as the case would admit of. The attorney-general answered my remarks, and the judges summed up the evidence, and stated the business to the jury, not in a very partial manner. The jury retired, and in about one hour returned with the verdict of GUILTY!

The sentence was soon pronounced, which was to this effect, viz. that I should stand one hour in the pillory, and remain three years confined to the house of correction, without the corporal punishment which generally is inflicted on those who are sentenced to said house.

[97]

Glazier Wheeler's sentence was the same, excepting an addition of twenty stripes, and to be cropt. Jones was sentenced for two years to the house of correction, and twenty stripes. Cook, for burglary, was sentenced for two years to the house of correction, an hour in the pillory, and ten stripes.

I was remanded to jail, there to contemplate the gloomy prospect before me, of spending three years in a state of close confinement. I expected this state of imprisonment would be in the common jail of the county, there being no other house of correction provided. Here the horrors of my situation began to open to my view! I saw an eternity in miniature before me, consisting of one continued scene of gloomy horrors. Shut from the enjoyment of society, from perform-ing a part among the rest of my fellow mortals, to make some estab-lishment for myself, in this state of dependance; and from tasting the sweets of liberty, for which we had so lately fought and bled.

How is this, said I to myself, that a country which has stood the foremost in asserting the cause of liberty, that those who have tasted the bitter cup of slavery, and have known from hence the value of liberty, should so soon after obtaining that blessing themselves, de-prive others of it? I know that it will be said, that for my crimes I am deprived of liberty, which is according to every dictate of justice; whereas America was only struggling for her natural rights, when exercising the principles of virtue.

I have no idea of calling in question the justice of the American cause, but only advert to the situation and feelings of the people in this state, to show that they feelingly knew the value of liberty; and therefore, it appears more strange that they should wantonly trifle with this valuable treasure. It has been abundantly said by the leading men in this state, that life without liberty is not worth the possessing. This was abundantly urged to the people in time of the war; and it was urged with great truth and propriety; therefore, that the same characters, upon a revision of the criminal code, with a pretence of mollifying those laws which were sanguinary and cruel, should substi-tute slavery for death, is to me, conduct truly enigmatical.

As this narrative will not admit of entering into a political dis-quisition of the subject, I shall content myself with barely stating facts, which have abundantly come to my knowledge, from seeing the operation of this system of servitude upon men. These facts I shall relate from time to time, as they naturally connect with the narrative; and I presume, sir, you will think with me, that political reasoning strongly marked this legislative act.

CHAPTER XV

"Deluge and conflagration, dreadful powers!
Prime Ministers of vengeance! chain'd in caves!
Distinct, apart the giant furies roar;
Apart; or such their horrid rage for ruin,
In mutual conflict would they rise, and wage
Eternal war, till one was quite devoured."

THE evening after my sentence, the prisoners in the room adjoining were endeavoring to make their escape. Their attempt was overheard by the jailer, who came into the room where I was, about 12 o'clock at night, with the high sheriff, who, with his drawn sword, threatened to put me to instant death for making the attempt to break jail. The cold contempt with which I treated his threats stung him to the quick; he lowered on me with an eye of malignancy. He cried, "Ah ha! Burroughs, you are in my power, and I'll make you know it before I have done with you." He by this time had learned his mistake, by hearing the prisoners in the other room crawling out of the hole which they had made. This circumstance serves to show the prejudice which the high sheriff had conceived against me, by his concluding, without the least evidence, that I was making an attempt to break jail; however, this I found was a pretty general opinion among people at this time, that I must be conversant in every species of outrage which was going forward, and consequently, when anything of that nature was known to be on foot, they were very confident of my being interested in it.

It was thought that the jail in Springfield was insufficient to hold me securely, and therefore concluded to remove me to the jail in Northampton, another half-shire town in this county; they accordingly put this determination in execution, removing all the prisoners at the same time. I was confined with a large chain around my legs, secured in the most critical manner, and then bound fast to the wagon in which I was transported, it being twenty miles between the two places. In this situation, carried through the country as a spectacle to the inhabitants, I will not attempt to describe to you my feelings, because I know the attempt will be in vain. There is a language of the heart which we cannot express, it so far exceeds the descriptive powers of speech; yet, by comparing our own feelings in different situations, we may give the nearest guess what our feelings would be under other circumstances; and hence by this rule only, can you judge of my sensations upon this voyage to Northampton.

It was on Sunday when we were carried through the country, on our journey to Northampton; and in the room of attending the usual solemnities of the day, people thronged the roads to see this procession. When we passed, the people would inquire with eagerness, who was the minister, being known more by that appellation than I was by my own name. When the minister was pointed out to them, some would shout with joy, considering that I was now detected, notwithstanding that amazing fund of subtilty which I could use when I had occasion. Their ideas of their own judiciary became highly exalted in their opinion; for, said they, "this man has been all over the world, playing pranks in all countries, but could never be brought to justice, owing to his amazing subtilty, until he came among us, and we have showed him what is what; he finds by this time, that we are not such fools as he thought for." Some examined my looks with great attention, to see if they could distinguish where that depth of knowledge lay which had set the world in an uproar. Some few dropped the sympathetic tear over our wretched state, apparently sensible that we belonged to the same human family with themselves, and were capable of suffering equally with others.

About sunset we arrived at Northampton, and were consigned to the abodes of misery. The ponderous doors growled on their reluctant hinges! The rattling of bolts, bars and locks, reverberating through the hollow apartments of this dreary abode, made such an impression on my mind, that with difficulty I supported myself under this situation. The appearance of the Cerberus of these infernal abodes was equal to every poetic description of the Janitor of hell. Hail, ye infernal powers! said I, who inhabit these regions; assemble your forces, gather your strength, and keep high carnival to-day, in consideration of those victims which have now fallen a sacrifice at your shrine.

[101]

I was confined in a room on the ground floor alone, and shut out from the possibility of seeing any company. This was a situation which left me to the corroding pangs of thought. However, these thoughts were, in the end, calculated to fortify me against impending troubles. I reflected on my imprudence at the time of trial; on the desperate voyage I had undertaken for the sake of befriending others; on the consummate folly in our plans for wealth; and upon the three years' siege I must now undertake against the walls of a prison. But, said I, what does it signify to complain? The die is cast; my fate is fixed; and at the close of three years, what will it matter, whether I have lived in affluence, or been confined in a dungeon? Does it now militate against my happiness to think that yesterday or last week I was in a disagreeable situation? The present and future are the only times for enjoyment. The present blessings we have in our power, and consequently, can partake of every joy they grant: the future we possess by anticipation; and it is thought by many, that the foretaste of pleasure by anticipation, is greater than the participation. At any rate, happiness is the pursuit of all, and it is evident that the nearer we can approach to a state of content, by the same proportion we approach to that happiness which we are in pursuit after; of consequence, the dictates of wisdom will induce me to throw aside care and trouble, let my present situation be ever so disagreeable.

Not long after I was confined in this jail, there was a man by the name of Rood put into the same room with me. This man had held a commission in the military department of Massachusetts, and was an inhabitant of a neighboring town; had a family consisting of a wife and one daughter, a young woman in the bloom of life, and a pretty handsome figure. This man, by mistake, having taken some cattle not his own, and appropriated them to his own use, some people were so impolite as to charge him with theft. This charge was carried before the supreme court, and there he was fined about seventy pounds, if I mistake not. As the circumstances of this Rood were somewhat embarrassed, he could not pay the fine which the court had laid upon him; therefore, the prospect was, that he must lie in jail a long time; until he should be able to pay his fine, and this he had no apparent chance for doing. This man had a genius somewhat singular. His stature was about six feet. He had an upright bold look; possessing a small share of learning. He was fond of using far-fetched and hard sentences, in order to appear like a man of letters. He was very fond of using high sounding words, and had a most singular talent of palming himself upon the vulgar for a man of real information. He was cunning, but not politic, sociable and amusing, but not edifying. Finding himself in this embarrassed situation, lieutenant Rood determined to extricate himself by any means which he should find in his power. As he was not possessed with those delicate feelings of uprightness, which would subject him to a hurtful system of honesty, he determined to have recourse to any measure which would answer his purpose.

We were soon joined by another, who was committed by the name of Warner; but I believe his real name proved to be Hutchins. This man was apprehended for passing counterfeit bank bills, and committed for trial, at the next court of quarter sessions, to be holden in the March following. This man was wholly destitute of literary knowledge, and also unacquainted with men and matters. He was simple, and destitute of intrigue, but possessed an inviolable attachment to secrecy, when anything of that nature was committed to him. He had a great share of enterprise, but was wholly destitute of system. Under these circumstances, I found many designing characters had made use of him as a tool to effect their nefarious purposes.

Having this company, that eternal series of ennui, which had hung like a leaden mountain upon me, was now in some measure removed. The privilege of conversation was now restored, and amusement in some measure occupied our minds. When I have been debarred the privilege of seeing and conversing with others, the bare sight of a man has involuntarily and unaccountably raised a sensation of joy in my mind greater than you can easily conceive. even when I had not a possibility of speaking to him. This, I think, is a strong evidence that we are all descended from one common origin, and that a certain attraction of cohesion operates upon the human race, and will so continue till we all return to that fountain from whence we originated, and form an union as perfect as is formed between the river and the ocean when their waters become one.

The scanty allowance of provision which we received at this place,

[103]

made us feel severely the pains of hunger. Those who had friends near them, commonly received an additional supply from them; but those who had only what our keeper allowed us, to supply the calls of nature, often felt the griping hand of hunger, in addition to other inconveniences. All these circumstances made me feel an inconceivable uneasiness at my confinement. I would walk backward and forward across the room by the whole day together, ruminating upon the possibility of making my escape. How I longed to be at liberty, is beyond my power to tell. Often would I wish that I was possessed with the ability of passing from place to place with the same facility that we could discern objects at a distance, in this place and that place. How quick would I then leave these hateful abodes, and wanton in the sunbeams of liberty. How easily could I then elude the iron grasp of this petty tyrant, who triumphs over the miseries of the wretched few under his control. Often would I contemplate upon the situation of the beggar, who gained his daily bread by the cold hand of charity, and yet walked at liberty, free as the air in which he breathed, capable of going to any place to which his fancy directs him, without let or hindrance; I compared his situation with mine, and in the comparison, I fell infinitely short of his state of happiness.

I was determined to try some measure for my escape from this place. I peeped into every corner of the room; I surveyed all the barricadoes with which I was environed; I contemplated every possible measure which occurred to my imagination. I at last concluded to begin my operation upon the chimney way, hoping that I could, by taking up the foundation of the chimney, get to the ground, and by that mean undermine the jail, and make my escape that way. I laid the plan before Warner and Rood, for mutual consultation and approbation. Warner, at once, entered into the scheme, and promised his assistance. Rood refused to lend his assistance, but encouraged us to proceed; suggesting that the thing probably might be accomplished. I soon saw into the drift of Rood. He determined to take advantage of our success, if we proved fortunate; if otherwise, he thought to exculpate himself by saying he had no part in the business. He had acted the part of a sycophant towards the jailer and the high sheriff from the time of his commitment, hoping through their intercession,

[104]

to gain some alleviation from the court of their sentence, at the next session.

Notwithstanding the assistance of Rood was not to be expected, Warner and I were determined to make the attempt immediately after the approach of night, as that was the only time in which we could work, without an immediate detection. Therefore, after the time of retirement, we pulled off our coats, and went to work with a great degree of energy, upon the stones in the chimney. We soon almost filled our room with stones and rubbish. In this situation, we experienced great inconveniences for the want of light, being obliged to have recourse to pine slivers peeled off from a board, which kept one hand constantly employed in feeding the blaze, lest it should be extinguished, which would at once defeat all our purposes. As I was the strongest of the two, I kept Warner feeding the light, whilst I labored like Sisyphus in rolling huge stones out of the chimney-way. Happy should I have thought myself at that time, if, Hercules like, I could have turned the course of some mighty river under the jail, to have assisted me with its force, to sweep away those huge rocks. I labored and toiled without intermission, till about midnight, when coming to a rock I could not possibly get out of the hole, I for a moment despaired of success, after straining with all my might a number of times to no effect. Rood, seeing the situation in which matters stood, jumped out of bed, and helped to lift the stone from its place, and then returned again into bed. I again renewed my labor, and had overcome the greatest part of the difficulties before us, when the light became extinct for want of fuel, the board being all consumed. I tried to pursue the business in the dark, but found it in vain, and therefore was obliged to quit our undertaking. How much would I now have given for a farthing candle! but wishes were as vain as our expectations were unfounded. The necessity of our relinquishing the pursuit was absolute, and therefore, with sullen reluctance, I yielded to the force of necessity. I did not entirely lose all hopes of succeeding yet by this method. As soon as daylight should afford an opportunity, I determined to renew my labor, and if by good fortune our Cerberus should not make us a visit till some time in the morning, I was still in hopes of making the breach soon enough to leave him to his own agreeable reflections, when he came to search our room, which he constantly did every day.

[105]

Therefore, at the dawn of day, I again renewed my labor with increased animation. I struggled and toiled with the huge rocks in such a manner as to establish the belief, that in the course of an hour I should again flit upon the wing of liberty. But O! horrid to relate! the thundering noise of the jailer, in opening his ponderous doors, throwing back the many bolts, and turning the keys of the enormous locks, at once defeated all my expectations of freedom. The mighty castles which I had been building in the air, came tumbling over my head like a sweeping deluge.

The jailer came into the room, and what was the scene pictured to his view? Rubbish, rocks, stones and dirt filled the room! Two men almost naked, covered with sweat and dust!

The door was again immediately shut, and the jailer retired, but his absence was almost momentary. He returned with a band of flinty hearted myrmidons to assist in the diabolical system of revenge. We [1] were taken by those patrons of humanity, tied to the grates, and received ten lashes each, on our naked backs, with a horse-whip. Immediately after this, we were put in the dungeon, where we lay two days, and were then removed to another room.

The day after we were confined in the dungeon, the high sheriff came to the jail, and threatened to put Rood into the dungeon with us; this threat had the desired effect. Rood declared he had given no aid, assistance, or advice in the business of breaking the jail, but on the contrary, used all the arguments and entreaties to induce us to desist, which were in his power: and moreover. said he. "when I saw they would not give up the attempt, I got out of my bed, and went to the window, in order to call the jailer but when Burroughs saw what I was about, he came up to me with his penknife, and threatened to stab me if I proceeded; therefore, I was obliged to desist."

This conversation happened to take place where I overheard it all. I called to Rood, in the midst of it, and informed him that he was a liar, that he had, in reality. been aiding and assisting in our efforts for breaking the jail; that had he conducted with ingenuousness in the business. I should have been willing to have him exculpated from blame; but when he manifested a disposition to heap additional censure upon me, for the sake of making himself stand high in the opinion

---

[1] Warner and myself.

of others, I supposed it a just tribute to my own vindication, to set matters relating to him in their true light. This I expected would be heard by the high-sheriff likewise, as they two were in conversation together; and my main object in making this declaration at this time, was to prevent Rood from building himself up in the opinion of the sheriff, at my expense.

When Rood found I had detected him in his duplicity, he entreated the sheriff to put him into a room separate from me; dreading, as I suppose, my just vengeance upon him, for his perfidious conduct. He promised on this condition, to give information concerning any attempt of the prisoners to break jail. He was, of consequence, put into another room.

The second day of my confinement, nearly night, I heard a terrible clanking of massy chains approaching towards my apartment. The door of the dungeon was opened, when lo! horrid to relate! a deformed Vulcan [2] attended with his grisly Cyclops, [3] carrying with them a huge iron chain, and all the tools for their infernal purpose!

I was ordered into another apartment, and to work went those engines of cruelty. They in the first place, made fast a flat ring around my leg, about six inches wide and an inch thick. This was connected with a chain weighing about thirty-six pounds and ten feet in length. The other end of the chain was fastened to the timber composing our floor, with a staple driven in with a sledge, which made the whole jail tremble. After I was fixed in this manner, they left me to my own reflections, inwardly exulting at their mighty power, in making a poor wretch secure from enjoying the cold comfort of hoping for better times.

O! ruthless mortals! said I, why so infatuated! Am not I a member of the same family with yourselves? Am not I capable of suffering the same woes with others? Place yourselves in my situation for a moment, and try to regale your feelings in such a condition. Even suppose a brother, a child, or any near relative, or friend, in my situation; would you conduct towards him as you now do towards me, who am a stranger among you? Surely you would not. Does not the language of nature, do not the principles of that benevolent

[2] A Blacksmith.
[3] A journeyman Blacksmith.

religion of which you make so great profession, teach you to treat the stranger with kindness? How then is it that you pinch me with hunger, mangle me with whips, confine me in a dungeon, etc., as though you envied me the enjoyment of the liberty of walking a room of twenty-feet square? You have confined me to a space of half that dimension; and this confinement too performed in the most cruel manner. Would any of you, who are walking at your ease, enjoying the sunshine of liberty, if placed in my situation, lie down tamely under the burden, and not exert yourselves for freedom, when you possessed a faint ray of hope, that you may obtain it by exertion? You who have never felt the burden of confinement, can have but a faint idea of its nature; hence, you esteem it as it feels to you, and treat those who are under its pressure, according to your feelings.

I lay in this dismal situation about a fortnight, if I remember right. My leg, by this time, was worn by the iron around it, till the skin was quite off. In this situation, I became entirely impatient. My sufferings I thought insupportable. I cursed the day in which I was born. I cursed my friends and all the human race, in the bitterness of my anguish! Well was it for Warner, that I was confined with a chain, at that time, lest haply I should have vented my rage on him in the overflowing of my distress. I roared with anguish! I raged like a Bedlamite! The obdurate heart of my Cerberus was not moved by my situation; he was terrified and durst not approach me. Yet that adamantine barrier which fortified the avenues to his soul, from the approaches of compassion, remained entirely unimpaired, and prevented the least motion of pity from disturbing his repose. There are certain situations of suffering which will make a man mad; will take away every exercise of rational conduct; will reduce him to a state of desperation; so that he will rush into the most desperate danger. This was my situation at this time. I was determined not to endure these trials any longer; and, in the language of the poet, to end them "by taking arms against myself, and all my woes at once."

I ruminated upon the means of accomplishing this design. Various were the plans which offered to my view, but none appeared so eligible to answer the state of my mind, as the terrible element of fire. Therefore, I determined to set fire to the jail, and Sampson-like, make a sacrifice at my death, which should atone for the cruelties I had suffered in my life!!!

The flooring of the jail was laid with two thicknesses of timber, each thickness being about fourteen inches, and over these timbers, a floor of inch boards. The boards which composed the floor I cut away, in such a manner as to be able to take up a piece about two feet long; the cracks between the timbers were about two inches wide, into which I dropped coals of fire, which fell down to the ground, twenty-eight inches below the floor, among shavings and other combustible stuff. The air drawing in strongly, at the place where the fire was, it soon began to rage with great violence. I replaced the board in its former situation; placed my straw, which served for my bed, on the board, and lay down with great composure, viewing my sufferings as fast hastening to an end.

The floor being so tight as not to admit the blaze into the room, it sought a passage elsewhere, and soon burst out, through the underpinning and blazed up to the height of the eaves of the jail, about twenty feet! this was a scene possessing more of the horrid sublime than anything I ever met with during my life.

At the dead hour of night, when all nature was lost in forgetfulness, as Young emphatically expresses it,

> "Night, sable goddess! from her ebon throne,
> In rayless majesty, now stretches forth
> Her leaden sceptre o'er a slumbering world;
> Silence, how dead! and darkness, how profound!
> Nor eye, nor listening ear, an object finds:
> Creation sleeps. 'Tis as the general pulse
> Of life stood still, and nature made a pause,
> An awful pause! prophetic of her end.
> And let her prophecy be soon fulfill'd;
> Fate! drop the curtain! I can lose no more."

In this situation, to see columns of smoke and fire rolling up with a majestic power, enveloping me around, was a scene which surpasses all description! I viewed the operation of the flames with a tranquil horror! I now felt myself exalted above the operations of the petty tyranny of those who had exercised the rod of severity over me.

Your reign, said I, will be short, and I shall not fall altogether un-revenged. It may serve as a memento to others, not to drive those to desperation, who have the misfortune to fall under their power.

I soon found that the fire had loosened the staple, which confined my chain to the floor; therefore, I was at liberty to walk from one end of the room to the other, contemplating the progress of this dreadful devouring element. By this time, the prisoners in the room overhead were awakened, alarmed, and began to cry out for help. The jailer was aroused, the inhabitants gathered, and the bolts, bars, and locks, were in motion. They immediately came into my room, and finding me loose, conveyed me into the dungeon.

Whilst I was in the dungeon, I heard the bustle among the people, in putting out the fire. From the exclamations of some, I thought the danger increased, and from the operation of others, I thought it diminished. My mind was wavering between hope and fear, till about 4 o'clock in the morning, when I found the noise decreased until it became entirely silent. I now concluded they had subdued the fire, and of course, I should be called to an account as disagreeable, as when I attempted to break jail.

The scene following, of all the scenes of my life, strikes my mind with the most distress in relating. To paint it according to the existence of facts, and the sensations arising from those facts, is an arduous task, too great for me to undertake, till I have refreshed nature with a little relaxation by sleep, and application to other objects, which will turn my mind a while from the disgust which the contemplation of this subject creates. Therefore, sir, accept my sincere wish for your welfare, my desire that you may never taste that cup of adversity, which I have drained to the dregs. I am, dear sir, etc.

CHAPTER XVI

" 'Tis only change of pain,
  A bitter change! severer for severe;
  The day too short for my distress! and night,
  E'en in the zenith of her dark domain,
  Is sunshine to the color of my fate."

AT 9 o'clock in the morning, I heard the usual tumult at entering the outer door of the jail. I saw a crowd were entering and passing along the alleyway, previous to their coming to the dungeon door! The door opened! The high sheriff, jailer, and about twenty more, entered! I saw by the appearance of things, that I must prepare for the worst possible event. The sheriff advanced with a cocked pistol. which he presented to my breast, and swore by God, that if I offered to resist, he would put me to instant death. He had an idea that I had become desperate, and would sacrifice my own life for the sake of ridding myself from the misery I was under, and obtaining revenge for the injuries I had suffered.

I called him a despicable, cowardly wretch, to advance upon a poor, helpless, unarmed man, in the manner he assumed. I told him I placed his utmost malice at defiance, and challenged him to do his worst. I told him I expected everything base and cruel from him, ever sensible that the ignoble spirit which possessed a coward, led to cruelty and barbarity. That I had been punished ignobly once, for nothing; and therefore, I determined he should have something for his next attempt which should make his cowardly soul tremble with fearful apprehension.

He ordered his posse to advance and seize me. They advanced and laid hold of me. As soon as they had made me secure, the sheriff took hold of my hand and twisted it round, so as to make the pain very sensible. I thought he would have wrung my arm off my shoulder. I was led out of jail in this manner, into the yard I was then tied fast to the grates, and stripped naked.

[111]

The reason why I was carried into the yard was, that this mild distributor of justice might have a better opportunity to give his whip full scope, without impediment. He improved his opportunity, and with a whip, commonly known by the name of hunting-whip, he laid about me with all his vengeance, for about five minutes. I then was taken down, and Warner put in my place, who received twenty lashes. We were then re-conveyed into the dungeon; when I was loosed from the iron I had about my leg, and in lieu of that, a large ring was put about each leg, with an iron bar running from one to the other. This bar was bolted to the floor. I then had an iron about my waist, and bolted to the floor: after all, I was handcuffed and pinioned.

The sheriff then came to take his farewell, and parted with some hearty curses for my incorrigible conduct. The curses he received back again with interest. I was now left to myself, a gloomy spectacle of helpless misery. This was in the month of December, in the year 1785, a remarkable cold month; and my confinement in this situation continued until January, 1786, being thirty-two days in the whole. Here I was deprived of fire, of clothing and exercise, till the time was nearly expired; and even the pitiful allowance of straw to lie on: but all this was nothing, compared with what I suffered with hunger.

Those who know the cruel effects of hunger, are the only people who can understand me when I relate these facts. But few people have ever felt its effects; therefore, should I relate this story to people in general, not many would know what I meant.

I had not been in this situation many days, before I began to experience the severe effects of the cold. As I could not stand, walk nor step, the only recourse I had to keep my feet from freezing, was rubbing them against an iron spike, a little from my feet, perhaps three inches; which had either never been driven into the floor entirely, or else had started back by some mean, the space of about four inches. This I wore very smooth with a perpetual friction. No person was allowed barely to look through the little aperture into the dungeon. This little hole was secured by a door, so as to hide every object from our sight.

About the seventh or eighth day after my confinement in this pandimonium, the pains of hunger became excruciating. Gladly would I have eaten my own flesh. I even had a hankering desire to get the excrements out of the vault, but that was out of my power. All my thoughts were occupied upon victuals. I could not conceive what I had been about through life, that I had not eaten more when I had the opportunity. I could not possibly conceive of the idea of a man satisfied with eating. That a man could be glutted with food, so as to loath it, was a fact established in my mind, by my own experience; yet, at this time, I could not believe it; indeed, I thought I knew to the contrary. Had I been possessed of an empire at this time, I should have parted with it in a moment, for a supply of food for the present necessity. It is said that hunger will break through a stone wall, but I say that hunger will carry a man the greatest length of anything in nature. It destroys the feelings of humanity, and makes a man a savage. It begets in his nature a ferocious feeling, which assimilates him more to the tiger than to a being possessing the milk of human kindness; therefore, take the mildest couple that ever lived, reduce them by famine to a state of extremity, and you will see the fond husband tearing from his beloved partner the food upon which her existence depends. Nay more, you will see, in this situation, the tender mother refusing her dying infant the smallest pittance of sustenance to its expiring entreaties!

Must not the mind of sensibility shrink with horror at a sight so dreadful? And this have I experienced in a land of christianity! A land where great professions of humanity and christian benevolence have been made! In charity to the inhabitants, I now believe they did not know the extremity of my sufferings. At that time I did believe it, and that they concurred in the business; but I know my situation did not admit of cool reflection and candid reasoning upon the subject. I begged, I entreated of the keeper of these infernal abodes for bread, but my entreaties were given to the winds. I raved. I swore, I tore, cursed and lamented; but all did not move his obdurate feelings. After the fifteenth day, the rage of hunger began to subside. Nature, tired with the struggle, gave way, and began her retreat. I grew faint and sick. There was a gloom hung over me, which is entirely inexpressible. Nothing did I ever feel of the kind before or since; and how to describe it to you now, I am entirely at a loss. I know if I undertake, I shall not succeed in giving you an image of the most distant resemblance.

I grew sick of life; I hated the idea of ever mixing again with the world; I wished for death with an impatient ardor. There is a situation, sir, when life is no more sweet. There are circumstances, under which life becomes a burden, and is no longer desirable. This was my situation. I began to console myself with the hope that my miseries would soon have an end in the arms of death. The approach of this grim tyrant now was the most pleasing object of my contemplation. Here I found a balm for all my wounds. "To rest from my labors" in this world, was the height of my wishes. Here was a pleasure in the prospect which assuaged the rage of my pain, and calmed the boisterous emotions of my mind.

I had now become emaciated to a skeleton. My beard had not been cut, during the time of my being in the dungeon; hence it was about two inches long. My hair had not been combed, which stood in every direction. From these circumstances, I had more the appearance of some savage beast of the forest, than anything appertaining to the human species. I now looked for the speedy end of my toils. I found my strength daily decreasing, and concluded that nature must soon march out of her fortress, and give entire possession to the king of terrors.

Matters being in this situation, one morning about 11 o'clock, I heard the outer door of the jail loosed from its bolts and bars. The door looking through the little aperture into the dungeon was opened, and the name of Burroughs was vociferated by the jailer. For him to have any business with me at that time of the day, was what had not happened for thirty-two days before, and what could be his business now, I could not conceive. The objects of life were so far out of my view, that I thought at first to pay no attention to this call, but upon more mature reflection, I rose up as far as I was able, and looked through the little hole. I there saw a man whom I did not recognize, a stranger. He called me by my christian name, when he spoke to me. Who it was addressing me thus familiarly I could not tell. I told him he had the advantage of being unknown to me, while I was known to him. He asked me if I did not know my uncle? I surveyed him with some attention, and at length saw he was my mother's oldest brother.

He appeared to examine my condition with as much attention as his situation would admit of. He entered into some general observations upon the nature of my folly in setting the jail on fire, and attempting to break out. He lamented the distressed situation in which he found me, and handed me two dollars to supply my present necessities. He then retired.

Immediately after this, the jailer's wife came into the alley, and told me if I wanted any victuals she would supply me with it. How this declaration sounded in my ears, you will more readily conceive than I can describe. To have a prospect of a speedy supply of food, again recalled the desire of life. My feelings were in arms, and all the vigor of desire was again rekindled in my bosom. I told her I wished for something to eat immediately; and on her informing there was nothing ready dressed, I besought her to fetch me some bread, that I might be eating, whilst she was making ready something else. She brought me a brown loaf weighing about four pounds.[1]

With what pleasure did I view this precious morsel approaching me. I half devoured it with my eyes before I got hold of it. How sweet was the taste! how exquisite the pleasure! Warner laid hold of the loaf and tore away about half the contents. Yes, said I, thou fellow sufferer! eat and be satisfied! the day of bitterness is over, we have the promise again of food sufficient to supply the calls of nature!

The bread was almost instantly gone, but the cries of hunger were not appeased. Soon however the wife of the jailer came with strong tea and toast. I was astonished she brought so little, but she understood my situation better than I did myself. We eat up the recruit of food in a moment. I entreated for more, but could not obtain it, under near an hour. When I had received my third portion, and we

[1] For humanity's sake, however, it is to be wished that this good woman had offered her starving prisoner food, before he had received the two dollars! Notwithstanding his aggravated crimes, and irritating conduct, there is no question but Burroughs received punishment far exceeding his deserts. And the savage treatment he met with, particularly in this prison, is enough to make one blush for the *christian* name!

had eaten it, Warner began to experience terrible pains in his bowels, and I thought, for some time, he must have expired under the operation.

The same characters who had made their appearance when I was bound in the manner described, now entered the dungeon again, and to work went hammers and files, and in about half an hour I was freed from the terrible load of iron under which I had groaned for thirty-two days.

When I was liberated from these irons, I had almost lost the use of my limbs; my feet would hardly answer my desire for walking; for both of them had been touched with frost, and the irons on one of my legs had been put on so tight as to cause a swelling, which ended in a sore about six inches long, and which has never yet gotten entirely well.

I was removed out of the dungeon into an upper room, which was much more comfortable than the one I had first occupied. Here I received food as often as once in three hours, through the next day. Yet I could not be satisfied; my appetite was keen as ever, even when I was so full as to prevent me from swallowing more. This continued to be the case for the space of a fortnight longer, when I found my appetite regulated upon the common scale of eating.

At this time, my uncle wrote the following letter to my father, giving him some account of my situation in Northampton jail.

"Charlton, January 7th, 1786.

"BELOVED BROTHER AND SISTER,

"I have been at Northampton twice within this month past; visited your son Stephen each time. The first time, I found him chained down in the dungeon, for attempting to burn the jail; and also for attempting, at another time, to dig through the chimney. I expostulated with him, with regard to his former conduct, endeavoring to show him his folly in trying to break and burn the jail. I obtained a promise that he should be let out of the dungeon. The second time I was there, which was this week, I found him in the common prison unchained. I found him very needy each time, and particularly the first, his allowance being very short. I let him have two dollars the first time, which I believe he made a good use of; the second time, I found him desti-

[116]

tute of a shirt; I got him a new one, and let him have thirteen and four pence in cash.

"As I am in a few days going to the General Assembly in Boston, it is not likely I shall see him again until spring, although I have lately been in something of a habit of visiting at Northampton. Being in haste and the bearer in waiting, shall only subjoin, that I am your loving brother

"EBENEZER DAVIS.

"REV. E. BURROUGHS."

After the receipt of this letter, my father wrote to an acquaintance of his in Northampton, by the name of Strong, to pay some attention to my needs, afford me what my necessities called for, and draw upon him for the amount of expenses incurred.

By some strange fatality, when this letter arrived, Captain Strong either thought, or wished people to believe he thought it a forgery of mine. He paid no attention to it; and the report was soon circulated, that I had forged a letter in my father's name and sent it to Captain Strong; and even at a very modern period, a gentleman of some eminence, from Northampton, has repeated this false report, in those places where he knew it must be attended with very disagreeable consequences to me.

And now, sir, permit me to digress a moment from the course of the narrative, and offer a few remarks upon the very singular scenes through which I passed in this jail. As you, sir, have been long in the practice of the law, you will more readily conceive of the illegality of these transactions.

The fundamental principles upon which our liberties and privileges are founded, are the trial by jury, that no unnatural and cruel punishments shall be inflicted, and that a person shall never be punished, but by due course of law. These leading principles, I believe, are never to be deviated from, except in case of rebellion, when the state is in danger; then martial law may operate; and even when martial law has its operation, it is necessary to have matters of fact established by evidence, and the voice of a majority of three, at least, to warrant a punishment. In the punishments inflicted on me, none of these preliminaries have been attended to, but I have been subjected to the arbitrary will of a petty tyrant. He punished when his inclination was for cruelty, and inflicted what kind his pleasure directed. It may be urged, that I had made myself liable to punishment, by my conduct in jail. This being supposed, which I by no means believe; yet, to punish me without a legal trial, was as absolutely contrary to every dictate of law and justice, as though I had been in fact innocent. It may further be said, that my sentence confining me to the house of correction, made me liable to the punishment of the master of the house at his discretion. If this be the case, we take away from one class of citizens a right, which we have very justly been tenacious of, and have subjected them to a state of as abject slavery, as the Negroes in the West Indies. And even if this doctrine is well founded, yet the injustice of their conduct will receive no extenuation; for Warner was punished equal in kind, though not in quantity with myself, although he was only committed for trial, and of course must be innocent in the eye of the law, until he should be convicted. As the narrative will not admit of treating this business largely, I have given you only the leading ideas, which possess my mind upon the subject, knowing your ability to state them in your own view, much more clearly and logically than what I shall do.

About this time Philips, of whom you have heard mention, was committed to this jail, and lodged in the room where I was first confined; likewise one Hinds was lodged in the room where I now was. This Hinds was committed for adultery with the wife of one Wallace, and the woman herself was kept in the common dwelling house of the jailer. One Norton, who was charged with the murder of a man by the name of Brown, was committed about this time, and confined in the dungeon. It appeared from all the information I could gather, that the circumstances of this business were of the following nature, viz. Norton being a house-joiner, was on a new building laying shingles, when Brown came by, and in a playful manner, threw stubble at Norton a number of times, which impeded him in his work. Norton was a man hasty and petulant in his temper. He told Brown if he did not desist, he would come down and give him a flogging. This threat induced Brown to continue his folly with more eagerness, to show that he did not regard Norton's threat. With this, Norton

[118]

immediately descended the ladder, came up to Brown, and a scuffle ensued. Some blows passed; at length Norton gave Brown an unlucky stroke, after which he never breathed again.

Norton, seeing that Brown was absolutely dead, made his escape, and left the country. He had been absent about twelve months, when he became known in some part of Connecticut, where he resided, and was apprehended and brought to Northampton for trial.

From experiencing the treatment I had received in this place, I had, through mistake, formed an idea that Norton would have no chance for justice at the time of his trial; I found likewise he entertained the same idea of this matter himself. I sincerely wished him out of their hands, and felt willing to yield him any assistance which was in my power.

Matters were in this situation when, one night about 12 o'clock, I heard a whisper as though it came from out of the room, calling me by name. I sprang up and ran to the window, but found the voice did not come from there. I then ran to the door, but there again was disappointed. Where the noise came from I could not conjecture, which still continued. I at last bethought me of the pump, leading into the vault, under the jail. I ran, and uncovering the pump, could easily distinguish the voice of Norton, who had gotten down into the vault. He entreated me to let him have a knife, for "by that," said he, "I can make my escape." Had it been a diadem, for aught I know, I should have parted with it, to have assisted him at this moment. I took the knife, and tied it to a string, and let it down. I then covered the pump, lay down, and reflected with a great degree of pleasure upon my affording some small assistance to befriend a human being whom I never saw. Truly, said I, this conduct has been guided by the principles of philanthropy. I soon fell into a sound sleep: my slumber was refreshing and sweet: I felt entirely at peace with myself, under the fullest conviction I had acted according to the plan of the good Samaritan. I did not know that any in the room were awake at this time; therefore, I thought myself the only person possessed of this secret. The next day, Hinds was taken out of the room where I was, and let into the alley with the woman, for a criminal connection with whom he was confined. They remained together about an hour, when he was put back into the room where I was. Soon after, I heard a number of people entering the outer door of the jail, and the clanking of chains, as though some infernal purpose was in agitation. I listened with attention, and soon heard the dungeon door open; when, to my surprise, they cried out that Norton was gone. I did not expect he would so soon have made his escape; and now felt the exultation of joy on account of his success. My joy was soon damped, by hearing another voice, soon after, crying out, "Here he is! here he is!" Norton, at this time, was so busy at work in the vault, that he never heard any of the uproar, until a youngster, putting his head down into the hole he had made, saw him at work.

They soon got him up and made him fast in irons: after this, they came into my room, took me out, carried me into the room where I was formerly confined, and there made me fast with my old chain. Here were Philips and Warner. Soon after the jailer had left us, I began to discover the amazing ability for contrivance which Philips possessed. He freed me from my irons in ten minutes. We then all went to work to make the hole larger through our pump into the vault under the jail. This we effected, to my surprise, in the space of about six hours, so that a man, when stripped naked, could let himself down through it into the vault. This hole was made in such a manner as entirely to secure it from the observation of those who perpetually searched the jail. Even should they examine the hole itself, they would not discover its being otherwise than what it was originally, so perfect was Philips master of what he undertook, of such a nature. We wrought with assiduity all the night following, and had made such progress in digging out, that we arrived at the stones of the underpinning of the jail, they being sunk about four feet into the earth.

The prisoners in the room out of which I was taken, and especially Hinds, were of opinion they heard a noise on the night that we were at work in the vault; but the other prisoners suspecting how the case really was, and being somewhat jealous of Hinds, endeavored to persuade him that it was a matter of mere conjecture, not founded in reality.

The next day, I found Hinds and his paramour were put into the alley together, as formerly. Placing myself in a situation where I could hear their conversation, I became acquainted with a very singular and curious circumstance, viz. that Hinds had entered into an agreement to discover whatever plan should be in agitation for the purpose of breaking the jail, and was to receive, as a compensation, liberty to be alone with his Miss one hour in the course of every day. That in consequence of this agreement, he had given information of my helping Norton to my knife, and that he was about breaking jail. In consequence of which information, Norton was discovered, and I was again confined in irons. Hinds told his prostitute, that he had heard the noise of somebody digging, and believed Norton was attempting to break out again. This noise, said he, continued through the whole night. After this interview, they were both replaced in their former situation.

Soon after this, the jailer, and a number with him, made a visit to the dungeon; carrying lights with them, in order to search every hole and corner. After about an hour's investigation. they gave up the pursuit as fruitless; concluding that Hinds was mistaken in his conjecture, or else the breach was made in another room. They therefore came into the room where I was confined, and after searching some time, concluded some mistake must have existed with regard to the conjecture of Hinds. The jailer even looked into our pump, and could discover no manner of breach which we had made: however, he thought that the hole was so large, as possibly to admit a small boy down it; and therefore determined he would make it more secure.

You will naturally ask the question, with regard to my irons, whether this was not a suspicious circumstance, as well as the noise? This business was fixed equally secure with the other. After I had been liberated from my irons by Philips, he made them answer a number of other purposes in the prosecution of his plans; and likewise prepared them in such a manner, that I could slip them on my leg in half a minute, so as to wear the appearance of remaining closely chained: this I always did when I heard the jailer entering, so that by this mean I remained undiscovered.

After the search was over, I called to one of the prisoners in the room with Hinds, Grinold by name, who was a person holding such conduct as Hinds had been guilty of in the utmost abhorrence, and related to him a simple account of facts respecting Hinds. Grinold immediately began an altercation with Hinds; they soon proceeded to

[121]

blows—and Hinds, who was as great a coward as he was a villain, soon cried enough; but this subterfuge did not answer his purpose. Grinold still continued to beat him, alleging that such conduct as Hinds was guilty of did not entitle him to the common usage under such circumstances.

In the afternoon, the jailer came into my room, and the blacksmith with him; and after taking up our pump, placed two bars of iron over the hole, and spiked them to the timber. This, I thought, was an effectual security against our ever again getting into the vault. But no sooner was the jailer gone, than Philips showed me how mistaken I was in my conjectures. Not more than six minutes after their departure, we had all the irons loosed from their place; and that was effected by us in this manner, viz.—We took the chain that was around my leg, and put it under one of the iron bars, and fetching it round, fastened it together over the bar, with a key made of one of the links. After this was done, we took an oaken bench, about ten feet long, made of a slab, as much as four inches thick in the middle, and put the end of this bench into the bite of the chain, placing it in such a manner as to gain a great purchase; we lifted the bar in an instant, drawing out the spikes with ease.

Immediately upon the setting in of night, we again went to work; but had not continued many minutes before the outer door of the jail opened, and in came a number of people, and passing our door, went up to the prisoners overhead. Here Hinds had an opportunity of giving the hint to the jailer, that he had something to communicate to him. Therefore, after the people had finished their business with the prisoners, the jailer took Hinds out into the alley, and there learned that we had broken again into the vault. Upon this information, the jailer came into the room, and removed all the prisoners into the dungeon, excepting myself, being in irons, so securely confined, that he remained at ease with regard to me.

After all matters were again settled, I silently let myself out of irons, went down into the vault, and wrought hard all night. By morning I had dug through the underpinning, gotten outside of the jail, and all that remained now, was to break through the frozen ground, which was about eighteen inches, as I conjectured. I thought my operations through this night had been so silent, as to prevent a discovery from any one; but I was mistaken. The least noise in the vault sounded strong through the pumps; these being the only apertures through which the sound could escape; therefore, its whole force was carried in one direction.

In the morning, the jailer took Hinds out of the room, where he had left him the night before, having put him into a separate room from Grinold, for fear of a repetition of that chastisement which he had so largely tasted the day before; and by him received information that somebody had been at work in the vault all night. After this information, Hinds was put back into the same room again, being a roommate with Rood.

About ten o'clock in the morning the jailer, attended with his blacksmiths, came into the dungeon, and removed the prisoners back again into my room. They searched the dungeon with a great degree of care, to see whether the prisoners had broken through into the vault, but not finding any breach, they were at a loss to account for the report of Hinds, not conceiving it possible for me to be the person, owing to my irons. However, after a while they came into my room, and searching the irons around my leg, they discovered the deception, seeing at once, with what ease I could take my irons off my leg when I wished. They then searched the iron bars which had been spiked to the floor, and found them pulled up. They looked at me with a stare of astonishment, not conceiving how it was possible for such a thing to be effected with what tools we had.

The blacksmith retired; and in about an hour returned, bringing with him an iron bar of twice the magnitude of the former, and six spikes, about twelve inches in length, and ragged, in such a manner, as to prevent a bare possibility of their ever being drawn. This iron bar he placed across the hole, and with a heavy sledge, drove in the spikes, looking round exultingly on me, saying "Burroughs, if you get down here again, I'll come and take your place." After he had driven in his spikes, and put all things in order, he came and examined my irons, fastened them on again, so as to prevent my getting loose, as he vainly boasted.

I now lost all hopes of liberty, by that method which we had been pursuing, viewing it impossible ever to get the iron from across the hole, if I should get free from my irons around my leg; but again I was taught to admire the vast ability of Philips; for before the outer door of the jail was locked, I was freed from my irons, and the bar across the hole was torn away. This was done while the jailer was shutting, bolting and locking the doors; so that the noise which we made, might be so blended with his noise, that it should not be distinguished by the prisoners overhead, viz. Rood and Hinds, in such a manner as to lead to a discovery. This had the desired effect. Not the least suspicion was entertained of our operations, so quick was Philips, in seeing every advantage which opportunities offered, for the prosecution of our purpose.

However, I found all the abilities which appertained to Philips, were set down to my credit, so strongly were all possessed with the opinion, that I was the soul of every enterprise of such a nature. And from the efforts which he made in this room, many were of the opinion that I had preternatural assistance. For, said they, "no irons will hold him, and no fortification will stand against him."

You will be curious, sir, I presume, to learn the method by which we effected such a surprising feat in so short a time, as to liberate me from irons, and tear away the huge iron bar which was spiked so strongly across our pump-hole. This I will give you a description of. You will recollect that one end of my chain was fastened to the floor, the other end around my leg, the length about ten feet; and the ring about my leg was flat.[2] Making the chain into a ring by the before mentioned process, we ran the end of our oaken bench into it, and placed the ring which was around my leg, under the bench, and bent it down tight to my leg; then turned it one quarter round and bent it back again. This we repeated three or four times and the ring broke. We immediately after this, hoisted the bolt confining the chain, by the same process. After all, we took up the pump, and fixed our chain around the iron, on the pump-hole, as formerly, and proceeded again according to the same plan. I thought it a piece of madness to think of drawing these spikes, and made observations to that amount. Philips paid no attention to what I remarked, but pursued his plan; and when we all jumped on to the bench, to pry up the iron-bar, the heads of the spikes flew off in a moment; the bar was torn from its place, and the whole jail trembled.

[2] The ring was an inch larger in diameter than my leg.

CONFINED IN THE DUNGEON

I now considered my escape as certain, having nothing but the frozen ground to break through, which I expected to effect in the course of an hour. Therefore, when night progressed so far in her course, as to carry people generally to their beds, we all stripped and went down into the vault, with as much silence as possible, that we might keep Rood and Hinds in ignorance of our operations; but this we found impossible. We soon heard them take off the cover from their pump, and listen to the noise in the vault. However, as we soon expected to make our escape, we did not so much dread their hearing us at work, not expecting they could give any information to the jailer till next morning, when we should be far from his restraining power.

We were vigorous in our operations till we had broken the frozen ground, so as to discern the snow. I communicated this circumstance to Warner, who was near me, and he imprudently, in the warmth of his feelings, told one near him, that in ten minutes we should be at liberty. This he spoke so loud as to be heard by Rood and Hinds. They hearing this, immediately called to the jailer, and informed him that we were breaking out. The alarm flew rapidly; people gathered into the jail-yard with lanterns, and discovered the hole, which was almost large enough for a man to pass through, whilst others entered the jail, and turned us all into the dungeon.

CHAPTER XVII

"Wake the lion's loudest roar,
Clot his shaggy mane with gore,
With flashing fury bid his eyeballs shine;
Meek is his savage, sullen soul to thine!"

OUR fond expectations of liberty were again blasted. We found ourselves confined in the dungeon, and two spies to watch all our motions. It appeared that Fortune delighted in raising my hope, in order to tantalize me with disappointment. There was a strange fatality attending all my undertakings! The most flattering circumstances were, in the end, attended with effects of the severest nature. Misery was my portion, notwithstanding every effort to the contrary. I now saw no way but that I must lay my account to wear away the three long tedious years, to which I was sentenced, in jail!

Early the next morning I was, contrary to my expectations, taken out of the dungeon, and re-conveyed into my old room, which was considerably larger than the dungeon, and there saw preparations for punishing me again with the horsewhip. I had a sharp pointed penknife about me, which had been often sought for in vain by the jailer. I pulled out this penknife, and opened it, and told the jailer I would positively put him to death if he dared to inflict that punishment on me again. I stood at this time, in one corner of the room, where I could not be attacked only on one side. The jailer ordered those with him to take hold of me, and secure me; but none chose to run the risk: for I had declared with equal determination, that the first who offered to approach me, should feel the weight of my arm.

Matters remaining in this situation, the grizzly looking tyrant was abashed and confounded, not daring to approach me himself, to execute any of his hellish plans; he therefore gave up the object.

About this time, the blacksmith and his apprentices came into my room, with all my former load of irons, to confine me as he formerly

[126]

had done, in the dungeon. Having succeeded so well with regard to the punishment of whipping, I determined to try the same experiment again, and see whether it would keep me out of irons. I therefore refused to have any chains put on me. The blacksmith came towards me in a threatening manner, with his hammer lifted, as though he would strike me; but seeing me stand, as though I was determined to execute my threat, with my penknife, he gave back. They soon left the irons lying on my floor, and all departed from the room. I expected they were gone after a recruit, but in this my fears were disappointed.

About one o'clock the same day, I was taken out of this room and put into the upper loft with Grinold. Philips and the rest, who were in the room with him, were taken out of the dungeon and put back into their former place of abode, after the breach was secured. I believe it was effectually secured this time, for I never heard of their breaking it again; but by what process they made it so strong as to prevent the prisoners from making another breach I do not know, never being put in that room any more. It was currently reported that the devil had assisted me, in my attempts to break jail. Many foolish people would apply to me for a discovery of matters unknown to themselves; as things lost, stolen, etc. And when I refused to pay any attention to their application, alleging that it was out of my power, they would look wisely at each other, and observe, "that I was not permitted to do such things, it being against the articles of my league!"

It being now the last of January, if I rightly recollect, news was brought us, that all the prisoners, who were sentenced to the house of correction, were to be removed to Castle Island, in the harbor of Boston, there to be confined to hard labor. This news had but little effect on my mind, being as yet entirely ignorant of the place, its situation, the state of the prisoners on it, or the treatment which I should receive there. The idea of being again carried through the country, in the manner I had formerly been, a spectacle to surrounding fools, gave me most sensible pain; but whether I should be in a better situation there, than what I was in at Northampton, was wholly unknown, and I had no evidence, by which I could form any conjecture.

Early one morning a number of deputy-sheriffs came into the jail, and bade us prepare for our journey to the Castle. They chained the

[127]

prisoners two together, placing the chain about one leg of each, then put them into a sleigh and drove off.

When I came to breathe a pure air, and to contrast the prospect of surrounding objects, with the gloomy mansions which I had left, you cannot conceive the ardor of my feelings for liberty. Every object which my eyes beheld was a loud proclaimer of my miserable state. Oh! said I, to myself, could I run about like yonder little boy, who, regardless of his privilege, loses its enjoyment; then should I feel like the lark, that escaped from its cage, flits into the air, and claps its wings for joy. I wondered people should feel so indifferent about my situation. I equally wondered at their not skipping with joy, because they were at liberty themselves. I thought if they had known the feelings of my heart, they would have arisen to a man and granted me that liberty which my heart so ardently panted after. It appeared to me sometimes that the sensations of my mind must be apparent to them, and that under this circumstance, they would actually grant me relief. Yet in the bitterness of my soul, I found these ideas all chimerical. Certainly, said I, did those very characters, who were instrumental in placing me in this state of confinement, feelingly know my whole heart, they could not resist the language of nature so far as not to wish me at liberty. I know that even the Pelhamites themselves would have cried, his punishment is enough—his sufferings are equal to his crimes. Then why will ye yet torment me? Why will you gall me any longer with the chain of slavery? The answer is, the course of law has brought you to this, and we cannot reverse its mandate. But, said I, what is law, but the voice of the people? And what is the voice of the people but the language of the heart? Does not every day's experience teach us, that cruel and severe punishments serve to harden, rather than reform the vicious? Ought we not to consider ourselves as members of one and the same family, and to adopt those rules and regulations among ourselves, as a society, which will in their operation, be congenial with such an idea? Surely, this is the idea which the language of nature strongly inculcates upon our minds. Should we not shudder with horror, if a father treated his child, as the laws of society treat each other? When do we hear of an unnatural parent chaining his child, confining him from the enjoyment of liberty, and placing him in such a situation, as to make him an object of contempt and scoff to the rest of his children, without feeling that indignation in our bosoms, which such an unnatural action merits? Between parents and children, the voice of nature is heard in its simple state, without being perverted by the sophistry of those, who are blind to the laws which bind mankind together as brethren of the same family. Is there not a spirit of nobleness in man which scorns the lash of tyranny, in whatever shape it appears, which manifests all the love and partiality of children, towards those laws, which discover the care and protection of a parent towards them? View the conduct of the parent of nature towards his children! "He causes his sun to rise on the evil and on the good, and sendeth rain on the just and on the un-just." He grants his parental kindness to all his children without dis-tinction, and watches over the wants of the smallest part of the works of his hands. Is his example worthy of imitation, or are we wiser than our Maker? I have often read with the highest delight a fable invented by Dr. Franklin, to show, in a familiar manner, the arrogance of man, in his attempts to place his own wisdom above that of Deity. The doctor represents Abraham as grossly abusing a stranger, whom he had invited into his tent, because he was an idolater, and did not worship God according to his method. The fable states, that at mid-night, God called unto Abraham and inquired for the stranger; Ab-raham recapitulated his treatment of him, which was done, said he, because he worshipped not thee. God took occasion, from this, to show Abraham the folly of his reasoning; for, said he, "have I nour-ished and cherished this man ninety and nine years, notwithstanding his rebellion against me, and could not thou, who art thyself a sinner, bear with him one night?"

As we travelled through the country, I again found the curiosity of people had brought them together in many places where we stopped; there a philosophic mind would have found ample scope for contem-plating the human character. We cannot discern the operation of the human heart in man, until we are in such a situation, as to prevent his wearing a disguise. This situation must be very abject, and then we become of so little consequence in society, that the notice of man is removed from us, and he acts in our presence without disguise; view-ing our approbation or disapprobation as immaterial to his prosperity. Under such a situation, the human character becomes really known,

[129]

and he who has ability with this knowledge to learn such regulations as will tend, in their operations, to promote the highest good of society, is called upon by that duty which man owes to man, to assert the cause of truth, with regard to these important points.

Under this view of matters, I have clearly stated my sentiments to you upon these subjects. I know you to be a man of so much observation as to know, that severe laws have the most fatal tendency, not only upon the criminal part of society, but likewise upon every member. Everything which tends to destroy the principles of humanity, serves to eradicate from the human breast that benevolence and compassion towards mankind, which is the bond of perfection in society.

When we see the father of a family conducting with mildness towards his children, treating them all as equal members of his household, and never permitting the ebulitions of wrath and malignity to operate towards any; at the same time, we see them inheriting their father's meekness and compassion Benevolence marks their ways, and harmony brightens all their paths. But on the contrary. where we see the parent becomes the tyrant, punishing the faults of his children with the unrelenting hand of rigor, executing judgment unmingled with mercy, we see a family possessing the feelings of cruelty, lost to the godlike principle of mercy, at war with themselves, and governed by those ferocious feelings which disturb the tranquillity of mankind. The same principles operate upon the great family of mankind. Where we find severe laws operating among a people. or mild laws executed in a cruel manner, we see the influence of this, upon the manners of the people, to be very great. It gradually roots out the feelings of benevolence and compassion, and in their room, implants the sentiments of cruelty and severity.

The body of mankind can judge of things only in a very partial manner. They are taught, in the first place, to revere the laws; they are taught, in the second place, to believe that the laws are founded in justice: from this consideration, they are led to treat others as they see the law treats its subjects: to cherish the same spirit which they see manifested in the execution of the laws: therefore, if the law, or the mode of executing it, is severe and cruel, they will of consequence imbibe a spirit of severity and cruelty.

Having treated these matters so largely in our conversation, it will

[130]

be needless for me to say more on the subject. I believe we are both agreed in this sentiment, viz. that the laws and the manner of their execution, do ultimately form the manners and morals of a people; and the best criterion to form an estimate of the laws and regulations of a people by, is their manners and morals.

On the first day of our journey towards the Castle, we dined at Belchertown. Here I found an assemblage of many characters. Some were led here by an anxious desire of seeing me perform some feats of dexterity in eluding my guard, concluding that I should not remain with them longer than to arrive at this tavern. Whether they expected I should evaporate in a flash of fire, or disappear in a cloud of smoke; or whether they thought I should, Faustus like, fix my guards, like pillars of stone, immovably, to some spot, until I could leisurely walk away, I do not know; but it was apparent that something they expected would be done. The least movement I made, their eyes were upon me; the least word I spoke, their ears were open, and their attention alive. When I moved, they made way for me, as though destruction would fall upon them if they obstructed my passage. It gave me pain to see the apparent fear that many manifested upon this occasion. I endeavored to persuade them that their fears were groundless, but all to no purpose. Some I found took this opportunity of showing their courage to the world, by letting the bystanders see, they were not afraid to insult me. One man even ran his fist into my face, making his boast that he would venture me, as great a man as I was, but took very good care to keep so far distant from me that I could not reach him, being chained to Glazier Wheeler, so that I could not move only when he moved; and the old man having the infirmities of age upon him, could only move with a degree of moderation. While the scoundrel continued his insults, one of the sheriffs came into the room, I think his name was White, and observing the unprovoked abuse, struck the villain across the head, with the hilt of a hanger, and felled him to the floor. This spoiled the fun of this courageous fellow.

After dinner was over, the landlady came to the high sheriff, and informed him that one of her silver spoons was missing, and she said it was impossible for any one to get it out of her cupboard, which had been unlocked, unless it was Burroughs; therefore, the high-sheriff set about searching me for a silver spoon, stolen out of a room, in which

[131]

it was known I had never been; but before the search was over, the good lady informed him that the spoon was found.

We soon moved from this and arrived that night at Brookfield. Here I found a little respite from that perpetual attention to the various whims, false opinion, and strange ideas, which people had formed of my character. But even here I was accosted by a grave looking old gentleman smoking his pipe in the corner. I had observed him sometime, sitting in silence, but now and then glancing his eye upon me; at length, taking his pipe leisurely from his mouth, spitting carefully in the fire, and adjusting his looks with some precision, he turned and addressed me as follows: "Burroughs, I have had a desire to see you, for some time; I have heard much of you. I know your uncle Colonel Davis, and had he given ear to my advice, he would have been a great gainer; but he did not, and the time is now passed for him to profit by his dear bought experience; however, I can give you advice, which you will find to your advantage, should you be endowed with wisdom to follow it. Your extraordinary conduct has made mankind form very strange conjectures concerning you, and many throw a great degree of blame upon your conduct; but as for myself, I cannot say I think your crimes unpardonable, or indeed very heinous, excepting one, and that was the flagrant transgression of the principles of gratitude towards the clergyman, whose clothes and watch you stole."

Here I interrupted the orator, in the midst of his discourse, by my ardor to set him right in his mistaken opinion of this business; I told him the story of my stealing a watch and suit of clothes from a clergyman was entirely unfounded, as no such circumstance had happened to any clergyman in this country; that this was an old anecdote, new vamped and handed to the world as a modern occurrence, the opprobrium of which a good-natured populace were willing to fix on me.

He looked me full in the face, with a sarcastic sneer, pulled a newspaper out of his pocket, and turned me to a paragraph relating that I was the person, who had stolen the clothes, watch, etc. After I had read the paragraph, the old gentleman said, "Now, Mr. Burroughs, I hope you will not undertake to correct my judgment again. When I form an opinion, it is not on slight evidence, therefore, since you have set up your opinion in opposition to mine, I shall let you pursue

[132]

it; you may repent when it is too late." He then turned from me, put his pipe into his mouth, and remained silent the rest of the evening, notwithstanding all my endeavors for a further explanation upon this business.

The next day we proceeded on our journey. In the course of this day, I could have made my escape, if I had been chained to anybody but Glazier Wheeler. I went out of the house where we stopped to dine, accompanied by only one person, and he, being impatient at staying out in the cold, went into the house, and we remained by ourselves as much as half an hour. I proposed our escape to Wheeler; but the severity of the weather, the infirmities of age, and the uncertainty of success, operated so strongly on his mind, as to deter him from concurring in my proposal. We returned, and I flattered myself, that this apparent instance of my peaceably remaining confined, when I had an opportunity of making, at least, a trial for escaping, would make my keepers more remiss in guarding me; but in this I was disappointed. I found the guard were all in commotion, when we went into the house, at our being left alone so long; and they took special care never to fall into the same error again.

In the course of this day, we made a stage at a public house where I found a number of the Pelhamites. They had been to Boston and were on their return. They were affected at seeing my condition! They dropped the tear of compassion! They pitied me! They offered me, as a token of their benevolent feelings, as much punch as I would drink. Whether some of their more benevolent feelings on the present occasion, did not proceed from the efficacy of the punch, which they themselves had drunken, is a question I shall by no means undertake to answer.

In the course of this day's journey, we met with Mr. Baldwin, minister of Palmer, of whom mention has already been made. The good old gentleman was truly affected: and, instead of reflections, which I expected, he lamented my untimely fall; wished I might meet with some alleviating circumstance in my sentence, before the expiration of my confinement.

We arrived at Little Cambridge, and tarried all night. The house where we put up was filled with people. I found the good lady of the house giving her daughters a lecture on the propriety of keeping

out of the room, where the prisoners were. But, as these young fe-
males possessed the curiosity natural to their sex, they endeavored
to persuade their ma'am that the danger which she feared, was more
in her fancy than reality. The prudent mother, however, cut her
daughters short in their arguments, by telling them, in the most peremptory manner, that they should not go into the room where Burroughs was; for said she, "he has a faculty to lead anybody astray:
why, there's Pelham now, where he preached—he undertook to preach
to people, that it was lawful for him to lie with all the women in
town, and he carried his point so far, as to lie with every man's wife;
and then ran away and left them; but if he should offer such a thing
to me, I'd show him he wan't in Pelham."

After this harrangue of the careful mother, her conduct through the
remainder of the evening did not manifest so great a fear on her own
account, as what she had shown on account of her daughters: but
whether she meant to give me an opportunity of making such proposals, as on her part would lead to a discovery of her impregnable
chastity, or whether her attention was the pure effect of humanity, I
shall not undertake to tell, not being in a capacity to give information
upon that subject, having made no advances towards her through the
course of a long tedious evening.

A sober faced clergyman entered into conversation with me upon
the events of my life. I found him entertaining all the acrimony attached to offended dignity. Says he, "What an enormous crime you
have been guilty of, by bringing an irreparable disgrace upon the order
of clergy, in assuming that character with all your vile hypocrisy about
you; and as though that was too little, you preposterously exhibited the
works of others and not your own. You have taken the most direct
measures to overturn all order in civil and religious societies, by making the character of a clergyman appear in a ludicrous point of view
to the world: a character, of all others, which ought to be held most
sacred: and which, of all others, has the greatest influence to the good
order of society."

My answer to the clergyman was to this effect. "Seeing, sir, that
you are professedly the ambassador and representative of him, who
has commanded us, 'in lowliness of mind to 'esteem others better than
ourselves'; who was despised and rejected of mankind; who was set

[134]

at nought by the rulers; and declared that his kingdom was not of this world: I say, sir, that seeing your dignity in this character is encroached upon by my conduct, I feel most heartily sorry for touching your highness in this respect."

The clergyman was stung with this reply, and retorted, that, "I might find that the government would teach me how to carry myself to my superiors. After I had been kept to hard labor on the Castle two or three years, my courage would be cooled, and my manners mended," etc.

We arrived at Boston the next day, about 11 o'clock; stopped and dined at the sign of the Lamb. I found many of my former acquaintance now shunned me, as though I carried some pestilential disorder about me. One in a particular manner, who was a classmate of mine in college, coming in sight of the sleigh, in which the prisoners were conveyed, and discerning me in the sleigh, stopped short; ran into a shop contiguous, and viewed me through the window with great attention.

After dinner, we were taken to the commissary's store, who provided for the Castle, and all the prisoners, excepting myself, received their clothes, which consisted of a parti-colored suit; I was entirely willing to be excused from receiving this bounty from the state.

After the clothing had been delivered, we were taken to Long Wharf, put on board a small sailboat, and left the mainland for the island, on which the Castle stood. As we put off from the wharf, the people standing on this, and the neighboring wharves, gave three cheers, declarative of their satisfaction in our leaving them for a state of confinement. We returned three cheers immediately after; endeavoring to retort their insult, by letting them understand that we were also glad to leave them, even for a state of confinement.

We soon arrived on the island, were conveyed into the Castle, our irons taken off, and we left to view the situation in which we were confined.

The island is situated three miles below the town of Boston, its figure being nearly circular, containing eighteen or twenty acres of land. The main channel of the river runs on the east side of this island, very near the shore, and not wider than would be sufficient for two vessels to sail up a-breast; of course, the east side of the island is

[135]

much the strongest fortified. A platform extends the greater part of the east side, on which are mounted cannon, twenty-four and thirty-two pounders. This platform is nearly the height of the island. Nearly on a level with the water, at full tide, is a place where another tier of cannon were placed, during the time in which the British had possession of it; but destroyed by them and never since rebuilt. The remaining part of the island is but very indifferently guarded by fortifications.[1]

The buildings, when I came to this island, were the governor's house, standing upon the most elevated spot on the island, under which was what was called the bombproof, in which we were confined; a stone magazine, barracks for the officers and soldiers, and a blacksmith's shop.

On this island I found a company of fifty soldiers, commanded immediately by three officers, viz. In the first place, Lieutenant Perkins, formerly holding the title of Major in the continental army. Secondly, Lieut. Treat; and thirdly, Burbeck, holding an Ensign's commission, if I mistake not, and doing the duty of gunner. The lieutenant-governor of the state was Captain of the company.

When I first came on to this island, there were in all only sixteen prisoners. The principal part of them were kept at work in the blacksmith's shop. The remainder did little or nothing. Our provision was one pound of bread and three-fourths of a pound of meat per day.

The officers who were in commission here, were of the following description, viz. First, Major Perkins, a man of about six feet high, well proportioned, and strong built; possessed with care, fidelity, and great attention to his duty, as a military character. He was a man of sentiment and feeling. His courage was unimpeachable, having tried it myself as thoroughly as was necessary to learn that circumstance. Notwithstanding his personal courage, he stood in such fear of his superiors in society, that he could not always maintain such a state of independency as to act himself. His military education had taught him obedience to his superiors, and he now maintained that principle with a degree of mechanical exactness. Major Perkins had a family living on the island with him. This family consisted of Mrs.

---

[1] The present state of this island is very different.

[136]

Perkins, whose amiable and compassionate conduct has left the most grateful feelings in my heart, and a number of children, how many I do not recollect.

Lieutenant Treat was a man about five feet ten inches in height, trim built, and slender; more fond of appearing in the fashion, with regard to his dress, the cock of his hat, etc., than he was to raise the garrison to the highest pitch of military fame. There was nothing very positive in his character. He was by no means a bad man, and as for his goodness, it did not appear with such eclat as to place him in a very conspicuous situation in society.

Ensign Burbeck may be described by comparing him to a petulant boy, of about fourteen years old, who had never been taught or restrained by parental authority. He was more fond of his dogs than of any other society; playing with them by the day together.

Immediately after my confinement on this island, I began to look about, to see whether a possibility for escaping remained. I viewed the building in which I was confined. It was made of brick, the walls of which were five feet thick, laid in cement, which was much harder than the brick themselves. I searched every corner for a spot upon which I could work without detection, our room being searched every day, to see whether the prisoners had made any attempt to break away. I at length hit upon a place. There was a chimney at one end of the room, grated in a very strong manner, about twelve feet above its funnel, which was sufficiently large for a man to go up. About three feet above the mantlepiece of this fireplace, I concluded to begin my operation. Here I could work, and not have my labors discovered, unless very critical search was made up the chimney. I had not been at work long before I had made a beginning of a hole sufficiently large to crawl through; I then took a board, and blacking it like the chimney-back, made it of the proper size, and put it into the hole, so that the strictest search could produce no discovery. The prisoners in the room with me were seven in number. These prisoners were all turned out to work about sunrise, when the doors of the prison were again shut, and not opened until 12 o'clock, when the prisoners came from work, and continued half an hour: they were then taken back again to work, and there remained until sunset. Therefore, I had as

[137]

much as sixteen hours in the twenty-four, in which I could work upon this brick wall, which work I continued, with the most unremitting attention.

The labor was incredible! I could, in the first place, work only with a large nail, rubbing away the brick gradually, not daring to make the least noise, lest the sentries, who stood round the prison, should overhear me at work, and thereby become discovered. One night I rubbed the brick so hard, as to be overheard by the sentry, standing on the other side of the wall. The alarm was immediately given, and the guard and officers rushed into the room to detect us in our operations. Fortunately, I overheard the sentry tell the sergeant of the guard, that Burroughs was playing the devil in the jail. The sergeant ran to inform the officers, and I had but just time to put my board in its place, and set down to greasing my shoes, when the officers entered, and with a great degree of sternness, inquired where I had been at work? I told them that I had been rubbing some hard soot off the chimney and grinding it fine to mix with the grease, and put on to my shoes. They laughed at my nicety about my shoes, that I should wish for sleek shining shoes in this situation. Major Perkins knowing my inattentiveness to dress, could not so readily believe that blacking my shoes was the only object in view; he therefore made a very strict search for some other matter, which should account for the noise the sentry had heard: but, after a fruitless pursuit of such an object, they gave over their search, concluding that one among the thousand strange whims which marked my character, had prompted me to set about blacking my shoes, at that time.

After they were gone, I felt as strong a disposition to laugh at them, for the deception under which they were laboring, as they did whilst present to laugh at me, for the whim of greasing and blacking my shoes. This temporary check was of the utmost importance in my further prosecution of this business. It made me more careful for the future, not to pursue my labors with too much impatient impetuosity, a failing I ever was subject to.

The prisoners in the room were merry on the occasion of my turning the suspicion of the officers so entirely from the real object to another very foreign from it. They thought it a manifestation of ability. In fine, I had gained such an ascendency over the prisoners, that they implicitly gave up to my opinion in all our little matters: and more particularly, when any contention arose among them, I generally succeeded in amicably terminating the difficulty without their proceeding to blows.

My conduct towards all, I determined should be marked with the strictest impartiality. I not only satisfied my own mind in the business, but likewise took the greatest pains to show them, that I meant to be an impartial friend towards all parties. When they fell into disputes and bickerings, I would address them to the following purport, viz. "Gentlemen" (even the convicts were fond of good words, and would listen when I called them gentlemen much sooner than when I addressed them by a less elevated epithet), "our situation you are all sensible is very miserable; do the best we can, it will not be tolerable; but when, in addition to slavery, we render our society hateful and irksome to each other, by falling into broils and wrangles, it then becomes a hell indeed, and answers the strongest wish of our inveterate foes. I know there are many circumstances calculated to harass and sour your minds; to render you peevish and petulant; to make you at variance with the whole race of mankind: but to indulge these feelings only renders your case worse rather than better; it gratifies your enemies and serves every purpose which they could desire; therefore, as wise men, I expect you will act with prudence, with regard to your own comfort and to the views of those who wish you ill." Even the convicts had reason sufficient to hear these arguments with attention, and they generally practiced according to this direction: so strong is that principle in all men to listen to the voice of friendship.

I determined to be more careful in prosecuting my labor on the wall for the future, and check that impatience which often hurried me on beyond the dictates of prudence. I now wrought with the greatest caution, and made slow but sure advances. After I had been employed in this business about a week, I found I could work to greater advantage if I had a small iron crow; therefore. I ordered one of the prisoners, who wrought in the shop, to make me one about a foot long, and sharp at one end. This he found an opportunity to do, undiscovered by the overseer, and brought it to me. I found that with this crow

[139]

I could pry off half a brick at a time without the least noise, after I had worn a hole with my nail, sufficiently large to thrust in my crow. The rubbish which I took out of the wall I put every night into a tub, standing in our room for necessary occasions, and this was emptied by one of the prisoners every morning into the water.

After I had labored with unceasing assiduity for two months, I found one night, after I had pried away a brick, that I could run my arm out of the prison into the open air. This circumstance made my heart leap with joy. After such a length of labor, to find my toils crowned with apparent success, gave me a tone of pleasure of which you can have no idea.

Upon examination, I found the breach through the wall was just below a covered way, so that it would remain unseen in the daytime, unless discovered by some accident. I had measured the height of the covered way by a geometrical operation, not being permitted to come near it: and this was done with an instrument made by my penknife; that penknife which had done me such excellent service in Northampton jail.

When the prisoners saw my measurement was exact, their idea of my profound knowledge was greatly raised; and they appeared to entertain the most sanguine assurance, that their liberty was certain when their operations were directed under my auspices.

After I had found the hole through the wall was entirely secreted by the covered way, I proceeded to make it sufficiently large to pass through.

After all this was accomplished, one difficulty still remained. The sentry standing on the covered way would undoubtedly hear us in going out at this hole; and moreover, if we should be so fortunate as to get, unheard, into the covered way, yet we must come out of that within five feet of the place where he stood, and therefore could not prevent a discovery.

Under these circumstances, we found it necessary to lie quiet until some rainy night should remove the sentry from his stand on the covered way, to some place of shelter. This was generally the case when the weather was foul or uncomfortable, unless some special cause should detain him to this particular spot. I recollect, that soon after the officers had found me blacking my shoes with soot, the sentinels kept their post, invariably, on the covered way, in every kind of weather; but they had, by this time, become more at ease in their feelings, and consequently would, at such time, retire into an alley leading through the bombproof.

CHAPTER XVIII

"Where now my phrenzy's pompous furniture?
The cobweb cottage, with its ragged wall
Of moldering mud, is royalty to me!
The Spider's most attenuated thread
Is cord, is cable, to man's tender tie
On earthly bliss; it breaks at every breeze."

WE did not wait many days for the happy moment, before we heard the sentry leave his station on the covered way, and enter the alley, for shelter from the rain.

About 11 o'clock at night, I made the necessary arrangements for the expedition. The island being in a circular form, I ordered seven men to go round it to the south, whilst I went round to the north. The reason why I did this was of the following nature, viz. There was a wharf on the western shore of this island, where the boats were kept, and a sentry placed over them. It was necessary, after we had escaped out of the bombproof, to procure a boat, in order to transport ourselves off the island; and as there were none, except what were immediately under the eye of the sentry, the only alternative which remained, was to make the sentry a prisoner, and carry him off with us. As this was a business in which some nicety of conduct was necessary, I chose to trust no one to execute it but myself; and therefore, ordered the seven prisoners round the island, a different way from what I went myself, and directed them to advance to within fifteen rods of the sentinel, and make a noise sufficient to attract his attention towards them. This would bring the sentry between me and the other seven prisoners; and when he was turned towards them, I should be at his back.

Having made these arrangements, all the prisoners silently crawled out of the hole, following them myself as soon as I saw they all had passed without any accident. We all met at the spot appointed. I told the men to be cautious, not to be in a hurry; not to be in any perturbation; but to proceed leisurely and considerately to the spot

[142]

appointed. I told them to be five minutes in getting to the spot. I then left them. I hastened round, and arrived as near to the sentry as I thought prudent, about one minute and a half before I heard the noise from the other men. At the noise, the sentry turned and hailed, "Who comes there?" No answer was made. Immediately on seeing the attention of the sentry turned from me, I arose from my position flat on the ground, and advanced as near as twenty feet, and lay down again. Immediately the noise from the seven men was again renewed; and the sentry's attention was fixed to the object of the noise. He again hailed in a very peremptory manner, cocked his gun, and made ready to fire. By this time I had arisen from the ground, and advanced to within about eight feet of the sentry, when I heard the piece cock, and saw him present it! I immediately darted at him, seized him in an instant, and clapped my hand over his mouth, to prevent him from making a noise, which should alarm the other soldiers on guard. When I first laid hold of him, he started, and attempted to get from me, making a noise through his nose as though very much terrified: crying "eh! eh! eh!" I told him that the least noise from him should produce instant death; that I would rip his guts out the first moment he proved refractory. After I had sufficiently terrified him, I took my hand from his mouth, and told him that no harm should befall him, so long as he behaved in a peaceable manner. I took his gun and cartridge-box from him. The other prisoners now coming up, we all went into the barge, carrying ten oars, and put off.

It was now about half an hour past twelve at night, it being extremely dark and rainy, and nothing to steer by, except mere conjecture. We were ignorant of the time of tide, whether it was ebbing or flowing, and consequently could not tell which way we drifted: however, we determined to row until we came to some land. I set myself in the stern sheets, steering the boat; Richards, the sentry, set in the bottom of the boat, between my legs. The gun with the fixed bayonet lay by me, and the cartridge-box hanging by my side. The other men were at their oars, rowing the boat. We had proceeded about far enough, as we judged, to be in the middle of the channel, between the island and Dorchester, whither we meant to direct our course.

It was now demanded of me, by one of the men who sat forward rowing the boat, what I meant to do with Richards? As I did not know where we should in fact land, I was undetermined in my own mind what I should do with him when I came to land, and gave an answer to that amount. The person asking this question, looking upon his escape as certain, began to put on airs of consequence, and answered me in a sarcastic manner, "Well, Captain Burroughs, as you have had the command until you do not know what to do, it is best for some other person to take it, who does know what to do"; and then turning himself to Richards, continued his discourse, "and as for you, Mr. Richards, you'll please to walk overboard, that we may not, after this, hear any of your tales told to your brother swads.[1] If you walk over without fuss, it is well, if not, you shall be thrown over, tied neck and heels."

When I heard this insolent treatment and dastardly language, I could hardly conceive what it meant. Unprovokedly to throw Richards into the water, was a manifestation of a language of the heart, which appeared to me so unnatural, that I could not believe the person using it, to be serious. Yet I could not conceive any propriety in using it in any other light. Richards himself was terrified. He began to supplicate me in the most moving terms, to save him from the destruction which was ready to fall upon him. His entreaties made such an impression upon my mind, that I should have given him my assistance, if I had been opposed by every man in the boat: however I did not yet believe he was in that degree of danger which he appeared to apprehend; but was soon undeceived by the three forward hands shipping their oars and coming aft.

I endeavored to expostulate, but to no effect. I saw they were resolutely bent on their diabolical purpose! I saw the disposition of the infernals pictured in their operations. I let go the helm, started up, and swore by the Almighty, that I'd send the first to hell who dared lay a hand on Richards. The poor fellow, at this time, lay in the bottom of the boat trembling with agony, and crying in the most piteous manner. The blood flew quick through my veins. The plaintive cries of Richards vibrated upon my heart, and braced every nerve. At this moment the first villain who had proposed this infernal plan, laid hold of me by the shoulder to prevent my interposing between Richards and the others, who were about throwing him overboard.

---

[1] A cant word signifying soldiers.

[144]

When I found his hand griping my shoulder, I immediately reached my arm over his back, caught him by the waistband of his breeches and dashed him to the bottom of the boat. The moment of my laying hold of him, I determined to throw him into the sea, and why I did not, I have never since been able to tell. After I had thrown him into the bottom of the boat, I caught the gun on which was a bayonet fixed; this I brought to a charge and made a push at the man nearest me, who drew back, took his seat at the oar, when all again was quiet.

We continued rowing until we struck fast on the ground, but could see no land. We left the boat and waded about until we discovered the shore. When we came to the land, we could not determine on what place we had fallen. We were soon satisfied, however, by the drum on the Castle beating the long-roll, and immediately after, beating to arms. We heard the alarm in that direction which plainly pointed out, that we were somewhere near Dorchester Point. We saw the Castle in an uproar, and all the signals of alarm which are usually made on such occasions.

After we had found where we were, the three men who engaged in throwing Richards overboard, left us, and went away together. I then told Richards that he might go where he pleased; that he must be sensible I had saved his life, even at the risk of my own; therefore, the dictates of gratitude would teach him a line of conduct which would not militate against my escape. This he promised in the most solemn manner. He was warm in his expressions of gratitude towards me. I believed him sincere. He departed.

In this transaction, I enjoyed a sensation of pleasure very exquisite. To receive the tribute of a grateful heart, flowing from a stream of sincerity, was a circumstance, which in a measure counterbalanced many evils, which I had experienced. We had all lost our shoes in the mud, in getting to dry land; therefore, had to travel barefooted. It was the space of an hour and a half after we had landed, before we found the way off this point of land; the night being extremely dark, and we all strangers to the ground.

After we had found the road, I told the four men who were with me, that the better way would be to separate, and every man shift for himself. This observation struck a damp upon all who were with me. They entreated me to tarry with them until the night following, when

[145]

they could have a better chance of getting clear of the country without detection; they feared falling into the hands of their pursuers if I left them. They felt a certainty of escape if I remained with them. My compassion was moved, and I acted directly contrary from what I knew was according to a system of prudence. We agreed to remain all together until the next night.

The day began to dawn, and we found it necessary to look after some place, to which we could retire from the observation of the inhabitants; all the men, except myself, being dressed in the uniform of the Castle, and of course, would be noticed by the first observer. Some proposed retiring into a swamp, and secreting ourselves in its dark recesses; some proposed the plan of going into the first grove of woods, and climbing up to the top of some trees, and securing ourselves that way. To these proposals I made the following reply: it is likely, that as soon as daylight has fairly appeared, the inhabitants of the country will be alarmed; and warm pursuit will be made after us; and every place, where the inhabitants will think it likely that we should hide, will be searched by them in the most critical manner. No places will be sought more thoroughly than thick swamps and high bushy trees; therefore, it will be our best way to hide where the people will not look after us, if such a place may be found. For my own part, I had rather take my chance, under present circumstances, in the open field than in a swamp or at the top of a tree.

The objects of the swamp and woods were immediately relinquished, and they all seemed content to leave the matter to my judgment entirely. We travelled on with rapidity about one mile further, and then came into a little thicket of houses, and a barn standing immediately on the road among them; this barn we all entered and found two mows of hay. I ascended one mow, and having taken up the hay by flakes, near the side of the barn, to the depth of six feet, three of us went down, and the hay fell back into its former situation, covering us entirely over at the same time. I had ordered the other two to go on to the other mow, and do as they had seen me. They accordingly went, and I supposed all secure.

Not long after this, there came a number of women into the barn to milk the cows. Soon after, I heard children round the barn, as though they were in pursuit of something with a dog. I soon found that a skunk was their object under the barn. However, when the women had finished milking their cows, the children were all ordered into the house, this day being Sunday.

To my astonishment and surprise, the two men who had gone to the other mow, now came over where I was, and told me, they could not find a place to hide; "and indeed," said they, "we do not like to be so far off, for it appears to us, that we shall be taken if we are!" How I felt under this situation you will readily conceive, by supposing yourself in my place, and people expected into the barn every minute to fodder their cattle! I jumped out of my place, told them to lie down in a moment, covered them over with hay, and returned into my place, just as the young men came into the barn to take care of their cattle. They came on to the mow where we were lying, and took the hay from it for their cows; but made no discovery: and yet, notwithstanding all this, one of our men, by the name of Burrel, whom I had covered over with hay, was asleep before the young men went out of the barn, and snored so loud, as to be heard; but the men did not know what noise it was, nor where it came from.

Immediately after these men had left the barn, I again jumped out of my hole, went to Burrel, who had uncovered his head entirely, waked him, and expostulated with him in the severest terms. "This is the consequence," said I, "of attending to your request of remaining with you. Your own heedless disposition, not only exposes yourself to be found, but likewise involves me in the same danger. Is it a matter of such indifference to you whether you are again taken, that you can tamely and calmly fall asleep at the moment when you are surrounded with danger? If no regard to your own safety will influence you on this occasion, yet, I should suppose you might pay some attention to my welfare, seeing it was by your earnest entreaty I continued with you, being influenced by no other motive than compassion towards you. If nothing else will answer, I will have recourse to the means which are in my power; and if I find you asleep again, I will positively put you to death; and this I think will be entirely just, if no other measure will answer to ensure my safety." I was of opinion this threat would answer the purpose, for which it was intended, viz. that fear would operate upon him so strongly, as to prevent his sleeping in such a situation for the future.

[147]

We lay quiet all the forenoon, without any accident: during this time, I endeavored to make some arrangement in my own mind for my future conduct. I concluded that I should be able to reach the state of Rhode Island by the next morning, when I should be no longer obliged to travel under cover of the night; when I could again mix with society, without viewing them as my open and declared enemies.

We heard the various bells ringing at Dorchester meetinghouses for the exercises of the day. The forenoon meeting was finished, and the first bell for the exercises of the afternoon was ringing, when a number of men came into the barn to put a horse into the chaise, standing on the barnfloor. The streets were full of people going to the meeting-house. A number of children came likewise into the barn with the men, and climbed on to the mow where we lay secreted, looking for hens' nests. At this moment Burrel began again to snore, which brought the children immediately to the spot where he lay, and his head being uncovered, they saw it, and cried out, "Daddy, daddy, here's the skunk! here's the skunk!" It hardly appeared credible to the old gentleman that a skunk should be on the haymow; he therefore manifested some doubt as to his children's report, but they were determined he should believe them, and affirmed it again with warmth, "it certainly is a skunk, daddy, for it has got ears."

The peculiar manner in which this was uttered, made the people, on the barnfloor, think something uncommon was there. They accordingly ascended the mow to the number of eight or nine, in order to satisfy themselves concerning this matter. By this time Burrel awaking, saw he was discovered, and began to pull the hay over his head. Those who were on the mow saw it, and were now convinced, that the children in fact had seen something that had ears. They took the pitchfork and moved the hay, which lay over these two men, and immediately saw that they were convicts, escaped the preceding night from the Castle.

The barn was instantly filled with people from the street, on the alarm's being given of these men. Through the whole scene, from the first opening of the barn by the men, who were about putting the horse into the chaise, till this time, my feelings were of the keenest kind. When I had succeeded with all my plans for escape thus far, when I had endured with so much patience, a course of such incredible labor, as what I performed in breaking through the bombproof; when I had furthermore, overcome the difficulties of making the sentry a prisoner, of preserving him from death, of finding the land we sought, through the thickest shades of night, and the uncertainty of being drifted out of our course by adverse tides; and then by a retrograde course of incidents, to be deprived of the object to which all these labors were directed, was a prospect which filled my mind with the keenest anxiety, and kept my fears in a perpetual state of alarm.

Burrel was a man of great stupidity, and I feared his senseless conduct more than anything else. You will wonder at my continuing with him! I wonder at it myself. My weak side was an inconsiderate compassion. I did continue with him, and too late I saw my error. However, I acted the foolish part in another respect, viz. by not taking him into the hole with me, where I could have kept him perpetually under my eye. He was very disagreeable, and the object of being freed from a momentary inconvenience was so powerful on my mind, at that time, that for this paltry consideration, I lost my liberty for more than two years.

I heard the children around the haymow with the utmost pain. I heard Burrel's snoring with indignation and horror! I now almost gave myself over for lost! But what were my sensations when the people ascended the mow and discovered these two convicts, plainly seeing who they were by their dress.

However, all hope of escape was not lost. I thought it yet possible to remain undiscovered, if the two convicts behaved with any prudence, seeing we were so far under the hay. The question was asked, "what had become of the other prisoners who had made their escape?" Burrel answered, that he should not tell, "but if they were anywhere in that barn, they are right down there." pointing with his finger to the spot where we in fact were. With this information, they began the search again, pitching the hay from the spot, till they came down to the place where we had been secreted. The feeble twig upon which my last hopes remained was now broken, and I sunk into a state of despair. All my fond hopes were lost in a moment, and I found myself only fallen into a state of greater wretchedness, in the room of being liberated from my former misery.

"Is this the reward," said I to the inhabitants, "for saving one of your number, but a short time since, from the devouring jaws of death, ready to swallow him up? But a little time since, he stood in need of my pity. I granted him that compassion which nature has taught me to show. I now stand in need of your pity; will you not grant what you, in a like situation, would request? Remember that this world is a state of revolution. You may yet see the time in which you will want the exercise of compassion, even from me, however improbable the present appearance. You would then lament not having shown that compassion which you would stand in need of yourselves. You can hardly imagine that my escape can produce any injury to you. I shall leave you, and shall never return to a place where I might be in danger of confinement. You who are parents, may have children in my situation; would not your hearts yearn with compassion towards a child in my condition? Would not you feel the most earnest desire, that some breast, softened by the tender emotions of compassion, would say unto your child, go—enjoy the blessing which nature bestows; wanton in the streams of liberty, and celebrate the day of jubilee? Would not the strong emotions of gratitude fire your heart, towards such a benevolent part of creation? Would not such a compassionate action appear to you more lovely than the beauties of the morning; more glorious than the sun in his majesty? This, surely you would say, is a narration of Deity; a spark of the fire of love, manifested by nature's God in the daily dispensations of his providence to man."

All my entreaties were to no effect. The minds of people were so fortified against every observation which I made. that the ideas of pity or compassion were shut entirely out. They knew not my feelings, therefore could not judge with regard to that conduct which I thought they ought to exercise towards me. They had never been in my situation, hence could not view it in its proper light.

We were all carried to a public house, and kept there until a guard came from the island and conducted us back again. Immediately upon our landing upon the island, I was ordered into irons. This was a circumstance proving the ideas existing here, of my being the soul of every enterprise; and indeed they had pretty good evidence to found their opinion upon, considering that I was the only person remaining in the room out of which we escaped, through the day, without being

[150]

turned into the shop to work; and their recollecting the circumstance, likewise, of blacking my shoes with soot, in order to account for the noise which the sentry had formerly heard; the reason of the noise being now more clearly understood than formerly.

The next morning we were all summoned, with great pomp and ceremony, before the three officers, sitting as a court-martial,[2] and there heard an enumeration of the crimes laid to our charge, which amounted to five in number, viz. first, breaking the jail; second, carrying the sentry from his post; third, taking the arms and ammunition of the garrison and carrying them away; fourth, taking the boat belonging to the garrison, and carrying it off the island; fifth, and lastly, deserting from our state of confinement. Of all these crimes we were found guilty, and received sentence of thirty-nine stripes for each, with the cat-o'ninetails, amounting in all to one hundred and ninety-five lashes; we however obtained a remission of ninety-five, and received one hundred only, the next day at sunsetting.

The three prisoners who went away by themselves, were likewise this day re-taken and brought on to the island, tried and sentenced; therefore, at sunsetting there were eight of us brought to the whipping-post, stripped and punished according to the sentence.

The sentry, whom we had made prisoner, had returned on to the island the morning after his captivity, and had given a very just relation of the events which had taken place while he was our prisoner; of consequence, when the punishment was inflicted on me, it was a name rather than a reality. The others, and more particularly three of them, were punished with great severity, the flesh flying off at every stroke.

[2] The law of the state of Massachusetts making Castle Island a place for the confinement of Convicts, had subjected them to martial law while remaining there.

CHAPTER XIX

"Enchanting pleasure dances in our sight,
And tempts us forward by a treach'rous light.
But while thy flattering smiles our thoughts inflame,
Thou prov'st to us a mere fantastic name,
A fair delusion and a pleasing cheat,
A gaudy vision and a soft deceit."

I FOUND that my humanity to Richards had made a partial impression in my favor, upon the minds of the people in the towns contiguous; but that impression was soon lost in forgetfulness, and no more remembered, when the event was a little removed from view by the hand of time. You may now hear my name mentioned a thousand times, together with a thousand circumstances respecting my adventures through life, without ever hearing the least mention made of this circumstance, though the fact was a matter of as much notoriety as any event of my life. You may hear the mouths of people filled with anecdotes relating to me, of the disagreeable kind, through all parts of the country. Nay, more, all the reports which have circulated through the world for many years past, of that species which serves to place the character in a vicious point of view, have been placed to my account, and are now related as facts not admitting the least doubt. Hence, the anecdote of the watch and clothes stolen from the clergyman, etc., etc., form a detail too long for me to insert in this narration. It has ever appeared that an ungenerous principle has influenced mankind to relate the dark circumstances which have composed my character; and that they have shrunk from the relation of any facts which have worn the appearance of my being clothed with humanity, as though the most baleful poison was attendant on such a relation. Such a fondness is there in the human heart to bring into view such circumstances, in the character of others, as will exalt themselves, in a comparison between their own conduct and that of others.

About this time the shops were fitted up sufficient to receive all the

[152]

prisoners, with conveniences for making nails. Therefore, I was put to work in the shops, and taught to manufacture nails; but the lessons which I received here had but little effect upon my progress in acquiring this noble art. That unaccountable stupidity which I ever possessed, had an unusual influence upon me at this time. It is true, I could make a nail equal to anything you ever saw, of the kind, in beauty and elegance; but the slowness with which I executed this, was a circumstance of great complaint by the overseer, not being able to finish more than five in a day; which cost more than ten times the value of the nails in coal and iron; therefore, it was determined, that I should be more expeditious in my work. I obeyed the commands of those who were over me. I made the next day five hundred nails; but they had as many heads and horns as the beast we read of in scripture. This did not answer the purpose intended. I was reprimanded in severe terms, but all did not signify. When I made good nails, I could not overgo five in a day, and when I made more, they were as varied, in form and magnitude, as the ragged rocks upon the mountains.

The plain truth of the business was here: I viewed the transactions of the government towards me, to be inimical and cruel. I felt none of that confidence in her treatment which a child ought to feel towards the government of a kind parent. I considered that she had declared open war against me; and would take every opportunity to oppress me. Under this view of matters, I meant to make those arrangements in my conduct, which we see one nation making in their conduct towards another, with whom they are at open war.

Whether I had just grounds to view matters in this light, I leave to your own judgment; meaning, with regard to that, only to relate simple facts. True it was, I had suffered many unusual, cruel and illegal punishments since I had been under the displeasure of the government; but whether the odium ought to be thrown on individuals or the government, I leave you to judge. I know my situation did not admit of that cool and rational thinking upon these subjects which real justice required; however, my design is not to justify that line of conduct which ought not to be justified; neither do I intend to criminate that conduct which I think justifiable; because some might be pleased to criminate it themselves. Viewing matters as I then did, I was determined to withstand every effort which my overseers should

[153]

make, to render me profitable in my situation; and how far I succeeded in my undertakings, you will be able to judge by the after relation.

About this time, the prisoners whom I left in Northampton for trial, came on to the island, according to their sentence, viz. Philips, Warner, Rogers, and a number of others, whose names I have forgotten. I was determined to defeat the business of making nails entirely; and accordingly entered into a plan for that purpose.

There was a large well about six rods from the shop, to which we used to repair for water. The well was 20 feet deep, and the water generally near the top. We took our nail-rods, broke them in pieces, put them into the water pail, carried them to the well, and flung them into the water. This we continued for the space of three weeks, until the well was nearly filled with iron. The return of nails did not half pay for the first cost of the rods, so that the commissary was determined to send no more rods to the island; supposing it a waste of the public property. However, the overseer urged another trial, and the commissary with reluctance, consented to send down a small quantity of nail-rods for the last trial. This circumstance I was informed of, by the boat-men, who went after the rods. I therefore exhorted the prisoners to stand this last trial with courage and perseverance. They universally promised to remain inviolate to their trust, and I pleased myself with the speedy accomplishment of my plan.

The universal excuse of the prisoners, for not returning more nails for the iron which they had received, was their inability. They constantly insisted upon it, that they could not make more nails out of the iron; all agreeing in one excuse, and all returning much the same quantity of nails, in proportion to the iron they received; it was thought that the business would not answer its design; and therefore was about being dropped. Yet the overseer was minded to try one more experiment, to see whether the business would bear a profit, or whether it would not. The law, regulating the treatment towards convicts on the Castle, had strictly prohibited the allowance of spirituous liquors, under any consideration; therefore, many, who had been formerly great drunkards, were now wholly debarred their favorite enjoyment; and moreover, being so long habituated to immoderate drinking, and being now wholly deprived of the use of it, they had experienced in reality, great temporary inconveniences, with regard to their health, as well as to the cravings of appetite unsatisfied. Hence, the prospect of spirituous liquor to these, would have a very powerful effect. This the overseer was sensible of; and accordingly, offered a gill of rum to every one who should return so many nails, out of such a weight of iron.

This bait I saw. I expostulated with the men to beware of the treachery. I used every argument in my power to convince them of the necessity of this self-denial. I endeavored to show them, that far from kindness, this rum was offered them as the most fatal poison they could drink. They were all convinced, and all seemed resolute to put in practice my advice. But when the rum was brought into the shop, and they saw the precious morsel before them, they fainted under the trial! They could not resist the temptation! They weighed the iron, and returned the full tale of nails; they drank the delicious liquid. They returned into the prison with exultation; they were rich; they felt far exalted above my situation; being able to gain a gill of rum a day; whereas, I was unable to perform one tenth part of the task required.

"Now," said they, "we shall be able to earn a gill of rum every day!" This appeared so great a state of happiness, when compared with what their case had been, that they were almost contented with their situation. They began to despise my wisdom; to think that my head did not contain so much as they were before inclined to believe it did. They exultingly said, "This never would have been the case, if we had followed your advice. We must have a little sense now and then, as well as you all the time." I had no disposition to contradict these haughty Patricians. "Perhaps, said I, before to-morrow morning you may find yourselves sunken to your former Plebeian state of servile misery." I had rather see the operation of such profound penetration, than undertake to contradict one of these Knights of the Pot, with all his greatness, armed capapee. I lay down in sorrow, repeating the following words of Young, as a lullaby to sooth my disappointed feelings:

"To man, why stepdame nature so severe?
Why throw aside thy master-piece half wrought,
While meaner efforts thy last hand employ?
Reason's progressive instinct is complete;

[155]

Swift instinct leaps—slow reason feebly climbs.
Brutes soon their zenith reach—their little all
Flows in at once—in ages they no more
Could know, or do, or covet, or enjoy.
Were men to live co-equal with the sun,
The Patriarch-pupil would be learning still;
Yet, dying, leaves his lesson half unlearnt."

After the prisoners had performed their task the next day, and returned their nails in full tale, to their astonishment and sore mortification. they found no rum was to be dealt out to them. They made
application for it, but received in return the bitterest reproaches and
heavy curses. They were given to understand that they should now
do their tasks, and that too without a reward. I found, when they
were shut into the prison at night, that they had fallen greatly from
their state of exaltation, which they felt the night preceding. They
were now not so rich, so great, nor so wise. They could now see the
propriety of my expostulations; but alas! they saw it too late.

Seeing the success of this experiment had such a salutary effect in
discovering the real cause why the prisoners had not been more profitable in their labors, the overseer thought to make me change my plan
of conduct as much as the others had changed theirs: but in this attempt, he found me possessing what the West India Planter would call
sullenness, or incorrigible obstinacy, in one of his slaves. Those who
felt friendly towards me would call it manly resolution; others, who
were inimical, would call it deviltry, wickedness, etc., so that it would
have as many names as there are different feelings towards one in
those who relate it. You, sir, may call it by what name you find
propriety will dictate. The fact was, that by length of time, I did not
become any more profitable in my employment.

About this time there was a change of overseers. The first, whose
name was Bailey, was by no means a bad man. He had something
of the petulant and whimsical about him, but this was only the ebullition of a moment. and his governing character was reasonable, humane, and feeling. In the room of the former, there came to occupy
his place, a man whose name was Rifford, ignorant, stupid, cruel, barbarous and unfeeling. He was a blacksmith by occupation, and hence
it was thought he would answer a better purpose to superintend the
nailing business than one who was entirely unacquainted with such

work. He had not been long on the island before the prisoners began to feel the severity of his arm. When he was offended, he made use of anything which he could lay his hand upon, to chastise those who gave him the offence; hence the prisoners were unmercifully beaten with clubs, tongs, bars of iron, or any other missile weapon which should come to hand. It was impossible to avoid the disagreeable effects of his anger. He would often be in a rage when no one could account for it; and at other times, would suffer himself to be treated in such a manner as no man of sense and dignity would allow: hence, I found the old adage, "It is hard to deal with a fool," most sensibly verified in this instance.

My prospects did not by any means reconcile my feelings to my situation. I yet panted for liberty with an ardor of desire beyond description. I viewed every situation in which matters were placed about this island. I endeavored to concert some plan to turn them to my advantage. I finally determined on making one bold and daring push to make myself master of the place. This plan I did not hastily enter upon, without first weighing all the circumstances which might probably attend such an undertaking.

There were at this time about forty-five prisoners confined in this place, a motley assembly of characters, from various nations in Europe as well as America. These were a class of people of the most abandoned principles, hardened in the school of vice and danger; consequently, I believed them to possess the most unshaken courage and daring fortitude, of any class of men inhabiting the globe. How I was deceived in this opinion you will learn by the relation following.

The bombproof, where we were confined, was about eighty feet in length, fronting the south, having only one door, which looked likewise to the south. A yard, with pickets, about six feet high, inclosed the front of our prison. The area of the yard was about one-fourth of an acre. This yard was made in a square form, and a guardhouse composed a part of the yard, standing in the southeast corner. There was a passage through the house, by which the soldiers on guard could come in and go out of the yard.

The ground around this yard was considerably higher than it was within, on every side except the west, where the gate was placed through which we used to go to our work in the shop. There was

[157]

a brass fieldpiece placed about ten feet from the guardhouse, upon the highest ground on the island, loaded with grapeshot, and a supply of ammunition constantly by it, for the purpose of preventing vessels from passing the Castle without liberty.

The governor's house stood on the bombproof, and having a walk upon the top of it; a sentry constantly stood there to observe vessels, etc.

A sentry constantly walked in the yard, to observe the motions of the prisoners; to keep them from coming out of the prison until the moment in which orders were given for them to turn out to work; to give the guard notice at such times, who were all under arms, the moment that our doors were unlocked. This guard consisted of a sergeant, corporal, and twelve privates.

There was a row of barracks a little distance north of the governor's house, in which the garrison soldiers lived. The officers' barracks were about forty rods westward of our prison, down the hill, contiguous to the water. The shop, where we were confined to labor, was about forty rods beyond the officers' barracks, in a southern direction. When we were turned out of our prison, to be taken to the workshop, three sentries attended us, who perpetually stood round the shop, to hinder any prisoner from leaving it. Here we continued till 12 o'clock, and were then taken back to the prison, where we continued half an hour, then returned to the shop in like manner, continuing our work till sunset. After we had finished our day labor, we were put into the prison, and confined according to the usual manner, by placing a couple of iron bars across the outside of our doors, making them fast by letting them into two staples.

Matters were in this situation on the island, when I concerted the plan of making myself master of this place. My idea was to watch some favorable moment, to rise on a sudden, and take the garrison by surprise, when they were most off their guard, and least prepared to defend such an attack.

I endeavored to weigh every circumstance relating to the time and manner, how to make this attack upon the garrison. I communicated my views to Philips, of whose courage and valor, I had the highest opinion. I had likewise the firmest confidence in his wisdom, to plan and pre-concert a system, which would embrace every advantage, that

[158]

the nature of the thing would admit. Various were our ideas upon the subject. Many schemes for executing our plans occurred; but none of them, when thoroughly investigated, but what had many difficulties, almost insurmountable. Once we had determined in our own minds to embrace the opportunity of coming from work, rush upon and disarm the sentries, who were guarding us, and with our hammers and the arms which we should take from the sentry, make a general assault upon the rest of the garrison.

This we found attended with the following difficulties, viz. The least unusual movement by us, would be discovered by the sentry on the governor's house, who would instantly give the alarm to the guard, and to the soldiers in the barracks, where arms were always ready; and they, being more in number considerably than we, and being all armed, would undoubtedly overcome us with ease, seeing they would likewise have the advantage of the ground, being at the height of the hill, and we at the bottom. But this was not all. The guard were within a few paces of that fieldpiece which commanded the island, and when once in possession of that, could subdue or destroy us, in opposition to every effort which we could make. Moreover, when we came from the shop to the prison, the commanding officer, Major Perkins, had ever his attention upon us, and observed all our movements with the greatest attention. This scheme was attended with so many difficulties which appeared insurmountable, that we laid it aside as impracticable.

We then thought of embracing the opportunity which Sunday offered to rise on the garrison. Every Sunday, the soldiers and prisoners were assembled in one of the barracks to attend divine service. The soldiers occupied one end of the barrack, and the prisoners the other. The garrison generally assembled without arms; and, of consequence, were not so formidable in that situation, as when they had their guns in their hands loaded, and bayonets fixed. The guard, however, kept their places, which rendered this project alike impracticable.

The greater number of the prisoners were at this time in irons; and of consequence, when we should attempt to make prisoners of the soldiers, a scuffle would unavoidably ensue; and, as they would outnumber us, we should have but a bare possibility of succeeding even with the soldiers in the barracks, seeing so great a proportion of us were in irons; and should we succeed in this respect, yet the guard would unavoidably be alarmed; and being in possession of the fieldpiece, they could, with the greatest ease, sweep us away.

These difficulties were thought too great to make the attempt upon the garrison in that way: they were of course given up as impracticable. We finally agreed upon the morning, as the best time to execute such an insurrection.

We were awakened by the overseer about halfway between daybreak and sunrise. Immediately after the words "turn out, turn out," had been given by the overseer, he retired, and was generally absent about half an hour, when he returned, and finding us all dressed, turned us out, and took us to the shop to work. The doors of our prison were not fastened in this interim. The guard were under arms, and the sentry walking backward and forward before our door, to prevent any from going out.

My reasoning upon the prospect of success attending this undertaking, was of the following nature: "It is now warm weather," said I, it being the last of May, or the beginning of June; "therefore, sleep has the most powerful effect upon man in the cool of the morning; this will prevent the officers and soldiers sleeping in the barracks from being so easily awakened and aroused. The first and most difficult object is the guard. They are, at such times, under arms, and therefore under a situation far superior to ours: but, as we could outnumber them, and as I entertained an opinion of the prowess of the prisoners, far beyond that of the soldiers, I think, pretty probable, we may succeed in making them prisoners. After that object should be effected, then it will be easy to become master of the fieldpiece, and when that is obtained, we are masters of the island at once. When we become masters of the island, we are in a situation which will place us upon a footing of no mean standing. We, by being masters of the garrison, become likewise possessed of the command of the harbor of Boston; of all the vessels going out and coming in; therefore, can appropriate them to what use we find the exigences of the times will require. We shall likewise be in possession of provision, arms and ammunition of every kind. Warlike stores will be in our power, of every kind, should we find occasion to use them. I think that the prospect of escape by

[160]

water, after we have overcome the garrison, will be more eligible than to attempt another fight by land: and as it will be in our power to arm a vessel, and equip her every way for defence, and a long voyage, it would be almost impossible, even should they pursue after and over-take us, to master us at sea. We shall likewise be able to prevent their following us from the harbor of Boston with any great strength, by blowing up the magazine, and spiking the cannon. In this situation, I would leave the inimical shores of America, and rather seek an asylum among the inhospitable inhabitants of Barbary."

These were the outlines of my plan; and I determined to make one powerful effort to carry it into execution. Either to lose my life in the cause of liberty, or else gain a glorious freedom. And now, sir, before I go on to the relation of this insurrection, permit me to make some reflections upon my situation, and the operations of my mind under it.

I had ever a warmth of feeling in following any object of pursuit, perhaps, peculiar to myself. From the first moment of my imprison-ment, I felt a degree of insupportable impatience at confinement, and an ardent desire of the enjoyment of liberty, entirely beyond descrip-tion. The various unfortunate attempts which I had made for the purpose of liberating myself, did not serve to cool my ardor for ob-taining this object; but my desires for liberty increased in proportion to the time of my remaining confined, and the misfortunes attending it.

Reasoning upon the various occurrences which had been closely con-cerned in bringing me to this state of wretchedness, and upon the mo-tives by which I had been actuated under every scene through which I had passed, I concluded that my punishment was greater than I ought to bear. And even at this day, I am under great doubts how I ought to have acted through all those trying scenes. I know much is due to government. Personal inconvenience is to be borne, rather than government should suffer any injury, and for this plain reason, viz. that upon the uninterrupted administration of justice by government, depends the welfare of the whole community. But there are circum-stances under which a man may be justifiable in opposing, at least, the despotic transactions of cruelty in government towards an indi-

[161]

vidual. Whether this was the case with me, sir, I leave you to judge.

I had suffered, during my state of confinement in Northampton, the most unheard of course of illegal cruelty, and that too in a very notorious manner; so that the branches of government must universally be apprised of it. And this punishment was inflicted likewise by one of the officers of government. Therefore, under such circumstances, whether I had not just reason to suppose the most arbitrary and unjust measures were prescribed against me by government, your own good sense will determine. This officer never received the frowns of government for his conduct, but remained in high favor to the day of his death: neither was I ever compensated for the injuries which I here received.

Moreover, when the scene was reversed, and one of their number became dependent upon my will for his life, his liberty, and his safety; and under that situation, I had put my own life at stake to save his; and had shielded and protected him from danger in the time of his distress; after this, as soon as I had fallen into the hands of government, what was their language? Why, that I should receive an hundred lashes at the post!!

I recollect to have read an account respecting a Turk, who was a slave in Venice. He was asked by a Venetian merchant, "why he wore that aspect of perpetual gloom on his countenance, and now and then appeared to struggle to suppress the starting tear?" The Turk replied, "Can it appear strange to you, that I should lose enjoyment with the loss of that which is the foundation upon which we build all our joy?" "What would you do," said the Venetian, "to gain your liberty?" "Ho, by Allah!" said the Turk. "name the conditions: place danger and death before me in their most horrid forms; and if I do not pay the price, then say that Hamlet is not worthy of liberty."

When I heard this story of the Turk and the Venetian, my feelings entered immediately into the meaning of the Turk's observations. I could there discover and read the language of the human heart, notwithstanding he was a Turk. My heart panted to tell him, "Yes, thou infidel Turk, get thee hence from the land of christianity, and enjoy the pleasure of liberty, even in thy unbelieving country."

His feelings were what mine had been: the language of the heart is the same among Turks and Christians, Jews and Gentiles, etc. etc. etc.

[162]

LANGUAGE OF THE HEART

"Shame on that heart that never felt
A fellow-creature's woes
Yet tenderly affects to melt
In pity—for a rose."

Sir, accept my most sincere wish for your happiness, combined with your family's, and believe me to be, etc.

CHAPTER XX

"O, cruelty!
Thy touch, thy dead'ning touch, has steel'd the breast,
Where, through her rainbow shower, soft pity smil'd;
Has clos'd the heart, each God-like virtue blest,
To all the silent pleadings of his child.
At thy command he plants the dagger deep,
At thy command exults, tho' nature bid him weep!"

IT was on Sunday, when I made my arrangements among the prisoners, for our great effort, appointing the morning following for the time of operation. There were 35 prisoners, in whom I placed the utmost confidence, as to their courage and undaunted resolution. Ten of whom I had selected to be with me in taking the guard; and twenty-five I had left to be headed by Philips, who were to repair immediately to the barracks, and secure the officers and arms; intending, if possible, to accomplish the business without bloodshed.

After I had made the necessary dispositions, I exhorted the prisoners, "to be firm and courageous; to abstain from all acts of cruelty, which were not absolutely necessary; and, above all things, to pay the strictest attention to the orders given, that all might act in concert; to abstain from spirituous liquors." And this I meant to make more certain, by knocking all the casks on the head.

As taking the guard was much the most difficult part of this business to execute, I had selected out ten of the most desperate fellows among the prisoners, to follow me. I told them that I did not wish for them to go farther into dangers than I went myself; that I expected them to follow and support me, as far as I went, and no further. To this they all agreed, without the least hesitation; and confirmed their agreement by the most solemn assurance, that they would remain by me till death or liberty. After all matters were adjusted upon this system, we went to bed with all our clothes on, so that we might arise the next morning, immediately after the door should open, and the

[164]

TURN OUT! TURN OUT!

overseer should depart. After I had lain down, the importance of the scene before me kept me from closing my eyes through the whole night.

> "Ha! not a breath of wind! no gentle breeze,
> To fan the darksome gloom! no ruffled wave
> Disturbs this silent port of life, nor moves
> The sleeping calm; a death-like silence reigns.
> Those storms of wrath, that oft by tyrants breath'd,
> Have shook the trembling world, now die away;
> In whispers lost—the froth of heighten'd pride
> Beats on the rocks, and wounds itself to death:
> The pomp of kings, the sycophantic breath
> Of soothing flatt'rers, and menial crowds,
> The voice of slander, the destructive blasts
> Of envy, self-distracting, softly seem,
> Like dying thunders in a distant cloud,
> Gently to vanish from the list'ning ear.
> Death, rigid death, impartially declares
> That man is nothing but a heap of dust,
> Clay-cold, insensible. Wipe from thy cheek,
> O man! the soft emasculating tear;
> For die thou must: just as by nature's streams,
> In easy mazes roll thin lympid tides,
> A tribute to the main. Thus art thou born
> For short-liv'd glory—pre-ordain'd to die.
> The thoughts of obsequies, convulsions, groans;
> 'Tis these distract thy soul. The kiss of death
> Is soft and harmless. Golden rest attends it;
> And soon dissolves the fearful dream of life.
> Nature's great law is death. As rising flames
> Seek their congenial place, and mount to heav'n,
> Thus haste we to our end. The bloom of youth
> Expels our infant years: then hoary age
> Encroaches on the man, and shuts the scene."

I waited with impatience for the approach of morn. This, of all nights through my life, appeared the longest. I often arose and went to the grates to see if I could discern any signs of day. At last the moment appeared! I heard the overseer enter and vociferate with great clamor, "Turn out, turn out," and immediately departed.

I arose with precipitation, and hasted to gather those who were destined to act different parts, in the business, into bodies by themselves. I observed a few got out of their beds with some reluctance. Philips I saw appeared extremely pale. I asked him what was the matter? He told me he felt sick. I answered, that the moment did not admit of attention to sickness. He came to the spot and took charge of his men. I ordered one of my men to secure the sentry in the yard the moment I gave the signal for starting. He took a stick about three feet long and two inches in diameter, and stood ready to execute his part.

When I came to the spot where I could observe the guard, I saw them under arms, and standing in the door of the guardhouse, with their bayonets fixed. This sight was by no means calculated to ensure our success; but not knowing what exertion would effect, I determined to make the push at all hazards. I therefore clapped my hands, the signal for rushing, and sprang forward towards the guardhouse, expecting the ten, whom I had appointed to that business, were close following me. The soldiers seeing me coming towards them, presented the points of their bayonets to prevent my entering the guardhouse. I parted the bayonets with my hands, and disarmed two men in a moment. This I did by a sudden jerk, when I caught hold of these two guns. I immediately turned the bayonets towards the soldiers, when they gave back, and I entered the guardhouse. I pronounced immediate death upon any one who dared to oppose me. I ordered them, in a very peremptory manner, "to lay down their arms and retire behind the guard-bed." They obeyed—two made their escape, and fled out of the guardhouse, giving the alarm to the officers and soldiers in the barracks, together with the sentry on the governor's house. When I entered the guardhouse, I carried with me two guns, intending to give one to the first who followed me, in order that he might prevent any of the guard from escaping through that door, and to secure the other myself: wishing to prevent any alarm, until the other party of twenty-five had time to get to the barracks; but imagine, sir, my disappointment and astonishment, when I looked and saw myself alone, without one of the prisoners to assist me!!

When I first started, Philips' courage failed. He turned and ran into the room out of which he came, undressed and jumped into bed. The rest, seeing this, were all struck with a panic, ran back and went to bed: thinking by this mean to make the officers believe, that they had no part nor lot in this business. Therefore, I found the guard my prisoners, and myself a prisoner to the guard.

I saw the soldiers and officers from the barracks, running towards

[166]

the guardhouse, with their clothes in the utmost disorder; some half dressed, and others naked, a shirt excepted. Seeing the day was lost, I turned, and ran out of the guardhouse, making again towards the prison. carrying my guns with me. The sergeant of the guard, who, but a minute before, had been begging his life in the most abject state of fear, now began to bustle towards me with his gun, as though he had been in close contest from the beginning, and intended to sacrifice me to his fury. He ran after me, hallooing, "Burroughs, you devil you, I'll kill you, I'll kill you." I turned indignant towards the coward, and threw my guns at him with the points of the bayonets forward. One of the bayonets took his hand, and entered the skin about an inch. At this, he bawled out in the bitterest manner, "I'm wounded, I'm killed!"

The officers and soldiers rushed into the prison, laid hold of me, and brought me again into the yard. Major Perkins with his sword, Lieutenant Treat and Burbeck with their rattans, were all lashing me at once, with the greatest violence. At this crisis, the sergeant, whom I had wounded, came up with his gun. and struck me over the head with all his might. The blood flew quick into my face, I moved suddenly towards the pitiful villain; at which he ran, making a noise more like a calf than a man.

I was then confined by a pair of heavy irons, commonly called shackles, taken to the whipping post, and there received an hundred stripes, which were laid on in a very serious manner, causing the blood to stream at every stroke, so that my shoes were filled by the time I was taken down.

This, sir, was a heavy stroke, too much even for my iron constitution to support. I fell under it. A fit of sickness succeeded, which continued about three months, making the prospect doubtful how my career might terminate. O! happy, thrice happy should I have been, had I fallen here! and closed the troubled scene of life! "O terque, quaterque beati. queis Trojæ sub mœnibus altis, contigit oppetere!" [1]

During my sickness, I had to contend with inconveniences of no small magnitude. There was no provision made for the sick; therefore, salt beef and bread were all the necessaries provided for me by

[1] O thrice, and four times happy those, who should be so fortunate as to die under the lofty walls of Troy! VIRGIL.

government. A medical gentleman, from the town of Boston, influenced by the mere emotions of compassion, visited me under this scene of distress, and administered to my necessities. The name of this humane ornament of nature I have forgotten, but think it was Elliot.

My back was extremely sore; and having a pair of heavy irons on my legs, I could lie in no other position than on my back. Major Perkins wished to liberate me from the irons around my legs, during the fit of sickness, but was absolutely forbidden by his superiors, until near two months after my punishment, when he was allowed to take them off.

My situation, and course of perpetual suffering, caused me to repine bitterly at the hand of providence. It appeared that I was marked out as an object for the heaviest strokes of misery to be reiterated upon, until I should be finally swallowed up by the power of their force. Why, said I, should all this befall me? Do these misfortunes happen as a punishment to vicious conduct? And am I so self-blinded as not to be sensible of my own unheard of wickedness? For certainly, if the wickedness of my conduct has been equal to my sufferings, I have been, of all mankind, the most abandoned. But, said I again, is this reasoning just? Do the wicked suffer, while the just are in a state of constant prosperity? Let us advert to facts for evidence upon this subject.

I believe that matters of fact will prove, that the best of men have suffered, in this state of imperfection, in an equal degree with the worst. We will instance Socrates and Aristides of the ancients, and the immortal Columbus, among those of a more modern date. Many instances might I produce even among ourselves, were it necessary; but one moment's reflection upon this subject is enough to confute the idea entirely, of a person's misfortunes being any evidence of his moral turpitude. Then why is it that some are marked out, in the course of events, to endure the heaviest strokes of misfortune in one continued series, is to me an inexplicable mystery in the course of Providence.

Since I started into life, how has my course been chequered! Even death, the last resort of the wretched, has fled from my approaches, as though cautious of his friendly presence, administering comfort rather than terror. Is it not strange, that death should join with

[168]

mankind, and even refuse the morsel afforded to his embrace, in order to fill up my measure of sufferings? When I set the jail on fire at Northampton, I thought it out of the power of malice itself to prevent the approach of the moment of my quietus; but was disappointed. I then expected to have found an end to my trouble, in the cold embrace of death, in the dungeon; and here I found the tyrant eluding my pursuit. When I rose on the garrison, it appeared to me certain that I should meet with death or liberty, but alas! in both was I deceived. Then surely, said I, this punishment added to sickness, must close the eventful scene; but, horrid to relate, I was reserved for woes, which yet untold, made my former sufferings vanish away, as not worthy of notice.

Are these matters painted to you, sir, in colors too high for the simple statement of facts? No, sir, indeed they are truths, the force of which I must feel while I set poring over the scenes; though they are past and gone, yet have left a mortal sting behind.

Soon after I was able to walk about, I was visited by a gentleman, whose name I never recollect without feeling that warmth of affection and glow of gratitude, which fills my soul with rapture. This gentleman's name was Summers. He was my father's sister's son. He commanded a vessel then in the harbor of Boston. He possessed an enlarged mind, which looked above the clamor of vulgar prejudice; and where he saw the course of humanity lead, he pursued his way, let it be ever so unpopular. This gentleman made me a visit, even against the custom of the world. He was the first relative that ever came or sent to me on this gloomy place. He saw my necessities. He administered to my relief. He poured the balm of consolation into my wounded mind. He conducted as a man ought to conduct, who is governed by a spirit of true benevolence. He continued to visit me from time to time, during the whole course of my confinement on this island.

Having been disappointed in my efforts for an escape, and that too by the cowardly, perfidious conduct of my fellow-prisoners, I pretty much gave up the idea of making any further attempts for my liberation; but concluded to reconcile my mind in the best manner possible, to the idea of wearing away the time of my confinement. I therefore told Major Perkins, that I would give up the idea of ever making another attempt for escape, if he would not put me in irons, give me the liberty of the island, and not subject me to the direction or authority of Rifford, the overseer. Major Perkins believed me sincere. He ever had occasion to believe what I told him, by way of contract, while I was under his care. He agreed to allow me the privilege, provided I would discover any attempt of the prisoners to escape. I told Major Perkins, that being under the same condemnation with the other prisoners, I had no intention to purchase any privilege at their expense. That I should by no means give them any aid in their escape; neither should I be a hindrance to them. After some days trial to obtain my promise for discovering any attempt of the prisoners to procure their liberty. without success. he agreed to my proposal; and gave me liberty of going to any part of the island, without a sentry to attend me.

This was a great degree of freedom, compared with what I had enjoyed; and therefore, most sensibly felt. My situation was as eligible as the nature of things would admit; and I, even in this state of servile wretchedness, began to look forward with the pleasing expectation of better days.

> "Whatever diff'rent ways mankind pursue,
> O happiness! 'tis thee we keep in view!
> 'Tis thee, in ev'ry action we intend,
> The noblest motive, and superior end!
> Thou dost the scarcely finish'd soul incline;
> Its first desire, and constant tho't, is thine!
> Our infant breasts are sway'd by thee alone,
> When pride and jealousy are yet unknown.
> Thou art, of all our waking thot's, the theme;
> We court thee too, in ev'ry nightly dream.
> Whither the roads that to perdition lead,
> Or those that guide us to the stars, we tread;
> Thine is the hope, the inestimable prize,
> The glorious mark, on which we fix our eyes."

About this time an incident took place, which gave me the most sensible pain. At a certain time, a number of people from Boston came on to the island, among whom was Thomas Cushing, son to the lieutenant-governor. When these people came among the prisoners, they asked money of them, as was the general custom. Cushing took a dollar out of his pocket, and gave it me; telling me at the same time, to give each of the prisoners a glass of rum out of the avails of the dollar, and departed without waiting for an answer. The prisoner, who had been instrumental in obtaining the money, entertained an idea of his being entitled to a larger share of the dollar than the others; and therefore proposed a division with me. My reply was, that the money was given to me for a particular purpose; and as I accepted the gift, I had implicitly pledged my faith to execute the trust reposed in me. I told him, that a glass of rum must be given to each prisoner, if the dollar would purchase a sufficient quantity for that purpose; and that I should perform that as soon as I could obtain permission of Major Perkins.

I accordingly made application to the Major, for liberty to give the convicts a glass of rum. He told me, that it was out of his power to grant my request at that time; but that Governor Cushing would be on the island in a few days; that he would consult him on the subject, and see if it would answer to grant such permission.

While I was waiting the issue of this business, Thomas Cushing came on to the island again; and the prisoner, Mount, by name, who had asked him for money before, now made application again for more money. Cushing answered Mount, that he thought it a shame for him to ask for money again, so soon after leaving a dollar with Burroughs for them all. Mount told him, that Burroughs had kept the money himself, and the other prisoners had received nothing. Cushing then asked for an explanation of the business. I told him how the matter was situated; and rejoined, that I would divide the money, if that was agreeable to his feelings. He left me without an answer. Not long after, Cushing being in company with a number of gentlemen in Boston, amongst whom was a Mr. May, a rational philanthopist; he, in a pompous declaration respecting his own excellent qualities of heart, related, that he had given three dollars to Burroughs, for the prisoners, and that Burroughs, had appropriated them to his own use, refusing to participate with any others in the benefit of the money. Mr. May entered with warmth into the subject, and when he saw me, expostulated upon the impropriety of my conduct; and when I gave him a simple narration of facts, he seemed to hesitate about giving credit to a report so different from Cushing's.

This circumstance, you may think, was of too small consequence to find a place in this narration; but the reason why I relate it, is the disagreeable effect it had upon my mind; having met with but few incidents which have given me keener sensations, than this trivial occurrence.

As the remaining part of my confinement was ended without any very remarkable occurrence, I will not dwell upon the uninteresting events; but only observe, that the terms of agreement between the Major and myself, were ever kept inviolate by both parties. I will, likewise, give you an extract of some letters which passed between me and my friends, while I remained here, and then pass from the disagreeable subject.

The first letter I received was from that uncle, who had relieved me in Northampton: It was to the following amount:

"Charlton, April 20th, 1788.

"BELOVED NEPHEW,

"I sincerely wish and hope, that your long and painful confinement may prove an advantage to you, by giving you time to reflect, seriously, upon your past misconduct. As that was in your thoughtless and youthful days, and as you have now arrived to the age of maturity, I beg of you to consider with yourself, seriously, what an awful and disagreeable situation you will soon be in, after you are liberated, if you should enter into an unlawful course of life. As you have now, by experience, tasted of the evil nature of transgression, and are now in a situation to figure to yourself the happy condition of those, who, by a course of honest industry, procure for themselves and their dependents, an honorable and honest living through life. I wish you may exercise that wisdom which nature has given you, to learn the difference between a regular life and a course of unlawful pursuits. You must be sensible. that you will not only render yourself happy by a course of regular conduct, but will greatly increase the happiness of your relations, and all who wish you well. We all hope and desire, that you will be so kind to yourself and to us, as to coolly and faithfully improve the good sense and reason which the all-wise Being has so bountifully bestowed upon you; and I think that under the influence of this reason. you will immediately after your liberation, repair to your parents, or to my house, or to some of your relations,

[172]

who can help you to business, and to those things you will be destitute of, and without which, you will be very uncomfortable. By doing this you will avoid many great and trying temptations.

"I am in no doubt but by a steady uniform course of well doing, you may re-establish your reputation, and again be a serviceable member of society. On the contrary, should you again, at this time of life, return to bad courses, every one would despair of your ever reforming, and you must be lost forever; which may the all-wise Being enable you to prevent, by a wise and virtuous course of life, for the future, is the sincere desire and prayer of your most affectionate uncle.

"EBENEZER DAVIS."

Soon after the receipt of the foregoing letter, I received another from my mother's youngest brother, to the following import:

"Oxford, May 12th, 1788.

"DEAR NEPHEW,

"A recent opportunity has given me the pleasure of hearing that your conduct has been good and unexceptionable, since your unfortunate attempt on the garrison. I entertain the most ardent desire that it may continue.

"Your long and severe confinement is almost at an end. Soon again you will taste the sweets of liberty, of which you have been deprived so long. I should advise you, by all means, to return to your friends. You are, and will be, destitute of clothes when your time of servitude has expired; therefore, without clothes, without friends, without money, and coming off the Castle with the prejudices which mankind entertain against one who has been confined there, you will find it impossible to gain a subsistence among mankind, in an honest way, without you come to your friends, who can help you to those things which you will stand in need of. I remain your affectionate uncle,

"JONATHAN DAVIS."

"Hanover, October 16th, 1787.

"DEAR CHILD,

"It is not our present object to lay open to your view the bleeding hearts of your parents. The attempt would be in vain; for it is wholly beyond the power of language to express. If the reports be true with respect to the atrocity of your conduct, we cannot but acquiesce in the measures taken by government to punish such acts, which are pregnant with ruin to the civil community. Did we pay attention to nothing but the yearnings of our hearts towards you; did we consult nothing but the dictates of natural affection; to part with an only son in this manner; to consider you as being lost to God, to your parents, and to your generation; is a consideration which would swell the tide of our sorrows, and render them like an overflowing deluge. But we fully believe, that our times and changes are in God's hands; that he has given us this cup of trembling, and that it becomes us to be still under this severe stroke of his rod. What further trials he may mete out for us, in his dealings with you, we know not; but this one thing we know, that in relation to anything that may concern you in future, it becomes us to cast all our care upon God and to leave you in his hands.

"When we recollect, that there is yet a probability, that we may see you again, and behold in your conduct the fruits of repentance for your misconduct; we cannot help feasting our hearts with such a pleasing contemplation. Nothing which this world could afford, would be greater comfort to us, than your return under such a situation.

"In the meantime, it is our ardent and pressing desire, that your behavior and conduct may be framed in such a manner, as to be to the good acceptance of those who are appointed to have the oversight of you, during the remainder of that servitude to which you are confined.

"It has ever opened the avenues of grief, and added fresh anguish to our sorrows, to hear of any attempts in you, to get free from your confinement by unwarrantable measures.

"It would be acceptable to us, to have a line from you, specifying the state of your mind, and what your purposes are, in relation to your future pursuits. In the meantime, take this as a testimony of love intermingled with the most heartfelt grief and anguish, from your afflicted and sorrowful parents,

"E. and A. BURROUGHS."

[174]

NO VERY PLEASING VIEW

"Castle Island, November 27th, 1787.

"HONORED AND DEAR PARENTS,

"Your favor of the 16th ult. was duly received. Were I to undertake to describe the sensations which it created, I know I should fail in the attempt.

"Notwithstanding my being considered as an outcast among mankind; and under that consideration, treated as the worst of villains, and vilest of slaves, yet it has not dissolved that tie of natural affection which binds me to those who gave me breath.

"To undertake a vindication of my conduct, is an object entirely out of my view at present; but I would suggest, the same natural course attends common fame, when applied to me, as it universally has done when applied to any other person or object; therefore, wish you to make those allowances, which candor will dictate under my peculiar situation.

"Could you read the language of my heart, you would there see the most sincere desire for your comfort through life. My situation is such, I am sensible, as to offer no very pleasing view to the minds of parents towards a child; yet, it is a situation, which at present is out of my power to alter. The time will come, when I shall again be called to act my part on the stage of life, as a member of the civil community; that time will discover whether the principles of virtue are the governing laws of my mind. I feel my task too arduous and difficult. Life's path is environed with errors, thick on every side. I shall have the passions and prejudices of a hard-hearted world to combat; whether I shall be competent to the task, is yet in the womb of futurity. It must be a most pleasing object with me, once more to mix with society upon honorable terms, and enjoy the blessings of friendship, after being shut out from those enjoyments this length of time.

"As to the object of my pursuits, after my time of servitude shall expire, I candidly declare, that I have not fixed upon any. I should receive any advice upon that subject, from you with pleasure.

"As to the state of my mind; I view myself as an inhabitant of a vacant desolate country. There are none amongst all the world to whom I feel that glow of friendship, together with an equality of

[175]

station which renders society pleasing. Long as I have remained in the converse and society of this motley collection of characters, of which the convicts are composed, yet I have no relish for their society.

"Should I receive no assistance from my friends, at the time of my departure from this place, I must leave the island absolutely naked; having long since parted with all my own clothes to satisfy the calls of hunger. I am, with duty and esteem, your affectionate son,

"SPEPHEN BURROUGHS.

"E. and A. BURROUGHS."

About three weeks previous to the expiration of the time of my confinement, my uncle Ebenezer Davis came to see me on the island, brought me some clothes, and gave me money sufficient to provide myself with what things were necessary to my making a decent appearance, and likewise to support myself on the road to his house. The happy moment arrived! How beautiful was that day! Of all the days of my life, this was the most beautiful and serene. The very heaven and elements were in unison with my feelings. I, for the first time, for the term of thirty months, dressed myself in clean, decent apparel. I heard the sentence from Major Perkins, "Burroughs, you are free," with a sensation of joy that is inexpressible. My heart bounded like the roe on the mountain! I went into the boat, the sea was smooth, and the wind was calm! the heavens were mild and serene; the sun was beautiful beyond description! the boat glided over the smooth surface of the waters with a facility that was enchanting!

> "Sweet memory, wafted by the gentle gale,
> Oft up the tide of time I turn my sail,
> To view the fairy haunts of long lost hours,
> Blest with far greener shades, far fresher bow'rs."

Having now ended in my narrative a tedious and bitter confinement, which lasted me three years and five weeks, I will here end this letter. I wish to make some reflections upon the nature of the punishment by servitude; and as that will take up too much time for this, I will reserve it for the subject of another letter. In the meantime believe me as usual, etc.

CHAPTER XXI

"Blest be that hand divine, which gently laid
My heart at rest, beneath this humble shed.
The world's a stately bark on dangerous seas,
With pleasure seen, but boarded at our peril."

A S I intimated to you, sir, in my last, that the subject of this letter would be a consideration of the nature of punishment by servitude; I now take up that matter in obedience to my promise. This is a subject of which I have felt the operation in some measure; and therefore, may be thought to know its natural effect upon the human heart, as well as most men.

The object of punishment ever ought to be the preservation of the good order of society, by a reformation of those who are disorderly through a vicious disposition, or a mistaken apprehension of matters. The honesty of a legislative body will ever point at that, and their laws will ever affect that where a sufficient fund of information directs their legislative acts. Whether the system of servitude upon its present establishment, does answer the purpose of producing a reformation in the disorderly, is the question now under consideration.

There was on the Castle an assemblage of characters from various parts of the globe: some old in iniquity, and others but timid beginners in the ways of transgression. Here, the objects of honor and promotion were reversed. In a winter evening's tale, you would not hear the feats of virtue recounted as a recommendation. These were objects treated with contempt. On the other hand, that person who could relate the most desperate and daring transgression of the laws of national justice, was considered the most honorable character among the prisoners; while those, who were novices in wickedness, shrank from an examination of their deeds, and felt a degree of littleness, because they had nothing worthy of giving themselves a name among those heroes of the night.

The natural effect of this you will easily conceive. Where our am-

[177]

bition leads we generally make progress. Those who would blush at the thought of their illicit conduct when they first arrived at the Castle, would now sooner blush at the small part which they have acted in the way of transgression.

They would listen with attention to the acts of those whom they considered as their masters in iniquity; this is a lesson but too easily learnt. Their whole object was, discovering and inventing means to carry their diabolical purposes into execution immediately upon their liberation. Finally, this of all others, was the most perfect school of vice that I ever saw. For a man to remain uncontaminated by this society, after continuing in it a number of years, he must have more solid philosophy than I believe mankind generally possess. Under these circumstances, how can this institution serve to reform the morals of men? Facts prove, that instead of becoming good members of society, the convicts have generally, taken to a course of the most atrocious transgressions after their liberation.

Indeed, the situation of the prisoners is such, when they are liberated, that all motives for doing well are taken away. They generally, at that time, find themselves naked, moneyless, and friendless. Their previous confinement on the Castle is a sufficient objection to their being employed in business; therefore, supposing them possessed of virtuous principles, what can such virtues do in this situation. They have the same necessities to supply that other men have, and where they find that government has not only confined them to servitude for a number of years, but has, moreover, taken away the prospect of earning a small pittance of bread by industry, will the feelings of nature allow them to consider any obligation which government may require, as binding?

I saw the effects of this system of servitude whilst I was a prisoner on the Castle. I published my sentiments upon the subject for the consideration of the legislature. Little attention was paid to my reasoning, in so low a situation. Had these sentiments come from one in a more exalted station, they might, perhaps, have been understood better, and the reasoning upon such a subject been more clear and convincing.

I will not detain you with any further observations upon this subject, but proceed in the narrative.

[178]

AT LIBERTY WITHOUT RESTRAINT

I went immediately to the house of Richard Devens, Esq. with whom I took breakfast, having received a previous invitation for that purpose before I left the island.

Immediately after breakfast, the good old man, taking me into a private room, entered into conversation upon my present prospects. I told him that I had concluded to repair to my uncle's at Charlton, who had supplied me with necessaries for my appearing again in the world. It appeared to rejoice him to hear that I was not left friendless. He said he had it in contemplation to help me, if no other person appeared for that purpose. He gave me counsel as a parent would give to a child. He appeared to be interested in my future welfare. He presented me with a dollar, wishing me to accept it as a token of his esteem, and good wishes.[1] After this, I immediately repaired to Long Wharf, where Capt. Summers lay with his vessel. I here met that philanthropist upon the shores of liberty, who had so often relieved my distress in a state of slavery. My sensations at this meeting were exquisitely pleasing. I tarried with him two days; and during that time an accident took place which gave me an opportunity of feeling the extremes of pain and joy in a very short space. The matter was this:

Capt. Summers coming into his cabin at a certain time, where he had left me, missed his watch, which he supposed he had left hanging in the cabin. He enquired of all the hands whether they had seen or taken his watch from the place where he left it. Their answers were in the negative. He asked if anybody had been on board the vessel that morning; they said no. I saw his countenance was troubled. He felt in a situation too delicate to know what measure to take. My feelings at this time were as disagreeable as though I had been covered with burning embers. I knew that the appearance must be that I had taken the watch. No other person could take it. The watch was gone. What a horrid figure of ingratitude I must now make, said I, in the mind of that man, above all others, to whom I wish to appear amiable! A single word was not uttered for the course of half an hour. A dismal gloom hung over the countenance of every one present; at length we were all relieved by the arrival of the mate, who

[1] Burroughs has given a true specimen of this gentleman's character through a long life. He has lately gone to receive the rewards of the righteous in a better world.

brought the watch on board, having carried it to a watchmaker to have some work done to it which was necessary.

The sight of the watch instantly dispelled the gloom from every countenance; we all felt the effects, as though a shock of electricity had operated upon us. Captain Summers burst into a laugh, patting me on the shoulder, saying, "one hundred dollars would not make me so glad as the sight of that watch."

My sensations were too violent for utterance; I could not reply; I felt wounded to death, that, even for one moment, a jealousy should remain in the breast of Captain Summers, of my treachery towards him; yet, what gave me such exquisite pain was, that circumstances were in such a train, that he could not avoid such a jealousy.

I visited a number of my acquaintance during this short residence in Boston; among whom was a Mr. Bingham, who was cotemporary with me in College. This man had a warm heart, friendly to mankind, scrupulously nice in every principle of justice, regulating his conduct by the exactest rules of propriety.[2]

After this I took leave of all my acquaintance in Boston, and measured back that road which, nearly three years before, I had been carried through, bound with chains to Glazier Wheeler. Before I left Boston, Capt. Summers offered to supply me with a sum of money, for my present necessities; but as I had a sufficiency already for my traveling expenses, until I should arrive at my uncle's, in Charlton, I declined accepting his offer, seeing he had been so bountiful towards me already.

It was in the month of September, when I walked through the country. To visit again the varied scenes of nature; to be at liberty, and

[2] Some of his old acquaintance were blamed by their friends for being seen in his company at this period; and it is but justice to state the motives of the former. They knew his excellent parents; they were sensible that the feelings of these parents were wrought up to the highest pitch, at this all important crisis, in the fate of their *only* son. Burroughs gave the most positive assurances of exerting all his powers to retrieve his character. Had his old friends forsaken him at this eventful period, what would he have done? Probably he would have immediately resorted to his former courses; and the doating parents would have accused these friends of being instrumental of blasting all their hopes. They also thought it their duty to afford the son all the support in their power, while he appeared to be in earnest to regain his reputation.

without the least restraint; ramble through the country, was a luxury of enjoyment which only those can feel who have been in my situation.

> "Hail, memory hail! in thy exhaustless mines
> From age to age, unnumber'd treasures shine!
> Thought and her shadowy brood thy calls obey,
> And place and time are subjects to thy sway!"

I arrived in Charlton the second day after my leaving Boston. As no immediate business offered, I concluded to turn my attention to manual labor, until some opportunity should offer for my attending to other business. I went to work among the common laborers of my uncle. This was somewhat mortifying; but I was determined to endure any inconvenience, rather than give the least idea to any of my friends that I was not willing to use such means as I possessed to gain an honest support. I continued in this business about one month, hoping to obtain a school in this or some of the neighboring towns, as soon as the season should approach for that business.

I will here give you an extract of a letter from my uncle to my father, about this time.

"Charlton, 25th October, 1788.

"DEAR BROTHER AND SISTER,

"Your son Stephen is now with me, and has been the greater part of the time since his having left the Castle. He works very steady with my folks on the farm. He has some prospect of teaching a school within this town, or in Oxford.

"He wishes you to write respecting your desire, relating to his further pursuits; whether you would have him try to obtain business in these parts, or return home, in order to enter into business with you. He appears to have ability for farming, and as you have a large farm, should he prove tolerable steady, he would greatly tend to ease you of a great deal of care and trouble; and it would, likewise, be advantageous to him.

"He must have some way for a subsistence; and there is none attended with less temptations than husbandry.

"A few days since, I received your letter by Mr. Curtis; previous to which, I had supplied your son with clothing, so as to come to my

[181]

house from the Castle; and agreeably to your desire, shall continue to supply him with what is necessary. I am your loving brother,

"EBENEZER DAVIS.

"REV. E. BURROUGHS."

"*Charlton, 25th October,* 1788.

"HONORED AND DEAR SIR,

"You will see by the date of this letter, that I am at liberty from the trying scenes of tedious confinement, which I have endured for such a length of time. The various occurrences of an unhappy course of misfortunes has left no very favorable impression upon the minds of the public concerning me. I know I have suffered greatly in your esteem in consequence of this likewise, which has added no small degree of poignancy to my sufferings. I hope to justify myself to you at least, by my future conduct. To a censorious world I have no idea of making the attempt, with an expectation of success.

"I have been in this place about one month, paying some attention to manual labor. I could wish for every degree of counsel respecting my pursuits at this critical juncture, that a parent can bestow. I remain with sentiments of affection and duty, yours, etc.

"STEPHEN BURROUGHS.

"REV. EDEN BURROUGHS."

Sometime in the month of November. I engaged to teach a school for one month in the town of Charlton. The inhabitants being fearful of employing me for any longer term, until they should find, by experience, whether I would conduct a school with regularity and propriety. I began this school with fifteen scholars; at the expiration of the month I had forty-five; I was then engaged for two months, which took all the public money which had been raised for the purpose of schooling. My wages for these two months were raised; and I found, to my no small comfort, that my conduct had given universal satisfaction. When the two months were expired, my school consisted of eighty-four members. A number of young men from various parts of the country had resorted to my school, in order to obtain the higher branches of education.

SETTLED IN BUSINESS

When the time of the last engagement had expired, the people composing this district assembled, and raised money for the continuation of this school one year longer; this was a thing entirely unknown before in that town. The season for schooling, heretofore in this town, was three months, in the winter, and the same length of time, in the summer. The summer school was taught by a woman, which school consisted of small children.

I now found myself settled in business, and rising fast in the esteem of those with whom I was connected; yet, under all these circumstances, I was by no means at ease. My mind was perpetually worried with fear, that some of the ten thousand of the unfortunate occurrences, which had heretofore befallen me, might again destroy my present pleasing prospects.

My former sufferings had left such an impression of horror on my mind, that I could not close my eyes in sleep, but what these terrible scenes would be present to my view, and I compelled to act them over again. For years after this, nay, to the present moment, sir, I often start from sleep, reeking with sweat under the intense misery of my fancied horror.

I will here give you a copy of a number of letters passing between me and my friends, and then pass on to more important scenes.

"Hanover, January 6th, 1789.

"DEAR CHILD,

"It is truly a matter of rejoicing to us, that the time of your severe trials, by a painful confinement, in a state of bondage, is now expired; and that you have now returned, once more to taste those sweets of liberty, which are always dear, next to life itself. But much greater joy will it afford us to see the evidence of your heart's being effectually turned from those ways which had well-nigh proved your ruin, in relation to both time and eternity; well knowing that without this, your release from a state of confinement, will finally operate to no other purpose, but bringing you into a state of far more awful bondage than you have ever yet experienced. In relation to any advice you desire from your parents, respecting your future objects and pursuits, we know not how to be any more particular than we have already

[183]

expressed to you in our former letters. You must be sensible, and every feeling of nature itself will teach you, that it must needs be highly acceptable to us to have you return home, and live with us, only provided you bring with you a child-like temper, and act out a spirit of genuine repentance, for your former conduct and ways. To invite your return to us on any other terms, we cannot, with any real sincerity of heart. And if it shall be agreeable to your inclination to return to us on the conditions here mentioned, your object in life must be pursuing the labors of the field. I have neither capacity nor inclination to introduce you, under present circumstances, into the business of any other calling in life. And in reference to such an object, you must necessarily consult your own talents and inclination; for any person, of your age and experience, can better judge for himself about the calling in life for which he is best furnished, than another can judge for him; and your own conduct, in relation to such an object, must be governed by your own judgment. We earnestly pray for your best comfort, in relation to time and eternity; and rest your affectionate parents,

"E. and A. Burroughs.

"Stephen Burroughs."

"*Charlton, February 25th,* 1789.

"Honored and dear sir,

"Yours of the 6th of January was received about a week since. My acknowledgments for your favor I have paid by the earliest opportunity.

"In the letter I wrote you last fall, you will recollect an intimation of my wishing for your advice upon my future pursuits in life. Not receiving any answer to that letter, I engaged in the school for a year, and cannot now leave it; my promise being given to keep it that term of time.

"In this undertaking, I consulted my uncle Ebenezer Davis, who was full in the opinion, that I ought to enter into the business, which then offered, on account of the uncertainty of having another opportunity of equal advantage.

"Your welfare and happiness lie near my heart, and should be exceeding glad to make you a visit, but at present such an object is out of my power.

"I remain in the bands of filial affection, your dutiful son,

"STEPHEN BURROUGHS."

"Rev. E. BURROUGHS."

"*Boston, December, 22d, 1788.*

"DEAR SIR,

"I received your letter, and gave it proper attention. I am glad you have, hitherto, met with so good success. You are sensible 'you must creep "again" before you can go.' I wish it were in my power, from good grounds, to encourage you with respect to business this way; but I have no disposition to deceive you. You will meet with better encouragement in the country than in town. I advise you to go to your father, as soon as you are out of business. He is able to help you, and I pray he may be willing. I rejoice to hear you conduct well; and, by all that is endearing in this, and in the future world, I entreat you to maintain your good resolutions. In the utmost haste, I am your sincere friend and humble servant,

"CALEB BINGHAM.

"Mr. S. BURROUGHS."

Matters continued in this train, without any material occurrence. I lived in the house of one Williams, a very considerable man in the part of the town where I taught the school. He was a man of a feeling heart, was ready to assist the needy, and administer comfort to the wretched. I was treated in this house, by the good old people, more like a child than a stranger. All the tenderness and care of a parent toward a child ever marked their conduct towards me. Sometime in the summer, D. Bacon received a letter from my father, the contents of which was to our satisfaction.

I had settled in my mind, to make my father a visit in the course of this summer; therefore, I hired a horse of one Curtis, formerly a clergyman, for this journey, and made my visit in the month of July, after an absence of nearly four years. To revisit again the scenes of early youth,

[185]

"Childhood's lov'd group, behold in every scene,
The tangled wood-walk and the tufted green,"

gave a pleasing sensation, tender and soothing. Not long after I had
been at my father's, my horse, playing in the pasture, fell and broke
his leg. This was a calamity which I felt in a very sensible manner.
I had grown so timid, that any object of misfortune was viewed in its
most terrible form. I started at every danger, and grew pale with apprehension. I have, since, wondered at my feeling this misfortune
so sensibly. In order to ease my mind, my father procured me another horse, and not only wrote himself, but added the testimonial of
one of his neighbor's, to his account.

I returned to Charlton, and the September following, was married
to the daughter of my uncle, Ebenezer Davis.[3]

This circumstance opened a new field of contemplation. To view
myself in the relation of a husband and parent; to feel the attachment
which such a relation constituted; you. sir, who stand in those relations
yourself, can more easily judge of my feelings than I can describe
them. When I became the head of a family, perfectly calculated to
render the domestic life happy; and saw myself established in such
business as would supply their necessities, I was satisfied; the height
of my ambition was gratified; I enjoyed a flow of uninterrupted felicity, for days and for months. The enjoyment of my fireside was
now a source of pleasure which I, before, had never a distant idea was
the portion of mortals. It was indeed too great to be of a lasting
duration. I received the warm congratulations of my friends on my
prosperity. Every event took place to please. All things swam gently
down the tide of time, and lulled my feelings to repose in the lap of
security.

I have made a transition in my narrative, over about a year of the
time after my marriage, without entering into particulars; having
drawn out the narration to such a length, already, as to fatigue my
own patience; and I believe, sir, that were it not for your tenderness
to my feelings, you would long ere this time have told me, "Burroughs,
your story being both lengthy and gloomy, it is time to desist."
Gloom is the chief I have to entertain you with in the after relation;

[3] This is a very respectable gentleman, a man of large property, and for many years
represented the town in the legislature of Massachusetts.

[186]

therefore, the most distant hint, that the story is too melancholy to give entertainment, I will discontinue.

I will here give you a few extracts from those letters of congratulation which I received in these days.

"Hanover, February 21st, 1790.

"DEAR CHILD,

"I have only the privilege to seize a few hasty moments, to inform you of our safe arrival, on the fifth day, from the time of our taking leave of you, and our friends at Charlton. It is impossible for the want of time. to be particular in any matter—would be glad to express our sentiments upon. That we are greatly comforted with the prospect of your being useful in life, would be superfluous to say. You well know that nothing can be a source of greater comfort to us, that pertains to the life that now is. We remember the kindness of your customers to you with sensible emotions of gratitude; and desire that our love may be presented to them. as opportunity may offer. Tell Mr. Williams that his kindness, and that of his family, has made a deep impression upon us. Inform Deacon Bacon, that my cordial salutations to him accompany this letter, as also to Elder Green. I have it in view to write to the deacon, as soon as opportunity will permit. At present the want of time forces me to a close; and with fervent prayers, that you and your companion may be taught of God, to walk as heirs of the grace of life, and for the highest comfort of you both, in relation to time and eternity: we remain your affectionate parents.

"E. and A. BURROUGHS.

"STEPHEN BURROUGHS."

"Hanover, March 20th, 1790.

"DEAR CHILD,

"It is needless to remind you, that whilst we behold a prospect of your being useful in life, in your present calling, we partake of that satisfaction, in the prospect, which proved in its operation, like a most reviving and comforting cordial. As soon as you come to know the heart of a parent, you will understand in a different point of view from what you can now, how the welfare of a child, is an object that is dear and precious, to such a degree, that in comparison to this, every other earthly treasure is of insignificant and trifling im-

[187]

portance. Amidst your present objects and pursuits that relate to the concerns and comfort of the present life; it would unspeakably add to our joy, to see the evidence that each of your hearts are reconciled to the character of that God who is the giver of happiness and the object of love to every soul, who is made wise to salvation. Whilst you are looking into the nature of religion, we wonder not, that you are oftentimes tempted to scruple, whether there is anything in religion, whilst you form an estimate of it by the lives of the generality of its professors. Whilst you discern that iniquity in its various shapes abounds amongst them, take heed that it does not prove a stone of stumbling and a rock of offence to you. If it should, it is a certain evidence that you have had recourse to a false rule, to form your estimate of religion by. If the things which you behold and hear, in the conduct and conversation of professors, operate in this manner, to worry and perplex your minds, and you are ready to enquire, 'Is there anything in religion? Can there any good thing come out of Nazareth?' I would only reply, in the words of Philip to Nathaniel, 'Come and see'; make the trial and then judge for yourselves. By making the trial, understand me to mean, that you look into the spirit of that temper which the word holds up to view, and let your hearts be fully reconciled to such a spirit, and governed by such a temper, and I well know you will want no other evidence to convince you, that in this wisdom there is such a treasure, that all the things you can desire are not to be compared to it. That you may both enjoy the happiness of the social life, in the mutual exercise of such a temper towards each other. is a prayer that is pregnant with the most genuine love that our hearts are capable of experiencing towards you. We remain your affectionate parents,

"E. and A. BURROUGHS.

"S. BURROUGHS."

"*Boston, November 20th*, 1789.

"DEAR SIR,

"I thank you for another letter. I am happy to hear you are so well married. I am glad to hear you say you have thrown away ambition. I am glad, likewise, that you retain it in so great a degree; for there are two sorts. You are ambitious of rising into fame upon

[188]

the basis of virtue. I charge you, fling not away that ambition. You may not rise, however, in the eyes of the world; but you will rise in yourself. For what more exalted situation can any mortal wish to arrive at, than to be able to adopt the words of the apostle, 'I have maintained a conscience void of offence both towards God and towards man,' or to that effect. This, you know, is what you and I must aim at, or we never can be happy; and with this, we shall be happy, however the world may think of us.

"People here are not yet disposed to believe you are reformed in reality. I will believe it; and you must, for once, disappoint the world. I feel greatly interested in your welfare. I seem to anticipate the joy of your parents at your reformation.

"It so happens that I am always in a hurry when I receive your letters, or I should be more particular.

"We have lost one of our children since I wrote you. I am afraid the bearer is gone, for I did not receive your letter in season.

"My compliments await your lady. I should be glad to see you both. The next time I go to Connecticut, I shall visit you. I am, dear sir, your faithful friend and humble servant,

"CALEB BINGHAM.[4]

"Mr. S. BURROUGHS."

"*Stratfield, February 2d,* 1790.

"SIR,

"I have received yours, and thank you for the respect you express,

[4] This letter, and a preceding one from the same, were published without the writer's knowledge or consent. The fact was this. The writer received a letter from Mr. Burroughs, requesting his opinion relative to the publication of his memoirs; intending, as he afterwards said, if that opinion should be favorable, to ask leave to publish these two letters, and four or five others. The answer was decidedly against publishing the memoirs, on the ground that the histories of rogues were frequently narrated in such an unguarded manner as to defeat any good that might be expected from their publication, the object being to show, with how dreadful a certainty vice and folly meet their reward. But the letter which contained this advice, as was the case with some others, directed to the same distinguished character, was stopped on the road, broken open and never arrived till the book was thus far in print. The work, however, on appearance, proved much less exceptionable than was anticipated; and it is presumed, if the reader will bear in mind that the writer is the hero of his own story, it will be found calculated to serve as a beacon for youth to avoid the like course, lest they meet a like fate—a vagrant and ignominious existence, constantly goaded by remorse and the dread of future punishment.

[189]

which also gives me great satisfaction for your acknowledgment to me, that I have been instrumental of giving you relief in time of distress, which is no more than a duty which rational beings are bound to do for each other, exclusive of the bonds of relation. I also rejoice to hear that your behavior is agreeable, and that you have gotten an agreeable companion, and that you are in prosperity. My business was such that I could not have an opportunity to wait on your father; please to excuse me to him, as I understand he is bound to your town before he returns. I wish to be remembered to your consort, your mother and your uncle Davis. These from your affectionate cousin,

"STEPHEN SUMMERS.

"Mr. S. BURROUGHS."

Thus you see, sir, that my portion of happiness was complete. All that was possible for man to enjoy, I now experienced; I was raised to the utmost pinnacle of bliss. But I was only raised to be thrown from my exaltation, to the deepest abyss of wretchedness and misery.

It appears to me that fortune, to show the extent of her power, had curiously interwoven a train of circumstances, of all others the most delicate; and of all others, the most calculated to make me vulnerable by her shafts.

From the Castle, from a state of confinement as a slave; from a state where I had suffered a course of unexampled cruelty; to fall among a people, of all others, the most agreeable, humane and benevolent; to find among them a readiness to give credit to all my virtues, notwithstanding the clamor against me; to make use of my abilities, where they found them useful; and to treat me as a member of the general family of mankind, was a situation, which rendered me most feelingly happy. Here I found a society which I could enjoy upon terms of that easy access, which renders it so grateful.

Here was a theatre upon which I had exhibited in such a manner, as to raise the desponding hopes of my friends, to a state of the most sanguine expectation, relating to the part which I should perform as a member of society. Here I had contracted such a tenderness for a fond wife and our helpless offspring, as to lose the desire for my own prosperity, in my anxiety for them. My own personal benefit was

[190]

now but a secondary consideration, and only viewed of consequence, as it contributed to render them happy.

Here I had a family; here were friends of near connection; and here was a society, among whom I enjoyed the social pleasures, in their highest perfection; consequently, I felt the most ardent desire to render myself agreeable, and endearing to all these.

At the moment, when I had obtained the highest pitch of my ambition, when I became completely happy in the enjoyment of all my heart's desire; to be hurled from this summit of happiness, and buried under the weight of one general wide extended ruin; to see myself in a moment, stripped of every enjoyment my heart held dear, and reduced back into that state of confinement from which I had so lately been liberated, was a situation in which all the powers of mind and strength of nature, operated and combined to render me completely miserable. Alas! thou unhappy companion of my life, how changed our prospects! but a little time since, when all nature smiled on our endeavors, to promote the welfare of our mutual concern, a rising family; even our hearts were exhilarated, our minds were soothed, and our souls filled with delight, with the playful smiles and opening mind of a tender infant! but alas! those scenes are fled—fled "with the years beyond the flood"; fled alas! beyond the reach of hope! No more shall my heart be made glad by the fond embrace. No more shall the sun rise to cheer my fond hopes, my rising expectations. But midnight and death shall howl their horrid dirges around my bed! misery and melancholy shall spread their sable veil over every part of my life, and after my exit from this stage of trouble, furies shall shriek a doleful requiem to my departure.

I find, sir, that I am wild and unconnected in my relation. The gloomy scene crowded upon me before I was ready to give it a place; and I, involuntarily, find my pen continually delineating those melancholy circumstances. I beg pardon for my irregularity, and will recall my wanderings. I am, sir, etc.

CHAPTER XXII

"A part how small of the terraqueous globe
Is tenated by man! the rest a waste,
Rocks, deserts, frozen seas, and burning sands:
Wild haunts of monsters, poisonous stings, and death:
Such is earth's melancholy map! But far
More sad! This earth is a true map of man:
So bounded are its haughty lord's delights
To woe's wide empire; where deep troubles toss;
Loud sorrows howl, envenom'd passions bite;
Ravenous calamities our vitals seize,
And threatening fate wide opens to devour."

IN prosecuting the design of this letter, I must confess that I am at a loss how to describe those events, of which I wish to give you a just idea. I know I shall fall infinitely short of my own wishes. The scene was so crowded with incidents, that it will be impossible to relate them in such a manner as to keep them clear and distinct, so as to render them entirely intelligible. Under this view, I have thought it the better way, to give you extracts of letters, relating to these events, interspersing them with some explanatory remarks, and filling up any deficiency by an additional relation.

To understand the after relation in as clear a manner as the nature of the thing will admit, it will be necessary to give you the characters of some persons who were active in my misfortune, and to begin with the chief engine of this business, viz. Israel Waters. This man was a near neighbor to me during my living in my own family. When Waters first commenced his career in life, he was extremely poor, illiterate, ill-favored, and of a sour, morose temper; hence he remained, for a long time, unknowing and unknown. A number of fortunate circumstances happening in the course of his business, he attained a handsome property. When he found himself to be a man of property, he grew unaccountably presuming and haughty. He had, heretofore, remained among mankind without attention or notice; but, now manifested an ardent ambition to start into consequence in the world.

MR. ISRAEL WATERS

His first effort was to rise in the military line. He stood for the command of the company of which he was a member, not sparing of his purse on the occasion; but was defeated in his pursuit. He then stood for the lieutenancy, and after a length of time, obtained his object.

The captainship becoming vacant a number of times, he endeavored, by the dint of electioneering, to obtain that office; his exertions were ineffectual, and he threw up his commission in a pet, and joined a company of horse.

Towards this company he truly acted a benevolent part, had his motives been a regard to the real prosperity of the company; but his after conduct made it evident, that electioneering was his object, in assisting various members of the company with those articles which their finances did not allow them to procure, without inconveniency. Notwithstanding every exertion which he made, the choice of the company fell upon a deserving man, and of course, he occupied the second place in this company.

Whilst he held the office of lieutenant in the company of light horse, the rebellion broke out which, you will recollect, was termed Shay's rebellion. This produced animosity among neighbors, and almost every man became a partizan. The militia were called upon, and Waters, with the rest of his company, went into service, against the insurgents. Here he had an opportunity of hearing much said in favor of government, and likewise against those who should oppose her measures.

Having been disappointed in all his efforts to become a man of that consequence in society to which his restless ambition had led him, he expected that he had now discovered the only sure road to preferment, viz. by making himself so strong a stickler for government, that he would be taken notice of, and promoted. Under this view of matters, not having ability to distinguish between a real and pretended assistance to the laws of the country, he became the pimp, rather than the friend of government.

My rising so suddenly and rapidly into esteem, had given this man great umbrage. "What," said he, "shall this mushroom of a night be rewarded and caressed by mankind, whilst I have been laboring years in the pursuit, and spent great part of my time and interest in this

[193]

business, and yet be neglected?" The comparison was too mortifying; and of course, he sought to remove that object from sight which gave him so much pain to view. He was but too successful in his undertaking.

He had made his calculation upon answering two purposes in rendering me obnoxious to the laws, viz. gratifying his own private spleen, and gaining the commendations of men in office, who, he expected, would be gratified at my downfall; hence, after my calamity, he made his boasts, that he esteemed the honor he had done himself in that business so highly, that he would not part with it for one hundred pounds.

Another character in this business, was one Elice Putney, an old girl, who had not borne the character of a Lucretia; and of consequence, finding herself at a low ebb, calculated to make some bold efforts to do away a jealousy there was remaining upon the minds of many, that she was by no means exposed to suffer on account of her virtue. No way appeared so eligible to this antiquated heroine, as to raise a report, of her having withstood some violent attacks upon the castle of her honesty. This being the case, you will hear in the after relation, how she succeeded in her undertaking.

The following character, who maintains a place most in dignity in this narrative, is Daniel Bacon. This man is as punctual in telling his great religious exercises as any man you will generally meet with. Take his own account for your evidence, and you will believe him to be the best man living; but when you examine him critically, by his works, you will find it necessary to place much to the account of human frailties, if you continue to believe in his goodness. He is a man possessing a very tenacious memory, relating to matters which make in his own favor, and the contrary, he has a happy faculty in forgetting.

His wife comes forward, in the next place, and clearly demonstrates that she is bone of his bone, and flesh of his flesh. They are both endowed with small mental abilities, timid and fearful of meeting with danger on every occasion.

About six months previous to my marriage, two daughters of D. Bacon attended my school. As I taught a school in the evening, separate from the common school, many scholars who attended in the day, likewise attended in the evening. After I had dismissed the school for the day, I generally made a practice of tarrying at the schoolhouse, until the time for opening that in the evening, in order to make some necessary arrangements.

More or less of the scholars, who lived some distance from the school, likewise tarried. At a certain time, the elder of D. Bacon's daughters remained with me in the schoolhouse, during the intermission between the two schools. A number of circumstances happening to throw a certain enjoyment full in my view, the temptation was too powerful. I fell before it. The fatal moment was past. It could not be recalled. After I had retired from school, the object had its full operation upon my mind. This was a moment of calmness. This was a moment in which the examination of my conduct gave me the keenest pain.

I considered that my situation had been the means of gaining easy access to her virtue. That she had been taught to put the most implicit confidence in my instruction. That the example, in me, would have a fatal influence on her principles of virtue. These considerations gave me no small degree of uneasiness. I lamented my untimely folly, but too late, I lamented it. I took the earliest opportunity of repairing the injury, so far as was now in my power.

Not long after this, the same opportunity offering again at the schoolhouse, I entered into conversation with the girl on the subject. I endeavored to give her a statement of my own views on the subject. I expostulated with her in the warmest terms upon the impropriety of ever swerving from the path of virtue. I intimated to her, that from the principles of integrity, as well as tenderness to her own welfare, I should keep this business a secret from every person living. It is true, I gave her no charge to keep this unhappy business buried in her own breast. I presumed, that the laws of delicacy and self-preservation would have been sufficient for such a purpose, but in this I was deceived.

She divulged the secret among some of her companions. By little and little, it gained ground, until it came to the knowledge of Israel Waters. He embraced the opportunity to make such arrangements with the parents of these girls as to carry his diabolical plan into execution. He pretended great concern for the welfare of the girl's character, and said he wished to save her free from imputation of blame.

Matters being under this situation, one morning about the dawn of day, I was awaked and made prisoner by a sheriff, Waters and a number of others. I was immediately carried to the house of Waters, and kept closely confined, until the evening succeeding, when there arrived two lawyers, one to act as justice of the peace, and the other to advocate the cause in behalf of the state. A circumstance somewhat curious, that these gentleman should come twenty miles to make inquiry into a matter, when there were four justices living within the distance of four miles, who were equally competent to make the inquiry.

I was brought before the justice and heard the complaint read, which contained allegations against me, amounting to a rape. To this, you may depend, I plead not guilty. When the girl was examined, she would not stand the test, but declared that I only had made the attempt to ravish her without success. To my astonishment, I found two others were called upon to give evidence, viz. Elice Putney, and a younger sister of the first mentioned girl. They all testified to the same import, that I had laid violent hands upon them, in various places, and exerted all my abilities to proceed with them to acts of iniquity: but they had made such noble resistance, as to overcome my greatest exertions, and fairly outmatched me in strength.

After they had finished their evidence upon these matters of offence, the justice made out my mittimus to jail, for trial at the next supreme court to be holden six months afterwards, for an assault with an intent to ravish. Notwithstanding, the court of quarter sessions had concurrent jurisdiction with the supreme court, in causes of this kind, and sat, if I mistake not, four months sooner. The girls, D. Bacon and wife, were bound over to give testimony at the sitting of the court, etc.

To undertake a description of my feelings under this situation, would be as fruitless as to attempt to give a blind man an idea of colors. I hate to dwell upon the scene, long enough to give you the general occurrences which took place. It makes my head run round in a maze, to dwell long enough upon these matters, to bring them again into view, so that I may state them in order. I rejoice that I may turn you to the perusal of some letters which will lead you into the knowledge of facts without my writing them over again.

"MY DEAR,

"After the scene of last night, you will not wonder at my feeling all the horrors of my situation. On the way, not a word said. All hushed with that dismal silence which betokens the feelings even of those whose occupation is cruelty. About midnight we arrived at the gaol, and after some difficulty, the Cerberus of this place of human woe was aroused, and procuring a number of his massy keys, the ponderous doors growled on their hinges, to open to my view and anticipation the regions of horror and despair. The doors were closed, and all the bolts responded to the iron force of their massy keys; the scene around me is beyond description; through the remainder of the night, my mind was overborne by the weight of what had taken place, in such a rapid succession for twenty-four hours before; nature gave way, and I sunk into forgetfulness. I awoke with the light, but not to stupidity. The mind became vigorous and clear, by a moments relaxation, all the avenues of sensibility were open; the positive and relative horrors of my situation came rolling upon me like a torrent of destruction, threatening instant desolation. All my flattering prospects in life, in a moment blasted. A wife whom I adore, an infant and only child, lost in a moment, by the merciful hand of justice! O! horrid profanation! To call that by the name of justice which nature recoils at with disgust. Is this the lot of man? To have his soul filled with complete happiness; to be possessed with every object which could gratify his remotest wish; in order to be thrown from the enjoyment of all, to render his misery absolute! I know your feelings upon these trying events. I know the various manœuvres which will be made use of, in order to prepossess your mind against my conduct, and of course in favor of the proceedings of those persons who have combined together for my destruction. In order to counteract their designs, I could have recourse to arguments, entreaties and persuasions; but all these I despise. If I possess your confidence to such a degree as that you will be able to resist the various efforts made use of against me, I then possess everything in you that I wish for, and short of that there is nothing for which I am ambitious. I wish to see you even in this

[197]

dreary place of confinement. I know you must be shocked at the prospect which you will find presented to your view, should you come to this 'place of torment!' but notwithstanding, I cannot say but what I wish to see you, even here; that is all the remaining comfort which now even glimmers before my eyes, and how long that spark of consolation may remain, I know not. If I should be deprived of it before tomorrow's dawn, not more strange should I esteem that than thousands of occurrences through which I have passed since I began my melancholy career in life. What a host of flattering friends and humble servants had I two days since, but now where are they? Not one who dares to show his head. The town of C——n will no more contend in what part of it I shall reside. So well do I know the baseness of the human heart, that for one shilling, I would part with all my chance of friends in this wide world (yourself excepted). And yet, whose prospects of unalterable friends were stronger than mine? Am I altered? Am I changed? Am not I the same in name and nature, in feeling and in sentiment? But my prospects are blasted, and my friends are vanished. Why do I write thus lengthy? Because it looses me from my situation for a moment. Write to me. Say anything to dispel the gloom for a moment, even if it be matters not founded in fact. I remain with tenderness and affection,

"STEPHEN BURROUGHS."

"MY DEAR,"

"I was mistaken in not valuing the friendship of those who made professions in time of prosperity. I find to my surprise, there are some real friends, and even those who dare profess it to the world: Strange! those who dare assert the cause of innocence, notwithstanding the power of oppressors! Captain I——r was here this day, and offered to become sponser for the payment of 250l. on condition of my being liberated till court. Cannot our friends, or relations, I might more justly say, be persuaded to give bail for the other 250l? I shall think it very surprising if strangers will show more kindness than the nearest relatives. I find that the opinion of the world is much more favorable than I expected. Many independent minds view this matter as they ought, according to the evidence which has been offered. For a girl to pretend that violence had been offered her six months before she makes the matter known, even to her nearest intimates, and seek the company of the person who had offered the violence, perpetually and continually, until just before the discovery is to take place, is to me a line of conduct hardly credible, and to the candid world appears ludicrous to the last degree. Yet, notwithstanding the ridiculous foundation upon which this matter rests, my enemies exult in the prospect of bringing ruin upon my head, by supporting the charge of violence against the virtuous, the modest and amiable L——y B——n; who, from her own story (did we not in charity disbelieve her), would make herself one of the most barefaced w——s, who disgrace her sex, and bring a blush upon the cheek of every modest woman. Yet, I know the world at large can believe an infamous report (however incredible in itself), so much readier than a good one, that my apprehensions have been much alarmed, by the great exertions which are now making, lest such an invincible prejudice should be raised against me, as greatly to mar the equity of the trial. I know upon that one circumstance, rests the whole expectation of my enemies; should they not succeed in that, they must fall with the rapidity of Lucifer; therefore, no pains will be wanting on their part, to effect their purpose in such a way; if I obtain my liberation by bail, I think they must be disappointed in their warm expectations. Strange that man should be so blind to his own happiness, and to the part he ought to act, as to use his exertions for the misery of his fellow. The ills of life by the common course of nature, are many, and hard to be borne; and our situation requires all the sympathy, commiseration, and compassion of each other, to render it tolerable; but, when to the common ills of life, the artificial cruelty of revengeful mortals is added, then is the cup of bitterness completely filled; then shall we find racks and gibbets, pillories and whipping posts. The inventors of those very engines of cruelty will boast of their superior lenity, declaring themselves with great ostentation, to be the happy few, who have ever known the feelings of compassion towards each other, exulting at the extent of their humanity, so superior to that of the Turks, Russians and barbarians. Mistaken wretches! And because they can find some more cruel than themselves, they deem this matter a sufficient evidence of their own great goodness; but should they for a moment make the comparison between their own conduct and the real standard of benevolence, viz. the conduct of Deity, how would they be abashed and shrink with astonishment at their own baseness. Where do we find prisons and tortures prepared by him, for offending mortals? Does he take advantage of every lapse which he sees in us to wreak his vengeance? Should he do this, how few would have the leisure to pursue his neighbor's destruction? Should matters turn out in such an unfortunate manner as to render it difficult to obtain liberation on bail, immediately, I wish you to come to W——r soon, if you find it can be affected without difficulty; otherwise, you will do well to defer your journey for the present. I remain, etc.,

"STEPHEN BURROUGHS."

"DEAR SIR,

"Yours of the 20th ult. came safe to hand. I read it with pleasure, because anything coming from you gives me pleasure; but more particularly, that which speaks your mind, and partakes of the nature of sentiment. You mention a desire to see me; I do not think I can come to W——r until court; the reasons are but too well known to you already, and these reasons appear to me conclusive; however, I wish to act with prudence and deliberation on the matter, and shall, therefore, await your opinion on the subject. The prospect of bail is entirely out of the question, owing to the influence of —— ——; however terrible such a condition, yet you must bear it; and I wish you may do it with composure, and not think of ridding yourself of confinement by any illegal measures. The fatal consequences, should you succeed, will be but too sensibly felt by me. The country you must leave. I must then remain forsaken, incumbered with a helpless infant, and what is more, uncertain what to hope for, or what not to fear. Almost any situation, to me, would be preferable to that. I tremble at the thought, that it is even possible for such an event to take place. Is your love towards me sincere? And can you bear to leave your country, to leave me and your babe, without a friend upon whom we shall have the confidence to rest for protection and support? I remain, in haste, your loving wife,

"SALLY BURROUGHS."

"MY DEAR,

"Yours of the 5th instant arrived yesterday; my feelings were

[200]

variously affected by its contents. Your intimation, of what comes from me gives you pleasure, was truly an intimation of the most pleasing kind to me; but, what was the difference of my feelings, when you tell me you shall not come to W——r until court. Do you imagine I can wear away five gloomy months without one drop of comfort, mixed in this cup of bitterness? Can this conduct be consistent with the duty you owe to me? Can it be consistent with that love which you profess, to forsake me in this time of difficulty? This is the time for trial, this is the time for the serious proof of the affections of our friends. I have seen your father twice since I saw you. I talked with him relating to his intentions concerning you, and whether he was willing you should come to W——r on a visit; he did not give me a decided answer, either in the negative or affirmative.

"He appears to be apprehensive, that so soon as my liberation takes place, I shall, with indignation, quit the country, and entirely leave you, or else carry you to regions unknown to him. Did he know the feelings of my heart on that subject, his ideas would undergo a revolution, and he would reason with more candor.

"In relation to my affection towards you, I think that you must be perfectly sensible, that it is stronger than the powers of misfortune. You ask me if I can leave you and flee my country? Would you ask the tender mother if she will leave her helpless infant? or the turtle dove, whether she will leave her mate? It is for you, my Sally, that I live; it is for you that I endure the ills of life. Should I leave you, what then would become of my Sally, the idol of my soul, the delight of my eyes? My soul shudders at the thought, and recoils with horror at the reflection! May the cold hand of death sooner close these eyes, so accustomed to sorrow, than such events should happen. You can hardly conceive of my feelings in this situation of wretchedness; they are like the boisterous ocean in time of tempest; confusion and distress, anguish and despair, perpetually assail me; I rave with madness, and grow sullen with disappointment. My sleeping moments often flatter me you are present. I awake to disappointment, and curse my dreams, for opening all my wounds afresh, and causing the blood of affliction to flow in streams anew. The clouds of darkness which now hang over us are thick and gloomy, but must not they be soon driven away? Will not that God, who knows the secrets of the heart, appear for

[201]

injured innocence? By the united advice of my friends, I have engaged Mr. S——g, of A——, rather than M——k. Sunday morning
—I have just opened my eyes from a pleasing dream. Methought I was
at liberty with you, and enjoying all the sweets of social life; the rapture of this scene overpowered my sleep, and I awoke! but to what
did I awake! to behold myself alone, environed by the gloomy walls
of a jail, composed of huge rocks and massy bars of iron, without the
hope of ever seeing you until court: I say wrong, I have hopes of seeing you soon, and must not be disappointed. You desire me to make
myself contented. You may as well desire the drowning man not to
seize on every substance within his grasp."

"DEAR SIR,
"Your favor of the 11th I received. It was with gratitude I received
it. You intimate a dissatisfaction at my declining a visit to you. But
think not, sir, that it is for the want of affection that I abstain from
coming to see you. The disagreeable necessity I may hereafter be
under, of subsisting upon the help of my friends, makes me fearful
of taking measures which will offend them. Notwithstanding, since
you so earnestly desire it, I shall try every proper measure to see you.
"I have heard that you have made attempts to break jail. I cannot
answer for the truth of these reports. I think it the better way to lie
quiet until court, however disagreeable the idea may appear, and not
run any risk by trying to extricate yourself from confinement by unlawful measures. Should you succeed, you would labor under very
great embarrassments, on account of leaving the country; if you have
any regard for an afflicted wife, or an infant child, once the delight
of your soul.
"It is impossible to conceive the anxiety that perpetually fills my
mind, relating to these unhappy events. Sometimes I am ready to give
myself over for lost, thrown out into a troublesome world, to endure
alone and unsupported, the hardships and distresses incident to such
a situation. But alas! how can I harbor such a thought? You certainly cannot wish to deceive me. You must be entirely sensible of
my affection towards you.
"I hear so many reports and observations that at times, my fears
almost overcome me. May God graciously support me under those

trials which I am now called to pass through. I remain, with the warmest affection, your loving, though afflicted and sorrowful wife,

"SALLY BURROUGHS."

"*December 28th.*

"MY DEAR,

"In answer to yours of the 21st, I have to communicate, that a degree of satisfaction was received in that letter, which is entirely inexpressible. There is a something in receiving testimonies of attachment and esteem, when we are in adversity, which is exquisitely grateful; on the other hand, to experience injury and abuse, at such times, is far more insupportable than when we are in common prosperity.

"Respecting those reports of my attempting to break jail, they are as unfounded as many others which have been in circulation. I have not the most distant idea, under present circumstances, of making any such attempt.

"You mention your anxiety, on account of the reports and observations which you continually hear made. To furnish you with what evidence the nature of the thing will admit, I shall refer you to that line of conduct which you have been acquainted with in me, from the knowledge you ever had of my person and principle.

"You entertain a fear of my abandoning you after my liberation. This appears to me strange. When I have once found a friend, I do not easily let him go, even in a state of the greatest prosperity. My soul was formed for friendship, and when I find a friend, who can endure the storm of adversity, I do not think there is, in the nature of things, an equivalent to be received in exchange, for such a friend. When you consider, that in addition to all these considerations, I stand in the relation of a husband to you, and of a parent to our infant; can there remain the most distant jealousy in your mind, that I shall forfeit all claim to every principle of integrity under these obligations!!

"Surely, my dear, if you take all these circumstances which I have mentioned, into your serious consideration, it will be an effectual bar against the effect of the suggestions of those meddling characters who wish to destroy your peace of mind.

[203]

"That you may enjoy every blessing, which the kind hand of providence bestows on mortals, is the fervent prayer of your affectionate husband,

"STEPHEN BURROUGHS."

"*January 3d.*

"DEAR SIR,

"Although I am at liberty from actual confinement, yet I partake of the affliction which environs you on every side. I wish it was in my power to grant you some relief; and could you point out any way, in which such an object can be effected, most gladly will I attend to it. It is now nearly two months since I saw you, and God only knows what I have endured since. It is not the want of friendship which keeps me from seeing you. My thoughts, by night and by day, are with you, and drink deep of the cup of affliction, which is set before us. I dread to . . . . I am determined to make you a visit as soon as conveniency will admit, unless you think the reasons against it are too great to be dispensed with. The conflict between . . . . has been greatly trying, but it is now decided. I am determined, in future, to regulate my conduct, according to the wishes of my unhappy partner, let the feelings of others be as they may.

"I shall wait with anxious expectations for your answer to this letter, specifying your wish with respect to my coming to Worcester.

"And now, dear sir, accept the advice of one who, in the warmth of duty and affection, feels ardently desirous for your welfare and prosperity.

"The time of your affliction cannot endure always. There must be an end to these trials. Therefore, sir, I wish you would compose yourself under your situation, and remain as contented under it, as the nature of the thing will admit. Look forward to happier scenes, that await us hereafter, in spite of all the malice of the demons of discord. It cannot render your situation any more tolerable, to suffer yourself to be thus overborne by the weight of your misfortunes. Let us bear with fortitude the stroke of misfortune. Let us show to the world, that we can rise above the malicious strokes of all our enemies. While I give this advice, I hardly know how to follow it myself. My sorrows

[204]

make me almost frantic with grief; but 1 am in hopes, that by long exertions, I shall be able to render them more tolerable. I remain, with constant fidelity. your loving wife,

"SALLY BURROUGHS."

"12th January.

"MY DEAR,

"Yours of the 3d inst. 1 gratefully acknowledge; in it I traced the marks of the truest affection. How grateful to my heart these tokens of esteem, in a time of adversity. There is a luxuriancy of enjoyment in sympathetic friendship, when the doleful knell of woe tolls in my ears, which beggars all description. In your letter, you advise me not to feel my misfortune. Do you know that we were both made to feel? And what nature has done, we shall find hard to undo. Your advice was founded, I know, upon the principles of true benevolence. but think you mistake, in some measure, the operation of the human heart. The most certain manner of lessening our agonies is, to give way before their pressure, and confess we feel their force. Fortitude is but a dream; for where lies the merit of being insensible to the stroke of adversity. or in dissembling our sensibility? If we are insensible, that is entirely owing to a happy constitution, formed by the hand of nature. This blessing is only obtained as the gift of heaven, in our formation. No art or assiduity of ours can ever acquire it. If we dissemble our feelings, we only endeavor, by artifice, to persuade others that we enjoy privileges which, in fact, we do not enjoy; and while we endeavor to appear happy. we feel all the pangs of internal misery, and all the self-reproach of endeavoring to deceive.

"Nothing is more certain, than that tears and groans grow out of pain; and when misfortunes oppress, it is our duty and interest to take refuge under such coverts from the storm, as we can obtain. To fly for support to friendship. To fly for support to wailings and lamentation, or to anything which will alleviate our distress.

"It is said by philosophers, that our passions are the source of all our miseries; this has been a subject of abundant declamation. I own that they are the source of all our misfortunes; but they are, at the same time, the source of all our pleasures: therefore, the study of our lives ought to be, not to dissemble an absence of passion; but to

[205]

repel those which lead to vice, by those which direct to virtue.

"Your visit was a most grateful circumstance: there is a pleasure in seeing you, even here, though intermingled with grief, which is a great alleviation to my state of distress. Next to seeing you, is the pleasure of receiving your letters. I wish you to favor me with this latter agreeable circumstance as often as conveniency will permit. I remain, with the warmest sentiments of affection, your loving husband,

"STEPHEN BURROUGHS."

"*5th February.*

"DEAR SIR,

"Yours of the 12th of last month was handed me this morning. Since I was at Worcester, I have written to Daddy Burroughs. I hereby send you inclosed a copy of my letter.

"You may think, that my anxiety for your welfare, led me to take such measures, in the course of my advice, as would not answer the purpose which I had designed. What I expressed, was the overflowings of my heart. You, undoubtedly, will make such use of it as your superior judgment will point out. I have the most ardent desire for your prosperity. I suggest such ideas for its accomplishment, as my weak capacity will produce. Perhaps I view matters too much on the dark side. But, when I take a view of what has happened to you since you came upon the stage of action; of the invincible prejudice mankind have rooted in their minds against you, and of the horrid effects of prejudice. I cannot but tremble at your approaching fate.

"We often view with horror the effects of superstition upon the mind of man, in matters of religion. We have seen the most sensible of men led into such acts of barbarity and cruelty, as have disgraced the human character, by the shocking influence of superstition. I find that superstition is not alone confined to matters of religion. Its rage is equally great against a character unpopular from any other cause. A character, however loaded with infamy, retaining the principles of virtue, is the greatest ornament to human nature, of any part of her existence. Many regard virtue only as it is attended with applause. Those who are really virtuous, regard it for the internal pleasure which it confers. Such models I wish were held up to view as worthy of

[206]

imitation.   Believe me to be, with sentiments of the sincerest affection, your loving and dutiful wife,

"SALLY BURROUGHS."

"HONORED AND DEAR SIR,

"You will hardly entertain an idea of my attempting to lay open to your view, the bleeding anguish of my heart; the distressed situation to which your son is reduced; and the agony of mind, I endure on that account; this is beyond the power of language.   It must require a very fertile mind, and an heart of great sensibility, even to figure, the most distant resemblance of this horrid situation.

"To give you some idea of these events.   About 3 o'clock in the morning, the room in which we slept was broken open by a man by the name of Israel Waters, attended by a sheriff, and a number of others, who seized your son, and with a very imperious tone, bade him get up immediately, and dress himself.   He was then conveyed to the house of this Waters, who was a near neighbor, or rather lived in the neighborhood, where he was kept through the next day, closely confined.

"It appeared that this Waters had, of his own self-moving will, inter-meddled in a matter in which he was neither mediately nor imme-diately concerned; had applied to a justice, living at the distance of twenty miles, to make inquest into these matters of charge, although a number of justices lived in the vicinity; had brought forward an at-torney to exert himself in the business, to your son's disadvantage; under these circumstances, you will not readily suppose that Waters acted from a principle of the strictest uprightness in this prosecution, neither sought for an impartial investigation of the business.

"The charges were truly of a heinous nature; but the evidences brought forward in support of these charges were of a kind too ridicu-lous to mention.   There may be something in this business, which is seen by the gentlemen of the law; but as for my own part, I cannot see the most distant color of evidence to support the charge.   Added to this, your son's conduct, ever since my acquaintance with him, has not borne the most distant appearance of such a principle, either in his treatment of me, or his conduct towards others.   Under these circum-

[207]

stances, you cannot wonder at my feeling very different upon this subject, from what many would wish, who have raised a clamor against him.

"And now, honored and dear sir, let me ask you, what would be your sensations, should your bosom companion be taken from you in such a barbarous and cruel manner, thrown into prison, there to remain confined a long time, without some benevolent friend would appear and give bail? I know the bail is excessive, but I can procure one half of the security from one of my neighbors; therefore, let me beg of you, sir, to come down and see your unhappy son.

"Were you under similar circumstances with us, would you not wish, would you not expect, that your parent would afford you relief under such a situation? I am perfectly sensible that you will run no risk, in performing this act of kindness.

"I do not feel a willingness to receive a denial to this request, so much depends upon your granting my petition.

"Had I the most distant jealousy, that any danger would attend this act of kindness, I should not presume upon this petition; but, as I feel the most unlimited confidence in every engagement being performed on our part, I cannot dismiss the subject without entreating you, by every sentiment of justice, of humanity, and parental affection, of compassion to the sufferings of your unhappy children, to listen to this request and grant my petition. I remain your dutiful, though afflicted and sorrowful daughter.

"SALLY BURROUGHS.

"REV. EDEN BURROUGHS."

I was confined, notwithstanding, until the sitting of court. When I was brought to the bar, I found three indictments against me, each charging me with an assault, with an intent to commit a rape. To the several charges I plead, *not guilty*.

At this time, there were on the bench, as judges, Dana, Robert Treat Paine, and Nathan Cushing; James Sullivan, attorney-general.

A large concourse of people had assembled on this occasion; and many evidences produced in behalf of the commonwealth to substantiate the charges which were brought against me.

After the evidences were gone through, on both sides of the question, and my counsel had made their remarks on the business, the attorney-general arose, and addressing himself to the audience, made some very severe remarks upon the town of Charlton, for employing me in the business of teaching a school; and observations, yet more severe upon the clergyman of the town (Mr. Campbell) for giving his approbation to such a business; and moreover, for even showing compassion to me under my present situation. Mr. Campbell, who was in court, arose, and begged leave of the court to offer one word, by way of reply, to what the attorney-general had observed, relating to him; Judge Paine commanded him to sit down. Mr. Campbell replied, "that he should by no means have made the request of addressing the audience upon this occasion, had not his name been drawn into question, in this very singular and extraordinary manner, being thus publicly charged with blame, and that too, in the most wanton manner, when it was no way connected with the cause upon trial; under these circumstances, he thought himself warranted to ask and insist, upon the privilege of answering the ungenerous aspersions which had been thrown upon his character." Without answering his reasons, judges Dana and Paine ordered him, in the most peremptory manner, to sit down. He accordingly desisted, and sat down.

To account for this very singular conduct, I will offer you what evidence I ever received upon the subject. Mr. Campbell, who was a man of feeling, had often expressed his sentiments upon my imprisonment, etc., as being too severe; this highly displeased Waters, and he threatened that Mr. Campbell should be disobliged at court, if he did not change his sentiments. This, I suppose, was the punishment contemplated.

After the attorney-general had finished his address to the audience and jury, he sat down; and Judge Cushing arose, and summed up the evidence to the jury in a very clear, candid and impartial manner. After he had sat down, Judge Paine arose and addressed the jury in a speech of an hour's length.

This was a subject, in which he appeared engaged to the last degree. In the course of his observations he took notice of every circumstance which made against me, either in the feelings of people or in point of law.

After him, followed Judge Dana, in a speech of equal length. After

[209]

exhausting himself, in persuading the jury I was guilty; after repeating the severe remarks against the town of Charlton and Mr. Campbell, he desisted.

You will take notice, that at this time, two juries were sitting upon two indictments. The next morning, one jury returned their verdict, guilty. The other, not guilty.

Immediately upon this, I was again indicted for two other crimes, founded upon the same facts, and supported by the same evidence, as was exhibited upon the former indictments, viz. "open, gross, lewd, and lascivious conduct." To these charges, I plead not guilty, but afterward, by the advice of my counsel, entered a *retraxit*, and plead guilty.

My counsel alleged, that one jury had already, upon the evidence, brought me in guilty of attempting to ravish; "that it would not be so extraordinary for them to find me guilty of the crime now laid to my charge. as it was for them to return a verdict against me on the other indictment; and if they should return an unfavorable verdict, the court, it was probable, would be more severe in their sentence, than what they would, should I throw myself on their mercy, by pleading guilty."

I objected to this for the following reasons, viz. "I am accused," said I, "of open lewdness. According to the account of the witnesses, everything which took place, was in private; therefore, how it can be said, that open lewdness is proved by this testimony, I cannot conceive. Open lewdness is everything of that kind which the law censures and punishes; therefore, it appears to me plain, that only a bare possibility remains for a jury to be so far led astray as to think the indictment supported." Notwithstanding these objections, my counsel did not alter their opinion, therefore, I submitted and plead guilty.

Immediately after this, the following petition was presented to the bench.

To the honorable, the Justices of the Supreme Court of the State of Massachusetts.

"May it please your honors to accept the petition of an unhappy female, borne down under a weight of almost insupportable grief. May a view of her distressed situation find the tender avenues of sensibility, and plead in her behalf, for mercy and compassion to attend the terrifying sentence of judgment.

[210]

A PETITION TO THE BENCH

"My husband, the tender companion of my life, is now about to receive sentence of your honors; and O! for the sake of mercy, the brightest attribute of the Deity; for his sake, who has been the kindest and tenderest of husbands, both in prosperity and the more gloomy moments of adversity; for the sake of my peace of mind, already torn with the most poignant grief; spare him, as much as may be consistent with the important trust reposed in your honors.

"I beg for his restoration to his family, as soon as your honors may think it consistent; and I will watch over him, with all the diligence of anxious solicitude, that he shall be a strict observer of the laws of the land, and a benefit to the community.

"May I not be permitted to suggest, that I cannot but view his conduct, with respect to the crimes of which he now stands convicted, in a very different light from what they appeared to the court; being particularly acquainted with circumstances which my relation to him prevents me from exhibiting in testimony.

"I have found his conduct, ever since our acquaintance, marked with strict fidelity, and must think, from his persevering conduct, for more than two years, that his prevailing desire is to be an unshaken supporter of the laws of the land.

"May the unerring fountain of wisdom guide your honors in the path of duty, and give you the consolation of being good and faithful servants. May the gentle influence of mercy be your portion through life and through an endless eternity. Thus prays your sorrowful and humble petitioner,

"SALLY BURROUGHS."

Whether all these things served to molify the feelings of the Bench towards me, you will more readily judge by the sentences themselves, which were to this effect: "That I should receive one hundred and seventeen stripes on the naked back; should stand two hours in the pillory; should sit one hour on the gallows, with a rope around my neck; that I should remain confined in prison three months; that I should procure bonds for good behavior for seven years, and pay the charges of prosecution."

I was remanded to prison. I was afterwards led to the place of execution, and suffered two-thirds of the punishment which was comprised in the sentence. A day was appointed for the execution of the remainder. Previous to this time I left the jail, the country, and my enemies, to their own reflections. . . .[1]

In addition to my account, I will subjoin an extract of a letter from a gentleman of high respectability, and an old practitioner of law, who was present, through the whole transaction, to a friend of his upon this occasion.

An Extract of a Letter.

We have undoubtedly many inducements to regular, honest and moral habits. I believe our liability to suspicion, when outrages against morality occur, or the deeds of darkness are developed without their author, and to the imputation of a thousand irregularities and vices of which we are entirely innocent, is not the smallest. The world, in general, for the same reason it calculates that the sun will rise to-morrow, because it rose to-day, imputes to him, who has been once in a fault, the commission of an hundred others.

This truth was very strongly proved to me, a few weeks ago, in the trial of S. B. at the supreme court, at Worcester. Three bills of indictment were presented against him for three several assaults, upon three young women, with a felonious, though baffled intent, each time to commit a rape. The charges were solemn. A cloud of witnesses was gathered round him, to bear testimony to the facts. The intended victims to his violence were there also. The prisoner, on arraignment at the bar, plead *not guilty* to the several indictments; and put himself on the country for trial. S. the attorney-general managed the prose-

---

[1] It was not prudent for the author, at the time of this publication, to relate the manner in which he made his escape from the prison in Worcester. It is presumed that no injury can now arise from a disclosure of the secret.

It is a notorious fact, that many people in the vicinity were of opinion that Burroughs was too severely punished; among whom were some of the first characters in the county. Burroughs was aware of this, and cherished secret hopes of deliverance. One night, about 12 o'clock, he says his prison door was forced open, and he was requested to depart. He walked out, and passed between two ranks of people to a great distance; the number appearing to him not less than a thousand. All this time there was a profound silence; and he departed, ignorant of the names of any of his deliverers.

cution on the part of the commonwealth; and S. S. and L. were advocates for the prisoner.

It was not to be wondered at, if the trial of the man, who preached the sermon on the haymow to the Pelhamites, of whom, while a prisoner on the Castle, many curious and diverting anecdotes had been told, and were still freshly remembered, had collected an uncommon assemblage of both sexes, of women especially; when we add the nature of the offence to the consideration.

The witnesses for the commonwealth were first examined. The three girls who had suffered the injury for which the prisoner was arraigned, were the most material. They told their stories so pertly, that their declarations seemed to be rather memoieter than impromptu. I do not recollect all the particulars of their testimony; but could not help reckoning up the strong inducements the poor girls had, to patch up as good a story as they could, to vindicate their own characters; enough of the circumstances of the transactions, through accident, or their own carelessness, had already leaked out, to render their virtue questionable; the world would make its own comments. The prisoner had been with them in private, and used them indelicately. If they had fallen unwilling victims to his lust, it was not their fault. But then, though their virtue remained as spotless as before. that indescribable something, that creature of our whims, that power to charm the men of this world, was weakened; and though they might still make as good members of the church, they would not prove such luscious brides.

One of the girls testified, that the prisoner (one evening, after he had dismissed his school, and after the other scholars were gone. she being left alone with him in the schoolhouse) attempted to persuade her to indelicate indulgences; took hold of her; behaved quite unseemly; and made some exertions to induce her to comply; not however, sufficient to require very strong efforts to prevent him, or cries to raise help, necessary; that at another time, afterwards, as she was returning home from school in the evening, in company with others, the prisoner overtook them, was riding, and, as she had some length of way to walk, persuaded her to get up behind him, offering to carry her home; that having rode some distance with her, he stopped his horse, and

[213]

took her from behind, and placed her before him; and behaved quite indecently; but that upon her resisting he desisted.

Another of the girls said, the prisoner one day finding her in the barn, had attempted the same thing much in the same manner.

The third said, he had enticed her one evening a few rods from the house, and they coming to a fence in their walk together, he took her up in his arms and lifted her over, and pulled her down upon the ground, and attempted familiarities similar to the others; that on her making resistance, he desisted. She did not cry out; and I have forgot whether she, or any of the others, gave any reason why they did not.

This is quite an abridgment of the testimony; but I believe it contains all the material facts and circumstances, and is accurate and particular enough to furnish data for an opinion upon the nature of the offences.

The jury who tried the prisoner on the first indictment, gave their verdict, *guilty*. The verdict of the second jury was, *not guilty*. The attorney-general then entered a *nole prosequi* to the third indictment; and the prisoner was immediately arraigned to answer to two new bills, charging him with open and gross lewdness and lasciviousness. To them he plead *guilty*. And it appeared to me, his conduct amounted to no more in either of the cases; though the court, in stating the evidence, and giving their opinion to the jury on the two trials, were strongly set against the prisoner. It will at any rate, I believe, be allowed, that if the prisoner merited the charge, he was, in one instance, quite original in the manner of the offence. Who, but he would ever have thought of attempting to commit a rape on horseback? Surely, if he had succeeded, the world might well say, he had fairly outquix-oted Don Quixote himself. And if B. had really attempted what the girl said he did, a few evenings before, in the schoolhouse, her consenting to put herself, a second time, in his power, was no very strong proof of her discretion. At least, we must suppose, her jealousy at the schoolhouse had not occasioned her very serious alarms.

The affair at the barn, and that also at the fence, were transacted so in the very neighborhood of help, if it had been wanted, as to render the charge of his having attempted to commit a rape, in either of those cases, incredible. We cannot imagine any rational being would attempt to commit such an offence in a place where, if proper resistance

[214]

was made and efforts used, he must certainly be discovered and prevented. And if such resistance was not made, he could not be concluded guilty of the crimes charged against him. I believe the conduct
of the prisoner, in these instances, if impartially scanned (allowing that
the girls told the truth) would be judged nothing more, than so many
resolute, earnest and persevering attempts to seduce them. With the
generality of those, who have heard of the conviction, it is possibly a
matter of indifference, whether he was really guilty as charged or not.
To them, the remembrance of many hard things report has said of
him, that he has been a prisoner on the Castle, would suggest the
probability that he had been highly culpable in this instance, and
produce their approbation of the verdict against him; especially, if
to these were added the consideration that the offence was at the lowest
estimation of it, a gross indelicacy, a high outrage upon all the rules
and principles of decorum and propriety.

It is difficult, in such a case as this, to extend to a prisoner at the
bar, circumstanced as B. was, all the liberality of that excellent maxim
which instructs us to presume the respondent innocent. Yet we are
all equally entitled to justice; though undoubtedly our courts are more
liable to do injustice to such a character as B. than to one that has
fewer blemishes.

Is there no material difference between the crime of seduction and
that of committing a rape? Neither of them are very praiseworthy, be-
sure; and each may be much aggravated by particular circumstances.
But our legislators make a wide distinction; and the difference is very
obvious to common sense. Is it material or not, that we observe a
distinction? I imagine the poor culprit, who is appointed to receive
chastisement for his crime, would not feel indifferent whether he should
be whipped or hanged for stealing.

Thus you see, sir, facts upon which you have to form an opinion,
relating to this very surprising trial. I have endeavored, so far as my
judgment would serve, to treat the characters concerned in this business with as much tenderness, as the nature of a faithful narrative will
admit. Wantonly to traduce a character, is a species of conduct I
wish by all means, carefully to avoid; and where it has not been
necessary, in order to give a true narrative of the facts which I
promised, I have studiously suppressed any such emotion.

Possibly these matters may not appear to you as they have done, and still do, to me. I know they cannot strike the mind of any, in that feeling manner. I have made but a faint representation of them. I cannot communicate those ideas and sentiments, by writing, so fully as what they appear to my view by contemplation. However, we are apt to estimate the feelings of others by our own, and judge that they will view matters in the same manner as we do ourselves. In this estimation we often find ourselves mistaken. Hence, it is thought by many, that that person who feels most indifferent towards an object, is in the best situation to form a true estimate, relating to that object.

I differ in sentiment with those who hold this doctrine. I know we are often hurried into error, by the operation of our attachment to certain objects. Our passions, our appetites, and our zeal combine to produce this effect; hence, many conclude that it is necessary to feel perfectly indifferent towards an object in order to form a true estimation of its quality. We must feel interested in an object, either directly or indirectly, in order to call forth our attention towards it, sufficiently to examine its merits. When we feel indifferent towards an object, we pay no attention to it, and of course remain ignorant respecting it; therefore, are incapable of forming a just estimate concerning it.

A person, who has no principle of humanity, or compassion, may hear of the exercise of cruelty. It is a report which finds no place in his feelings; he is indifferent as to its existence; therefore, we readily see, that he would be an unequal judge as to the merits of the report.

Having a mind of sensibility, I know these matters will have their due operation on your feelings, and under this consideration, I shall ever receive your observations with attention, and pay due regard to your ideas, upon any matter wherein you may think different from me.

That there is such a thing as right and wrong, I believe is not called in question by any; and that we are all, in some measure, capable of judging with propriety upon this subject, is equally allowed. That we may, and are led astray many times, in forming an estimate of the principles of distributing justice, is a truth I shall by no means deny; but then we have all, I believe, a sufficient knowledge to distinguish upon the general principles of justice, at least, where we allow the operation of reason, without the embarrassments of prejudice.

REACTION OF A SENSIBLE MIND

When we find a private person injured by a public body, many circumstances are combined to lead the candid mind astray in the investigation of such a subject. Here error is most likely to take place. Popular clamor will be raised against the injured person; this is like the noise of the waters of Niagara; this swallows up the small voice of the individual.

We find the great Alexander, when the leading man of the world, committing acts of cruelty, injustice and oppression; a prospect of which, at this day, makes the blood curdle with horror; yet, those very actions were extolled in the most extravagant manner by his cotemporary sycophants; and mankind gave him the most flattering encomiums, where they ought, upon the simple principles of right, to have execrated his conduct. This is a specimen of public opposition to private individuals, and the effects that follow, which I believe will hold good pretty generally, even in our days. Public characters are as liable to the malignant passions as other men; they are as prone, likewise, to be led astray, by the various causes that serve to lead mankind astray, as others; but when they find themselves in an error, they falsely suppose, that it derogates from their dignity to acknowledge their error, and repair the injury which they have perpetrated, or even to have it suspected that they have been in an error. How false this system to the dictates of reason; how can the human character appear in a more exalted point of view, than by showing a readiness to acknowledge and repair the injuries which our own misconduct has occasioned?

I recollect to have read an anecdote of Julius Cæsar, which places his character in the highest point of exaltation of any part of his conduct. It was of the following nature. One day, when Cæsar was in the forum, surrounded with the patricians, or nobles of Rome, a certain slave belonging to him sought his manumission from his master. Cæsar being employed about weighty matters of the commonwealth, paid little attention to the solicitations of his slave. After repeated importunity, to call the attention of his master to the subject which lay so near his heart, the slave received a denial to his request for his freedom. When he saw that no further hope remained, he reproached his master in the bitterest terms; and this too in the most public place in the city of Rome.

[217]

What was the conduct of the truly great Julius at this time? His attention was called to the examination of his conduct, in order to see whether the reproaches of his slave were founded on good grounds; or whether they were the mere ebullitions of wrath, proceeding from disappointmnt. On the examination, he found he had really injured the slave. His reply was such, as will support his fame as long as the name of Julius Cæsar is known. "You are right," said he, "in reproaching me for not doing you justice; it is the only alternative you have for redress. I grant you your freedom because I ought. I further grant you six hundred sestertii, because you had the fortitude to accuse me of injustice when I was guilty!"

Will not this conduct appear admirable to every candid mind in love with truth? A very erroneous idea prevails with many, that men in eminent stations never ought to have their conduct called in question until the last extremity. This I am sensible is a doctrine very pleasing to many who possess places of eminence, and maintain them, perhaps by the strength of it. But that man who can adopt the words of Brutus, in his answer to Cassius, "for I am wrapped so strong in honesty, that your words pass by me like idle winds which I regard not," will never feel himself exposed to lose his influence upon society, or be injured by the closest examination into his conduct.

CHAPTER XXIII

"Calamities are friends; as glaring day
Of these unnumber'd lustres robs our sight;
Prosperity puts out unnumber'd thoughts
Of import high and light divine to man."

I HAD determined to end my narrative for the present, with the foregoing letter, but, as my journey to the westward is prolonged another week, I will devote my leisure moments, during this week, to form a farewell address to the best of men and the dearest of friends.

Perhaps you may feel somewhat interested in the continuation and issue of my narrative. Your intimation of such an idea has had a powerful operation on my mind to induce me to gratify your request. You wonder I do not publish. Are not these scenes too disagreeable to be called again into view, and more particularly into public view? I wish I could forget that they had ever existed; yet I cannot say that I am entirely without some consolation for these afflictions. They have learnt me a lesson which no other school can teach. They have learned me to feel the woes that others suffer. They have learned me to contribute of the small portion which I possess to alleviate the distresses of others; and in this, sir, there is a sensation grateful beyond description.

It is not without pain that I view my prospect of leaving you and your agreeable family for a season. Were it not for the prospect of being sooner able to provide for my own family, I think no motive, however lucrative, would induce me to leave my present agreeable situation; but, sir, notwithstanding I am surrounded with this agreeable society, and in it enjoy a great portion of happiness in the social line, yet I cannot feel entirely at ease, whilst my family is at a distance.

We find that this situation appears desirable from the time of our first coming upon the stage of active life, until we settle in a matrimonial state. Both sexes are looking forward to this as the end of their pursuits; and when due attention is paid to the business, and such

[219]

connections formed as the laws of nature enjoin, I believe, that man arrives to the greatest state of happiness he is capable of enjoying. It has ever appeared to me, however, surprising, that so little attention has been exerted to form such connections between the two sexes as are congenial to nature. I am inclined to believe that no one need be left destitute of a partner, entirely calculated to render each other as happy as what things in this world will admit, should a regard be had to tempers, feelings, views, etc., previous to forming the matrimonial connection.

Various are the objects which occupy the attention of mankind in their pursuits after happiness; none, perhaps, more than riches and power. When these are obtained, they give a momentary spring to enjoyment; but soon the soul reverts back to its former state, and is left without any greater sensations of happiness than what are enjoyed in a state of poverty and impotence; therefore, but a very small difference remains between the poor and the rich, the humble and the powerful, as to actual enjoyment.

Did we act as philosophers, we should turn our attention from those objects which a length of experience has taught us are futile in our pursuit of happiness; and place our thoughts upon such subjects as are calculated by nature to grant us that enjoyment which we are ever seeking after. All this may be found in friendship; and the greatest friendship is formed in the intimate connection of matrimony.

We find many times jars and feuds taking place in families. The husband and wife drag on a life through a course of bitter recriminations. From a view of these matters, many are led to despise and ridicule the married state. Were we to reprobate every condition in which some do not happily succeed, there is no calling or pursuit in life, but what would fall under our animadversion. But one striking evidence, in favor of the happiness enjoyed, even in the most disagreeable matrimonial connections, is, that a separation is dreaded, and never had recourse to, only in cases of the last extremity; as Young pertinently expresses,

> "Like peevish man and wife,
> United jar, and yet are loth to part."

I believe, sir, you will think me very wandering in my observations, and preaching a doctrine to one who stands in little need of instruction

[220]

upon this head; seeing your family connections are such, that you need no arguments to enforce the necessity of enjoying yourself in your situation. I know, sir, your situation in that connection, is peculiarly agreeable; therefore, I considered that you would not only see the truth of my observations, but likewise feel it; and it is a pleasure to preach to those who feel the truth of our doctrine.

I have determined here to give you a relation of some events which took place in the course of my life, in point of time, some earlier than where I have arrived; but, which could not be introduced in the course of the narrative, without interrupting the order; therefore, I concluded to omit it, until some convenient time, in which I should not break in upon the relation of that chain of events which appeared to be more closely connected together. I give you the relation of these incidents, in order to illustrate one of the reasons why popular prejudice had arrived to such a pitch against me.

I was one day travelling in Massachusetts, and late at night, put up at a tavern where I was a stranger, as I apprehended. Soon after I arrived, being fatigued with the journey of the day, I retired to rest. This was previous to my marriage. About ten at night, I was awaked by somebody at the bedside. Upon my opening my eyes, I recognized the person as an old acquaintance whom I had not seen for several years. I asked him where he lived, how he came there, and by what means he became possessed with the knowledge of my being in the house? At these questions he stared at me with a countenance of surprise. He asked me where my wife was? I was equally surprised at this question. "How," said he, "do you wish to conceal the matter from me? I am acquainted with the circumstances of your marrying —— ——, of your carrying her away, and to endeavor to hide it from me, argues no very honest design in you."

You will not wonder at my surprise being increased by these observations. I told him his conversation, to me, was wholly unintelligible, that he talked to me of a wife, etc., that I never was married, and what he meant by his observations about —— —— was an enigma to me, never before hearing the name of such a person; that I was an absolute stranger in the town, and supposed myself equally unknown in the house, until I was awaked by him.

This declaration brought on an explanation. He told me, that a

[221]

man calling himself Stephen Burroughs, had been in that town, had become acquainted in a respectable family, had, in opposition to all the efforts of the family, married a daughter and carried her away; alleging, that he was going to Hanover to live with his father, and that they had received no information from their daughter since.

I observed to this young man, that I thought it surprising, that he should be deceived by the artifice made use of; that he certainly must have known whether the person was in fact what he pretended to be. He answered, that being absent on a journey during this time, he never saw the person; that had he even been at home, the deception might have passed undiscovered; for no one doubted as to his being the person whose character he had assumed; and without accident had thrown him in my way, I might never have seen him.

After this conversation, the young man left me, and soon again my eyes were closed in sleep. I had not slept more than an hour and an half, or two hours, before I was again aroused from sleep by the same young man; when I had awoke, I saw in the room an old man and his wife; they approached the bed, the woman broke out into the bitterest lamentations, crying, "it is not he, —— is ruined, gone off with a vagabond, no one knows where." The father's countenance was a picture of distress, though his sorrows did not break forth with such ungovernable rage. Here was a scene truly affecting. The distress of the parents was exquisite; and what gave the greatest poignancy to their sufferings was, they were left without hope.

Whether they have ever found their daughter, I am not able to say, having never seen or heard from them since.

At another time, passing through a part of Connecticut, I called at a tavern for some refreshment, where I had been previously acquainted; I was asked, with some surprise, how I had made my escape from jail? This question immediately introduced a dispute between the landlord and myself. He affirming that I had been committed for theft, and I with equal assurance denying it.

This dispute produced so much noise, that I was apprehended and carried back to jail, as they supposed; but when we arrived, what was the surprise of my landlord, and the constable, when we found the Stephen Burroughs who had been committed for horse stealing, quietly remaining where he was first confined.

[222]

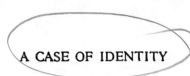
good name!
bad luck!

A CASE OF IDENTITY

The facts upon which this laughable mistake took place, were of the following nature, viz. a certain person had been apprehended and committed to jail, under a suspicion of horse stealing. My landlord, who had formerly known me, heard that a person, by the name of Stephen Burroughs had been committed to jail. This immediately fixed an idea in his mind that I was confined under the suspicion of theft.

For some reason, the person, who had been committed, chose to assume my name and character, which circumstance not only deceived my landlord, but likewise caused the report to be circulated that I was detected in horse stealing.

Had I conducted the business a little different, when I was accosted by the landlord, perhaps the matter would never have come to an explanation. He did not seem inclined to apprehend me. at first; but, when I treated his assertion with some harshness, he manifested a disposition to let me know that I was in his power; and that he would exercise that power, unless I soothed his resentment by more gentle measures. How he felt when the mistake was discovered, you can more easily conceive than I can describe. His sensations were not of the most agreeable kind, you will readily imagine. Indeed, sir, I felt a degree of compassion towards the man under that situation, notwithstanding his conduct had not been of the most grateful kind.

A number of instances, similar to these, have occurred since I came upon the stage of action. You will readily understand what consequences would naturally proceed from such events. I found the world ever ready to give credit to such reports. When mankind had once formed an unfavorable opinion, it was hard to eradicate such an idea, even by the most pointed evidence.[1]

I recollect at a certain time, when I was among a people who did not know my real name and character. Among them I gained a credit and standing of the pleasing kind, long before my real name became known.

[1] About the year 1808, a respectable gentleman, of Boston, accosted me one day, saying, "Your old friend Burroughs has got into jail again." I asked him where? He replied, "at Johnstown, in the state of New York." I told him he must labor under a mistake, for Burroughs was certainly then in Canada. He was quite piqued at this, and answered with an air of triumph, "Sir, I cannot mistake; for I am now direct from Johnstown, and *know* that the noted Stephen Burroughs lies there in prison!!!"

MEMOIRS OF STEPHEN BURROUGHS

I happened at this time to become acquainted with a certain physician, who came from a part of the country contiguous to where I had formerly lived. In the course of our acquaintance he told me, "that he was acquainted with a certain character by the name of Stephen Burroughs, who, of all others, was the most singular. That he was a person possessed of the greatest abilities of any man he ever knew." In order to illustrate more fully the truth of his observations, he related many anecdotes concerning me, of the humorous kind, which I had never heard of before. "How I had deceived many people in the most surprising manner, and to the general diversion of the country. How I would still continue to deceive them, notwithstanding all their precautions against me. How I would steal from the rich and give to the poor; and that people were afraid to prosecute me, because I would ever find some shift to evade the business; and would, moreover, always steal again from the person who had attempted the prosecution; however," continued the Physician, "I could ever discern in his countenance the features of design. There ever was the appearance of deceit in his looks; and I should have known him to be a rogue, had I never heard of his character. I believe," continued he, "that the countenance of a man is a strong index of his natural disposition; as for instance, if you will permit me to make the comparison, without conceiving that I am attempting to flatter, I never saw a more striking contrast, than between the designing, deceitful countenance of Burroughs, and your open, frank, and candid countenance. I have generally found men wearing such characters after acquaintance as the expression of their countenances had indicated in the first place." You will readily conceive, sir, that I smiled at the harrangue of this physiognomist. He remained at ease in the enjoyment of his own opinion for a while; but the bubble soon broke, and he was fairly exposed to public view, without the thinnest veil for a covering. My real name and character were soon developed to the public, and all his knowledge in physiognomy was discredited immediately; and even a great share of that science of which he was really master, fled at the same time. So fickle is the multitude; so prone to run from one extreme into the other. This simple circumstance produced the fall of the poor physician.

Thus we see, sir, that every person, be his situation in life what it

[224]

may, is more or less exposed to revolution, misfortune and disappointment. Those very means which we make use of to answer our purposes of promotion and exaltation are often the direct and only causes of our calamity. We all wish to be happy, and all use such means to obtain happiness as our judgment points out. From daily experience we learn how incompetent we are, to form right estimates of the various effects which will follow the measures we pursue; therefore, he who depends upon the uncertain occurrences of events for his happiness, builds upon a very slender foundation, and will most assuredly find the chances run against him.

> "For these pure joys the world can never know;
> In gentler climes their silver currents flow.
> Oft at the silent, shadowy close of day,
> When the hush'd grove has sung his parting lay;
> When pensive twilight in his dusky car,
> Slowly ascends to meet the evening star;
> Above, below, aërial murmurs swell,
> From hanging woods, brown heath, and bushy dell!
> A thousand nameless rills that shun the light,
> Stealing soft music on the ear of night.
> So oft the finer movements of the soul,
> That shun the shore of pleasure's gay control,
> In the still shades of calm seclusion rise,
> And breath their sweet seraphic harmonies!"

I have often wished that my memory was sufficient to retain a recollection of all the mistakes which I have either made myself or have seen others make, during the course of my life. From such a circumstance, I think I should be able to learn, whether any general cause existed in nature, which produces our miscalculations, or whether they always arise from a general weakness of the mind, which is incurable. From what observations I have been able to make, I rather think the evil may in some measure be remedied, but I believe not entirely cured.

Should we lay a right foundation for happiness, and rear our super-structure upon that foundation, we should all find an indescribable advantage arising from such a procedure. I have once before hinted, that mankind were generally in pursuit of riches and power, in order to render themselves happy; that this pursuit is not calculated to contribute to our happiness, but on the contrary, to miltate against

[225]

it, will appear evident, when we take a candid view of the subject.

That all mankind are descended from one common origin, and partake of the nature and feelings which are common to each other, is not only allowed by the united voice of all, but is likewise demonstrated by the united voice of nature, perpetually crying in the bosom of every person. Being all descended from the same origin, we are all upon the footing of brethren of the same family, entitled to equal privileges and immunities. Being members of one and the same family, we have a common interest in the prosperity of each individual which composes this family. This is the language of nature; however, we may have our minds perverted by error and corruption; hence, we find a language speaking within us, that we cannot silence; a language that speaks strongly in terms of compassion towards those in imminent distress. Who can stand still and see another fall into the fire, without reaching forth the hand of assistance? Who so insensible to the pleasures which he derives from society, that he will retire from them with indifference! Are not all equally dependent on each other for the comforts which are enjoyed in life? Has not our great parent constituted the order of things in wisdom, so that by following his laws we arrive at the most exalted state of perfection which things in this life admit?

It is a truth, I believe, apparent to every one, that all cannot possess power and riches; nay, the greater part must ever remain without these acquirements; therefore, he who strives for power and riches, endeavors to take from the general good of the whole, and appropriate to his own use. He endeavors to invert the order of nature, by depriving others of equal privileges, in order to add to his own, and by inverting the order of that wisdom which has bountifully provided for all her children, misery will ensue, confusion and disorder will run through the body, and many inconveniences will be felt by every member of the community. On the contrary, when we feel the affection of brethren towards each other; when the welfare and prosperity of each member of society become, in a measure, our own, how changed the scene! how happy the prospect! Our griefs become lessened by communicating them to others; our joys are increased by the participation of our friend! The disgraceful passions of hatred, envy, malice and revenge are lost for want of support.

[226]

THE UNITED VOICE OF NATURE

When we set out in life, under the auspices of this disposition, and pursue such a course, we are in a situation not to lose our enjoyment by every puff of misfortune. We are inaccessible to the malignant passions, the great disturbers of human repose. In this line of conduct, we follow the directions of nature, and answer the purpose for which we were designed. Property, even riches, acquired by industry, (not by power) are of use to contribute to our happiness; by rendering us capable of lessening the necessities of our brethren and fellow members of society.

> "O ye blest scenes of permanent delight!
> Full above measure! lasting beyond all bound!
> A perpetuity of bliss, is bliss,——
> Could you, so rich in rapture, fear an end,
> That ghastly thought would drink up all your joy,
> And quit in Paradise the realms of light.
> Safe are you lodged above these rolling spheres;
> The baleful influence of whose giddy dance
> Sheds sad vicissitudes on all beneath."

These ideas, to me, have ever appeared as matters of high importance; and I wish to see some abler pen go deeply into the subject, and try the experiment thoroughly, to see whether mankind can be reasoned into their own good. Should you, sir, devote a few of your leisure moments to such an object, it might be attended with very salutary effects. It is said, "that mankind are daily growing in useful knowledge." Perhaps this may be true in a partial sense; but it appears to me, that the state of society in the days of the Spartan and Roman governments, was much more congenial to nature, than what we are under at present. At least, we do not find such striking instances of affection towards the public welfare, among any of the modern patriots, as what was instanced in the conduct of Lycurgus, Regulus, Cincinnatus, etc. etc.

I have just hinted at a number of subjects in the course of this narrative which may appear to you somewhat mistimed, considering the primary object was barely a narration of facts. Yes, sir, this manuscript will ever be a memorandum of those subjects, at which I have barely hinted; and as your attention is occupied by your station in society, with political objects, there remains a bare possibility of such a memorandum's being of service, in calling some of those subjects into view; as this country is happily situated, on many accounts, to pursue political inquiries, without the embarrassments attending preconceived opinions and settled systems; I feel the more desirous that the truth of these observations may be decided by experiment. Should they be productive of good to the community, even in the smallest degree, I shall feel the benefit of an essential reward, for suggesting those things. Should they, on the contrary, be found to be a system of error, I shall place them to the account of the many mistakes I have made through life, and rest satisfied that I have wished to have them productive of good.

Whilst I am absent, you will have sufficient leisure to peruse the manuscript and detect the errors which I have been guilty of, and rest assured that I shall ever receive any suggestions of yours upon that head as an additional mark of that sincere friendship which you have ever manifested.

After you have sufficiently perused the present narrative, if you should wish for a continuation, I will attempt to gratify you as soon as my situation shall again become so settled as to admit of writing.

Entertainment of the highest nature, generally consists of a due variety, and I find people most fond of buying books of entertainment, where novelty, melancholy, humor, joy and triumph are interchangeably the leading features; hence, Clarissa Harlow is condemned for being too gloomy. Young's Night Thoughts fall under the same censure. The critics say there is a want of a variety; that our compassion is wounded, but never gratified; that our disgust is excited against certain characters; that the rewards of vice are set forth, but nothing on the pleasing side; that virtue is not rewarded; that our compassion is not relieved, and that of course we feel nothing but painful sensations. All these observations, I know, will apply with propriety to my narrative. I should have been glad to have interspersed something of the pleasing kind among the relation of misfortunes; but I could not do it consistently with the character of one, who had a regard to truth in his history.

Should I pursue hereafter the history of the remaining part of my life, you may not be more pleased than what you are with that already given. It is true, that I passed through many scenes entirely new, and partaking in some measure of the humorous kind; but that uninterrupted course of severe trials, which I have experienced from the beginning, never forsook me until I arrived in this hospitable town, where I have met with that attention and kindness which has in a measure been a counterbalance to my former misfortunes.

This observation, I believe, may not be misplaced, that whenever I have suffered a temporary respite from the stroke of calamity, my feelings have been more alive to the enjoyment of my situation. The comparison has ever been striking, both to my view and feelings; and of consequence, all the force of happiness had its operation upon my mind without any impediment.

Another observation, I believe, ought to have a place here, viz. that our minds, after giving way to the strokes of calamity a while, will regain their vigor and pristine state of tranquillity, under the most trying situation; hence we often find among our slaves (I blush to write the word) a degree of tranquillity and evenness of temper which is wanting in the more exalted stations of life. Visit the prisons, and you will find many in those situations who are desperate, wearing in their countenances a content of insensibility produced by despair.

I recollect when I was in the dungeon at Northampton, and every prospect of relief was out of the question, that I felt a degree of calm or sullen content, under my situation. I really thought that I rejoiced in it, "because," said I, "the end will soon come to all my sufferings." These were my sensations, so long as the prospect of better days was out of the question: but as soon as the sound of relief had reached my ears, these images fled like the "baseless fabric of a vision, and left not a trace behind."

The mind, when out of her bias, is ever struggling for a state of rest, or tranquillity, and according to the strength she possesses, gains that situation sooner or later. There are but very few minds, but what will gain that situation ultimately, let the strokes of adversity be ever so heavy. It is true, that some are overpowered; the powers of their minds are broken, and they either become delirious, or else sink to the grave under the pressure of misfortune. Of all situations in life, that is the most dreadful, which produces death or delirium, by those wounds which the mind has suffered. You intimate, sir, that you wish me to give a particular description of the people in the dif-

[229]

ferent states, their manners, their local peculiarities, their particular customs, their economy, property, industry, genius and tempers; likewise, the nature of the soil in different parts of this country, the price that land bears, the quantity and kind which it produces, the different methods of agriculture, the different facility of obtaining a living, etc.

You require of me a task which I do not think myself competent to perform with accuracy; however, in my next attempt, after my return, I will endeavor to gratify your request in as great a measure as my opportunity furnished materials for, when I made the tour of the United States.

My situation was such, when I made a journey through the states that I had an opportunity of observing many things which other travellers have not; on the other hand, travellers in general, have an opportunity of observing many things in the course of their travelling, which I had not; therefore, sir, if you can gather anything from my observations on those subjects which you have requested, either profitable or amusing, I shall be highly gratified with my performance.

Baron Trenk observes, that he once travelled in his coach through Poland; that he thought he was acquainted with the people, with their manners and genius. But afterwards he was compelled to travel through this country, in a most abject situation, and under the necessity of begging his bread; then it was he discovered his mistake. He found them to be another, and very different people, from what he had apprehended in his former tour. So true it is, that mankind will wear the veil of deception, generally, in all countries.

My situation, in respect to property, was somewhat similar to the Baron's, in his last tour through Poland, but to the honor of humanity be it said, that in many places, I found a very different reception from what the Baron met with. Yet, in some instances, the unfeeling heart wore a prominent appearance in the character of the inhabitants of the country.

In different states, I found a great difference in the manners and morals of the people; in their refinement, feelings and sentiments; and in different parts of the same states, I found this variation equally great. The causes which produce this, I will not undertake to assign; however, shall wish to hint my ideas respecting it when I enter on that subject. Could the causes of these variations be traced, and clearly

[230]

understood, they would be of the utmost service to society, and an object worthy the attention of every benevolent mind.

There is something in the system of education yet undiscovered, which, I believe, would have the most effectual operation upon the world of mankind, in forming their minds in such a manner as to render them fitted for the enjoyment of society, without the interruption of those irregularities, which overthrow the happiness of the social state. That denomination of people called Quakers, have brought their mode of education to the greatest state of perfection of any class with whom I have been acquainted. We find a state of the utmost order among them, and this too, founded upon the most simple principles. Their manners and conduct savor very strongly of their education.

Having never been educated to the business of farming, it cannot be expected that my mind was sufficiently enlightened upon that head, to make such inquiries and observations as would tend to throw light upon the subject; though perhaps this might afford an inquiry of the greatest utility to society, were it taken up and pursued by some one able to perform the task. True it is, that many different methods are made use of in agriculture; these methods are in a measure local, retained by those who have been in the custom of using them, and parted from with reluctance for others, not so common, but perhaps more useful. What circumstances of that kind came to my view and observation, I will mention. Perhaps you may draw some ideas from them which may be new and useful, but I have no expectation that you will many.

Relating to the subject of land; the price which it bears in different parts of the state, the quality, situation, convenience, etc. which it possesses, its quality and kind of produce, the net proceeds which it averages to the possessor, in different places, are all objects which have claimed a considerable share of my attention, when opportunity has invested me with a chance for observation. I have, moreover, had my attention much occupied by the different degrees of industry and economy which have marked the characters of different people.

It has been the practice of the greater part of writers to speak in general terms, respecting the subject of which they are treating; this mode has undoubtedly its advantages; but perhaps it may not embrace

[231]

all the advantages which a more minute description would afford; as for example—should a writer, in general terms, describe the state of Georgia as a fruitful country, abounding with the conveniences and luxuries of life, etc. the reader would undoubtedly obtain an idea of its being a country in which property might be acquired with a degree of facility; yet he could hardly form an accurate estimate of the particular occupation or business which would afford the most considerable and ready profit. Whether a capital would be absolutely necessary in order to prosecute business, and if necessary, how large that capital must be. He could not form an estimate of the difference in the profit, which he would realize by relinquishing business in one state and removing to another; as for instance, from New Hampshire to Georgia; and of consequence, could not determine with propriety upon such an object, should it be presented to his view. On the contrary, should the cost of an acre of land, in the state of nature, be shown, the cost to render that acre productive, the profits which the land would afford, both in New Hampshire and Georgia, then the reader would be possessed with data by which he might state his calculations, and form an accurate estimate of the object of acquiring property, both in Georgia and New Hampshire, and learn the advantages, if any, that one would have over the other, and how great that advantage would be.

Thus likewise, by a minute description of the price which articles of importation bear in the two states; the price of those for exportation; the quantity and quality of those articles; the demand for them; the facility of importing and exporting; the price of living; the mode of dealing, etc., would give a sufficient fund of information for any one to decide upon the subject of merchandise in either state; so likewise for mechanics, and every other employment which admits of profit.

This is a system of writing which I do not recollect ever to have seen; and I have somewhat wondered at the circumstance. There are advantages to be derived from such a method, sufficiently great to claim the attention of the literary world; and I believe such a method would afford more useful instruction to the philosopher, the politician, the farmer, the mechanic, and the merchant, than any other which has been made use of. This method draws the picture of men and man-

[232]

ners to the life, and gives every man an opportunity of viewing, and making his own reflections upon it.

When we are, in this manner, made acquainted with countries, men, manners, customs, etc. in the more minute departments, we have data to form our own opinions relating to the various causes which produce the different effects upon society, and are not dependent on others for an opinion respecting them.

When I travelled through the states, my situation and circumstances did not admit that extensive opportunity for information and observation upon these subjects which my propensity led me to desire. However, what observations I was in a capacity to make, I paid the strictest attention to form, with as much accuracy as my judgment would allow. I did not settle down upon an opinion until I had satisfactory evidence of the just principle upon which it was founded. Should I ever again travel through the states, I should devote my attention greatly to such an object; and endeavor, upon the most thorough plan, to investigate all the little secret springs which set the wheels of society in motion.

Should the population and emigrations into these states be as great for one hundred years to come as they have been for the same time past, what an amazing multitude must this continent contain! Nature seems to be swiftly hastening forward her events to fill up the measure of time!

Here is a vast field for the philosophic eye to view. Perhaps there may be more effected for the good of society, during the continuation of the American settlements, improvements, inventions and experiments, than ever took place at any other, or perhaps at every period, since time began. The philanthropist will be induced to labor with redoubled exertion in this field, owing to the animating prospect of success which he will have in view, as a reward for his labor.

Did the philosopher have nothing more in view, than his own particular benefit, this would be a sufficient motive for him to be incessant in his researches after that knowledge and improvement, which would tend to the general good; there is a general connection which does, and must exist in the world: and no man discovers and communicates useful knowledge to mankind, but he himself will reap the advantage.

No discovery, in its crude state, but what admits of improvement.

[233]

When it is flung open to the world, every person has the opportunity of amending, improving, and altering, as judgment and experiment will dictate, until it is brought to perfection; and then every member of society enjoys the privilege which such improvements produce.

A stronger motive than all these considerations has its influence upon the mind of the real philosopher. To view himself as able to promote the happiness of his brethren, the common stock of the human race; to see himself contributing to increase their joy, comfort and prosperity; to behold the various circles of society wearing countenances vacant of care and remorse; to see the tender connections among more intimate degrees of consanguinity indulged in their utmost latitude, without the cloud of care to intervene, or the corroding sting of disappointment! This is a luxury of enjoyment, a feast of pleasure, beyond the utmost conception of the voluptuous epicure! And the more deeply we dip into these enjoyments, the keener is our appetite for their relish. These bring no alloy, no pain, no disease. No evil attends their indulgence, no repentance grows from their use.

And now, sir, permit me to address this wish to you and family—that the perfection of all these grateful sensations may be enjoyed by you in their fullest measure. That as your family increases, their opening minds may drink deep of this principle, and enjoy the effects so long as they continue to occupy a station upon the stage of mutual dependence. That the most striking examples of filial, parental, connubial, and fraternal affection may pervade the whole body; and when such a series of time has rolled away, as to admit you among the higher order of beings, in that state where we are but little acquainted, may the memory of you and family be called into view with the most grateful emotions, and pleasing sensations. I remain, dear sir, with sentiments of the warmest esteem, your much obliged, humble servant,

STEPHEN BURROUGHS.

THE END OF THE FIRST VOLUME OF THE ORIGINAL EDITION

CHAPTER XXIV

"Thus the lorn wretch, by ignis fatuus led,
   Pursues the gleam which charms his lonely way:
Nor, till destruction whelms his hapless head,
   Suspects the dangers of the treacherous ray."

I WAS determined, when I left Worcester, to quit the country in such a manner as to leave no traces of my route behind. I intended to go to Long Island, in the State of New York, and there reside, until I could look about me a little; see what was to be done; and where I could procure a place to move my family.

All the day, following my escape from confinement, I lay in the woods, unknown to any person whatever. At the close of the day, I repaired to a friend, who carried me about ten miles on my way; and, at parting, gave me directions how to pursue my route to the best advantage; informing me where to take a road, not so much frequented, but much nearer than the main road.

At this time I had with me fourteen dollars in cash, one shirt, a pair of breeches, a pair of stockings, boots, waistcoat, and gown; all which I had on. This comprised the whole of my wardrobe, and all the property I had about me.

Not long after leaving my friend, I turned into a road, which I supposed was the one pointed out, and pursued it with diligence, until I came to a pair of bars. The night, by this time, became extremely dark; the sky being overcast with thick clouds, and the rain beginning to pour down in torrents. I did not suspect my being in the wrong road; but found the way much less frequented than I had expected, from the direction of my friend. I concluded, likewise, that I should meet with more difficulty in following the footpath, than I had contemplated before the night had become so extremely dark. I got over the bars, however, and pursued my course, until I found myself in the midst of a swamp, composed of brakes, mire, and rocks, without any path to direct me, or knowing what way to extricate myself. I tried

[235]

to find the way out of this swamp by measuring back my former course. After repeated trials, I found it impossible. The more I attempted to find the way back, the deeper I found myself involved in difficulty. Sometimes I would plunge to my knees in mud; I would then cautiously seek for a rock, and crawl out of my filthy predicament, by its friendly aid: and yet, by taking one incautious step, I was plunged headlong into the mire. With this difficulty I struggled about four hours, when I once more found myself, on dry ground.

How much does our happiness depend on our reasoning with propriety upon the various subjects which offer themselves to our view! When I had again got my foot upon dry ground, I felt exceedingly happy, notwithstanding I was wandering alone through this dreary night, drenched with rain and covered with mud; notwithstanding I had torn one of my boots in such a manner as to let my foot to the ground at every step; and had, likewise, torn my foot almost as bad as my boot.—Thus we may enjoy happiness in the most forlorn situation.

I sought diligently for a path, or some directory by which I might again find the road. I soon found myself in a footpath, which I pursued until I was led into a large frequented road. I judged that, by this time, I had travelled between twenty and thirty miles, since I had parted from my friend. I expected I was in the state of Connecticut, and far enough from the place of my acquaintance, to travel through the day without being known. I passed by a large house about the breaking of day, which appeared to be a place familiar to my eye; but could not recollect myself so as to determine where I was. I passed on a little further; and, what do you think, Sir, was my astonishment, when I discovered myself in Oxford (a town adjoining to Worcester) walking, with hasty strides, back to prison; being now four miles nearer Worcester, than I was the preceding evening, when my friend left me.

I immediately turned my course, and left the main road, and made my way towards Douglass-woods (a wild, barren forest). As the rain yet continued, without intermission, and the morning, of consequence, was dark, I believe I was not seen by any person. I ran, with the utmost speed, about an hour and a half; and concluded, that, by this time, I had nearly arrived into the State of Rhode Island; when, again, to my utter astonishment, I was about re-entering the great road which led back to Worcester, near where I had left it, "What," said I to myself, "am I mad? Am I divested of every ray of reason? Am I designed for destruction, and led to it by infatuation?" The truth is, I was so bewildered by my wanderings through the night that I had lost all ability to calculate respecting the points of the compass.

Under these circumstances, the only way I had to pursue, was to take the most open and direct road to Douglass Meetinghouse. It was now about 10 o'clock in the morning. The rain had ceased, and the sun broke out from the clouds, and shone very warm, it being now the month of June. Having been without any refreshment through the night preceding, after enduring such a course of fatigue, you will not wonder at my feeling faint and weary, by this time, for the want of food.

After I had travelled some distance in the town of Douglass, I intended to procure some refreshment. This I calculated to obtain at a private house, considering I should be more exposed to be seen and known by the variety of company that might be at a tavern. I therefore called at a small, snug house by the wayside.

No sooner had I entered this house, than the man, starting up, exclaimed, "How do you do, Mr. Burroughs?" This salutation very much disconcerted my feelings; which being perceived by the man, he answered, "that I might make myself perfectly easy; that no person should molest me while I tarried at his house; that I might remain there as long as I desired." And without asking whether I was hungry, ordered his wife to get some victuals ready immediately. I was apprehensive that all this seeming kindness was only an intended delusion, with an expectation of procuring help to carry me back to Worcester; and more especially after he told me he was going on my way about four miles. My suspicion was so strong against him that I intended, the first opportunity, to pretend an occasion to step into the bushes, and by this means, make my escape.

After I had refreshed myself we set off together on our way. Finding the country entirely open through which we passed, I could not put my intended flight into execution; not finding any bushes by the way. After we had travelled about two miles, we were met by two men, one of whom I knew, being on the Grand Jury at Worcester, at the time of my trial; the other was a Justice of the Peace, to whom my fellow-traveller introduced me, expressing his satisfaction, at the same time, that I had got out of "their damn'd clutches."—The Justice and Juror gave me their hands; hoped it was for the best that I was at liberty; wished I might meet with kinder treatment; and so left us. At this moment I felt a mountain's weight removed from my mind. I was satisfied that my fellow-traveller meant me no injury. I felt, likewise, that people generally viewed my treatment at Worcester as I did myself.

We travelled together until my fellow traveller arrived at the place of his destination. We there parted with expressions and feelings of reciprocal friendship.

After I had left this man, and had taken a view of the incidents of the day, I began to think that people were generally informed into the nature and particulars of my trial; and from that information had conceived a disgust towards the Court, and a desire that I might elude, as much as possible, the effects of the sentence against me. Under this idea, I determined to travel openly, and to wear no disguise on my journey to Long Island.

On the evening of this day, I arrived at Gloucester, a town in the state of Rhode Island, and put up at the house of one Owen. Immediately after, I went into a shoemaker's shop, hard by, in order to get my boots mended.

The shoemaker gave me a pair of slippers to wear while my boots were mending, which were so small that I could scarcely put my toes into them.

When I had returned into the house, the landlord, who was an impertinent fellow, having his curiosity excited by my looks, dress, etc., asked me from whence I came; who I was, etc. In the simplicity of my heart I told him all the circumstances relating to myself. Owen observed that many people had accused him of affording shelter to the insurgents, at the time of Shays' rebellion; but that he would be damned if they brought any such accusations against him again. After he had made these observations, he went out, and in about half an hour, returned with a Constable and Justice of the Peace. I was again interrogated by them respecting the circumstances of my leaving Worcester, etc.: to all which I gave a simple detail. So strongly was I infatuated.

After I had ended my narration, Owen, the Justice and Constable retired into another room, to consult what measures to take. There was a traveller at this time, who had put up at this house, and was in the room where the consultation was held. He soon came into the room where I was sitting, and beckoned me out. I immediately obeyed his motion, and received information that a plan was in agitation to carry me back to Worcester. This hint was sufficient. I was roused from my stupidity; and immediately left the house of my good landlord Owen. My boots were in the shoemaker's shop. I had nothing I could wear on my feet. I could not travel in my slippers. I must walk barefooted.

Under these embarrassments, and by no means so refreshed by rest as to feel vigorous for another night's travel, I again began my pedestrian exercise. Soon after I had set out on my night's walk, the rain began again to descend in torrents, which continued through the whole night. I found the pain from walking excruciating. My feet had been miserably torn the night before. The gravel over which I had to walk, was sharp; and the darkness of the night prevented my seeing the stones and rubbish against which I perpetually dashed my feet.

Notwithstanding the pains which I suffered, the solitary situation in which I spent the night brought the various scenes into view, through which I had passed in such a disagreeable succession. The events of my life I found still chequered with the most surprising variety. One moment lifted on the pinnacle of hope, and the next, dashed into the vale of despondency.

I have (said I) passed through a series of trials at Worcester, the parallel to which is not to be found in the history of man. To be indicted for the attempt to ravish, and those bills predicated upon such circumstances as were exhibited in testimony, is to me altogether unaccountable. What is still more unaccountable is, the determination, anxiety, and pains of two of the Judges to have the verdicts returned against me; and even to terrify any who should look towards me with an eye of compassion. But what winds up the scene to the great climax of astonishment is, that a Jury should be so far wrought upon by such measures as to return a verdict against me.

As though one thunderbolt was not sufficient to fall upon my devoted head, I was again brought forward to answer to two new bills of indictment, accusing me of the same facts, but calling them by another name (viz.), open lewdness. You, Sir, will be more able to judge of the propriety and legality of this transaction than I. This is a crime but little known in our country. I do not recollect of ever hearing of a trial for such an offence, before I was called to answer to a charge of that nature. I had then but a moment's time for consideration; but am more confirmed, upon further investigation, of the propriety of my first ideas upon the subject (viz.), that it must be an *open* transaction, in order to come within the nature of the crime. I am sensible the nature of this crime has ever been, in a measure, left indefinite. All I recollect ever having seen upon the subject, by any of the writers on criminal law, was in Hale's Pleas of the Crown. He explains the crime by saying, that it is such conduct as "those were guilty of, who showed themselves naked, in the balcony, on the king's birthday": or to that purpose. This, I think, is sufficient to show, that *openness* is an essential part to constitute the crime; and that unless the lewdness be open, it cannot be punishable by law. One circumstance is worth noticing by the way, viz. Daniel Bacon and wife testified, under solemnity, at the court of inquest, that on a particular night, (they were very positive as to the particular night) their daughter was out and not to be found; a number of months afterwards she told that she was with me at that time; though when inquiry was first made, she gave a very different reason for her being absent, too indelicate to find a place in this narrative. As this was somewhat of a memorable night, on account of a number of circumstances, I recollected my being in company with a gentleman of undoubted veracity the whole time in which it was possible for me to be with the witness, according to her testimony. I produced this gentleman, who made oath to this fact, before the Justice by whom I was committed. When the trial came on at Worcester, before the Supreme Court, the father, mother, and daughter, had then very ingeniously forgotten on what particular night the transaction took place; but only remembered it was sometime in the month of June. I believe, Sir, you will understand, by this time, there was not the greatest partiality in the Court, in my favor; and that I did not stand any very extraordinary chance for simple justice upon this business. After the trial was ended on the part of the Jury, it appeared that the sentence was as extraordinary as the trial. Happy for the world that the heart is not always callous to the feelings of justice or compassion! How different was the treatment I received from my kind entertainer at Douglass? Can the mind, fraught with compassion, look upon his conduct but with the highest veneration? We see in him, the operation of the laws of nature, unsophisticated by the pomp of dignity, and the violence of passion. He saw no fatal consequences of the ruin of society, of the destruction of morals, and of the overthrow of virtue, by my escape. He wished me happy. He wished me liberated from misery. He saw no danger arising to himself, as a member of society, or to any other, from my obtaining this. He acted accordingly. How contrary to this was the conduct of Owen! Because *he* had borne an imputation of blame, he would render me back again to misery; not because justice required, or the laws of humanity called for my apprehension; but because he should suffer additional blame in entertaining me at his house, under such circumstances. Where will this principle lead, but to the commission of every species of wickedness? When we make our conveniency a rule to infringe upon our neighbor's privileges, we shall not fail to rob him of his property, health, and life, when our conveniency shall call for such a transaction.

After travelling until near day, I turned off from the main road, and took a path which ultimately led into a large open field. In the midst of the field I found the bottom of an old stack of hay, and a yard of crooked fence around it. I took a large flake of hay, and laid it on some rails which I had fixed for that purpose, and creeped under it, to shelter myself, in some small measure, from the rain. I was, by this time, so far exhausted by the fatigue of travelling, and the pain of my feet, that I could not proceed any further; therefore I crawled under this flimsy shelter, with more pleasure than many feel in retiring to a bed of down, hung with rich tapestry, and lulled to sleep by the enchanting sound of music. I had scarcely laid my head to the ground, before I was fast locked in the leaden arms of sleep. All things were lost to my knowledge, until about 10 o'clock, when I was aroused from my profound slumbers, by the repeated cries of men. When I first awoke, I expected that Owen and his gang had made pursuit after, and had overtaken me. But how it was possible for them to trace my route to this place, was wholly a mystery. I was not suffered, however, very long, to contemplate on this subject. I was ordered to turn out. There were three men around me. Owen was not one of them. I found that I had travelled twenty miles since I left him; and therefore concluded myself out of danger from him, and from being known by the men who were with me. I was determined not to run into the same error here as I had at Gloucester, by relating my name, situation, etc. I demanded of the men what they wanted of me? They soon informed me, that their design was to carry me to Providence, supposing me to be an accomplice with George Irish, who had been committed to Providence jail, on a suspicion of counterfeiting bank bills. A number of his accomplices had made their escape, for the apprehension of whom a reward was offered. Being found by these men, in such a situation, they suspected I was one who had fled on the before mentioned account. I endeavored to convince them that so far from being an accomplice with George Irish, I had never seen him. I believe they were pretty thoroughly convinced of their mistake; but still supposed that some extraordinary cause had brought me to this place; and therefore talked of carrying me to Providence. I was sensible I should be recognized in that town; and of course, should be exposed to the danger of being carried back from thence to Worcester. The men perceived that I was unwilling to be carried to Providence; and being desirous to make me turn to some account, began to banter me upon the price I would give for my liberation. I expostulated with them upon the cruelty of exacting money for my liberation; but my expostulations were in vain. I found they were bent upon carrying me to Providence unless I would buy them off. After much altercation upon the subject, they consented to release me for eleven dollars. I gave them the money and they went off.

After I had got rid of my disagreeable companions, I again walked on as well as the soreness of my feet would allow. I had travelled about a mile, when I began to feel extremely faint for the want of food. I therefore determined to go into the first house, and obtain some refreshment, if possible. I accordingly entered a house, hard by the wayside, and asked the woman of the house, if she would permit me to take a dinner with her. My appearance, my lameness, etc., had a strong effect upon her feelings. She gave me a pleasant dinner, and said many things to sooth and comfort me. She wanted to know more particulars relating to my circumstances than I wished to communicate. After I had rested myself awhile, and was about making ready to compensate the good woman for her kindness and refreshment, she desired me to sit down for a minute. She then went into another room, and soon returned with a pair of thin shoes, belonging to her husband, tolerably good, and presented them to me. I offered to compensate her for the shoes and dinner; but she refused to receive anything, alleging that, "thy necessities are greater than mine; and when thou seest one in distress, and hast it in thy power to relieve him, remember that he is thy brother."

I was struck with astonishment at the nobleness, combined with simplicity, of this woman's sentiments. Did mankind view the relation they stand in to each other with these sentiments of benevolence, and act accordingly, how changed would be the miseries of life, to scenes of the most pleasing contemplation! There, said I, is religion, manifested in a clearer manner than what Ridgley has displayed in his whole body of Divinity. There is virtue; there is benevolence; and finally there is everything which ennobles the human character.

After I had left this house, I travelled on again; but so great was the embarrassment I met with from my feet, that with all my exertion, I did not travel more than four miles through the remainder of that day. My feet were too much swollen to admit of my travelling with my shoes on; I was, therefore, under the disagreeable necessity of carrying them in my hands. This was on Saturday; and I concluded, that resting one day without travelling, would serve to recruit my feet so as to be able to wear my shoes. And as I should have a plausible pretext for lying by on Sunday, I determined to appropriate that time for such a purpose.

I found it would be impossible for me to travel in this country without giving some account of myself, or disobliging the people at whose houses I should call; and therefore found it necessary to fix upon some system, and be uniform in it. To pass for an inhabitant of any of the towns in New England, I was constantly exposed to meet with people, who would either be an inhabitant of, or acquainted in the town from whence I pretended to come; and this leading to a discovery of the

[243]

deception, people would be led to form unfavorable conjectures concerning me, perhaps, more than they ought. Under these circumstances, I thought it best to pass for a foreigner, and lay the scene of my birth, etc., in London; as the probability would be, that I should not often meet with my fellow townsmen of that place; and even should that be the case, I could still act my part without detection as a member of that great city; it being easily accounted for that I should not be acquainted with every individual in such a populous place. My birth, place of abode, etc., I fixed in Leadenhall Street. My real parentage, connections, etc., I retained, only transporting them to London. Some account I must give for my leaving England, and coming into America, and for my present forlorn situation. I concluded that the real account, with a little alteration, would answer, only changing the place of action. Moreover, as this last information would be considered by people in gen ral, as a delicate point, they would be more willing to receive their information by distant hints.

I had determined to wear this character until I could introduce myself into business, and obtain an establishment for my family; until I could, likewise, see the operations of the world towards me, under my real name. I expected that in this situation I could form a better estimate of what would be prudent for me to do, as I should then be in a capacity to learn the feelings of the public towards me; and what would be their treatment, should I discover myself and reassume my real character.

I entered a tavern and called for entertainment over night. Soon after I had been in the house, I discovered the landlord was sick. After inquiry, I perceived that he had the remitting fever, which I mentioned in the course of conversation. This aroused his attention, and he enquired eagerly whether I was a doctor? Thinking I might reap an advantage from this profession on this occasion, and being persuaded I could help the man, I assumed the character of an English physician with no small degree of parade. I was fortunate in my administrations, which gave seasonable and effectual relief.

I tarried here till Monday morning, and to my no small satisfaction, found I could travel with my shoes on my feet. When I departed, I was rewarded with a French crown for my medical assistance. About noon this day I overtook a man dressed in clean, neat apparel, carrying a bottle of rum. He accosted me in the following manner. "Shipmate, will ye take a drop of rum to cheer your spirits this warm day?" I did not wish to treat his friendly salutation with neglect or contempt. It has ever been a principle by which I have wished to regulate my conduct, to treat the sentiments of benevolence with attention, let them be manifested in ever so singular or uncouth a manner. Accordingly, I accepted the benevolent invitation of this Hibernian. Not being possessed with an appetite for rum, I only put the bottle to my mouth, and offered to return it; but my fellow-traveller refused to receive it until I had drank again. "And now, sir," said he, "I am an Irishman myself. I have lived in this country fourteen years. I married a fine girl here, and have five fine children. I tell you, sir, they are as likely children as any in the country; and this is allowed by all. I served my time in Dublin with a weaver. My father was a weaver; and indeed he thought no little of himself at that business: but one bloody day I bate him at weaving; at which the old man orthered me to fetch him a pail of wather, and he poor'd it on the ground. This he kept doing till I fatched forty pails of wather: then the old man took and gave me a bloody bating. At this I run off and 'listed for a soldier, and came into this country. But, sir, you look like one in distress. Are ye of this country?" My answer was in the negative, but told him I was from London. At this the Hibernian jumped towards me, seized me by the hand, and shook it in such a manner as to feel that he was in earnest. He observed that we were old neighbors; for London, said he, is but a short bit from Dublin.

After our mutually recognizing each other for old neighbors, he looked at me with an arch significance, and observed, that some misfortune he presumed had brought me to this country. I told him, it truly was so; that an unfortunate contest had rendered it necessary for me to leave the country. "O ho!" said he, "you fought a duel?" I assented. "By J——s," said he, "did you challenge him fair?" I did. He then seized my hand again, and declared he was satisfied that I was a good fellow. "And by the Immortal," said he, "you shall go home with me, and I will keep you a fortnight, and then will put a dollar into your hand. I am determined to fight a duel myself with a bloody rascal, who sold me a cow, and told me she was farrow, and all the time she had a calf in her; and you shall go and be my second."

[245]

You will readily conceive that this invitation did no way comport with my views and desire. I had recourse to a number of excuses to elude the force of it. The Hibernian was not willing to accept any apology I could make; and it was with difficulty I obtained my release from this knight of the bottle. However, after marching and countermarching some length of time he gave up the pursuit, and let me depart with the honors of war.

Thus I found it difficult to pass without great obstructions in my first essays upon the plan which I had studied with so much caution, and which I thought might be pursued without interruption. Sir, my best wishes wait on you.

CHAPTER XXV

"Bent on destruction, and in love with death!
Not all these luminaries, quench'd at once,
Were half so sad as one benighted mind,
Which gropes for happiness, and meets despair."

AFTER I had freed myself from my troublesome companion, I hastened on to Stonington Point, in order to find passage to Long Island. When I had arrived, I found the prospect of such a passage not very flattering; and therefore determined to go to New London, a town fourteen miles distant, where I was informed a packet ran regularly once a week. In the course of the next day I arrived at New London, where I immediately went on board a boat ready to sail for Long Island. Early the next morning we arrived at Sag Harbor, the only port of entry on this island.

I now supposed myself on ground where I should no longer be exposed to the cruel lash of the envenomed tongue of slander. I supposed myself in a situation convenient to begin my operations in order to establish myself in business. I passed here for an Englishman lately from London, forbearing to subjoin the word *new*. My name was demanded. I told them it was Stephen Edenson (my father's name being Eden). The people therefore called my name Edenson. I acquiesced in the name.

I began to inquire for a vacancy where a schoolmaster was wanted. I had not long made the inquiry, before I was accosted by a gentleman, who introduced himself to me by the name of Havens. I was informed by the landlord of the inn where I had put up, that the gentleman was Judge Havens of Shelter Island. After inquiring from whence I came, my education, my age, my objects, etc., he informed me that he lived on Shelter Island, about three miles from that place; that the island contained about thirty families; that they were destitute of a school, and wished to engage an instructor: "therefore," said he, "if you wish to accept the chance, I will use my influence in your

[247]

behalf on the island, that you may obtain the school. It will not be an object of any considerable consequence, only to give you a temporary standing among us, until you become acquainted with the ways and manners of the people of this country, and learn the objects which may offer for your attention."

I accepted the offer made by Judge Havens, and took passage with him in a boat going to the island. When I arrived, I found the island lying nearly in a circular form, containing, by estimation, about 8000 acres. On this island lived the number of families as mentioned before; among whom were three, by the names of Nichols, Dearing, and Havens, who were the chief proprietors of the island. There was a tavern kept by one Havens, in the middle of the island. He likewise kept a small store of goods in his house. This man possessing many singularities, which rendered him a person on whom the attention of strangers was naturally drawn, I think it necessary to give you some further description of him.

This publican was extremely fond of being in the secret of every man's business and circumstances, and not only so, but likewise to have it thought so by others. So strong was his desire for knowledge in all the minute circumstances which relate to any one, that, whenever a stranger entered his house, his first conversation would be directed to his name, circumstances, connections, etc. Should the stranger chance to carry a portmanteau with him, or a bundle of any kind whatever, he might lay his account to have it searched, even before his face. His thirst for conversation was insatiable. His tongue had almost become a perpetual motion, and what rendered this circumstance highly disagreeable was, that he was so deaf that one must halloo with great strength in order to make him hear any answers to his innumerable questions. He was fond of showing his sagacity by understanding half answers, and motions of the head and countenance. Hence he frequently obtained strange ideas of the occurrences of the times, etc. Notwithstanding this humorous side of the picture, the reverse was drawn with many virtues. He was a man of unshaken integrity in all matters in which he was concerned, either of a public or private nature; much attached to order and regularity as a member of society, rigidly just in all his dealings, and a constant promoter of the means of general information. Under these circumstances, many laughed at his

[248]

the island

foibles, and at the same time revered his virtues. Mr. Nichols was born to a state of affluence, and was happily connected with a most agreeable family. Col. Dearing was in possession of a large estate, encumbered with considerable debts, which, by a system of strict economy, he was annually decreasing. This man possessed good information respecting his domestic matters, beyond which his capacity did not extend. He was extremely haughty, and a presbyterian bigot.

I found the secluded situation of this island had a very decided influence upon the manners of its inhabitants. By not having that constant opportunity for intercourse with other parts of the world, they became extremely attached to their own peculiar manners and customs, to a degree of bigotry, which was very disagreeable to a stranger upon a first acquaintance. I found that want of ease and accessibility, of that candor and liberality, which so peculiarly characterizes a people of refinement. Notwithstanding, when these difficulties were once surmounted, I found them a people possessing many excellent qualities of heart.

effect of seclusion

The principles of economy were pretty well understood by the inhabitants of this island. Their soil was not so luxuriant as to preclude the necessity of economy. An acre of this ground would produce, upon an average, fifteen bushels of wheat, and twenty-four bushels of Indian corn. It afforded a moderate supply of grass for neat cattle; but the productions of a dairy, which might be made considerably profitable, were entirely neglected. Their improvements in agriculture did not appear to be making rapid advances towards perfection. Their situation was under most excellent privileges, as it related to marketing their produce, and obtaining their returns; it ever being convenient to send to New York by vessels from their own shores. Land on this island sold about eight dollars the acre.

no dairy

I obtained a school at the moderate price of six dollars per month, together with my boarding, washing and lodging. I entered upon this office with no very sanguine expectations of making a permanent establishment for myself and family. Yet it was a resting place from severer trials. I was retired from the world and sheltered from the storm, which had been so abundantly poured upon my devoted head. I was in a situation, I thought, too inconsiderable to raise the feelings of jealousy, or alarm the most selfish mind. Yet in this I labored un-

teacher's pay

[249]

der a mistaken apprehension. A son of the innkeeper, who had formerly taught a school on this island, was much mortified at my introduction into a place which he had once filled, and which he wished to occupy again. He considered me as a person of very little consequence, being poorly dressed, and was attentive to treat me accordingly. He frequently gave me invitations to assist him in the labors of the field at my leisure hours from school. He carried his politeness so far one afternoon, as to threaten to turn me out of the house, if I would not assist him in raking hay. But my tranquillity was not much injured by these circumstances, knowing this spark to be totally destitute of the power which he threatened to exercise; and otherwise too inconsiderable to affect my interest with the people.

My situation was such as to excite the greatest anxiety of the innkeeper to develope a character which appeared to be somewhat veiled in mystery. His assiduous attention to my concerns was marked with the most noticeable circumstances. He would often throw himself in my way, in order to assure me how much he felt interested in my welfare, and likewise of the unbounded confidence I might place in him, in any matters which might partake of the nature of difficulty or secrecy.

By half answers, innuendos and shrewd suggestions, the old man had obtained a most surprising idea of my history; and sorry am I to say it, too much was acted on my part, to communicate this unfounded system of ideas in his mind. These were secrets of too great magnitude for him to comprise in his own breast, without pain of the greatest kind; therefore, to ease his mind of the enormous load under which he groaned, he imparted his trust to many of his friends. However, they were not convinced that they had obtained all the circumstances which related to my life. They therefore entered into a plan to pursue the discovery; and accordingly agreed among themselves to persuade me to write to some of my acquaintance in England, or some of the British dominions; and Uncle Jim, as the innkeeper was called, was to send the letter, by the way of New York, immediately to the place of destination. Uncle Jim's deafness discovered to me the plot which was so ingeniously concerted, and the part which he was to maintain in it. Being apprised of the design of this jacobin club, I easily entered into the plan, and made it a scene of great amusement. I

A DISAGREEABLE SITUATION

wrote a long letter to the Right Honorable Lord George Montague, etc., etc.: I filled the body of the letter with high encomiums upon Uncle Jim and his family, more particularly his daughters. This was touching him upon a string which vibrated to the centre of his heart. His favorite object was the beauty of his daughters and the excellency of his family. The old gentleman was running over full of satisfaction upon the discovery of these mighty state secrets. He began to contemplate the probability of his becoming known to the first families in the British dominions, and of obtaining the whole budget of secrets relating to them; and likewise the office of an agent to transact their business.

These circumstances brought me into a situation somewhat disagreeable. I was reduced to a condition in which I was obliged, in some measure, to give countenance to those representations which I found had obtained among the people at large. The fact was, that for my own diversion, I had given rise to those ridiculous ideas which had taken such deep root in the minds of those who were concerned in the *letter plot,* that I found no small degree of danger in receding from the ground which I had first taken.

As I became more acquainted with the people on this island, I found their curiosity more exercised in penetrating the secrets of my pretended history. Their continued questions on this subject growing more and more irksome, I found, that by my own imprudence, I had involved myself in a disagreeable and ridiculous situation.

About this time I became acquainted with a man called Doctor Havens, possessing this appellation by courtesy, rather than by merit in the science of medicine. He put two of his children under my care as an instructor. As his character will appear several times in the course of this narrative, it will be necessary to give you some general sketch of this man, previous to my proceeding to particulars in which he was concerned. As I have hinted, this man was very ignorant; of a mind, by nature, sordid and clownish in the extreme; possessing no feelings of delicacy or propriety; yet very ambitious of introducing his family into the high and more refined circles of life. Being governed by no principle, he ever used such means as came in his way, to further his objects, without any reference to their quality or merit. He would appear generous and hospitable to such characters as he

[251]

thought would promote his interests, or further his objects; but to others he appeared in the native hue of selfish penury.

You will readily conclude that a man of this cast would not be idle under circumstances of such a kind as those in which I was involved. Often I had invitations of the warmest kind to make his house my home. When I made him visits, I was treated with a degree of hospitality truly grateful. I often found him indirectly hinting that my present situation of apparent poverty did not preclude my attention and success among the ladies who were standing in the market for marriage (by the way, the Doctor had two daughters in that predicament), and of introducing myself into business, by which I could maintain a family, and support a reputation of credit among the people; observing with great sagacity, how different matters of such a nature were in this country from what they were in England. He gave me an invitation of commencing business in partnership with one of his sons, in the mercantile line; observing that, could I raise 500l. by the help of my friends, he would let one of his sons carry on the business for me for half the profits; intimating that such an offer was generous on his side, as the weight of the business would lie upon his son, until I should become acquainted with the mode of doing business in America. I found to my surprise, the most pointed enmity existing between this man and his only brother, who was his nearest neighbor, and also between the two families. I was by no means backward in manifesting my astonishment upon the occasion; but by the representation of the Doctor and his family, was given to understand that his brother Constant was, of all the various works of nature, the worst, the most unnatural and inhuman. This reason quieted my astonishment, but did not satisfy my feelings. Finally, the clownish bluntness of the old Doctor served to cover many vices of the mind, which would have been suspected sooner in one possessed of politer manners.

This man was as avaricious for information into the subject of secret history as his namesake, the innkeeper; but their motives for obtaining this information were very different. The one sought it for the gratification of internal feelings; the other for the opportunity of turning such a circumstance to his advantage in adding to his property, or promoting the advancement of his family. The Doctor had no embarrassment of delicacy to surmount: he came immediately to

[252]

the point, and insisted, *sans ceremonie*, to be initiated into the whole system of secrecy. He was not to be turned off by a polite evasion, or an intimation that the matters, into which he inquired, were not to be divulged. His professions of friendship were unbounded; his assiduities of attention were innumerable, and his feelings really appeared to be interested in my behalf. He gained my confidence so far, as fully to believe that his professions were sincere, notwithstanding many intimations from others relating to his general character. Yet I never esteemed him as a confidential friend, owing to his want of abilities more than uprightness, in my view.

[margin note: Confidence in Dr.'s intentions]

Judge Havens was another character who made his appearance upon the stage of action at this time; but performed a very different part from the others who have been already mentioned. He was a man of science, and by no means affected with the mania of discovering secrets. A close application to study had produced in him a habit of appearing absent in company, unless the subject of conversation turned upon some branch of science; then he became animated and instructive.

[margin note: About Havens]

He lived somewhat secluded from common access, owing to his continual perseverance in the pursuit of science. His genius was not brilliant; but his unabating industry supplied the defect. He thought with metaphysical accuracy upon every subject which he undertook to investigate; which often produced too great a degree of refinement in his theories for the convenience of practice. He was a man of delicate feelings, though not so suddenly moved as many others of a more volatile constitution. His integrity as a public character was inviolate. As a private companion, he was pleasing and agreeable; and, as a member of society, he was useful and beneficial.

This was the pleasing side of the portrait. The reverse was not greatly darkened. His temper partook somewhat of the obstinate. He was ambitious of popularity, and somewhat timid in pursuing those measures which might render him unpopular, however justice might call for them. In some of his transactions in the field of love, his moral rectitude had been censured by the inhabitants of the vicinity; and as that was a subject of too much delicacy for me to introduce to him, I never heard his observations upon it, and therefore had but a partial idea of the matter.

Thus stood the principal characters with whom I was immediately concerned as an instructor for their children. I pursued the business with close application; and, as I flattered myself, with a degree of reputation. I had not continued long in this situation, before my kind entertainer, Uncle Jim, introduced the idea of my writing for the periodical publications of the press. This subject did not find an agreeable place in my mind. I was a stranger in the place; ignorant of the prevalent ideas of the country, their political and moral character. Moreover (strange as it may seem from my conduct), I wished to remain as little known in this place as possible, and therefore declined the proposal. Yet I found the old gentleman so tenaciously attached to the plan, that I was quite surprised; however, from the drift of his discourse upon the subject, I had concluded that his idea was, to appear himself as the author of the business, proposing to copy the pieces in his own handwriting, previous to their going to the press, and to have the matter known only between him and me. The old gentleman, on this occasion, not only professed a great disposition for secrecy on his part, but also enjoined the like on me, in the most pointed and earnest manner.

Under this view of the matter, I consented to his proposal. I began my literary task under the name of the Philanthropist. I had proceeded as far as the fourth or fifth number, before anything of note took place in consequence of these publications, excepting the pleasure which Uncle Jim apparently enjoyed in transacting the business, under the veil of secrecy. At length, a clergyman of Southampton, taking the alarm at some sentiments here manifested, published a very spirited answer to them. A reply on my part was then unavoidable. The clergyman answered my reply, and I rejoined to his answer. By this time the attention of the public was excited to the controversy, more than to the merit of the publications; and they were of course anxious to know the combatants. It was known at the printing office, that Uncle Jim uniformly brought the Philanthropist for publication; and also that the manuscripts were ever in his handwriting. These circumstances turned the eyes of the public upon him; and he possessed the fortitude, for some time, to retain the secret; but at length it became a burden too heavy for him to support alone. Therefore he imparted it to some of his intimate friends, who compassionately re-

[254]

lieved him from the cumber, by dissolving the charm of secrecy, and giving the matter to the public.

I now found a retreat the only place of safety; and therefore withdrew my lucubrations from the press; and here ended the matter, as it related to me in the character of the Philanthropist. But I had, by this time, excited the attention of the public, and every one was ready to make his own comments upon a character so new; having, by direct and indirect means, given myself a character very novel; and my intimate friends had highly embellished the superstructure which my fancy had reared. There were almost as many different opinions concerning me as there were persons to form them. But none of the various conjectures happened to light on the identical character which I had sustained in reality, though the publications from Worcester relating to my confinement, trial, and escape were among this people.

didn't really man him

I found no prospect of making an establishment for my family on this island, the encouragement for instructing was so small; and as that was an object of the utmost consequence to me, I turned my attention to some other place. I made application for a berth, when my time should expire on Shelter Island, at a number of places; and at length found an opening in a parish called Bridghampton, a part of Southampton, on Long Island. At this place I engaged to teach a school at the price of twelve dollars per month, without the privilege of board or any of its appendages. I engaged to begin this school in two weeks after the time of my teaching the other should expire, which time of intermission I had determined to appropriate to the purpose of revisiting my family, and learning the operation of things since I had left them. As this time approached, my anxiety to put my intended visit into execution increased to such a degree as to deprive me of sleep.

I lived, at this time, in the family of Judge Havens. I endeavored to enter into his character and disposition; and to penetrate the governing principles by which he was actuated. After I had satisfied my mind upon these heads, I determined to lay open to his view the whole of my situation, and consult him upon that line of conduct which he should think advisable, in order to answer the object which lay so near my heart. I had fixed upon the time, in my own mind, to unfold

[255]

this circumstance. I came prepared from school at the intended time to put in force this resolution. But while I walked leisurely from the schoolhouse to my lodgings, which was about one hundred rods, it occurred to my mind into what a disagreeable situation I had once been involved by communicating such a secret; how possible, and even how probable it was I might be deceived in my expectations from Judge Havens, notwithstanding my favorable predictions towards him; how often I had been egregiously deceived by the conduct of certain characters when the prospects of life were changed; how he must be surprised at coming to the knowledge of real facts relating to me. Under this view of the matter, I shrunk back from the scene, and durst not proceed. I concluded still to let matters of this kind lie in a state of secrecy, until I had been back to Charlton, and learned the feelings and sentiments of mankind concerning me.

My time of engagement was almost expired. I soon expected to recross the Sound, and measure back my former steps to Charlton. This last part of my time seemed to move with leaden feet. I had not heard from my family, connections, or acquaintance, since I left them. I had not written to them, nor had I dared to inquire after them, or any of the inhabitants living in that part of the world. Therefore my desire to see them was beyond the power of language to express. At this moment, when my wishes were almost gratified; when the object of my most earnest desire was almost within my power, I was suddenly taken sick with the remitting fever.

This stroke was too much for my utmost fortitude to endure. I sunk under it. I felt the weakness of a child. It struck me in a part which I was not prepared to defend. I could not bear the thought of submitting to a fit of sickness at the present juncture; but sad necessity taught me that I must endure what I could not avert. My fond prospects were blasted; the painted vision of enjoyment fled from my view. The little money which I had, with so much perseverance, scraped together for my small excursion into the country, was likely to be all swallowed up by the expenses of sickness, which must eventually preclude the possibility of my returning to my family. These circumstances, which foreboded the most dismal prospects, left but little consolation to my feelings. The fever and melancholy made rapid havoc of my constitution.

GIVING NATURE HER WAY

Under these circumstances, Doctor Havens made me the offer of quarters and attendance at his house, until my recovery. I accepted his offer, and was removed to his house accordingly. As I had ever been averse to loading the stomach with medicine in cases of sickness, I now pursued the same course, and invariably adhered to my old maxim, of "giving nature her way," until the ninth day, when, by the help of a generous constitution, the fever formed a crisis, nature predominated, and the disorder abated. Doctor Havens was willing to give himself airs of consequence from this speedy decision in my favor, although he had only given me two potions of the cortex Peru, and that after the fever had abated. I was so far recovered as to set out on my intended journey on the twelfth day of my sickness, much against the advice of Doctor Havens. Before my departure, I called upon the Doctor for my bill for board, attendance, etc.; his answer was to the following effect (viz.), that as twenty shillings was due to me from him for schooling his children, and as he expected to send them to me again, at Bridghampton, and to receive special attention to them at all leisure hours, he would rest the discharge of my bill upon that ground. I acquiesced with his proposal, under an apprehension of his having his full due; the price of boarding, washing and lodging being eight shillings per week; and as I was at the Doctor's two weeks only, and my situation such as not to cause a great degree of special trouble, I considered the addition of eight shillings more per week to be a full compensation for my receipts. Therefore, as his bill under this settlement would amount to thirty-two shillings, there would remain a balance of twelve shillings in his favor, which he expected, and did receive by my extra attention to his children afterwards.

I was somewhat disappointed when I called upon the Doctor for a settlement. By the course of his conversation, when I came to his house, he clearly intimated that he would make me welcome to the favor. And moreover, his abundant professions of friendly attention were sufficient to induce me to expect that he would not demand pay for my boarding, etc.; considering my peculiar situation (he being a man himself in easy circumstances), and the particular and pointed declarations of friendly assistance which he had made, almost at every time I had seen him during my residence on the island. However, I esteemed his demand no more than strictly just, and considered his

[257]

calculations to befriend me, operating in some other channel, to which I had not yet been introduced.

The time had now expired in which I was to begin my school at Bridghampton. However, I could not reconcile my mind to the idea of relinquishing my visit to my family; and accordingly sent on word that sickness had disenabled me from opening my school so soon, by a fortnight, as my engagement had specified. Under these circumstances I entered on board the boat to recross the Sound to New London, having given the people to understand that I had heard of a certain *friend* of mine being somewhere in the state of Massachusetts, to whom it was very necessary for me to make a visit.

I was entrusted with some letters to a gentleman in New London; and immediately after my arrival in the city, it being five o'clock, P. M. the same day, I set about discharging the trust by delivering the letters. When I arrived in New London, I felt fearful of being known, and wished to be seen as little as possible.

The reason of this desire was of the following nature, viz. being in doubt of the operation which a knowledge of my real character would have upon the feelings of the people where I had engaged to teach a school; and likewise ignorant of the representations the public would make on that head; I did not wish yet to put the matter to a trial, until I should have further opportunity to establish myself in the place. There were people with me from Long Island, and therefore should I be recognized by any in New London, it would develop the business immediately to those who were with me, and the knowledge of this matter would reach Bridghampton previous to my return.

Thus stood matters in New London. I had determined to deliver the letters and immediately leave the town. I accordingly set out for the house of General Huntington, the gentleman to whom the letters were directed, in company with one of those who came with me from Long Island. This companion I wished handsomely to drop, but found myself unable. As I was walking through the street, I observed a number of gentlemen standing together, and observing me with attention. I immediately concluded that I was discovered and known. However, I walked by without appearing to notice them; when I heard one of them uttering with an emphasis, "By G——d, it is Burroughs!" This satisfied me as to the truth of my first conjecture. I wished, more

[258]

and more, my companion gone; but to no purpose: he still remained with me in spite of all my efforts to the contrary.

I found that those who had observed me with so much attention, were following after me, and continued at but a short distance, until I came to the house of General Huntington. When I went into this house, they made a stand in the street before the door, until I came out; when they immediately came up to me, and, in the language of friendship, inquired after my health. I was agreeably surprised to find two of my college classmates among the number, who were practising attorneys, attending the Supreme Court sitting in New London.

When they accosted me by my name, I gave them to understand they were mistaken. The greater part understood the reply, and went away as though satisfied with being convinced of their mistake; yet one, by the name of Bulkley, one of the before-mentioned college classmates, remained firm to his integrity, and declared that he *knew* it to be me; "that he thought it to be me before he heard me speak; but since then was entirely certain." At this moment, there was passing by a man by the name of Hyde, a new made Justice of the Peace, belonging to Norwich, who being led into the subject by Bulkley, manifested an ardent desire of convincing the world how prompt he was in the execution of his peace-office. He called for assistance, laid hold of me by their help, and conveyed me to the Attorney-General, Mr. Coit. My companion from Long Island was terrified at seeing all this; and learning nothing more than that I had changed my name, he came up to me with a woeful aspect on his countenance, and said, "A'nt you sorry you changed your name?"

The others who had first accosted me, and more particularly, William Hart, my college acquaintance, concluding where Hyde and his gang were conveying me, hastened to the Attorney-General before we arrived, in time sufficient to give him a just statement of the matter. When we arrived at the house of Mr. Coit, I found a large gathering already there. I had now given myself over as lost. I concluded that my detention and reconveyance back to Worcester, were quite certain. The extreme state of weakness to which I was reduced by sickness rendered the prospect of escape hopeless. I saw the rigor of my confinement increased, and the severity of my punishment by no means diminished. I saw another series of cruel sufferings before me, of which I could not even conjecture an end. Hyde exulted much in the part he had acted, concluding, as I readily understood, from his conversation, that he had done himself immortal honor. He took the utmost pains to exhibit me to the view of the surrounding spectators as a monster of iniquity, and as a devil incarnate, in order to enhance his own merit in the act of confining me from society. He told many anecdotes relating to me; of my stealing horses, committing rapes, etc., etc. With all, he wound up, with an anecdote of his own experience. "When I was riding through the state of New Hampshire, some years since," said Hyde, "I saw a man standing in his door at Charlestown, who took me to be Burroughs.[1] I was on a very fine horse, and the man called out to me, Burroughs, where did you get that horse? I made no answer, but rode on; when the man called again, Damn you Burroughs, if you do not stop, I will stop you! But continuing still to ride on, the man ran after me, and overtook me; when I turned about, and demanded what he wanted. The man, by this, discovering his mistake, begged my pardon, observing, I thought it was one Burroughs, a great horse thief; and I have no notion of being stopped as I ride the country on such a fellow's account."

After Hyde had ended his harrangue, the Attorney-General demanded if my name was Burroughs. I told him it was. He enquired further if I had been confined in Worcester jail, and from thence had made my escape. My answer was in the affirmative. He then demanded where I had been since; what doing, where going, etc. To which I gave him a simple statement of the truth. He then made a reply which will leave a grateful monument of esteem in my mind, so long as his name is retained in my powers of recollection. "Mr. Burroughs, we in Connecticut feel ourselves interested in the fate of every man, and wish him to be happy in promoting his own good, combined with that of society; and where we find him making that his object, we wish to assist him forward, rather than throw any obstacle in his pursuit. As this appears to have been your object for the summer past, and as you are still inclined to pursue it, it is my duty to encourage such a pursuit, and not hinder it; therefore you may consider yourself at liberty to depart. I have heard your history. I have been made

[1] Esquire Hyde was about 5 feet 8 inches high.

acquainted with your trials at Worcester. I have wished, and still wish you a happier lot."

At this instant I felt the weight of a mountain removed from my mind. All the horrid prospects of confinement, punishment, etc., immediately vanished. The sunshine of hope burst with full splendor upon my soul, and filled me with so great a measure of joy, that, in my debilitated situation, it almost overpowered my strength; and, with difficulty, I prevented myself from fainting. Indeed, sir, it was a state of enjoyment so great as to render it truly painful. The prospect flashed on my mind the idea of again enjoying my family, connections and society; and the possibility of maintaining them, by my industry, without danger of being interrupted.

I returned to Mr. Coit my warmest acknowledgments of gratitude for his humanity. Yet my tongue did not utter the thousandth part of what my heart dictated. I was overcome. A universal tremor shook my frame; and I was glad of a moment's ease by retiring, and hiding my feelings in my own bosom. When I had left Mr. Coit, and arrived at the Coffee-house for lodgings over night, I found there my Long Island companion, who, finding me liberated from confinement, began to think that changing one's name was not so flagrant a violation of the laws of Connecticut as he had, at first, apprehended. I stated to him my desire that he would not, on his return, make any mention of the occurrence, or that he knew anything relating to my possessing another name. He promised a compliance, and much to my surprise, kept the secret inviolate.

Early next morning, I went on board a packet boat going up the river, as far as the little city of Norwich, fourteen miles directly on my way to Charlton, where we arrived about noon. After our arrival, I immediately set out on foot, and reached fourteen miles further that afternoon. I put up at a house where the people were strangers, as I then conceived, in the town of Canterbury. During the course of the evening, by some conversation that passed in the family, I began to conjecture that I was in the house of an old acquaintance of my father. Previous to my retiring to bed, the man of the house came home, who was before absent; and I readily recognized the countenance of Doctor Knight, although I had not seen him since I was of the age of seven, being about the space of twenty years.

[261]

The Doctor conducted me to the bed where I was to sleep, and I embraced that opportunity to discover myself to him, hoping to gain some intelligence which might be of consequence, either relating to my family, or the public opinion, and measures which had been taken since I left the country. I was, however, unsuccessful in my object, not gaining any intelligence upon either of those points. I arose early next morning, and departed, after being made welcome, by the Doctor, to my lodging.

I found a fever perpetually hanging about me, and the worry of travelling constantly increasing it. But my feelings were so much interested in pursuing my journey, that my judgment had lost its force; and I travelled with an unabating diligence, until midnight, when, to my no small satisfaction, I arrived to the abode of my family. This scene I shall never presume to describe. Your own fruitful imagination will do more justice to the subject than is possible for the power of language to perform.

I tarried here two days, and found my health constantly declining. I began to grow alarmed, under an apprehension that I might have a severe confinement by sickness in this place, and by that means, be discovered, and committed to Worcester jail. Therefore I procured a friend to carry me on horseback, into the state of Connecticut, where we arrived about midnight, at the house of a distant relation in the town of Thompson. Here I tarried until the close of the next evening, and then began my journey again on foot. However, I found my weakness so great, I could not proceed more than two miles that night. I stopped at a house about 9 o'clock in the evening, and went to bed immediately; but found little rest through the night. A fit of the fever and ague came on me; and after that the sweat poured from every part of my body in the most copious effusion. In the morning I was scarcely able to rise from my bed. However, I dressed myself, and after procuring horses, I again set off for Plainfield, about twelve miles distant, in order to take the stage from thence to Norwich. I arrived here about noon, but so very weak that I was under the necessity of going immediately to bed. Indeed my disorder began to increase so rapidly, that I pretty much despaired of returning to Long Island for the present, and concluded that I must be confined by a fit of sickness. A fit of the fever and ague came on me again, and after that the copi-

[262]

ous discharge of sweat. I felt more at ease when the sweat had ceased, but by no means strengthened. However, I determined to set forward again at the arrival of the stage.

About 4 o'clock in the afternoon I took a seat in the stage, and set off for Norwich. I found in the stage a gentleman of the law from Boston, travelling to the west. After some introductory conversation, I was satisfied that I was not recognized by him, although we had formerly known each other. After I was satisfied in this respect, I gradually introduced, as though by accident, the topic of conversation which lay near my heart (viz.) the singular trial of one Burroughs, at the sitting of the Supreme Court at Worcester in their April term. I manifested some surprise at the conducting this trial by the court, if I had been rightly informed into the matter. He allowed my information to be correct, but defended their conduct by the singularity of the character they had to deal with. His ideas upon that subject were of the following nature, viz.

"This Burroughs was, of all characters you ever heard mention made, the most singular. He has led a course of the most barefaced and horrid crimes of any man living, even from his childhood, to such a degree, that his own father has desired the courts to show him no favor, and wishes, for the good of society, to have him confined perpetually, as the only possible means to prevent that course of horrid transgressions which he has perpetrated ever since he has been capable of acting. After an innumerable train of instances in which he was guilty of stealing, counterfeiting, robbing, adultery, etc., etc., he was apprehended and sent on to the Castle. In this situation, as though confinement had made him tenfold worse than formerly, he often threw the whole garrison into a state of alarm; burnt the buildings; wounded the soldiers, some, it was supposed mortally; and finally made his escape. After his escape, no property was secure from his grasp; no virtue was proof against his wiles, even to such a measure that he became a general nuisance to society; and the country arose in its own defence and confined him in jail.

"Such a character you will not wonder was very obnoxious to the court, and they found it necessary to take the most decided measures to bring him to justice; for even under this load of infamy, he had planned his matters with that address and dexterity, by means of the

[263]

testimony of his accomplices, that, with the utmost difficulty, the court obtained his condemnation. After that they determined to lay a sentence upon him that should keep him confined for a long time; but in vain. He soon made his escape, and is now acting the same scenes of excess over again. Finally, you cannot enter into the merits of this trial, so as to understand it thoroughly, unless you should become really acquainted with the villain; then you would be sensible that too great exertions could not be made against him."

The carriage at this moment broke down; and all the passengers were under a necessity of halting, until another was brought to take them up. Under this situation, William Hart, Esq. came riding up, and saluted me by the name of "Burroughs." Aghast and astonished, the poor lawyer rolled his eyeballs in wild dismay. The apparition of Macbeth's Ghost would not have been so terrible to this son of the long robe, as the sight of that identical man, whose picture he had so pleasingly drawn. "He believed he could walk to Norwich much easier than wait for the carriage." He made his obeisance to the company, and marched off. As low as my spirits had been reduced by the gloomy prospects presented by my increasing sickness, I felt them exhilarated by this curious circumstance. I laughed aloud, which conveyed the sensations of my heart to this knight of romance; but he did not tarry for any further explanation. He pursued his course with diligence, and was soon out of sight.

We were directly reseated in another carriage, and drove on with speed; but did not overtake our lawyer. He had either stopped by the way, or made greater progress on foot than is common for men who are not impelled by extraordinary motives.

The stage set me down at Norwich Landing, and continued its route to the town. This night I found the fits of fever and ague increasing, and my strength continually abating. The next morning it was with difficulty I reached the boat bound to New London, where we arrived about two o'clock, P. M. I here found that I could not proceed any further, but must submit to the force of sickness, and lie by until I should be better able to move.

CHAPTER XXVI

I WILL here leave the course of my journey, and go back a little, to take notice of some circumstances necessary to be noted in order for you to entertain a clear idea of my present prospects, and future hopes. As the object of making provision for my family was the prevailing wish of my heart, I had flattered myself that the salary which I should receive for the school would be sufficient, with close economy, to support us, in some small state of comfort. Under this view I had proposed the plan of moving my family to Long Island; but, previous to such a measure, my wife's father had agreed to make me a visit, to view my prospects, and then determine whether prudence would allow of such an attempt. As the money which I was to receive for the school was the only dependence which I had, I felt not very sanguine in my hopes at this time, because, as long as I should remain sick and unable to teach the school, I was earning no money; and was, moreover, involving myself in debts which must be discharged with the first money I could raise from my labors. My sickness would probably prevent my keeping the school where I had engaged, as the proprietors wished to have it opened, at furthest, by that time, and I had presumed already to overrun it by a fortnight.

I was confined, by sickness, about a week in New London, before I found myself recruited in any measure. As I felt extremely anxious to gain intelligence relating to the school in Bridghampton, a matter on which much depended in my then present situation, I once more attempted to cross the Sound. I found the motion of the boat very irksome; and before I had reached the Long Island side, I was again attacked with a severe visit of the fever and ague, attended with the most violent effusions of sweat immediately succeeding. After I had again arrived at Sag Harbor, I betook myself to bed, and after the space of five or six hours found myself so far recruited as to be able to ride to Bridghampton. When I arrived at this place, I found they

[265]

had engaged another instructor despairing of my return, and he had appointed the day for opening the school.

This circumstance was a matter of great disappointment, inasmuch as I could not proceed further for want of money or health. I represented my situation of distress to the person, Johnson by name, who had engaged the school, with some hope that he would relinquish his appointment, and look for another situation; but all to no purpose. He remained steadfast in his resolution, and all entreaties were ineffectual. I now concluded my labors were at an end; that I had nothing left but to wait patiently the time of my exit from these continued scenes of woe.

> "Nor dreadful transition; though the mind,
> An artist at creating self-alarms,
> Rich in expedients for inquietude,
> Is prone to paint it dreadful. Who can take
> Death's portrait true? The tyrant never sat.
> Our sketch all random strokes, conjecture all;
> Close shuts the grave, nor tells one single tale.
> Death, and his image, rising in the brain,
> Bear faint resemblance; never are alike;
> Fear shocks the pencil; fancy loves excess;
> Dark ignorance is lavish of her shades;
> And these the formidable picture draw."

In this situation I lay two days, unable to rise from my bed. I found the people in this place desirous of my instructing their school, if they could by any means get rid of their engagement with Johnson. They had formed a favorable idea of my performance in that line by the character I had sustained in that capacity on Shelter Island. the place being only five miles distant, and Johnson being a total stranger in the country. Therefore the people of this district sent to another part of the town, who were destitute, and wanted a schoolmaster, informing them that one was to be had by applying immediately, and mentioned Johnson as the person. It was likewise mentioned to him that application would be made from another part of the town, where the presumption was much stronger in his favor for high wages, etc. Johnson eagerly swallowed this bait, and accepted the invitation immediately after it was given. The committee who were appointed for this purpose, learning, however, that there was another person present, who

[266]

was a candidate for a schoolmaster, and who they found, was to teach the school in the middle district, provided they could get Johnson off their hands, began to query about the propriety of having the choice themselves rather than the middle district, seeing Johnson was already engaged. This motion, I found, by no means comporting with the feelings of Johnson, or the people of the middle district. He wished to take the western school, and the people of the middle district wished the same. This produced a warm altercation between the two committees; but they finally agreed upon me as the person to decide the contest; and I chose to abide where I was. This accordingly settled the dispute. What influenced my choice was, the solicitation of Johnson, who was now as anxious to leave this situation, as I was the day before to have him.

In a few days, I was so far recovered as to begin my school. My health, however, was so low as obliged me frequently to lay it by, sometimes for the space of half a day, and sometimes for a whole day. As this was a stage upon which some of the most surprising transactions were performed of any I have met with, it will be necessary to give you an idea of the leading characters.

And I will begin with a person that will appear most frequently, and who performed the most conspicuous part in those matters particularly relating to me, viz. Rev. Aaron Woolworth. He was a clergyman, settled in the ministerial office at Bridghampton, and who resided near me, during my continuance in this place. This man was about the age of eight and twenty; had been the preacher to this people about six years; had a wife and three children. His wife was the daughter of the aged and venerable Doctor Buel, minister of East Hampton, a town adjoining; and was, like her father, a person of a good natural disposition, although possessing moderate abilities. Mr. Woolworth was of small stature, diminutive in his appearance, his features somewhat irregular, but his countenance displaying a great share of vivacity and spirit. His voice in conversation and in preaching was harsh and unharmonious. His gestures and deportment, at first view, were somewhat awkward and clumsy; but beyond this veil was soon discovered a pleasing companion, and interesting associate. His genius was brilliant: his mind was active and full of enterprise. As a reasoner, he was close and metaphysical, but as a declaimer, he was bungling and

[267]

weak. His passion for an unlimited influence over the minds of his parishioners was so great, that every other feeling fell a sacrifice to it. Any circumstance that obstructed this favorite motive he sought to remove, be the consequences what they might. He was impatient of contradiction, and easily irritated. He had a thirst for associating with such characters as were rich, or who even made a splendid appearance; hence his intimate associates were the following characters, viz. Deacon Hedges, a man of extensive property, of small abilities, either natural or acquired; the whole of his information being comprised in his own circle of property. This man was avaricious in the extreme, sordid and clownish. Yet no man made more flaming pretensions to the exercises of religion than he. He ever took the lead in public worship in the absence of the clergyman. One would draw the idea from his prayers, that he really was but a sojourner in this world, seeking for another and better country; and that he viewed all things in it as dross and dung. Yet to see the same man, on another day, one would be led to conclude that this world was his god, and its goods his inheritance. I will relate one or two anecdotes concerning this man, and pass from the disagreeable picture.

At a certain time, a man from New York had bargained for all the cheese belonging to Deacon Hedges, at the price of six pence the pound, and had paid him some earnest money, but had not taken the cheese away. A few days after, another man, on the same business, called on the Deacon, and offered him seven pence per pound. The Deacon seemed somewhat embarrassed, and to hesitate; but finally told the man that his cheese was all engaged. Upon which the man was retiring, but the Deacon observed, before he had left the house, that it was possible Mrs. Hedges might have some cheese for sale. The man stopped, and the Deacon went into another room, where he remained some time; and at length Mrs. Hedges made her appearance, and sold three thousand weight of cheese for seven pence per pound; and when the other man called for his cheese, the Deacon had but two hundred and fifty weight that he could possibly spare.

At a certain time the Deacon was sick, and apparently nigh unto death. Under this situation he was visited by a Jew, who bore him no very great affection; and was asked whether he felt himself willing to submit to the stroke of death. To which the Deacon very readily answered in the affirmative. "Vel, vel," said the Jew, "you be one very remarkable man. You be villing to die yourself, and all your neighbors be villing you should."

Judge Hurlbut occupied the second place in Mr. Woolworth's esteem. This man likewise was a person of very moderate abilities, full of religious professions, but not so careful to commend himself to the consciences of others for his honesty, as many who make no cloak of religion to cover a base heart.

Sometimes in the course of last war, he was appointed an agent for the crew of a privateer sailing out of New London, to sell the prizes, divide the money, etc. This circumstance placed property in his hands to considerable amount. At the close of the war, he left New London, came to Long Island, purchased a farm, erected handsome buildings, and lived in a state of splendor for a while. But after I had lived on the island for the space of two years, the owners of the privateer began to lay claim to the property he had made use of, belonging to them; and he was obliged to relinquish his farm, buildings, etc., and retire into obscurity, to support himself by the exercise of his trade, being educated a saddler. With all this he did not by any means discharge his debts.

Capt. Post was the third man who made his appearance in this group. He had commanded a privateer during the war; but had not been very successful in his enterprises, owing to an extraordinary degree of caution not to be drawn into an ambuscade by any vessel he might chance to spy during his cruising. Towards his own men he was courageous in the extreme, if tyranny and barbarity are marks of courage. Towards the enemy his heroism was not so clearly established, owing to his great caution not to be thrown into the way of its being put to the trial. However, some small prizes fell into his hands; and it was currently reported that, at least, his own share of these prizes came to his possession, besides some small *donations* from the private property of the officers who fell under his power.

At the close of the war, he found himself able to purchase, in company with two others, a brig of about 150 tons burden, in which he followed the West India trade. It happened surprisingly, that in every voyage, he involved his owners in debt, but grew rich himself. This scene continued until one, more wary than the other, gave up the use of his part of the brig, and refused to assist in fitting her out any more. Notwithstanding, the other owner continued his aid, until he became bankrupt; and Capt. Post yet remained possessed of a considerable farm, and the most elegant buildings of any in the country. The brig was then sold, and the avails divided among the several owners. Capt. Post descended from parentage extremely low and poor; accordingly his education was rough and uncouth. Yet he possessed a strong desire to be thought a man of information and importance. This frequently led him to tell large, pompous stories, of which himself was ever the hero. He was a great swaggerer over those whom he found calculated to bear it; but to others he was supple, cringing, and mean. A man using the most rough, uncouth, and blasphemous language before those whose good opinion he did not wish to retain.

Surprising as it may seem, these three were the most intimate companions with whom Mr. Woolworth perpetually associated; which you will consider as being no very strong mark of his prudence, let his taste be ever so vitiated, or assimilated to such company. Having completed the picture of the four principal characters, it will be only necessary to give a slight sketch of a few others.

Doctor Rose, who kept a house of entertainment, was better fitted, by nature and acquirement, for a printer, than either for a physician or tavern keeper; being the best calculated to gather and distribute *news* of any man I ever knew. He was a man of very superficial abilities in his professional character; a professed friend to every one, but sincere to none; versatile and unstable in his disposition, and a libertine in practice.

Elias Halsey, one amongst many of the same name, was a person descended from a family in moderate circumstances, who pursued a system of industry and economy, thereby obtaining a comfortable support. His education was not great; and his opportunities for learning men and manners were small: notwithstanding which, he had a genius which was brilliant, and a great thirst for information. He was a person of keen feelings, hasty passions, and a good heart. The turbulence of his passions often led him astray in the exercise of his goodness. He failed in system, and of course, was not always stable.

Deacon Cook was the leading character of a small society in this place, denominated Separates. Between these two societies there was the greatest animosity; and as Deacon Cook was the principal member of the Separates, the other party blackened his character with the vilest epithets that language could utter. He was an old gentleman, treading hard upon eighty. Time had brightened his locks with pure silver; but his age was no protection from the tongue of slander. As the line of his conduct which was open to my view, gave me a far different idea of his character, so the facts to be related hereafter will form data for your opinion in relation to the same matter.

The character of the people in this place was of the following description, viz. uniform, contracted, and uninformed. Economy was practised here, upon the closest system, by far, of any with which I was ever acquainted. Necessity, in a measure, produced this effect. The people were so extremely attached to their own modes and customs, that it produced a fondness for their own society and disrelish to other customs, beyond parallel; hence emigration from their internal population was less frequent here, than in places elsewhere. Therefore the country had become populous, and the soil so exhausted as not to be luxuriant. The land was generally divided into small parcels amongst the proprietors, from forty to ten acres. Under these circumstances, rather than emigrate into those parts where land was in greater plenty, they contented themselves with living close, poor, and careful. Notwithstanding, they were a people under thriving circumstances, every one living within his income, be it ever so small; and their poor-tax was the smallest, for so populous a place, of any on the continent. Could useful manufactories be introduced, and three quarters of the inhabitants turn their attention to them, retaining their industry and economy, I do not know the place where they could be made more profitable, as labor and provisions are extremely cheap for cash. The means for acquiring property here are few, and very simple; no mechanical branches being pursued, but barely to answer the necessities of the inhabitants, such as shoe-making, tailoring, and blacksmithing; all other pursuits being common hand labor.

This people are at the lowest ebb in their improvements, either in agriculture, manufacture, or domestic economy. They are the genuine picture of ancient times, when their land was first settled by its white inhabitants. These effects are produced, in a great degree, by their insular situation.

Among these people I was about beginning my career again upon the active stage of life; and to establish a line of business which should render me a support for myself and family. I accordingly commenced my operations under such circumstances as will better appear to you from what I have related, than by what I can, by any other means, describe. I had not, at best, any glaring prospect of accumulating an independent property.

After I had pursued the business of instructing this school about three weeks, my wife's father, according to agreement, came to Bridghampton. My school at this time was crowded with scholars, and the prospects were fair; yet my name and character were veiled in secrecy, and what would be the event of the disclosure of this matter was still a doubt; and to remove my family to Bridghampton must, in its natural effect, finally reveal it. Therefore it was thought best for my father-in-law to lay open this circumstance, together with my general history, to the people, in order to see its operation, previous to my family's coming to me. Accordingly we pitched upon Mr. Woolworth as a proper person to whom we should unfold this matter, and consult him further what was to be done.

We accordingly waited on Mr. Woolworth, to whom I introduced my father, and left them together. I tarried away about two hours, and then returned; and found that the whole matter had been laid open, to which Mr. Woolworth had given a favorable ear; and promised his assistance during the time I should choose to remain among *his* people. His influence, I knew, was weighty, and would be of the utmost consequence. It was thought best to call a meeting of the proprietors of the school that evening, and for Mr. Woolworth to be present, and lay open the whole matter to them. This plan was accordingly put into execution, and the most favorable consequences apparently produced.

However, I found that the world was in a state of ferment, at the recital of this strange news. The people on Shelter Island had found themselves thrown out in all their conjectures. Uncle Jim was abashed; Doctor Havens was confounded. Judge Havens was the only man who appeared unmoved in the general tumult. A letter I received a few days after will give you a better idea of the matter, than anything else.[1] This was a fine subject for the relish of Doctor Rose. He had

Nov. 14th, 1791.

[1] SIR,

I have thought that it would not be uninteresting or disagreeable to you to receive some account of a remarkable event which hath happened here since you left us. You must know that, not long since, a remarkable phenomenon appeared within our hemisphere. But this was not anything which was to be seen in the starry heavens; but was confined altogether to our mother earth, and partook of the *moral* world as well as the *natural;* and was conveyed to us by water; and might properly be designated by the term *character;* the particulars of which I will detail to you.

He was the son of a clergyman of reputation, and born in Leadenhall-street in London; and received his education in the London schools, where he was taught Latin, English grammar, arithmetic, and various other branches of science; was patronised by Mr.———, a gentleman of great distinction in that city, and who represented the city in Parliament; and had lived six years in a compting-house, with merchants who carried on the Russia trade; and at some time in the late American war, his worthy friend and patron, Mr.———, had entered into the laudable scheme of attempting, in some degree, to emancipate the Irish, and relieve them from the intolerable burden of the British yoke; and, to effect this purpose, had written a pamphlet, entitled, "The political necromancer, or the popish plot detected," which he, the above mentioned character, had copied off in his own handwriting, and had privately caused fifty thousand copies of it to be printed and dispersed all over Ireland; which had, in a great measure, the desired effect. The Irish were roused, and the English obliged to make concessions. This conduct had greatly incensed the British ministry. The pamphlet was deemed a libel; and the author of it, when discovered, was sure to suffer the utmost vengeance of the British government. For a long time this remained undiscovered, but was at last disclosed by a journeyman printer; and our character was obliged suddenly to leave his nearest and dearest connections, and take refuge in a foreign country, to save his worthy friend and patron. Chance threw him in the way of his friend Capt.———, who brought him out to Nova Scotia, where a thousand guineas reward were offered for him by the governor. But his friend provided means to convey him privately by water into the American lines. Here he suffered a dismal disaster; for the Captain who was desired to do this, behaved like a villain, and robbed him of his chest, in which were all his clothes and money, and in particular some bills of exchange on a noted house in Baltimore; and then sat him on shore, forlorn and destitute; and, to add to his afflictions, he was obliged, the ensuing night, to walk thirty miles through mud and mire barefooted, and in a dreary dismal way, to avoid a horrid plot which had been laid to entrap him. He was conveyed from thence by a friendly Captain, to Rhode Island, and had now taken shelter in our Isle and wished our protection and friendship. To some of his more intimate friends, he hinted that he had left behind him in England, a connection of the tenderest kind, a young lady of the most amiable qualities and exalted virtues, with whom he was on the eve of a marriage. To this account I will add some description of his person. He was tall, handsome, genteel and agreeable in conversation and manners; appeared to be a man of reading and extensive information; was well acquainted with the world; and the natural endowment of his mind appeared to be such as might render him an ornament to the country in which

[273]

a full employ for a number of days, and actually grew fleshy under the pleasing effect. People flocked to his house for information. He was never weary in stating in order, in opening and expounding, the whole of the news on this extraordinary circumstance. Notwithstand-

he lived, and a useful citizen. To the public he appeared in the double capacity of the *Philanthropist*, calling upon all mankind "to co-operate with him," in the establishment of the principle of universal benevolence, on the ruins of superstition; and of an *Observer*, to support his works against the rude assaults of criticism. Various was the opinion of the public concerning this character; some supposed it not at all founded in truth. All seemed to entertain suspicion. For my own part, I reasoned on the subject to myself, and said, "It cannot surely be possible that so many natural endowments should be wholly destitute of the moral sense; but perhaps the truth may be, that he is some person of our country, who hath been to England, and hath left it suddenly on account of some swindling trick." But in the midst of this variety of speculations upon a character so new and extraordinary, how sudden and surprising the change! Fame opened one of the doors of her temple, and from the northeastern corner of our hemisphere, blasted upon him with her trumpet, and suddenly this pleasing character "vanished like the baseless fabric of a vision," and in its room was exhibited another of the most hideous kind! A thousand rumors floated upon a thousand tongues, and every one of these was infamy! He had committed a rape! had counterfeited money! was a notorious cheat; was a liar; was a rascal; was a villain! had committed theft; had stolen a watch and suit of clothes from a clergyman; had dared to assume the sacred function when he was unworthy; murder and sodomy were alone excepted from the black catalogue of his crimes. I have heard of him before, said one; I know all about him, says another; his whole life has been one series of enormity, cries a third; he has been disgraced by his public punishments as well as his crimes, says a fourth. In the midst of this uproar, being actuated by the principles of philanthropy, and from a conviction that he had not yet abandoned himself, I determined to stand the poor man's friend in the hour of his distress and calamity. Stop, gentlemen, say I, stay your rage; pray hearken to reason. The devil is not so bad as his picture.— "But he has committed a rape certainly," says one. "Not quite so bad neither," say I (and then endeavor to extenuate it by saying that it did not amount to a force, and that I understood that the young woman swore falsely to plaster over her reputation)—"But he has counterfeited money, and been a notorious cheat," says another. "Something of this kind has perhaps happened," say I, "but this was owing to his extreme necessities." "The rascal has called himself an Englishman all this while," says a third. "He only forgot to insert the word *new*," say I; "he is a New Englishman."—"The villain has altered his name," says a fourth. "He sprung from Eden," say I, "and therefore may, with propriety enough, be called Eden's son." "He is a d—d liar," cries one, "his head is a perfect magazine of lies."—"You ought to consider that having laid a wrong foundation, when he came to build up his superstructure upon it, and embellish the building, and ornament it in all its parts, these must necessarily be wrong likewise." To one and all I say, "the gentleman has been in a wrong road for some time; but I am inclined to believe that he has turned short about, and has now come into the right path; he is now at the bottom of the hill, pray give the man a chance to come up again, and get upon a level with his fellow-citizens." By arguments like these, at one time ing my school flourished, and all things seemed to subside into a peaceful calm.

At this time I had in money but one half dollar, and no other property to help myself, excepting the anticipation of my wages. With

facetious, at another time serious, I endeavor to smooth over every difficulty, and make every circumstance appear as favorable as possible. This, I think, is acting according to the true principles of benevolence and philanthropy; and I doubt not that in future he will "co-operate with me" to render these exertions in his favor of the most lasting benefit to himself, and to his nearest and dearest connections. You will perhaps wonder why I should so far interest myself in this person's good or ill fortune. This requires some explanation. You must know then, that the secret of his birth and character was, by private communication, made known unto me for a long time before it was known in this part of the country. It was evening when I first received this intelligence, and notwithstanding my former suspicions, I was struck with grief and astonishment. How, said I, art thou fallen! fallen like lightning from heaven, O Lucifer, son of the morning! All thy anxieties and fear lest Sir John Temple should discover thy being in this country, are no more! No longer shalt thou dread the malice and persecution of thy British enemies! No longer shalt thou dread the effects of a British outlawry! The doctrine concerning libels shall no longer prove thy ruin! The mighty fabric which thy imagination hath been so long building, shall soon vanish, like the morning dream, and pass away, with the years beyond the flood. How will the *sons* and *daughters* of the uncircumcised triumph when they come to hear of this! Tell it not in Gath! Publish it not in Askelon! With thoughts and reflections like these was my troubled mind tossed to and fro almost the whole of the ensuing night. I put the case of this unfortunate stranger home to myself, and my breast was touched with sympathy and compassion. How easy, said I, is it for a man to go from one step to another in the path of vice, until he is brought to the brink of destruction! How often have I, by my imprudence and folly, needed the forgiveness of others, and shall I not be of the like disposition towards him? Shall man, poor vile man, vain of his own self-righteousness and virtues, presume to be less merciful than his Maker? "But," said prudence, "perhaps this man, for whom you have so great sympathy, has abandoned himself to all manner of vice and immorality, and deserves not the pity or compassion of others. There is nothing impossible in this; and if he should return here again, perhaps you had better join in the public clamor against him, lest your own character should be contaminated." "No," said I, "it is possible the contrary may be the case, and I will give him a generous credit for his future virtues." With thoughts like these was I deprived of rest until my mind found consolation in the following ejaculatory prayer: "O thou Preserver of men! deliver him from all those sins which do most easily beset him. Bring him back into the right road. Restore him to himself, and to his friends, and to his country: and if he should again return to seek our protection, grant that he may no longer be stigmatized and scandalized as the vilest of men; and may no cold or formal reserve prevent me from giving him friendly and decent admonition. If it be thy holy will and pleasure, may I be the happy instrument of reclaiming him; and may Jesus of Nazareth wipe all his dismal stains away.

Mr. STEPHEN BURROUGHS.

[275]

this I hired a house for my family, of Mr. Elias Halsey, the person aforementioned, and bought 126 lb. of beef, 140 lb. of pork, two bushels of Indian corn, and one of rye, with six cords of wood for my winter's store. With this provision for my family I remained till they arrived, which was about the beginning of winter; and my wife brought money only sufficient to defray her expenses till she had crossed the Sound, and arrived on the island. My health, at this time, was again on the decline. Pulmonary complaints had taken hold of me, and constant fever attended, together with great effusions of sweat immediately after closing my eyes in sleep, which were so great as to drench the sheets in which I lay.

At this time I had opened an evening school, and thirty scholars attended. When I used to dismiss the school at ten o'clock in the evening, I would find myself exhausted to such a degree that I could scarcely reach home; and it would seem that I should never again enter the schoolhouse; but this was the only mean in my power for the support of my family. Wretchedness stared me in the face. When I stopped the school, absolute want was close at my heels. Therefore in the morning I would again renew my endeavors to attend to business. This scene continued for six months; every night despairing, and every morning renewing my efforts; and, strange to tell, I remained about at one, neither better nor worse; and continued every day in school, from nine in the morning till ten at night.

I found the winter on this island uncommonly severe. The surface of the ground is extremely level, and no intervening hills or woods to break the force of the wind coming in from sea; hence it becomes the most subject to violent uncomfortable winds of any place I ever saw. In addition to this, the buildings on the island are set up high from the ground, without any underpinning or banking, and not very tight, and, of course, are very cold, being thus unfortified against the winter. In addition to all this, my wife was put to bed this winter, of our second son, and of course, our family was increased with additional expenses. Notwithstanding the six cords of wood, together with the provisions in the first place, had reached to the utmost extent of my finances, a few potatoes excepted; and I could not, till the month of April, replenish my store.

These were times to which I now look back with astonishment, and wonder how I lived: how we kept soul and body together. Yet I went through, and continue now perhaps as well as though I had lived in the palace of a king, feasting on the rich viands of his table. For my own part, my state of infirm health precluded the necessity of much food.

At the opening of the spring, Doctor Havens put four of his children under my care, and they continued with me for the space of two years; to whom I paid unwearied attention for their advancement in literary acquirements. The Doctor now again renewed all his former professions of friendship; and called on me constantly to enliven the declarations of esteem. However, my neighbors and acquaintance constantly warned me against the connection, alleging that I never should close my accounts with the Doctor without difficulty. I observed, with some surprise, that he did not attend to settle his quarter bills; yet I could not give credit to these admonitions, until bitter experience taught me the lesson.

During this time I had formed a most agreeable and intimate acquaintance with Mr. Woolworth. I found him a man of very pleasing parts, and an entertaining companion. His conduct on my first acquaintance had endeared him to my feelings; and his after treatment had confirmed and increased those sensations. I also became acquainted with Mr. Dagget, minister of Southampton, who had written so spiritedly against the "Philanthropist." By these two clergymen I was violently attacked upon the subject of the ideas there manifested; but not feeling any strong desire for the support of the sentiments given out, and likewise knowing the pieces to have been written in an unguarded manner, I waved the challenge to combat, and did not enter the lists with these knight-errants.

Some time after this interview, I fell in company with these same gentlemen again, when they attacked me with more determinate resolution to bring me into action; but I still kept them at bay, without closing in the contest. Seeing this, they demanded of me my religious sentiments. Not complying immediately with their demand, they accused me of Universalism, than which nothing could be more criminal in their view. This was a circumstance of which they had been somewhat jealous, owing to my wife's father being strongly in that sentiment. However, their accusation produced no discovery, and we

[277]

parted no wiser than before. Yet the whisper circulated in some measure among a few particular characters, that I was suspected of entertaining sentiments of universal salvation; until a good old lady, who had heard the report, put them all to silence by observing, that "he can't be a Universaller, for he is quite a civil man."

At the opening of spring I found myself in a situation, from my salary, to provide for my family in some little state of comfort, superior to what we had enjoyed the winter preceding. We saw our little ones smiling around us, and a prospect of being able to provide for them comfortably. Do you, sir, know this pleasure? Indeed, you do not; you cannot. You never yet saw the time when you expected your little ones to perish before your eyes, or otherwise be thrown upon a barbarous world for charity, whose cold approach suffers thousands to droop and die, before she extends her hand to their relief. This I have seen. I have felt these truths. I have shuddered with horror at the prospect. I have wished myself and family at rest in the silent grave. Under such circumstances my soul revolted at the idea of a long life. Horror stalked around my dwelling. Wild dismay was my pillow companion. The most excruciating agony perpetually harrowed my almost exhausted spirits. To be relieved from such a situation; to see these frightful images chased from my view; to see all these threatening dangers past and gone, brought on a situation, of all others, the most calculated to render me sensible of my present felicity; and to give me those feelings under it, which no other person can experience, unless his situation had been similar to mine.

My school, through the winter, had been large, and had made rapid proficiency in learning. Satisfaction was the necessary consequent among all my constituents; and prosperity was now the general prospect. One circumstance seemed but slightly to interrupt this harmony. The evening school, which continued through the winter, was composed of elder members, who wished to perfect their education by attending to mathematics, geography, and rhetoric. In paying attention to the latter, they had committed to memory a comedy of "A Bold Stroke for a Wife." After practicing it for a while in private, they formed a purpose to exhibit the performance in public. As there was no situation, the meetinghouse excepted, convenient for such an exhibition, it was determined, after consulting some of the leading men in the parish, to have the comedy performed in the meetinghouse. It was accordingly performed before a crowded audience.

Deacon Hedges had not been consulted on this business. He lived in a remote part of the town. He was much offended at the circumstance. He viewed the house *polluted* in consequence of the performance. But this difficulty died away, without much flowing from it of any kind.

As I have heretofore hinted, the people on this island were very illiterate, making but a small calculation for information, further than the narrow circle of their own business extended. They were almost entirely destitute of books of any kind, except schoolbooks and Bibles; hence, those who had a taste for reading, had not the opportunity. I found a number of those young people who had attended my evening school, possessing bright abilities, and a strong thirst for information, which would lead to rapid improvement, had they the opportunity. Therefore, under circumstances like these, I felt very desirous to devise some method to remove the evil. It was a subject of frequent conversation with the various characters into whose company I happened to fall. No plan, however, was yet adopted. I mentioned the expedience of a Sunday school. That idea was immediately rejected, on the principle of its being unprecedented in the place. I proposed to devote Saturdays for the instruction of those who could not attend through the week; but that trenched too hard upon the economical system. I endeavored to persuade the young people to buy books; but the greater part being yet minors, that could not be effected without the assistance of their parents, which assistance could not be expected on account of the *expense*. I finally thought of using my endeavors to persuade the people into the expediency of raising money for the purpose of collecting a number of books for the use of the young people of the district. I laid this plan before Mr. Woolworth for advice. I had often conversed with him on the subject before. He did not encourage me in the pursuit. He said the people would not consent to it; that they had no idea of the benefit of books, or of a good education; "and you cannot persuade them to anything that is *new*, or that is attended with *expense*. I have tried this matter myself. I have had the assistance

[279]

of Judge Hurlbut; but all did not effect the purpose; a library they would not have. I believe our influence is much greater with the people than yours."

Under these discouraging prospects I had about relinquished the idea (though reluctantly) of attempting any plan to assist the young people to procure a tolerable education. I was in conversation one evening with Mr. Halsey upon this subject. He was a man of shrewd discernment and excellent judgment. "Mr. Burroughs," said he, "I have for some time observed your attention to the welfare of your school with some surprise. It has not been thus with former schoolmasters. They have ever manifested a desire to do as little for the school as they could consistent with their engagements. I am sensible of the advantage of such a plan as you propose, of having a collection of books for the common use of the district. I wish you may succeed in your friendly endeavors. I believe you may, if you pursue right methods. Mr. Woolworth, it is true, has made sundry attempts to establish a library in this town; but a number of circumstances have been unfavorable to his plan. In the first place, he has made the price of a share much too high; in the room of forty shillings it ought to be twenty. The people in general will then likely become proprietors; and for such people the library ought to be established, because they are not able to supply themselves with books in any other way. We who are ignorant of the benefit of a library, may be willing to risk twenty shillings; but forty would terrify us.

"Another reason why Mr. Woolworth has not succeeded is, that people are afraid they shall not be gratified in such books as they want, so long as he has the lead of the business. They generally expect the library will consist of books in divinity, and dry metaphysical writings; whereas, should they be assured that histories and books of information would be procured, I have no doubt they might be prevailed upon to raise money sufficient for such a purpose."

These hints from Mr. Halsey were clear in my view, and his reasoning decisive. I determined to improve from it, and once more renew my plan and exertions. As Mr. Woolworth was my counsellor in all matters of moment, I again made application to him, and sketched out the plan for his opinion. He still manifested his doubts about my succeeding. He added, "Certainly, you cannot expect your influence

[280]

among this people to be equal to mine. I have tried the project faithfully, and have not succeeded." However, after reasoning with him
upon the subject for the space of two hours, he ended with this observation—"If you find that *you* have influence enough among the people
to effect your purpose, I will become a member of *your* library." Thus
we parted.

CHAPTER XXVII

HAVING now a little leisure on hand, owing to a school vacation, I determined to devote that time to the purpose of visiting the people of the district, and offering and urging upon them my plan for a library. Much to my satisfaction, I found the people willing to grant their aid to this business, after I had informed them into the nature of such books as should be procured, and into the advantages such a matter would afford them. However, I had to renew my promises often, before they could feel certain that their money would be appropriated to the purchase of histories, etc.

In the space of a few days I had raised forty pounds, which I supposed adequate to the purpose first intended. I then applied to Mr. Woolworth for his share of the money, and to inform him of my success. I felt a degree of exultation in the hope of surprising him in the most agreeable manner, with the news of my succeeding so happily. But what was my astonishment and dismay, when in a cold disdainful manner he observed, "that I was very officious to gain influence among *his* people." However, he paid his money, and we parted with feelings, on my side, very different from what they were when I was going on this visit.

I immediately advertised the proprietors of the library to hold a meeting for the purpose of selecting a catalogue of books, and to make rules for the government of a library, etc. At the day appointed we all met. After we had entered into some desultory conversation upon the business, it was proposed and agreed to choose a committee of five, to make choice of books. Mr. Woolworth, myself, Deacon Cook, Doctor Rose, and one Matthews, were chosen a committee for this purpose. Immediately after we had entered upon business, Mr. Woolworth produced a catalogue of books of his own selection, and told the meeting that he had consulted all the catalogues of the book stores in New York, and had chosen the best out of them all for this library; and called for a vote upon his motion. The meeting voted in the affirmative; upon which he proposed to proceed upon the business of forming rules for the regulation of the library.

I now felt myself in a most disagreeable and delicate situation. Mr. Woolworth was a character, of all others, I would not willingly disoblige. To take any measures to stop his extraordinary efforts, I knew, would offend him in the highest manner; and to remain a silent spectator would be at once renouncing every claim to integrity, inasmuch as I had promised the proprietors positively, that histories, and books of information upon secular subjects, should give the leading cast to the complexion of the library. Mr. Woolworth was fully availed of this circumstance. His reasoning, as it appeared to me, was after this manner (viz.), that as the support of myself and family depended on my school, and as his influence was so considerable that he could essentially injure me in that respect, he therefore concluded that I would sacrifice every other consideration to my present support; and would not, of consequence, dare provoke his resentment by opposing his measures with regard to the choice of books for the library. If that should be the case, the people who had placed confidence in me would see it delusory, and that I would not or could not be instrumental in aiding their measures when opposed to him. The natural consequence flowing from such a circumstance, would be to appreciate him, and depreciate me in their view; a matter which now lay near his heart, fearful that my growing influence would lead the attention of the people from him to other objects.

The contempt with which he treated me, as a member of the committee, together with the rest, was what I would have submitted to, with patience, on my own account. But when I viewed all the other members silent under the indignity, Mr. Woolworth not deigning to consult any upon his catalogue, I found the imperious hand of necessity laid upon me to advocate the cause of those who had paid their money on the faith of my promise.

I requested the favor of Mr. Woolworth to see the catalogue he had selected. After running it through, I perceived that the conjectures of the people had not been ill founded respecting the choice he would make for them. His catalogue consisted wholly of books upon the subject of ethics; and did not contain a single history, or anything of the kind. I observed, in the mildest manner, that this catalogue was

[283]

essentially different from the minds of the people, or else I had misunderstood them; that I was apprehensive they did not understand themselves when they passed the vote; but that should the mistake lie on my side of the question, I was willing to stand corrected; yet, at least, we had deviated from the first plan. Upon this Mr. Woolworth observed, that "he hoped *his* people were not dependent on *me* to know their own wishes; that he wished I had modesty enough not to consider myself spokesman for *his* people; that he believed *he* was as well acquainted with them, and understood what books would suit them as I did."

You will naturally conclude that observations like these had no very pleasing effect upon my feelings. I was determined, however, not to be bullied out of countenance until I had reached the mark for which I had started, which was to learn the feelings of the meeting, and to act accordingly. Mr. Woolworth was moderator, and consequently, I could not call for the minds of the people collectively by a vote; but applied to the members individually, and asked them if they were satisfied with the vote they had just passed; to which they universally answered in the negative.

When Mr. Woolworth found them decidedly against their own vote, he plead for an adjournment, which was readily granted, and the meeting was adjourned for a week. After the present meeting was ended, a number of the members came to my house to consult upon the business in private, which they dare not advocate openly against Mr. Woolworth. I found they were somewhat surprised at my daring to speak publicly against the measures of *the minister*.

A few days after, there was a general collection of people, on account of a woman who was delirious, absconding, and hiding herself in the fields. Mr. Woolworth and myself met together on this occasion, for the first time since our library meeting. He attacked me with some warmth, on account of my conduct in opposing him, and told me decidedly, that should I not withdraw my motion at the next meeting of the proprietors of the library, and remain silent, I should there find things that would make me tremble; and that I must lay my account soon to leave the country. During this conversation, Judge Hurlbut joined us, and began to address me in the following manner: "Mr. Burroughs, do you expect to come here among us, and attempt to direct our matters, and set yourself up above all the first men in the country, after we had taken pity upon you, a poor miserable vagabond, turned out of all countries where you have resided, and a disgrace to the people among whom you ever lived?"

An address like this, I apprehended, was calculated to affect the feelings of any man who had feelings, and at the same time manifested such a disposition as sunk Judge Hurlbut into abject contempt, in my view. I found, by this time, a clamor raised, which filled the neighboring towns, that I was trying to fill the library with books of corrupt principles; and more especially with the writings of Deists and Universalists; and consequently was determined to shut out all good books. This declaration was constantly in the mouths of Judge Hurlbut and Mr. Woolworth.

Matters were in this situation at the appointed time of the adjourned meeting. I found that a large number of members were added to the body of proprietors; so that by this time, the whole number amounted to nearly or quite a hundred. This had taken place by the instrumentality of Mr. Woolworth, who had spent a great part of the week of adjournment to gain new members, in order to give himself a majority among them, by the addition of his friends, and more particularly such as he deemed influential.

The meeting was opened by Mr. Woolworth, who stated to them the excellency of his own collection of books, and the vile means I had used to make contention and division among his people. He was about calling for a vote of the meeting, when I endeavored to gain a hearing, but to no purpose. He proceeded to put his motion to vote; and, to his infinite mortification, saw but fifteen hands raised. He did not call for the contrary. I then found an opportunity to address myself to the meeting, and stated to them my reasons for wishing for a collection of books in the first place; the methods I had taken, and the plans I had pursued; but added, "As the business has now become much more extensive than I, at first, had entertained the most remote idea, I think the plan of the library ought likewise to be extended, and more latitude given in the choice of books, that we may, in this way, gratify the taste of every member, making this the leading object of attention, to obtain such books generally as are most conformable to the taste of the majority of the society. I have made a selection from

[285]

a number of catalogues of such books as appeared to me suitable to the first design of this institution: however, I did not proceed so far in this choice as I should have done, had I known of the considerable addition which has now taken place. I will read to you, gentlemen, the titles of the books, and then describe them to you in a summary way. Should any book be thought of by any one, which he may wish to have introduced, I think it reasonable for him to have the privilege, so far as his money will extend in the purchase, to introduce his book, when no special objection shall lie in the way."

After I had ended these observations, I proceeded to read the titles of the books. After a course of time, I came to "Brooks' Writings": at which Mr. Woolworth declared that to be a book, together with the others, totally inadmissible: "For," said he, "no one can understand it, he writes upon such subjects, and in such an obscure manner; and all Burroughs' books are of the same cast." Knowing that the "Fool of Quality" had been read by some present, I made the appeal to them, whether that was a book obscurely written. At this question Mr. Woolworth started, and demanded if Brooks was the author of the "Fool of Quality." For so ignorant was this critic, that he did not know the books he undertook to condemn.

After I had finished my catalogue, this method was finally proposed, and adopted (viz.), that two others should be added to the committee, and that the meeting should be adjourned again for a week, to give the members of the committee time for information; that another meeting should again be held, and a choice of books made after the following manner, viz. that each member of the committee should have a negative upon any book which was offered for admission, and thus proceed until all were satisfied with the books.

During the time of adjournment the clamor still increased against the books which I had offered for the library. Mr. Woolworth and Judge Hurlbut were in a state of great activity on this subject, and their perpetual cry was, "that I was endeavoring to overthrow all religion, morality and order in the place; was introducing corrupt books into the library, and adopting the most fatal measures to overthrow all the *good old establishments.*"

At the next meeting, the different members of the committee had collected a catalogue of books, peculiar to their own taste. Deacon

Hedges brought forward, "Essays on the Divine authority for Infant Baptism," "Terms of Church Communion," "The Careful Watchman," "Age of Grace," etc., etc., all pamphlets.—Deacon Cook's collection was, "History of Martyrs," "Rights of Conscience," "Modern Pharisees," "Defence of Separates," etc.—Mr. Woolworth exhibited "Edwards against Chauncey," "History of Redemption," "Jenning's View," etc. Judge Hurlbut concurred in the same. Doctor Rose exhibited, "Gay's Fables," "Pleasing Companion," "Turkish Spy"; while I for the third time recommended "Hume's History," "Voltaire's Histories," "Rollin's Ancient History," "Plutarch's Lives," etc. I carefully avoided, from the beginning, offering any books of the sectarian kind, or that would have a tendency to lead the readers into religious disputes.

After we had assembled together, we chose Dr. Rose for our clerk, and on his being appointed, Mr. Woolworth proceeded to order him to insert in his entries, books of his own choice, without even deigning to hear the opinion of any other member of the committee upon them. I endeavored several times to call his attention to the books of my catalogue, but in vain. Doctor Rose proceeded to obey his orders with punctual exactness until Mr. Woolworth had finished his catalogue. He then addressed the meeting, and told them that the *committee* had made choice of the catalogue of books then presented, and called for a vote of the meeting whether they would accept it. They voted in the affirmative.

After the vote was passed, I arose and addressed myself to the meeting in the following manner: "Gentlemen, it is with no small degree of pain I have been a spectator of what has passed at this meeting. I have here seen a departure from every principle of propriety in the choice of your library, and you giving countenance to it by your vote. I in the first place felt anxious to befriend you in the collection of a small number of books for your use. I consulted your feelings and interest in the matter, and promised you my faithful support in promoting such a choice as you would desire. In obedience to my promise, I have pursued such measures as to incur the highest displeasure of Mr. Woolworth and associates, and subjected myself to the highest insults, to the most virulent lash of slander and malignity, and to the threats of being turned out of town with infamy and disgrace; all

[287]

these evils I could have borne with patience, because I have the consolation of doing what I ought, and likewise knowing that truth must finally triumph over error; but to see you relinquish thus tamely those privileges which you have manifested such a desire for, and which are so clearly your right, is a circumstance truly mortifying. However, as this is the second instance of the kind, I think myself clearly absolved from my first engagement to procure you books according to your taste. I truly feel very much disappointed in the loss of my object, and therefore shall decline any longer considering myself a member of the library. As I have the money in my hands, every member may receive it again, when he requests it. You cannot then complain that your money has been applied to uses contrary to your wishes. In thus doing I acquit myself of every obligation which my promise had laid me under to you. I wish you may profit by your library: I wish it may claim the attention of all classes, more particularly the younger, and inspire them with a thirst for information and improvement; but I fear that these consequences will not so readily follow, as I once expected. In the room of hurting the institution, I promise you, gentlemen, that I will give it every aid which I can consistently. A poor library is better than none."

After I had closed, Mr. Woolworth replied in the severest and most pointed terms. He observed "that I had very generously promised my aid to his library. He wished me to remember that my aid was not wished for. They felt perfectly able to manage without me, and if I would not consider myself of so much consequence in that place, I might meet with better treatment." He likewise demanded the money which I held to be delivered over to him and not to the individuals. However, his demands were not complied with. I gave each member his money, and departed.

In the course of this evening, about half the members of the library came to my house, and desired me to take their money and send to New York for such books as were contained in my first catalogue, observing, that Mr. Woolworth's collection was such, that they would not be members of his library. I demanded why they voted for it, so long as it was contrary to their wishes; their answer was, that they were loth to offend Mr. Woolworth, for if they did, he could *out talk* them. I consented to their proposal, but observed, that probably the other so-

[288]

ciety would send to New York for their books, and we might, by purchasing the whole together, obtain them cheaper, and after the books arrived, then each library receive its own. This idea met with their approbation, and it was agreed upon that I should, the next morning, wait on Mr. Woolworth, and lay the plan before him.

I considered Mr. Woolworth the morning preceding, as much out of temper, so far as not to treat me with common decency; how he would feel and conduct this morning was a matter of some doubt in my mind; however, I was determined to observe such measures towards him as to make it manifest that still the remains of gratitude were sufficiently strong in my heart, to act upon the most friendly terms. I was very sensible that the plan which I was about laying before him would embrace his interest as well as mine, and that there could not be any reasonable objection to it.

When I arrived at his house, I found that time had by no means cooled his rage. He there said and performed actions which, for the honor of the cloth and of human nature, I do not choose to repeat. He utterly refused to pay any attention to my proposition. He threatened me with immediate expulsion from the place, provided I did not retrench my measures, or if I proceeded to purchase the books for those who had left his library. My answer to these many threats was of the following tenor. "I feel myself, Mr. Woolworth, founded upon too just a principle to be subject to the motive of fear, therefore you will save yourself some fruitless labor to drop that subject and never resume it. One circumstance has weight on my mind, in my conduct towards you. When I first came into this town, you then conducted me like a friend. I then stood in need of assistance. I felt the benefit of your kindness; I felt grateful on the occasion; I ever have most sincerely wished to manifest those sentiments by the most friendly line of conduct towards you. I still wish it. Therefore I conjure you, for your own sake, for the sake of my enjoying those sensations of pleasure which will naturally flow from acts of benevolence, that you would conduct so as to leave it in my power to show a friendly part towards you.

"You cannot but be sensible that self-preservation is the first law of nature, and if you continue as you have done, to use every effort to injure me in the public opinion, it is a duty I owe myself and family

[289]

to justify my conduct to the public, and this ultimately will be at your expense, for if they entertain an idea of my conduct as being founded in justice, they will of course, consider you as a false accuser, malignant character, and revengeful person. How such an idea will operate, you must be sensible, if your passion for revenge has not wholly deprived you of reflection. Finally, sir, I wish to be in such a situation as not to injure you either directly or indirectly."

After I had closed my observations, I saw a sneer of contempt sitting on his countenance; he answered, "You wish not to injure me? I despise your exertions. What do you think you can do, you poor miserable wretch! towards injuring me? I suppose you wish for me to make terms with you; you forget yourself, that you are a miserable fugitive and exile from your own country, and here by the means of my protection."

I left the house of Mr. Woolworth hopeless and melancholy. To see the effects of his ungovernable rage, was an object truly distressing to any feeling mind. To see him thus blindly pursuing his own ruin to gratify his revenge, especially being a clergyman, the professed ambassador of the King of Peace, was an object of contemplation of the most disagreeable kind.

> "I grant the deed
> Is madness; but the madness of the heart.
> And what is that? Our utmost bound of guilt.
> A sensual unreflecting life is big
> With monstrous births, and suicide, to crown
> The black infernal brood."

I made report to the members of our library that the object which we first contemplated was now entirely out of the question, and that it was necessary of consequence to have a meeting in order to take further measures for our own internal regulations. and procuring the books in question. A meeting accordingly was warned to be held at my house the third night succeeding, where the members accordingly met, and we were proceeding on business, when Mr. Woolworth came among us. He did not now appear with that overbearing haughtiness which he had at first assumed. He seemed moderate and rational. He observed that he was apprehensive our measures were not calculated for the general good. "While we are pursuing the object of two libraries I fear we shall fail in both; being divided, we shall in our operations militate against each other, and finally both come to the ground." In answer to this we observed, "that every idea we entertained on the subject was to purchase such books with our money as we wished for. This was a right which we inherited from nature, and which we did not intend to give up; and so long as we could not be indulged in this privilege in company with him, we had separated and set up by ourselves; yet we were willing to purchase our books together; nay more, have them all kept in one library, if that were thought most expedient, so that after we had read our books, they might have the privilege of them, so far as they esteemed it a privilege, and we of theirs under similar circumstances."

To these remarks Mr. Woolworth answered, that he felt himself entirely contented with them, and further observed, that he would use all his influence with the other members of the committee to have our proposals acceded to, on condition of our remaining still with regard to the purchase of the books, until the sitting of the committee, which would be in about a week. We readily complied with these proposals, and consequently all further proceedings were at present suspended.

At the sitting of the committee, I came forward with our proposals, without entertaining the least doubt of their being readily acceded to; but, sir, imagine my astonishment when I heard Mr. Woolworth reprobate the idea in the most pointed manner, in open violation of his positive promise to the contrary. He insisted upon it, that it was departing from the dignity of their character to form a coalition with malecontents; that it was contrary to their powers to admit such books into the library; and finally, that no other way remained but for us to pay our money into their hands, and rest the business with them to buy such books as they should choose. I expostulated with Mr. Woolworth upon such a line of conduct; upon its unreasonableness and absurdity; but all to no effect. He tenaciously adhered to his first position, and I finally proposed the expediency of calling another meeting of the proprietors, and laying the business before them. This was equally opposed; but the rest of the committee now began to even dare to dissent in opinion from Mr. Woolworth, and a meeting of the proprietors was accordingly warned.

About this time the term of my engagement, as a schoolmaster, was

[291]

now expired, and Mr. Woolworth and Judge Hurlbut made a visit to all the inhabitants of the district, in order to dissuade them from engaging me again; however, this visit produced no effect; my school again was full, and matters went on as usual in that line.

At the meeting of the proprietors it was proposed and readily agreed to on our side, though with great reluctance on the part of Mr. Woolworth, to fling by everything which had been done, and begin anew.

Mr. Woolworth had brought forward at this time a collection of books much better than formerly, having taken about twenty out of the catalogue which I had at first exhibited. This collection I generally recommended, and observed many things in its favor, but still I offended; I was given to understand by Mr. Woolworth, that he did not wish to have *his* catalogue owe its reception to *my* recommendation. Out of all the catalogues now present, we made a selection of books to the mutual satisfaction of all parties; and by the way, every individual volume of my first catalogue was comprised in this. The books were sent for, and matters seemed to subside into a sullen calm.

CHAPTER XXVIII

THINGS remained in this situation for some time without any material alteration. The affairs of Judge Hurlbut began to grow embarrassed, and he was often in want of money for transacting his small necessary concerns. Under this situation, he proposed to a committee, which we had for the purpose of making additions to the library, the sale of some books out of his private library. The committee, upon his earnest recommendation, purchased a number, among which was the "History of Charles Wentworth." If you have ever read those volumes, you will recollect a deistical treatise in one of them, as severe and ingenious as any extant. I heard soon of this new acquisition, and on the day for drawing books I asked some if they had seen that book; they answered in the negative. I then turned to the part referred to, and showed them some passages. Aghast, in wild dismay, they started back with horror! Had Afric's grim lion, with his shaggy main erect, and jaws bedaubed with blood, met them full in the way, they would not have manifested greater signs of fear. To see the holy religion of their ancestors vilified thus by a vile caitif, enkindled their eyes with rage, and their cheeks flushed with anger! To see their library, now their common resource for information, thus corrupted by the vilest heresy, and blackest poison, after they had taken such unwearied pains to obtain one, pure as nature's simple fount, or the gurgling rill rolling its lucid streams over the brightest pebbles, was a sight which made every feeling of holy wrath burn with fury against the unknown traitor. They were loud in their clamors to the librarian to know who was the author of this abominable deed. At length, they heard that Judge Hurlbut was the man; he, who but a little time before was so fearful of my corrupting the youth with bad books, that he filled the whole country with uproar, lest I should effect such a purpose; that man, who was the constant companion and fellow-laborer of Mr. Woolworth to keep the library pure from deistical writings!!!

[293]

A knowledge of this circumstance flew with the rapidity of lightning among the people. All who had read the book condemned it to the lowest part of perdition, and a meeting of the proprietors was instantly called, to extirpate so monstrous a production from the face of the earth.

When we were once more assembled, Mr. Woolworth opened the business with a lengthy harrangue upon the subject. He labored the point with the utmost exertion, to save his friend from condemnation. He went largely into the merits of the book, and said, "As but a very small part was upon the deistical strain, the other, entertaining narrative, he had no idea of its being attended with fatal consequences, and had it not been for Burroughs, who is ever fond of making mischief, you would not have known that the book contained anything bad in it; but there is a peculiar strain of malignity in this man, which ever seeks for and embraces all opportunities of creating difficulties among the first and best characters. He had kept this parish in an uproar almost ever since he has resided among us, and if you continue to have your minds disturbed by this man's machinations, you will find the parish soon ruined and broken to pieces."

I now arose in answer to Mr. Woolworth's observations, and said, that "I had now heard some remarks which had surprised me more than anything else through the whole course of Mr. Woolworth's very extraordinary conduct. It was a justification of Judge Hurlbut in that transaction, which amounted to the whole of what he had accused me, though wrongfully, of intending, and of condemning in me that conduct which he had extolled so much in Judge Hurlbut. But what is the most extraordinary, is the avowed principle upon which he justifies his friend the Judge. He says you would never have known that the book had been a bad one if I had not told you!! He appears to be entirely willing that you should have bad books, to be cheated out of your money, to be wronged, imposed upon and abused, provided there is nobody wicked enough to tell you. Is this a doctrine, gentlemen, which sounds agreeable to your ears, and particularly from your spiritual leader, from your guide and director in the paths of truth? If your ignorance would be an antidote against the poison of such books put into the library by Judge Hurlbut, why not the same reason in my favor? And why will not the epithets of mischief-making fellows, apply as readily to the reverend gentleman and to his friends, for representing *my* books in that light, as what it will to me in representing his book in its true light? And much more so when you take into consideration, that *their* statements are false, and that mine have the full force of fact before your eyes. They have taken the liberty upon bare suspicion, to make loud clamors against my books, or else they *pretended suspicion* as a cloak to cover some other design; be it which way it might, the example is the same; and they have been the leaders in it, therefore out of their own mouths they are condemned.

"It has ever remained with a doubt on my mind, whether Mr. Woolworth and Judge Hurlbut acted honestly in the great fears which they pretended to possess respecting my choice of books; and as it is necessary for you to know whether I do act towards you openly and candidly, I was very glad of the opportunity which presented for you all to see and judge for yourselves. Let my sentiments upon the book be what they are, I suppose it necessary for you to know its contents, and by whose instrumentality it came into our library.

"It has been urged abundantly upon the other side, that I ought not to intermeddle in your concerns, seeing I am in so great measure a stranger among you. You, gentlemen, I expect are the judges with regard to this doctrine, and if it be founded in truth, then you will undoubtedly withdraw from me that confidence which you have heretofore placed in me.

"Whether the Rev. gentleman and his associates refer in their reasoning to any known established law or custom of the country, or to the general nature of the matter, I know not. If the former, I would thank them to point it out; if the latter, I will observe that they themselves are not natives of this place, and what particular period they have fixed for a previous residence before one may be concerned in public matters, I would likewise thank them to describe. For my own part I can see none, especially in matters that are clear and obvious to every common understanding. Why a man should be prohibited from contributing his assistance to the public welfare because he is a stranger, is a mode of reasoning beyond my reach.

"Finally, gentlemen, the whole course of treatment which I have received from Mr. Woolworth and Judge Hurlbut, from the first commencement of the plan for a library, has been injurious, abusive, un-

[295]

manly and indecent; yet their conduct on the present occasion oversteps all the former instances, in its glaring wickedness. You, gentlemen, have the book before you, you understand its nature. I wish to have you treat it according to your discretion. I feel no anxiety about it on my own account."

It was then motioned to have some of the obnoxious passages read before the meeting, but this was overruled by Mr. Woolworth, Judge Hurlbut, Capt. Post and Dr. Rose. It was then put to vote, whether the book in dispute should be excluded the library, and the negative was obtained by a large majority. The truth was this: there had been so much said respecting the book, that each individual was anxious to gratify his curiosity by seeing this phenomenon; and each one who had read it, was more afraid for others than for himself, therefore it was determined that the book should remain a member of the library, in order for each one to be gratified by the perusal.

The Sunday following, Mr. Woolworth took up the subject in the pulpit, and labored through the day to convince the people that it was their duty to banish me from their coasts. After the exercises of the public service were over, I addressed the people, and endeavored to confute the ideas brought forward by their clergyman, and to show the injurious nature of his treatment concerning me, and the unrighteous conduct which he had been guilty of from time to time, and especially his falsehood and duplicity in going contrary to his promise at the time of my meeting his committee for the purpose of a union. Deacon Hedges demanded of me whether I meant to accuse Mr. Woolworth with lying. I answered that I did. The Deacon then answered in a menacing manner, "We will see who lies. It is high time for us to stir if it is come to this, that our minister must be accused of lying."

The next day I saw a large gathering at the house of Dr. Rose, and curiosity led me among them, to learn the occasion of so large a meeting of people without any public day or appointment. Upon entering the house, I perceived Deacon Hedges addressing the people in the following manner: "One Burroughs has come into Bridghampton, and conducted in a very *obstropolous* manner; he has accused our minister with lying, and is a Universaller. He is a very bad person, for he was whipt and cropt and branded in his own country for a rape, and he has acted a great deal worse here than he did there, for he has quarrelled with the minister, and said he lied, and has tried to break up the town. They turned him out of their country, and we must turn him out of our town, for he's a vile fellow, and not fit to live among us, and ought to be kicked out of town long ago."

Mr. Halsey was present, and answered the Deacon in the following manner (viz.), "Do you expect, Deacon Hedges, that Mr. Burroughs' leaving this town will settle the difficulties prevailing here? If you do, you mistake the point. Mr. Woolworth has been guilty of open and premeditated falsehood, and Mr. Burroughs has brought the accusation justly against him. These are truths to which I am personally knowing, and to which I can bring a number of substantial witnesses; therefore, the scandal will lie upon your minister, notwithstanding all your persecution against Mr. Burroughs; and whilst you are thus endeavoring to injure him, you involve yourself in still greater difficulty, and will have the blot of disgrace more apparent on your minister, than what it would be, had you let this business rested easy as possible." "Dare you, Mr. Halsey," said Deacon Hedges, "take the part of that villain?" "I dare," replied Mr. Halsey, "advocate the cause of injured innocence, wherever I find it, let the power of the oppressor be ever so great." At this Capt. Post made towards Mr. Halsey in a swaggering manner, giving him to understand that he would chastise him for his insolence; but being mistaken in the person whom he undertook to frighten, he tamely shrunk back to his seat.

Judge Hurlbut now proposed the plan of bringing an action of slander against me, for charging Mr. Woolworth with lying, before the Supreme Court, "And there," said he, "we will twist him, unless he will retract what he has said, and confess that he has been the author of all the difficulty in Bridghampton."

I was at this time so profoundly ignorant of law cases, that I did not know to the contrary but what an action would lie in this case; and that a Judge of the Court should be equally ignorant, was a circumstance to me of no small surprise; yet so it was that the *learned* Judge really thought an action of slander would lie against me, for accusing his *minister* with lying.

However, the terror of a lawsuit did not produce the desired effect, and the meeting broke up in confusion. The next day the following letter was received by Mr. Woolworth, from Deacon Cook.

[297]

"Bridghampton, May 28th, 1793.

"To Mr. Woolworth.

"Sir,

"I have thought, ever since we were both on the library committee, that you were unjustly trying to make contention, and if possible, a division among the proprietors; and I am witness that you pushed hard for a division into parties, in sending for the books, for no other reason than because you could not gain the sovereignty of putting in or shutting out such books as you thought fit. I tell you plainly, sir, that your authority, or knowledge in wisdom and grace is not sufficient to rule men's consciences at such a rate. It is evident that because you could not do these things and beat Mr. Burroughs, you are pursuing Haman's plan to hang poor Mordecai.

"It is a truth apparent to your hearers, that in preaching and in conversation you envy Mr. Burroughs, and try to get him away; but we defy your rage, and tell you plainly that he has as good a right to stay here as you, or even your friend the *learned* Judge. We know Mr. Burroughs has benefited this people ten times as much as ever you did. You could not have obtained a library without his assistance. If we may judge by your behavior, were the laws of the land on your side, a persecuting Saul would not go before you. Does this behavior comport with the principles you *pretend* to preach?

"I believe, were the case put to trial, there would be as many votes for your leaving this town, as there would be for Burroughs. Look at your congregation. There you may see that things do not wear the face of union. but the people will not tell you these things decidedly; they are not plain and faithful to you.

"We cannot but notice how true your zeal has been in carefully guarding against bad books. Look at that abominable blasphemous one which the Judge put into our library! I tell you that until you have taken up these stumbling blocks, you can never be my minister. Such people as you, say and do not.

"You may set your heart at rest. Mr. Burroughs is able to maintain by argument or even a regular life, so far as we know him, his own cause, against any accusation which you can bring.

UPROAR IN THE MEETING

"I don't wonder that St. Paul charged Timothy about receiving a *novice*, who is in danger of being puffed up. Pray let you and I think seriously of these things.

"J. Cook."

After this letter had been read by Mr. Woolworth, it was at once determined to call in counsel; therefore Judge Hurlbut, Deacon Hedges, and Capt. Post were called upon to weigh and determine upon this important letter. After they had gone largely and *learnedly* into the business, it was voted, *nem. con.*, to be a *libel* against government, and that it ought to be burnt by the common hangman. They further determined, after the most candid investigation of the subject, that no way remained for a settlement of these sore and grievous difficulties, but by expelling me, who was the author of all iniquity, from the coasts; it was therefore determined on the next Sunday to warn a parish meeting for the aforesaid purpose.

The business was again resumed by Mr. W. in the pulpit, where he went largely into the propriety of not suffering such a person as I was to remain in town, and more particularly to teach a school. After the meeting was ended, Deacon Hedges mentioned the parish meeting to be held on the Thursday following, for the purpose of "clearing Rev. Mr. Woolworth's character from the charge of one Burroughs."

On the day appointed, the parish, together with a number of spectators out of town, were universally convened at the meetinghouse. Deacon Hedges opened the meeting with some abusive language against my conduct, and immediately Mr. Woolworth arose and addressed the assembly in a speech of an hour's length, where he exhausted all his powers of abuse, in pouring forth the most vilifying epithets against me, which language could form, apparently intending to bury the idea of his own guilt in the odium cast on me; however, his rage in this attempt was detrimental to his health; it proved a powerful emetic, and this stopped his career.

After he had ended, I arose to reply in answer, but the house, which before was profoundly silent, was now in a state of uproar, from the confused noise of talking, by his partisans, and by repeated orders to me from Deacon Hedges and Judge Hurlbut to be brief. This produced a resentment on the side of my friends, which flung the house into an uproar, which continued for some time; and my utmost endeavors were necessary to prevent a serious engagement between the two parties.

After this was in some measure appeased, Deacon Hedges proceeded to tell all who were for Mr. Woolworth to draw off upon the east end of the meetinghouse, where about one-third of the congregation retired, and the rest kept their seats. Seeing this did not answer his purpose, he ordered all those who were for Burroughs, to go to the west; at which an equal number went to the other end, and the remainder retired out of the house. After this, those at the east end of the meetinghouse proceeded to choose a committee of twelve, to take such measures as they should deem necessary to settle the difficulties and clear Mr. Woolworth's character. The leading members of this committee were Deacon Hedges, Capt. Post, etc.

The next day at evening, the following paper was handed to me.

"At a meeting of a committee, chosen by the parish of Bridghampton, for the purpose of clearing up the character of Rev. Aaron Woolworth, held at the chamber of Dr. S. H. Rose.

"DANIEL HOWELL, Moderator.

"HENRY PIERSON, Clerk.

"Ist. Voted, that it is inconsistent with the safety of the parish of Bridghampton, to have Stephen Burroughs remain an inhabitant in it any longer.

"2nd. That if Stephen Burroughs does not remove by the 17th of next month, this committee will take such measures as they shall see fit in order to remove him.

"3d. That Stephen Burroughs be served with a copy of these resolves of the committee.

"HENRY PIERSON, Clerk.

"*Bridghampton, May 30th, 1793.*"

I know, sir, you will smile at this *bull* of the Bridghampton committee, and at their profound erudition in law knowledge, considering they had a Judge for their counsellor in all their proceedings. This

[300]

peremptory mandate had but little effect on my conduct. But I found my neighbors, and the parents of my scholars were much alarmed at the event. They were afraid the power which the committee assumed, was absolutely in their hands, and that I should be turned out of town by might and main. These matters disturbed my school for some time; reports being frequently circulated by the adverse party, that I was about flinging by all business, and would forthwith move out of town. Yet after a while the inhabitants found that my school would continue steadily, and therefore they sent their children.

The 17th of next month, the time appointed by the committee for my removal, drawing nigh, and no signs of my obedience being manifested, it was thought necessary for Judge Hurlbut to gain further light into the powers of the committee, and what course they must take in order to effect their purpose. He accordingly applied to Ezra L'Homedieu, Esq. clerk of the court, and from him received information that the only mean of effecting their purpose was, to expel me by the *poor act*. Big with this information, the learned Judge returned to his constituents and made his report. Daniel Howell, the moderator of said committee, then signed a complaint, directed to Judge Hurlbut and Henry Pierson, Justices of the Peace, alleging that I had no sufficient means for the maintenance of myself and family, and consequently was in danger of being chargeable to the town for a maintenance, and prayed for my removal therefrom. Accordingly an order was granted by these two *Justices* for my apprehension and appearance before them forthwith. The order was executed, and I was brought before them, when they inquired with great magisterial importance, what business I followed for a living, and what means I had for support. After they had gone through with their interrogatories, they withdrew, and in about five minutes returned and informed me, that in their opinion I was liable to become a town charge, and therefore ordered me to remove by the 20th of July, and on failure, declared they should grant their order for my removal.

I was ignorant of the statute of New York upon this subject, therefore applied to an attorney living in Southhold, about fourteen miles distant, for counsel and information. The contents of which were contained in a letter received from him a few days after.

[301]

"SIR,

"Having made a *bona fide* purchase of the value of thirty pounds, you have gained a legal settlement, from which you cannot be legally removed; therefore, should you be illegally removed, demand and take a copy of the warrant, and give notice to one or more of the overseers in writing that you appeal from said order to the General Sessions of the Peace, to be holden at Southhold on the first Tuesday in October next, of which take a copy and be able to prove the service: also give notice in like manner to the signers of said warrant, that unless satisfaction is made you within one month, you shall commence an action against them for the recovery of the damages you have sustained by your illegal apprehension, confinement and removal: and if satisfaction be not made, I think it advisable to prosecute both the signers and executors of such warrant. I am, etc.

"DANIEL OSBORN.

"July, 17th, 1793."

Upon this information I strained my credit with my friends, and by the addition of my own little savings, raised the thirty pounds, which I immediately appropriated to the purchase of land. Information of this I transmitted to the Justices, and likewise a notification of my appeal from their judgment to the Court of Sessions. However, one thing had almost escaped my memory, viz. the evening following my examination before the Justices, I waited on Judge Hurlbut, with two of my neighbors, men of substantial property, who offered to give any security which should be required, to indemnify the town from any charges on account of me and my family. This was done that the world might be satisfied how consistently these men acted in obedience to the oath of a Justice of the Peace, in trying to remove me under a pretence of fear of my becoming chargeable to the town through poverty. They refused to accept the security.

When the committee were informed of my becoming a freeholder, they appeared much disconcerted, and at a loss what measures next to pursue. Matters rested in silence for some time, and I was apprehensive that, baffled in their measures, they had given up their object in despair; however, they still held their meetings in secret, and to the great entertainment of the curious, a neighboring woman of infamous character frequently met with them. At length I was notified by one of the committee, who came to my house on the business, that Mrs. Aldridge, the name of the woman, had sworn a rape against me before Judge Hurlbut, and that unless I absconded immediately, I should be taken by a warrant, which had already been granted, and was now in the hands of the constable.

My family were very much terrified at this unexpected stroke of infernal conduct. My neighbors flocked in and advised me immediately to decamp and leave the country, in order to save my life; "for," said they, "Mr. Woolworth and his party will take your life, let the event be what it may."

I thought the better way, however, not yet to leave the country, but risk the event. I knew the consequences of taking such a step. The party against me would then be gratified in every wish. They would see me driven away, loaded with the greatest infamy, and themselves possessing every advantage to bury their own wickedness under the odium which they would cast on me, and none could prevent it.

As this was a matter wholly unfounded in truth, I did not believe the abilities of the woman whom they had chosen as the instrument of their wickedness, sufficient to carry the business through, without detection; and Mr. Halsey assured me that he would render me every assistance in his power through the trial. I therefore waited patiently the arrival of the officer, expecting to be carried to jail, to remain until the sitting of the next supreme court of *Nisi Prius*.

This circumstance prevented the continuance of my school. None expected I could attend to any business again until after court. I waited in this situation a number of days without any further movement. I was surprised at not being yet served with the warrant; however, after a time, I heard the warrant was not founded upon the crime of rape, but of an "assault with an *intent* to ravish"; "O!" said I, "you are about endeavoring to bring the Worcester scene again into view; a pattern well suited for such vile purposes!" This being a bailable matter, I gave over the idea of a jail.

Whether the warrant granted in the first place by Judge Hurlbut was for the crime of ravishment, and afterwards he thought it better calculated to answer his purpose, to lay his crime in the warrant on a

[303]

lower grade, or whether the warrant was the same and the report incorrect, I cannot determine.

The officer not yet making his appearance to serve the warrant, I was determined to go to him, that the difficulty might terminate, and I be in a condition again to attend to my school. I accordingly went to his house, and desired him to serve his precept, if he had one in his possession. He of consequence made me a prisoner, but added, that as he was then busy, he could not attend to go with me before Judge Hurlbut, and desired that I would meet him there at sunsetting, and give in my bail. I told him that I would comply with his request, but added, "that I felt a little surprised to be treated in such a manner, after being apprehended on a criminal process. That I had been made a prisoner before on such an occasion, but had ever been guarded with the most sedulous attention." Gelston, the officer, replied, "that in common cases he conducted very differently; but under present circumstances, if I made my escape and left the island, he would be answerable for all the difficulty which should arise, and if I was determined to stay, he had no doubt of my meeting him according to agreement.

I expostulated with him upon the wickedness of the conduct to which he had become an abettor. "You, Mr. Gelston, have bound yourself by oath to execute the functions of your office without partiality, affection or favor. The nature of this office is to preserve the peace, apprehend and secure offenders, etc., and every idea attached to your office is comprised in this general conduct, viz. to guard the innocent from the attacks and injuries of the wicked. This being the general complexion of your duty, are you not prostituting yourself to the vilest of measures, by being instrumental in prosecuting those plans which are so notoriously founded in wrong, as influencing your conduct towards me in such a manner as to throw a temptation in my way to elude the decision of law upon this business, thereby declaring this to be the object of the party whom you serve? Is not the language of the party, to whose service you are devoted, so notorious that you have not mistaken its meaning? viz. that they are not grieved for any law which they apprehend is broken; that they are not desirous for the punishment of an offender; but are anxious to lay hold of any pretence to get rid of a man whose openness they fear, and from whose

[304]

resolution they shrink back abashed. What shall we think of a man, who being a Judge of the court and Justice of the Peace, shall conduct in the manner which Judge Hurlbut has done, and that too in such a notorious manner, that not a child in Bridghampton but what would be at once sensible that every purpose would be answered in his mind, should I leave the country; and moreover you would be justified. nay, be applauded for giving me the opportunity. and being instrumental in furthering my escape."

Mr. Gelston barely observed, "that he felt no great inclination to enter into inquiries respecting the *motives* by which those were actuated who granted precepts. He should ever obey them, and leave the consequences to those who granted them."

We parted, and at the time appointed I met Gelston at the house of Judge Hurlbut. in company with Mr. Halsey, who became my security in the sum of one hundred pounds for my appearance at the court of Quarter Sessions. I found Judge Hurlbut determined to recognize me to appear before that court, of which he was Judge, rather than before the court of *Nisi Prius*, which sat some time sooner, and which always took cognizance of matters of such a nature.[1]

After matters had progressed to this point, I found my enemies extremely mortified at their terminating so differently from their calculations. I again resumed my school and continued for some time in peace; but the tongue of slander did not cease, the exertions of my enemies for my destruction did not abate; they now saw that the matter must come to trial before a court of Judicature, respecting the crime for which I stood charged; therefore they determined to affect that by prejudice in which they should fail by testimony.

After holding frequent meetings in company with Mrs. Aldridge, the committee resolved that Mr. Woolworth should make a journey to Massachusetts and effect an investigation of the reports there in circulation against me, and bring them forward to Long Island under such a coloring as to take hold of the minds of people in that place; Mr. Woolworth accordingly set out on his *ministerial* mission.

---

[1] It will be well to notice, that no court of inquest was ever held by Judge Hurlbut upon this business when I was present, fearing I suppose to bring the witness before me, lest I should gain some advantage, by her telling those things which would militate against the cause afterwards.

[305]

When he arrived in the state of Massachusetts, he began his complaints in the bitterest manner, stating that I had come to Bridghampton, and after being used by him in the kindest and most humane manner, I had returned the blackest ingratitude; had made difficulty among his people, and endeavored to effect all the disturbance possible; and endeavored to deceive the people about my former character, etc.

Under this view, he requested a Mr. Storrs, minister of Longmeadow, who was bound to Hanover, to call on Mr. Wheelock, President of Dartmouth College, and after relating to him the enormity of my conduct on Long Island, requested a statement of my character in writing from him. True to his trust, Mr. Storrs called on Mr. Wheelock, and made known his business, without any hesitation, or regard to the feelings of delicacy, notwithstanding my father was present at the time; however, for an excuse for Mr. Storrs, perhaps he had been led into the general error which Mr. Woolworth had spread among his acquaintance, viz. that my father had become my inveterate foe, wishing me in prison rather than at large.

Mr. Wheelock remarked to Mr. Storrs the impropriety of his intermeddling in a contention between Mr. Woolworth and me, and declined doing anything in the business. Finally, after a painful and laborious pursuit after something to answer his purpose, Mr. Woolworth returned home, with only his own story, which he had inserted in a Springfield paper, in order to give the business a little less the appearance of design, and brought that paper to one Frothingham, printer of Sagg Harbor, for him to republish in the Long Island *Herald*. This curious publication was in the following words:

"Springfield, (Massachusetts), June 25th.
"The celebrated Mr. Burroughs, who, some years since was convicted of counterfeiting hard money and passing of it in this town;—of borrowing a certain worthy parson's garments, watch, etc. under pretence of being a clergyman and clad in a manner unsuitable for him to perform the sacred functions of his office, and leaving his benevolent friend in exchange for those articles, this consolatory text, "Thou shalt seek me early but find me not," is now on Long Island, in the state of New York, taking care of a large school. This villain, after spend-

[306]

ing a few *agreeable* summers on Castle Island in consequence of counterfeiting, committing theft, etc. again sallied forth into the country in order for a change of amusements.

"By his artful insinuations and through the credulity of the inhabitants of the town of Dudley, in the county of Worcester, he procured the charge of a school, a trust of the most delicate nature. Here he had an excellent opportunity of 'teaching the young idea how to shoot!' He improved it, and presently after was lodged in the prison at Worcester, tried on three separate indictments for attempts to commit rapes on the bodies of his young female scholars, was convicted and sentenced accordingly. Two-thirds of his punishment was inflicted, and a day appointed on which he was to receive the remainder; previous to which he broke jail and made his escape."

How this conduct may appear to you, sir, I cannot tell, but to me it seemed a stretch of wickedness beyond parallel, taking into view the circumstance of Mr. Woolworth's being acquainted with this fact, viz. that the greater part of this advertisement was entirely false, and done with an intention of creating an invincible prejudice in the minds of those, before whom my cause of assault must soon come for trial. Added to this, the cry was raised against me, that I was abandoned by all my former acquaintance, even by my own parents, being despised, rejected and entirely disowned by them. This assertion was made by Mr. Woolworth, in the most positive and categorical terms. In the midst of this uproar and clamor, my father, mother, and wife's father, came to Bridghampton, on a visit—Abashed and dismayed, my enemies slunk into silence; my friends, who had heard these dismal reports, now came flocking to my house in order to satisfy themselves in what manner I was treated by my own parents.

About this time the sitting of the Court of *Nisi Prius* took place, at which presided the Hon. Judge Lansing, Nathaniel Lawrence, Esq., Attorney-General. I attended this court, in order to lay the libellous publication produced by Mr. Woolworth, as above stated, before the Grand Jury, in order for them to prosecute as a breach of the laws of the state. I waited on Mr. Lawrence in the first instance, and laid the matter before him, and received his decided opinion, that the matter was a notorious breach of the law of the state, and ought to be prosecuted. However, immediately after I had left Mr. Lawrence,

[307]

Judge Hurlbut entered into private conversation with him; and I heard them very earnest in their discourse, but could not distinguish the meaning of their words. The next day Mr. Lawrence sent for me and gave me to understand, "that he should not assist in bringing forward a bill of indictment on the subject of my complaint. That he had been informed by Judge Hurlbut that the matter contained in the publication was true, and that my conduct had been of a similar nature since I had resided on Long Island; that I was now bound over to Court for a crime of a most enormous and aggravated nature, of which there was not the least hesitating doubt of my being convicted; and that the publication had been brought forward under a real necessity of preventing the ruin of the people of Bridghampton."

I replied to Mr. Lawrence in the following manner. "I feel, sir, myself injured in a very peculiar manner, by the statement made by Judge Hurlbut, and the resolution you have taken on the subject. I have been oppressed by certain characters in Bridghampton, among whom Judge Hurlbut is one, in a very barbarous and cruel manner; no means, however wicked and cruel, have been neglected to effect their purpose: this series of difficulties is too tedious to relate; I have been much reduced in my circumstances by them. I had but a competency before, but now am reduced to a situation in which I have nothing to spare from the necessities of my family. Had not this been the case, I would not have brought this matter forward in behalf of the state, but would have commenced a suit in my own behalf; notwithstanding, I really flattered myself that the laws of my country would have protected me from injury, even in my state of penury. I am willing to risk the action on the falsehood of facts stated in the publication; and moreover upon the falsehood of the facts stated by Judge Hurlbut respecting my being proved guilty of those enormous crimes which he has related." Mr. Lawrence waved any further conversation upon the subject, and the next day I went, as my only remaining resource, before the grand jury. After considerable conversation on the subject, I was dismissed. The Attorney-General being sent for soon after, I had leave to withdraw my papers. It will be well to note, that one of the Bridghampton committee was on this jury; whether by accident or design, I leave you to judge.

The Solicitor for the county being present at this court, I inquired of him whether other bonds would be necessary, provided a continuance of my cause should be granted at the time of my being called upon by the court of Quarter Sessions; or whether the old bonds were sufficient, until the cause came to trial. I was informed that the old bond was sufficient under such a circumstance, without the necessity of a renewal. The reason of making the inquiry was produced by a witness then being sick whom I depended on, and danger remained of her continuing unable to attend at the time of trial.

The Court of Quarter Sessions was attended but by one attorney as a general thing, the Solicitor for the county excepted, who was likewise clerk of the court. This attorney, whose name was Skinner, I applied to, in order to pre-engage his assistance at the time of trial. He promised to assist me, but I yet gave him no retaining fee.

As the time of the sitting of the Court drew nigh, much noise was made about my absconding, and many frightful reports were made to Mr. Halsey that I should break my bonds and leave the country; however, these machinations proved ineffectual: Mr. Halsey paid no attention to the reports; nay, he carried his confidence so far, as to furnish me with horse, saddle and bridle, in order to ride to the place where the Court was held, being thirty miles distant from my abode; alleging, "that if I was determined to abscond, he would place me in a situation of doing it with facility."

As I feared, the witness upon whom I chiefly depended, was unable to attend, and consequently, I had drawn up the resolution of moving for a continuance of the cause until the next term; but judge, sir, my surprise, when I arrived at court, at finding the attorney, Mr. Skinner, to whom I had spoken for assistance, engaged on the other side, to assist Mr. L'Homedieu the Solicitor; therefore I was left alone, and unsupported by any. The Judges presiding, were J. N. Havens and John Hurlbut.

I was called to the bar and answered to my indictment. I then pleaded for a continuance. The attornies on the other side made answer that they should bring no objections; and demanded further security by new bonds, or that I should be committed close prisoner until next term. In my answer I observed, that I had endeavored to gain intelligence upon this subject from Mr. L'Homedieu previous to the sitting of court, owing to an apprehension of my being likely to want a continuance, on account of my principal witness at that time being in a state of lingering illness, and received information from him that I should have no need to renew the bonds, in case of a continuance. Depending on this information I came on, unprepared with any security, expecting that I had done everything which could be required; therefore, the matter rested thus with me, viz. that I must either go to trial without the assistance of witnesses, which I could not do with safety, or else be committed close prisoner to jail until I could send to Bridghampton for bondsmen, which would be attended with difficulties I did not know how to encounter, not only on account of the confinement, but likewise on account of the expense attending the business under such circumstances; under this view of the matter, I prayed the indulgence of the court to let the business rest as it was until next term.

My prayer was not granted, yet I was indulged with a continuance until the next morning to make the best arrangements for my defence. One of Bridghampton committee was present at this court, who came to my lodgings in the evening, and desired a private conference with me. He endeavored to state to my view the dangerous situation I now stood in, observing from what I had seen I might clearly discern that the whole court was against me, and that I should have no chance for an acquittal. "You know, Mr. Burroughs, that the whole of this difficulty has arisen in consequence of your obstinately persisting in continuing in Bridghampton, when the committee had requested you to move away. It has ever been the determination of the committee to remove you by some means, and you see to what the difficulty has already arisen. We do not wish to have you confined in jail, if you will only be wise for yourself. If you stay and stand trial you can't entertain a hope to the contrary, but what a jail will be your portion. You see the leading characters in the court against you. You see that Mr. L'Homedieu has already treated you with open insult, which the court allowed, and has your attorney on his side. You have no witness in your cause, and no chance to get any. You have no person to assist you in managing your trial, and two powerful lawyers against you; besides all this, the court is against you. You have put your great dependence on the integrity of Judge Havens, but you may depend that he is determined not to befriend you, since he sees so many against you. Mr. L'Homedieu has great influence upon his mind, and he will not go contrary to his opinion. If you should leave the country, the business would come to an end without any further difficulty. Your bondsman would never be prosecuted, and the whole business would die away of its own accord. I heard Judge Hurlbut say myself that Mr. Halsey should never be hurt if you left the country. If you should live to get through this difficulty, we shall never leave you until you quit the town of Bridghampton; therefore my advice to you, as a friend, is to leave the country this night, and never more return; if you do not accept this advice, you may depend you are undone forever."

After Mr. Hains, the name of this person, had done speaking, I answered him in the following manner: "You have observed, Mr. Hains, that *friendship* has influenced you to give me the advice which you have just now uttered. Well did the wise man observe, that the 'tender mercies of the wicked are cruel.' Influenced by your friendship, what a horrid picture has it produced!!! You advise me to abscond and leave the country, under the peculiar circumstances to which your wickedness has reduced me; loaded with the infamy of a crime, of which you know me to be innocent, and to leave my family with those who have not shown the common sympathy, which we find among savages; moreover, you advise me to forfeit all claims to confidence, by betraying my friend, who has been my security, into your power. You promise me, that no harm shall befall him, in consequence of my elopement. Can I place confidence in the promises of such characters, who have violated all the laws of propriety, integrity, humanity or decency!!! When I take into consideration, Mr. Hains, the character which Mr. Woolworth professes, viz. a minister of that gospel, which teaches meekness, mildness, benevolence and charity; when I view you, Judge Hurlbut, and the rest of the committee as members of the church over which he presides, under the most solemn covenant to govern yourselves according to the laws of benevolence and equity, which are taught by your professed Master; and contrast your conduct with your solemn profession and covenant, it fills my soul with a species of horror too great for utterance!!! Did you believe a Power existed who would eventually punish the wicked, fear would keep you within the bounds of moderation. Either madness

[311]

and infatuation have taken hold of your heart, or else you disbelieve every article of your mock profession.

"I firstly and formally pursued what appeared to me to be my duty, in relation to the causes of our difficulties in Bridghampton. I have never intentionally swerved from that line of conduct since, neither do I ever intend it. I am sensible that every measure has been taken which malice could dictate, in order to involve me in difficulty by this prosecution. Mr. Woolworth in the first instance has circulated through the country a libelous publication, calculated to raise an invincible prejudice among the people, who must compose the jury, by whom I shall be tried. You have exerted yourselves to strengthen this by the unceasing tongue of slander and calumny, in hopes of effecting that by prejudice, which you could not by a fair trial. You have likewise very ingeniously manœuvered to bring me to trial without the assistance of evidence or counsel. As for Judge Havens' being influenced by party cabal in this matter, I do not yet fear it. Be the consequences what they may, I shall risk the trial, and abide the consequences."

After Mr. Hains had retired, and I was left alone to a cool reflection upon my present situation, it filled my mind with the keenest anxiety. I saw myself brought into a most disadvantageous situation by the unmanly treatment of the Solicitor against me. I saw myself under a necessity of going into jail, or else going to trial without any witness. I expected that the next day the probability was strong against me of being confined in close jail. Under this view. said I. "what must become of my family? They are already reduced to indigent circumstances by the continued interruption and extraordinary expenses which the difficulties have created. I have vainly flattered myself with considerable help from my friends, in whose cause I embarked in this difficulty. When my business shall cease, the support of my family is cut off, and they are left without resource: left in a barbarous land, the hearts of whose inhabitants are made of more than savage inhumanity."

A view of this business kept my eyes from closing through the night. I tumbled from one side of the bed to the other, in hopes of finding a moment's respite from my perplexity in some easy situation; but alas! I tumbled in vain.

[312]

CHAPTER XXIX

"O! days of pain! while here,
How tasteless! and how terrible when gone!
Gone? they never go; when past they haunt us still;
The spirit walks, of every day deceas'd,
And smiles an angel; or a fury frowns."

EARLY the next morning I again appeared at the bar, in order for trial; the courthouse was very crowded. No witness was examined, whose evidence amounted to anything, on either side, excepting the woman, who was the chief instrument in this business. After she had gone through with her testimony, and the questions had been asked on the other side, I proceeded to cross examine her; but she would not answer any question I put, until Judge Hurlbut had given her a lead to her answers. Upon many questions she was totally silent until she was ordered by Judge Havens to give an answer. After the examination was through, I proceeded to make some observations to the jury, but was continually interrupted by the attornies on the other side, ordering me to keep to the point, until Judge Havens commanded them to desist and let me proceed. After I had ended, the attornies on the other side labored the business with great earnestness to induce the jury to find me guilty. They ended, and Judge Havens commanded the jury to retire and make up their verdict. After an hour's absence, the jury returned their verdict, Not Guilty of the charge, but guilty of an assault only. The verdict, returned in this manner, threw the cost of prosecution on to me, which amounted, together with the fine which the court imposed, to twelve dollars and one half. Not being prepared with the money to pay this sum, Mr. Gelston, the sheriff, advanced the money for me, and I was dismissed.

I left this place about sunsetting, and rode hard until I arrived at my own abode. I found my wife up, and a number of the neighbors at my house, though it was now the latter part of the night, waiting with impatience and solicitude, listening to the sound of every step, to

[313]

hear if possible how the matter had terminated in relation to my trial, the news which had already arrived being of the most disagreeable nature. As my horse approached the house, they came out at the sound of his steps to learn who it was, and if it was any one by whom they could gain further intelligence from the River-head (the place where the court was held); finding the horse was approaching the house, they concluded some messenger was coming with news: they therefore drew back into the house, waiting in fearful suspense, till the event should be announced!!!

Whilst they were in this situation, conceive, sir, if possible, their surprise, when I appeared among them. They started, as though doubtful of the evidence of their own eyes. When they heard my voice, they crowded around, to learn the final catastrophe. I had maintained my fortitude unshaken until this moment. All danger being now over, and I returned once more into the bosom of my family, and to the society of my friends and neighbors, brought on those sensations which I cannot describe, but which overpowered my resolution, and became too heavy to support; tears flowed from my eyes in abundance, when I could scarce tell the reason why.

> "Hast thou ever weigh'd a sigh?
> Or studied the philosophy of tears!
> (A science yet unlectur'd in our schools!)
> Has thou descended deep into the breast,
> And seen their source? If not, descend with me,
> And trace their briny riv'lets to their springs."

My enemies were greatly mortified at the unfortunate termination of all their labors for my ruin. I had struggled with the difficulties until I had overcome them; though at the expense of my domestic provisions. It was now thought that Mr. Woolworth and his party, being so thoroughly baffled in all their endeavors, would yield to necessity, and give over their machinations. However, I soon found him. together with Judge Hurlbut, again intriguing among the parents of my scholars, and endeavoring to detach them from the school. They were successful in some instances, but not in a sufficient degree to answer their purpose. Therefore Judge Hurlbut and Henry Pierson, Justices of the Peace, granted a warrant for the removal of me, my wife and children, as likely to become poor. My wife and two children were taken and carried from the island to New London, in the state of Connecticut, and there left. Gelston, the officer who executed the warrant, manifested the most brutish and indelicate conduct towards my wife, during this scene. He came after and transported her in a horse cart to the vessel which was employed to carry her to Connecticut, being a distance of five miles, and insulted her during the passage with the most obscene and abusive raillery. However, when he arrived at New London, he found the corporation so far from receiving my wife and children, and sending them on from town to town, according to the directions in the warrant, that they informed Gelston that he must find security for all costs the city of New London might be put to on their account. This at once disappointed the prospects of the party, and my wife and children returned the next day to Bridghampton.

You may possibly wish to know how it happened that, as the warrant commanded Gelston to remove me as well as my family, I was not carried away with them. The reason was this. I found it extremely difficult to support my family, under the embarrassment which I, by this time, found myself; therefore had resolved, if they were determined to carry my family away, that they would soon arrive among their friends, where they would tarry until I should get my affairs somewhat settled, and my business so arranged, as to afford them a comfortable support. That disencumbered from the necessity of their immediate support, I could make myself easy under almost any situation, and accordingly could practice a system of much closer economy, in order to bring my affairs into a better state. Under this view, I had determined to keep out of the way myself, when my family were taken from the island. However, I have since suffered the keenest remorse on the account of letting my family be taken away, by such barbarians, without risking the consequences of being with them.

As the winter was now approaching, I found myself straitened in my necessary stock of provisions, fuel, etc., for the winter consumption. There were some debts I had due, but particularly one of Dr. Havens, to a considerable amount, on which I depended for the support of my family. I accordingly made application to the Doctor for a settlement, but to no purpose. I endeavored to bring him to a reckoning, that our accounts might be adjusted, being now almost of three years standing; yet my efforts were ineffectual. I stated at large the disagreeable situation of my affairs, and the necessity of the debt for the support of my family. However, I yet obtained nothing more than empty promises.

During the winter I continued my school, which was not large, and by the closest economy, made shift to get through with tolerable comfort; but distress now began to stare me in the face. My wife was in hourly expectation of bringing another wretched infant into existence. The provisions which I had laid by in the fall were all consumed. My wages during the winter were all taken up in discharging the debts which my lawsuits and other difficulties had brought upon me; nothing now remained excepting the debt of Dr. Havens, which amounted, if I mistake not, to about eight pounds. This debt I had tried to collect, without effect, for six months. I for the last time wrote him word, that I should leave the account in the hands of Esq. Rogers to collect, if he did not forthwith settle the matter. The Doctor had the effrontery to come to my house and tell me, "that I was hated so much in that country, that I could not collect a debt." He offered me five dollars if I would pass receipts. I rejected this offer with that disdain which such an unworthy action merits. Upon this, Dr. Havens left my house, and repaired immediately to Mr. L'Homedieu, for a special warrant for me to be brought before him, for an action of debt; testifying, under oath, that I owed him, and that he was in fear of my absconding, and that thereby he should lose his debt. This oath being necessary to entitle the plaintiff to a special warrant.

I was taken with this warrant, and brought before Esq. L'Homedieu immediately. I plead for an adjournment, alleging that I had material witnesses to cite, and offered security for my appearance; for I could have proved the offer of five dollars the day before for a settlement. This request was denied; I had the disagreeable necessity of going to trial immediately.

Doctor Havens here exhibited an account against me for attendance, nursing, boarding, washing, lodging, etc., during the term of twenty-one days. His charge for board was three shillings per day, for nursing six, for washing and lodging one and six pence, and for attendance and medicine, ten shillings. You will please to recollect that this account was for services during my sickness of the fever and ague, and remitting fever, which had all been settled; first, by its being done out

[316]

of kindness, and secondly, my discharging the Doctor's school bill during my teaching on Shelter Island.

Bridghampton committee attended this court, and made themselves very busy in interfering in the trial. The cause finally went to the jury, who abated much the price which Doctor Havens had put to his items, and yet after all, left a balance against me of 23 shillings. When judgment was given against me, there remained no more fear of the loss of the debt by my absconding. I was left at liberty and retired to my own home, in a state of desperation. I could not view my own family without feeling the frantic rage of grief, more cruel than the sting of death. My all was gone. My only remaining hope forsaken me, and my family in such a situation as to need the solace of comfort. I was in a state of horror through this night, totally indescribable. To add to this scene of woe, Gelston came the next morning with the execution, took our bed and bedding, and sold them at public vendue, to satisfy the execution, which amounted to four pounds.

This was the winding up of all the scenes of horror through which I have ever passed. I now saw myself sunk under a weight too heavy to endure, without any prospect of recovery. To behold my innocent helpless children hanging about my knees, with fascinating fondness and affection, endeavoring to cheer and dissipate the horrid gloom that overspread our brows, ignorant of the ruin which was hovering around; Oh, God of mercy! this was a scene too great for mortal strength! I could look death in the face with composure, but this scene deprived me of manhood. I lost all fortitude under it, and could not withstand the tempest of passion, which entirely overthrew every remaining spire of resolution. I now saw my wife and children thrown upon the charity of a merciless world for support. I was unable any further to contribute to their maintenance. My business was interrupted, my property exhausted, and my health and strength were wasted. A state of universal debility had attended me for more than two years; pulmonary complaints. together with symptoms of universal decay, had increased upon me to such a degree, as to render me incapable of business. Gladly would I have resigned my life, but revolted at the idea of leaving my family without the consolation of one solitary friend to solace them in their distress. Oh, helpless innocence, said I, to what a state of wretchedness have I reduced you, by making you companions

[317]

in my wayward fate. Would to God the days of my joyful union with you had been barred by the irreversible laws of nature! Notwithstanding no joy had been so great, no pleasure so exquisite as domestic felicity, yet the pangs of their disappointment, the horrors of their situation overpower every consideration of past enjoyment, and make me loathe its recollection! Which way to turn, of what course to take I could not determine! All was darkness, gloom, night, wretchedness and despair.

As the throw of a desperate gamester, I determined to make application to Mr. Woolworth, Judge Hurlbut, and the committee. "Possibly," said I, "gratified in their desires, their breasts may at last be touched with compassion, and they will commiserate the victim who has fallen a sacrifice at the shrine of their ambition"; but, alas! this application was productive of nothing but the bitterest taunts, irony, and reproaches; added to this, I received the swaggering declamation of Doctor Havens, triumphantly exulting under the idea that he had outwitted me; and effected that, at a single stroke, which all Bridghampton had been in vain pursuing for more than two years.

This had the effect to arouse me from that state of stupid languor and insensibility, under which I had servilely crouched for some time. I erected my head, and reproached myself for falling under the burdens of misfortunes, which were produced by pursuing the course of rectitude. What, said I, shall honesty and integrity flee ashamed from the face of vice and wickedness? forbid it justice; forbid it fortitude. Shall we only pursue virtue when her paths are strewed with flowers; and the cries of the multitude are in our favor? "Rather," said I, "possess that virtue, under the exercise of which we stand against and overcome whatever difficulties may be thrown in our way."

I now began to arm with resolution, to look about and see what means, could yet be used, and determined to devote what little remaining ability, I yet possessed, to the advantage of my family. I had often received invitations from my quondam friend, Joseph Huntington, Esq. to come to Georgia, and commence business in that country, as affording a much fairer opportunity of making an establishment for my family. My friend Huntington being in the practice of the law with a large run of business on hand, was under peculiar advantages to afford me essential assistance to such an object.

[318]

PLANS FOR DEPARTURE

Under all circumstances, I concluded that the only measure I could adopt, would be to accept of this offer, and travel southward as soon as the trying hour of my wife's sickness in childbed was over. Possibly, said I, a change of climate may alleviate my difficulty, or hasten my end. In either case it will bring doubtful circumstances to a certainty, and should I eventually be taken away, the probability will be, that my wife's father will then make provision for his daughter, when no one is left to do it. Should I happily succeed in recovering my health and gaining an interest for the support of my family, it would be infinitely preferable to tarrying in Bridghampton, and suffering a thousand deaths in preventing one. Moreover, by going such a distance, I might illude the disadvantages of a thousand reports, floating upon a thousand babbling tongues, loaded with gall and bitterness. Already has the propensity among mankind to depreciate the merit of others, been carried to such an alarming height towards me, that whoever performs an evil deed to me, thinks he is doing "God service."

I made a statement of these views to my wife. Many objections occurred, but after maturely considering the subject, her reason triumphed over her feelings, and she aided me with counsel to strengthen my yet irresolute mind. One great difficulty yet remained, which was hard to remove, viz. how to provide against the expenses of sickness, as we were now in a state wholly destitute. After ruminating some time on this subject, with no small degree of trouble of mind, I at length determined to make a visit to William Hart, Esq. of Norwich Landing, lay my situation open to his view, and peradventure his heart would be inclined to compassionate my situation; he had ever appeared as a person possessing the milk of human kindness. I was not deceived in my estimate of his feelings. He compassionated my distress: he gave me ten dollars: he moreover wrote to an acquaintance of his in New York, recommending me to his attention. With this small sum I hastened back to my family, with feelings triumphantly delightful. I found my exertions crowned with success so far as to produce a remedy from the impending evil of being destitute of help in time of sickness. I waited the usual time of expectation, nay, I waited three weeks longer than the natural period in rotation; but the hour of sickness and delivery did not yet arrive. The stock of money which I had laid by for this purpose, was now expended, and no prospect of gaining another supply. To stay longer and starve with my family, I knew was fruit-less and in vain. I determined therefore immediately to hasten my departure from this inhospitable clime, and seek support in a distant country. The time I fixed for my leaving this place being now estab-lished. the fortitude of my wife began to fail. The prospect was so dreadful before her, and the time uncertain when we should again meet, or whether we should ever again see each other, that she sunk under it. She roared with anguish through the night. The children were terri-fied at seeing their mamma in such distress. They wept to keep her company, yet little thought of the harm that was around them. You, sir, are a father! yet you know nothing of these feelings. Distress such as that can only give you a sense of them.

I used my endeavors to administer comfort in this dreadful situation. I called the attention of my wife to the fluctuating scenes of time, that such prospects could not always last; that the darkest times are soon followed by the rising sun; that she lived in a country where they dare not let her starve. Miserable objects of comfort!! While I was endeavoring to administer this consolation (cold consolation) I felt the want of assistance myself. I proceeded till my faculties of sensa-tion were stagnated by the dint of grief. My eyes were set with hor-ror; my teeth gnashed with anguish; my tongue clave to the roof of my mouth, and I could not pronounce a syllable. O! God of mercy! on me alone pour out the full vials of thy wrath. Let me alone sustain the fury of thy decrees, and avert thy vengeance from these who prat-tle innocence in every lisp of the tongue.[1] At earliest dawn I tore myself from my family, I hastened on board a vessel, and sailed for New York.

These are scenes at which nature sickens; yet they are scenes of na-ture. For the mind, in the cooler moments of reflection, to investigate the secret source from whence originated such cruel sufferings, and apply a remedy to this disorder, is performing a part truly humane. The first emotion, we are apt to feel, under the impulses of misguided passion, towards the author of such calamity, is vengeance; but, alas! vengeance may gratify the impulses of passion, but cannot correct the

---

[1] This violent sensation of grief was caused by the exclamation of my little child, who, seeing the distress of his mother. and learning that I was going to leave her, cried, "Don't go away, dadda, for if you do mamma will die."

[320]

evil. Had not the most besotted ignorance bewildered their minds, they could not have conducted as they did. Although some were reputed men of information, yet by making advances in error and cultivating wrong pursuits, they made themselves more the children of darkness, than nature's simple sons. They had become more estranged to the voice of reason. and shut out from light, by stronger bars of darkness. Wisdom teaches us all to consider each other as children of the same common family, and that our true happiness is promoted *only* by the welfare of all; that there is that connection between the various members of this family, that no one can suffer without involving, in some measure, the family in the difficulty.

Mr. Woolworth had been educated and habituated in the opinion. that the character and station of a clergyman was great and sacred; as he observed to me on a certain occasion: "A clergyman," said he, "is the ambassador of the Lord Jesus; he is clothed with his authority in that character, and therefore ought to be treated with that respect which such a character claims; therefore any attempt to oppose, or bring a minister into contempt, is committing a crime immediately against God. and ought to be punished as the most destructive of any which could be committed."

These sentiments were disseminated among the people who were leagued against me; and I believe they conscientiously thought it their duty to destroy me by any means, be they what they might. Under this view, it is not to be wondered that extraordinary and violent measures should be adopted. The consequence of such treatment towards me awakened the feelings of passion, and when passion is the leading feature on both sides of the contest. but little reason will be called into exercise. Cool deliberation will give place to the wiles of subtilty, and the disorder will increase rather than abate.

I have many times since lamented my want of patient perseverance, in endeavoring to convince my persecutors of their wrong, by the cool dictates of reason, and in pursuing some measures with too much warmth against them. where, in fact, I found that jealousy had miscolored their transactions to my mind. Error once seen ought to be corrected. The pruning-hook should never be laid aside, then we should live up to the condition of our nature, which requires a state of improving and progressing in knowledge till time shall cease. Had

[321]

Mr. Woolworth laid aside the idea attached to his preconceived errors, and given the subject a free discussion; looked into the nature of man, his feelings, and state in society; and considered the nature of that doctrine which he undertook to inculcate, as an ambassador of the Lord Jesus, I know his native good sense would have flung a load of error from his mind, "whose heft would sink a navy." The full evidence of truth would have blazed upon his understanding with irresistible force. He would have remembered the command of his Master, "Love thy neighbor as thyself"; and in this command, he would have seen *that* wisdom and propriety, which will render society perfectly happy, when it becomes perfectly obeyed. But on the contrary, he had taken his position in error, he had pursued this error without giving himself liberty to examine its merits, until he raised a fortification of darkness around his mind, and consequently excluded the approach of truth. Under circumstances like these, the energy of his mind was perverted to inhuman purposes. He spread wretchedness and desolation around him, and became a partaker in the general calamity.

What a different effect would a contrary line of conduct have produced! By nature he was made for social pleasure and enjoyment; to receive and communicate happiness in the mutual display of a benevolent mind: had he pursued nature, in the matters relating to our unhappy disputes, in the room of producing noxious effects, it would have been attended with the most salutary consequences. This line of conduct would have produced the most feeling evidence upon the minds of his connections, of the real dictates of wisdom. They would have been mutual helps to each other in making improvements, in this progressive state, upon that establishment. They would individually have contributed their share to have kindled the flame of pleasure, social enjoyment and benevolent satisfaction; and so fast as ignorance was removed, they would have found themselves in a situation of bestowing and receiving the permanent establishment of a lasting happiness.

Ignorance is the great source of evil; and where men pursue a course founded in error, ever so far, in the room of acquiring wisdom, they make further removes from it, and become more and more strangers to light and knowledge; more and more stifle the voice of nature within them, by shutting the avenues of information; fixing in their vain

[322]

imaginations their own opinions, as the test of information; saying to investigation, "Hitherto shalt thou come and no further, and here shall thy proud waves be stayed."

A state of prosperity is much more fatal to the growth of wisdom than the bitterest adversity. Under misfortune the mind is called into a state of active exercise. That dependence which mutually subsists between the members of society, is not only seen but felt; and no truths are so well understood as those we feel; the evils of misfortune are known; the operations of the heart and the exercises of the soul in this state of mutual dependence can there be traced. Whereas in the days of lazy prosperity, the objects presenting to the view, are personal gratification, and a listless inattention to the welfare of mankind, owing to the want of a stimulus to call the powers of the mind into exertion upon such subjects as they feelingly find is productive of happiness.

We find in history many striking examples of this truth. At the time of Alexander's mounting the stage of action, and performing his part in the busy scenes of life, he was humane, benevolent and kind, to an extraordinary degree. Prosperity and adulation made him forget that he was a man. His conduct would make the feeling heart wish that the arrogant assertion of not being a mortal, had been true; in order that the character of human nature had not been stained with those scenes of injustice and folly which must leave an indelible blot upon our escutcheon, which time can never purify. The yet more amazing folly of mankind had fixed the title *Great* upon this inhuman wretch. Had mankind seen with the wisdom of Agesilaus, king of Sparta, they would have blushed at giving such a name to one of the most improper subjects then in being. When the king of Persia was called *great* in the hearing of Agesilaus, he would ask, "How can he be more *great* than others, without he is more *just?*"

Perhaps nature had not ever been more bountiful in furnishing any characters with the talents requisite for communicating happiness to mankind, than appeared in Pompey and Julius Cæsar; however, an uninterrupted course of success, and its constant attendant adulation, called their attention from their true interest, made them ambitious of being more than man, and in the pursuit of the object of this ambition, they sank infinitely beneath the meanest slave. Even the bloody Nero,

[323]

when a commoner, was so strongly affected with objects of human calamity, that when it became necessary to sign a death warrant, he lamented his ever learning to write, because thereby he must do a deed so repugnant to his nature.

Nothing in the ordinary course of things has so direct a tendency to pervert the bounties of nature in the human mind as exaltation, prosperity and adulation. Nothing has a more direct effect to learn man wisdom, than often to experience those events which teach him that he is a *man*. From this view of human nature we see the wisdom of those governments, where they have made provision for calling men frequently from office, to mingle again in common society; to feel and experience the weaknesses, dependencies and connection which exist among each other.

I found the most difficulty in reconciling my feelings towards Doctor Havens, even upon the benevolent system. With him and his family I had maintained one uninterrupted course of friendly offices during my acquaintance with him. In a number of instances, when his misfortunes required my friendly aid, I exerted myself with the greatest ardor in his behalf. One circumstance I will relate. The doctor had a daughter, who being unfortunately in a state of pregnancy, by a young man who utterly refused to marry her, a universal gloom of despondency hung over the family under an apprehension that the matter would become public, and leave a blot upon the family. Under this situation the Doctor entreated me to do something to relieve him from his difficulty. I entered warmly into the business, I visited the young man, I exerted my eloquence in painting the situation of the young woman, together with that of the family. I expostulated with him upon the injurious nature of his conduct, in betraying that weakness which by nature he was created to protect. I spent day after day in this pursuit. After he had utterly refused to comply with any other terms, than to make provision for the child, I still would not give up the point. I saw him and wrote to him with all the powers which I could call into exercise by my tongue and pen. My exertions proving fruitless, the Doctor formed a very extraordinary resolution to obtain revenge upon the young man. He concerted, in company with his daughter, the plan for prosecuting him for a rape; but applying to Mr. L'Homedieu on the business, obtained information, that under *such circumstances,* such a prosecution could not be carried into effect; therefore the Doctor was necessitated to sit down contented under his disappointment.

The source of all the evils arising from the Doctor's conduct, I can now clearly impute to ignorance, both natural and acquired. He was, among men, the most stupid and unfeeling. His capacity admitted the least improvement of any man with whom I was ever acquainted; his prejudices the most rooted and stubborn; and his system of thinking the most singular. He ever considered the perfection of the human character consisted in an ability to subvert an adversary; he ever appeared to think it laudable, and a striking instance of wisdom, to use the most nefarious means to obtain a favorite, if the means and end were immediately connected. His sensorious appetite upon the failings of others had no bounds; but when the tables were turned on his own family, the least obloquy was the greatest crime. The sufferings of others had no place in his mind, but his own trials were objects which called for universal commiseration.

I believe you think by this time, I am drawing the picture of a man consummately *ignorant;* and that a consummate degree of folly was the fruit of this ignorance, and that an equal degree of stupidity will ever keep him consummately ignorant. The picture is the most disagreeable that ever I have met with in human nature, and I do not believe many equals are to be found.

CHAPTER XXX

April 23d, 1794.

I LEFT Long Island with those heart-cutting pangs that a person of feeling must experience under my situation. a family behind me, consisting of a wife, and two small children, and my wife in hourly expectation of being put to bed of another, in a state of such poverty as not to have the value of one dollar of provision in the house, and no way to procure any more; and myself again launching out into the world without a single dollar to help me forward, and no business to apply myself to in order to procure me sustenance for one day. I took a passage with a man by the name of Fordham, for New York, who followed the business of carrying passengers from the east end of Long Island to New York. His price for the passage was one dollar, and each passenger to find his own sea stores. I took on board with me a few hard biscuit, hoping the passage would be short, and that I should stand in need of but little provision; but in the room of its being one day. it was lengthened out to seven. by calms and contrary winds. so that by the closest economy, my biscuit were entirely gone by the fourth day; and one of the passengers by the name of Du Val, perceiving my necessitous situation and anxiety in consequence, made me the butt for his ridicule the remainder of the passage, to my no small mortification, for I found the master of the vessel took part in and favored the sport, under an apprehension, as I suspected, that I was not able to pay him for the passage, and moreover was fearful of my making application to him for more provision, since my own was all exhausted. This I bore, because I could not help it, for I knew his suspicion was rightly founded about my own provision, and of consequence he was the only person to whom I could apply for relief, and apply I must, or starve. After much solicitation, I obtained half of a three pound loaf, with which I made out until I arrived at New York. where I put up at a public house. and called for a supper, having left my trunk on board the vessel for want of a dollar to pay .

my passage. After I had supped very heartily, as may be supposed, I retired to rest. or rather to bed, to have the more leisure opportunity of reflecting upon my desperate situation, and to fall upon some plan for my future conduct. In this situation I had a chance to take an uninterrupted view of all the difficulties that attended me, and the miseries to which I was reduced; a family left among barbarians, who, under the sanction of religion, would willingly cut their throats, as they had under that sanction already reduced me from easy circumstances, and from a situation in which I could comfortably support my family, to my present condition; my name scandalized in the most infamous manner, by those hellhounds of despotism, among those who were no way acquainted with me but by those reports; destitute of money, of business and of friends; and all my dependence upon the recommendation of my worthy friend Hart, to a gentleman in New York by the name of Huntington. as an object deserving charity.

This was the nature of the prospect as it then offered to my view. Under this prospect the burdens of life appeared too great for mortal strength, and gladly would I exchange this life upon the presumption of finding a state of rest in the grave. But to desert a family under such a situation! unprovided with the bare necessaries of life! my soul started back with horror from the contemplation of such an object. After nature had been a long time fatigued with the anguish of these prospects, she at length being exhausted, sunk to rest. Early in the morning I set out with my letter, to deliver the same to Mr. Huntington; and while I was on the way thither, my heart was in a state of palpitating anxiety, for fear that some of the ten thousand accidents which daily happen should interfere with my obtaining assistance from my present and only prospect. But my fears were much abated after delivering the letter, and his telling me to call at 10 o'clock that morning. I returned to the tavern with a cheerful countenance and ate a breakfast with a renewed appetite. I did not fail to call precisely at the hour appointed, and to my inexpressible joy received from Mr. Huntington ten dollars. The clouds of poverty were dissipated in a moment, and for a few moments I beheld myself sufficiently rich to answer every gratification of my heart; but this delusive vapor soon vanished, for I found. after paying my passage and expenses at the tavern, that my heap of treasure began very apparently to diminish.

[327]

I had by this time determined to bend my course to Georgia as fast as possible, in compliance with the solicitations of my friend Huntington, who was in those parts in the practice of law. But to perform a journey of a thousand miles with my finances was apparently a difficult task, but to proceed on as far as my money would carry me, was what I thought best, and then perhaps there might offer some prospect of my obtaining business of some nature which would enable me to earn by my industry sufficient to carry me on again. With this resolution I paid my passage to Philadelphia in the stage wagon, and bid farewell to the state of New York in which I had spent so many pleasing and painful days. I found by this time my health, which never was good in that state, grew better, and after a very agreeable passage, arrived at Philadelphia the next day about five in the afternoon, where I put up at one Wm. Elliot's, at the sign of the cross-keys, whom I found to be an attentive and agreeable publican. My money was here all exhausted, consequently I was under a necessity of trying some measure for another supply. There was a member of Congress in Philadelphia, by the name of Learned, who was partially acquainted with my misfortunes, and of consequence, I expected he would relieve them. I accordingly made application to him, stating my circumstances and views to him in as concise and plain terms as I was able, it being then evening, and he engaged for company (as he said) told me to be at the lobby of the Congress-house, at the time of their going in, and he then would see me again. Accordingly I waited in the lobby at the time appointed, for the space of three hours, with an anxious mind, before he made his appearance. He told me at once, after I saw him, that he had a damn'd expensive family to maintain, and therefore could not afford any assistance to beggars. My feelings any person will more readily conceive upon this occasion than I can describe. I told him I did not wish him to injure his own family or give to me as a beggar, but to afford me temporary assistance until I could be under a situation to help myself, and if he would do that he should ever find that I possessed a grateful heart; but all my entreaties were in vain, and I was forced to leave him with a heart almost bursting with grief and indignation. I then knew not what to do, or which way to turn for a subsistence, as my situation then was, being a stranger in the city,

[328]

and no person to recommend me to business, which was absolutely necessary, in order to obtain any.

After pondering a long time upon the gloomy prospects before me, I bethought myself of another person of whom there was a probability of obtaining some help. This was likewise a member of Congress by the name of Niles, from the state of Vermont. This gentleman was an intimate friend of my father, and accordingly I was in expectation of his advancing a small sum of money, and taking a draught upon my father for the same. This man possessed a sincere good heart, and was a man of great metaphysical talents; his economical system had raised him from a small beginning in the world to possess a handsome competency. His education had been such as to prepare him for the clerical function, in which character he had exhibited for a number of years, so that the most striking features in his character were his great fondness for close metaphysical reasoning, and a habit of great economy in his domestic concerns, and had so long practised upon this system, that any variation from it in a person's conduct, or any want of success in a person's undertakings, were in his view perfectly wrong. This was the man to whom I applied for assistance, as my ultimatum. I described my circumstances to him in as clear terms as possible, and afterwards told him of the request I wished to make. Without giving me an answer either in the affirmative or negative, he went on with a lengthy discourse to prove that my system of economy had been wrong, drawing a comparison between *his* prosperity and my adversity, and then pointed out a certain line of conduct that I ought then to take up and observe, and offered to assist me in prosecuting such; but as his plan had many things in it which I could not reconcile my mind to, and more particularly the length of time which would intervene, before I could provide for my family, I took the liberty of reasoning with him upon the better plan which I had marked out in my own mind. This was touching him in the tender spot, and he told me he was happy in not having the direction of my conduct; that I must do as I chose, but that he had no idea that my father would answer any draught upon him, and therefore could not advance me any money. In as great a proportion as my hopes had been flattered with the expectation of relief, in the same proportion did I feel the keenness of the disappoint-

[329]

ment, when I was refused the supply which I sought for. I at this moment viewed myself in a state of desperation, and had an inclination of rushing into the streets and commencing war with the whole human race. When I took a view of the world, of the pomp and splendor which surrounded crowds that perpetually passed before my eyes, to see them roll in affluence and luxury, inhabitating lofty houses, with superb equipages, and feasting upon all the delicacies of life; under these affluent circumstances, withholding from me what would never be missed from their abundance; myself destitute of every necessary of life, and looking in vain to those who from their superfluity could spare enough to relieve my distress and feel no diminution in their own property, brought to my mind a train of ideas that were desperate and horrid, and almost reduced me to a state of madness. Under this situation I could not suppress the overflowings of my feelings. My eyes lighted up with indignation, my countenance was fortified with despair, my heart was swollen to that bigness which was almost too large for my breast to contain. Under this situation I arose with a tranquil horror, composedly took my hat, and politely bid Mr. Niles farewell. I believe the desperate emotions of my heart were apparently manifested to his view by my countenance, his apparent immoveable insensibility relaxed, he put his hand in his pocket and handed me three dollars. This act of kindness in a moment melted the ferocious feelings of my heart, and I burst into tears; all those desperate sensations vanished, and I again found myself a man. With this small sum I determined to leave the city of Philadelphia, and still pursue on towards my destined place of abode. I paid my tavern bill, which I found much smaller than I expected, and afterwards took the Baltimore stage-wagon, and went on as far as a town called Warwick, about half way to Baltimore. Here finding my money again gone, I was under the necessity of stopping at Hogson's tavern, under a pretence of being too unwell to pursue my journey any further. I found at this house a young gentleman by the name of Hawley, who was originally from Connecticut; and having more confidence in him on account of his coming from the same part of the country with myself, I told him my circumstances, and begged him to point out some way for my relief, if possible. I had it in contemplation to obtain, by his assistance, a small school, or an opportunity of tending a store, writing in an office, or something else, by which I could raise a little money; but no such chance offering to his mind, I accepted of a dollar which he gave me, it being all he had, and at the same time manifested a sincere desire to give me further relief, had it been in his power. With the dollar I paid for my lodging and breakfast, and left money sufficient for my trunk to be brought on in the next stage-wagon; this taking again all the money I possessed, I pursued my way on foot without being much burdened with the weight of my cash. I travelled on moderately, and had a leisure opportunity of taking a retrospective view of my life, of the many vicissitudes to which I had been subject from my first commencing an active part upon the great stage of the world. I took a view of the virtuous and vicious among mankind, of rewards and punishments, as they were distributed through the world, and could find no general rule in which rewards were given to virtue and punishments to vice, but that good and ill fortune was promiscuously scattered through the world without any reference to virtue, merit, or vice. I at this moment examined my own heart to see whether I was suffering a punishment due to any evil which I had done; I carefully viewed all the transactions of my life, and the motives which actuated me to their performance, and after canvassing the subject maturely, I could not find an accusation that my heart brought against me. That I had done wrong in many instances, through imprudence, the impetuosity of feelings, and a misconception of things, I was perfectly sensible; but that it had uniformly and ever been my desire to render good, rather than evil, and to avoid injuring every person, so far as my judgment would serve, was a truth my whole soul responded to with pleasure. Why then it was, that my fortune through life should be marked with such striking instances of misery, was a mystery to me in the dispensations of events, that I could not reconcile to my feelings of right and wrong. These reflections had so wholly engrossed my mind, that I had almost forgotten my situation, until I was aroused from this reverie by the calls of hunger. I had now walked on till almost night without eating, and began to grow faint and hungry. What to do I did not know. Money I had none, and to ask for victuals like a common beggar, was a mortification I was loth to submit to; yet this was the only alternative to which I could have recourse; and observing a large house near the wayside, I was determined to

[331]

make my first essay in it. I accordingly fortified my mind with all the resolution possible, to go through the operation, and then made my way into the house. I found the inside of the house elegant and well furnished, and a lady sitting in the front room, who appeared to be the mistress of the house; notwithstanding all the resolution I had mustered on this occasion, I had almost failed of making the attempt of asking for victuals, and had determined once in my own mind to leave the house without mentioning any business which brought me there; but finally I made my request known. My countenance, which was always a strong index to my feelings, I believe at this time betrayed my inward sensations. The lady immediately ordered her servants to set the table; while they were laying the cloth, I perceived the curiosity of such a request, coming from a person genteelly dressed, and whose manners were not of that rough nature as those of common beggars, had raised an anxiety in her mind to know more of my circumstances, and the reason why I was in the situation in which I then appeared. She said, "I presume, sir, you have been unfortunate." I knew the purport of her question, and this question was apparently asked for the purpose of knowing *how* to give relief. To see the immediate promptness with which she sought to relieve me, to see her solicitude to know in what manner she could afford me farther relief than by supplying me with food for the present moment, had divested me of all resolution, had reduced my feelings to a woman's weakness, and it was with difficulty I restrained a shower of tears; so that I was unable to return her any other answer to her question, than "Yes, madam." My feelings had taken such a turn as to divest me of an appetite, which a few minutes before was very great, so that I was unable to make but a sorry meal, from a full table. Her frequent invitations to eat, and anxiety to know if anything else would suit me better, but added to my present exquisite feelings, and it was with the greatest difficulty, I uttered the monosyllable "No." After I had finished my repast, I arose to depart, when she gave me a warm invitation to tarry until Doctor Maxwell came home (who I found was her husband), and he would, she said, endeavor to relieve me from my difficulty; but finding I did not incline to tarry, she desired me to stop a moment, and immediately fetched from another room two dollars and half of a French crown, with a desire that I would accept them, adding,

[332]

she was sorry it was out of her power of doing more, by the Doctor's being absent. This was too much for my resolution to support. The tears, which had for a long time been restrained, now found free vent, in spite of every effort to the contrary. I was unable to speak: I bowed and retired. Never did a wretch in the hour of danger more fervently pray for his own salvation, than I did for the peace and happiness of this ornament of human nature. Yes, thou lovely image of the God of benevolence! may thy gentle bosom never feel the corroding pang of sorrow, but happiness, exquisite happiness, be thy never failing portion.

I travelled until half after nine o'clock at night, and put up at the house of a gentleman by the name of Black, where I was treated with the utmost hospitality and attention. Here I had recovered my appetite so as to eat a very hearty supper, and the next morning I breakfasted as heartily again. Mr. Black gave me a warm invitation to spend the day with him, which I declined, and calling for my bill, he bid me welcome to the whole, telling me he was happy any time in waiting upon gentlemen at his house, and wished me to call whenever I came that way again. I travelled on from thence without anything further occurring worthy of remark, until I arrived at Chestertown, having money sufficient to pay my expenses thus far. Here again I was reduced to the want of a penny; and knowing I must do something, or give up all further hopes of success, I determined to try my luck among some of the people of eminence in Chestertown, by stating my wants to them, and working upon their philanthropy. I accordingly waited upon Mr. Ferguson, principal of the College in that town, with an account of my circumstances, and to my great satisfaction, he told me he would advance five dollars, if that would be of any service. This gave me an opportunity of taking the stage-wagon again for Baltimore, as my trunk had by this time come on. I accordingly took my leave of this worthy friend to humanity, and set out for Baltimore, where I arrived the same day, and put up at the house of one Stark. Here again I found myself in my common situation (viz.), destitute of money. I found the way in which I had travelled to be the most expensive way of any; and of course, prudence dictated the plan of trying if possible to obtain money sufficient to carry me through my journey, by water, which would be a much cheaper conveyance. I accordingly applied to several merchants, one after another, who had

[333]

connections in New England, to advance me twenty-five dollars, and take a draught for the same upon some of my friends there; but my application was fruitless. After showing that great fondness for knowing all the particulars relating to my situation, which is peculiar to New England characters, they appeared to be satisfied, and calmly told me that it did not comport with their view to help me to any money. I had tried such a number of my countrymen and failed of success, that I almost despaired of obtaining any further supplies, and concluded that here my travels must end; yet one more expedient came into my mind. I had found, as will be perceived by the relation already given, that the native inhabitants of Maryland possessed that noble hospitality which was more conspicuous in them than in any of the people of states in which I had been; I therefore concluded to apply for once to some character who was a native inhabitant of Baltimore. I accordingly waited on Luther Martin, Esq. Attorney-General of the state, who immediately, upon knowing my desire, answered with all that god-like nobleness of humanity, which appears greater than royal pomp, that I should have what money I wanted. This threw me into such a delirium of ecstasy, that I hardly knew what I said or did. He counted me out thirty dollars at my request; and when I came to write an obligation for the same, my whole nervous system was in such a tremor, I could not execute the business. Mr. Martin perceived it, and relieved me by doing it himself. He, to add to his hospitality, politely invited me to dine with him that day, it being then early in the morning, which invitation I accepted. I now considered myself in a situation capable of performing the long wished for, the long sought for object of my desires (viz.), to arrive in Georgia, at the residence of my friend Huntington, where I had no doubt of every necessary assistance, both for present need and future prospects in business. I accordingly applied at the wharves for a vessel bound to Georgia, but found none going short of eight or ten days; this was somewhat of a disappointment, on account of the delay; but supposing I had money sufficient to pay my expenses in town for that length of time, and likewise the passage, I felt tolerably contented. At noon I went and dined with Mr. Martin; but not before I had met with somewhat of a singular accident. Having a little leisure on my hands from the time of making the necessary inquiry for a passage, till noon, I took a stroll through

AN IMPERTINENT QUESTION

the town, in order to take a view of it, and the public buildings in a particular manner. After viewing the market house, church, etc., I went to view the jail. Whilst I was taking a look at it, there came a gallows-looking fellow out of that part of the building, which was occupied as a dwelling house, and in a very imperious tone, demanded my business. The looks of this fellow plainly demonstrated him to be a candidate for a patient of a public executioner. I answered his demand with this reply, "that my curiosity had led me there to take a view of the building, and if I was not transgressing any rules of the place, still wished to gratify my curiosity." He made me no answer, but went into the house, and soon there came out an elderly looking man, genteelly dressed, and politely desired to know if I wished to see the jail. My answer being in the affirmative, he told me he would give me every assistance in pointing out whatever was worth observation. I gratefully accepted his offer, and we took a turn through the jail and garden adjoining, where we took a seat at his desire. Here he entered into a detail of some of the crimes of the prisoners, and among the rest related the adventures of one Davis, who was then in confinement for theft. I asked what sort of a man Davis was for height, looks, etc., and told him I knew a man by that name in the Eastern states, but not of his description, who had left the Eastern for the Southern states. As the time had now elapsed for my being at Mr. Martin's, I told the person who was giving me these lengthy accounts, that being engaged to dine with a gentleman by particular invitation, I felt myself under a necessity of leaving him; but if he would drink anything for his trouble it should be at his service. He requested to know with whom I was going to dine. This question I conceived to be a piece of impertinence, but could not yet think it was designed, and therefore told him. Upon this he told me he was well acquainted with Mr. Martin, and that he would not dine for two hours yet to come, and wished me to sit with him yet longer. This request in such a manner, attended with the circumstance of his impertinent question, made me conclude his company would be no longer gratifying, and I accordingly told him I should not stay any longer. I arose from my seat to go through the house, as that was the only way out of the garden, and he followed me. When I came into the house, and was met by the first person, who accosted me about my business, and he,

[335]

together with the other, caught hold of me, and told me I must stop. At this time there came four more likewise out of the room adjoining. My indignation at this treatment was aroused, and I told them that whatever their prospects might be about abusing and robbing me, they would find to their cost they had the wrong person in tow, and that should their bankrupt circumstances prevent any remedy by civil process, yet a criminal prosecution should teach them to use strangers with common civility. At this, there appeared another character, who styled himself a magistrate, and inquired into my coming there and asking after Davis. I told him if he wished to know the matter for any valuable purpose, I would tell him; but if he wished to be an instrument in carrying on the farce of rascality which had been begun, I felt no disposition to give him an answer. He protested his innocence as relating to any farce, said that this Davis had been apprehended with strong suspicions of his having accomplices, and that therefore it was ordered by the court, to apprehend any person who should come and inquire after him. I then related the circumstances which brought me there, and why I asked concerning Davis; at this the *magistrate* concluded I might be dismissed. After I had departed, and came to reflect upon the farce which had been acted, the humor of the circumstances, and the perfect propriety with which every character had played his part, it raised a laughable disposition in my mind, and dissipated every feeling of revenge which I had before entertained.

The next morning I thought it necessary to look into the state of expenses which would attend any ten days' residence, and accordingly applied for my bill at the tavern, which to my astonishment amounted to three dollars and a half. Finding this to be the case, I concluded it necessary to decamp immediately, while I had any money remaining to carry me away.

Not being able to obtain a water passage, I again betook myself to the stage-wagon, and continued my course to Alexandria in Virginia, without any material occurrence. Here I put up at Wise's tavern, and found that the stage would not travel south from here, for the space of six days, therefore was reduced to the necessity of tarrying that term of time. During this I found my tavern expenses, together with what I had already paid, would swallow up all my money with which I had calculated to reach Georgia. Accordingly I became extremely embar-

[336]

rassed, and began to cast in my mind some way to extricate myself from the difficulty. Matters being thus situated, there came a gentleman into my room, belonging to the back part of Virginia, and offered me a tract of land, containing 25,000 acres. Immediately a thought occurred to my mind, suggested by the impulse of necessity, viz. to get this land into my hands, and with the avails thereof to answer my present necessities, and after a course of time discharge the demand which might occur in consequence of the purchase. I inquired the price at which he held the land. He informed me that he held his land at fourteen pence the acre. Intending to buy so cheap as to be able to sell again upon such terms as to be in a condition to discharge my debt, if such should occur, I replied to this amount, "that being on a journey I did not carry money about me for such an extensive purchase; but if he felt himself willing to take my obligations to become due. one third in three months. one third in six, and one third in nine months, I would take his land at a shilling per acre; and more than that I would not give. After some debate upon the subject, the person (his name is gone from my memory) concluded to embrace my offer, and accordingly writings were made and executed, and I invested with this extensive tract of land upon the credit of my own obligations, none of whom became due short of three months.

CHAPTER XXXI

I NOW felt myself in some measure relieved from my state of penury; but my property was in no measure in the situation which was necessary for my present circumstances. Accordingly I began to cast about in my mind some way to appropriate this property, or at least a part of it, to raise the necessary cash for my journey. Whilst I was under these cogitations I was accosted by a Mr. Patten, (if I remember rightly the name) a Scotch gentleman, for the purchase of my land. and he offered, without hesitation, to give me the same price which I had become obligated for, and to pay me cash in hand.

Cash in hand, of all other offers, was what suited me the best, and I immediately closed with his offer. I made and executed the deed directly, and he counted out four thousand one hundred and sixty-six dollars, and two-thirds.

At this sudden and surprising reverse of fortune, my mind was in a state which I hardly know how to describe. I saw before me a heap of treasure far beyond what I had ever been the possessor of before, even in my most prosperous days. But a moment before I had been at my wit's ends to know how to raise money sufficient to carry me out of Alexandria. Now I saw myself, in my imagination, in possession of an independent fortune. sufficient to support myself and family with economy through life: my heart was fascinated with the prospect of being able immediately to return and relieve my family. I concluded upon this measure, and bid farewell to Georgia. I immediately applied to the stage office for a seat to Baltimore, and whilst I was taking my money from my pocket to pay for a seat in the stage wagon, it suddenly rushed into my mind, for the first time, that all the money which I then possessed would soon become due to the person of whom I bought the land. This thought dashed all my prospects in a moment, and I suffered the infinite mortification of finding all my animating hopes of returning to my family, blasted in a moment.

A VICTIM OF ROBBERY

I withdrew my hand from my pocket, made some excuse for not taking the seat in the stage, and returned to my lodgings. Here I endeavored to call my thoughts together and adjust my pursuit to my situation. A thought soon occurred of speculating upon my own paper. I therefore repaired to the man of whom I bought the land, and after some preliminary discourse, told him that I would pay him immediately, providing he would make me a handsome allowance. He finally agreed to allow me a discount of one hundred and fifty dollars upon my notes, and I accordingly paid him the money.

Finding myself now in possession of nearly one hundred and fifty dollars, I again began my journey southward. In travelling through Virginia, I uniformly met with that polite attention from the gentlemen of the country, for which they are so remarkable, and which renders their society so extremely pleasing. Nothing of unusual moment occurring whilst I was on my journey through this state, I shall not detain your attention with the relation of common events.

In passing through North Carolina, I put up for the night at the house of one Smead, on the banks of the Neus River. Being about to depart the next morning, I discovered my trunk broken open, and on examination, found a bundle of fine clothes taken out, and with it one hundred and ten dollars, it being all my money, excepting two or three dollars which I had in my pocket. I tried all measures for the recovery of my money, which offered any prospect of succeeding. The Supreme Court then sitting in Wilmington, I laid the matter before Judges Ash and M'Lay, but found no circumstance of alleviation from any measures which I took. I was again reduced to very deplorable circumstances, and did not know what further to do. My case was generally known. Yet no man offered to assist me in any measure, until a young gentleman, by the name of Huntington, and another by the name of Bowen (a clergyman), gave me sufficient to discharge my tavern bill at Wilmington, which in the course of twenty hours had amounted to the enormous sum of three pounds ten shillings. The name of this conscientious landlord was Dawsy.

I contracted with the skipper of a coasting sloop to fetch me to Charleston, in South Carolina, for four dollars, and put my trunk into his hands as a security until I should pay him the money. We arrived soon at Charleston, and being partially acquainted with a Mr.

[339]

Thayer, merchant, I applied to him, and he humanely assisted me to go on to Georgia.

When I entered Washington it was evening, and I looked with eager desire to behold some situation resembling such as my fancy had pictured in my own mind for my friend Huntington's. My soul was attuned to the soft harmony and tender touches of friendship. I had pictured in my mind a thousand tender expressions and pleasing observations, after meeting once again, which would mutually pass between us. Eight years had elapsed since we had seen each other. We both had passed through many unusual and trying scenes during that period. We had both a great store of amusement for each other in the relation of our adventures, more particularly those where the feelings of the heart were deeply interested. And what greater pleasure can exist than granting pleasure to our friend? I now fancied the end of my trying pilgrimage had arrived, and that I should here find a resting place from further trouble. I eagerly inquired of the first man I saw for a direction to the house of Mr. Huntington. I was informed that Mr. Huntington did not live in Washington, that his family had gone to the New England states, and that he was in South Carolina, or else gone on to the northward after them.

This information was like the sentence of death. My blood revolved back to my heart in death-like chills, and I saw nothing but destruction staring me full in the face; a total and absolute stranger, not so much as knowing a single character in this state from hearsay; again become destitute of money, and what further to do, or where to go, I was totally at a loss. In the room of making a sudden establishment for my family in this country, I saw no prospect of providing for my own bare necessities.

By this time you will begin to think that I was the sport and plaything of fortune, and that she delighted in tantalizing me with false hopes in order to see how great was my fortitude to endure disappointment. However, as Esop says in the fable of the frogs, "It might be play to her, but it was death to me."

I put up for the night at the house of our friend Terondet, and ruminated on my situation, and upon my plan of operation for the future. I arose in the morning and began to inquire of my landlord into the nature and situation of the country, and the prospect of obtaining business. I learned in the course of inquiry that the academy in this town was destitute of a Rector, and that General Williamson was Principal of the commissioners superintending the academical affairs. To him I therefore applied, and introduced myself as a person wishing for business, and offered to act in the capacity of Rector of the academy.

The General asked whether I had any credentials by which I could show my ability as a Rector, so as to ensure his confidence. I answered in the affirmative, and said if he would give me an opportunity I would exhibit them. At this answer the General looked me in the face as though he was waiting for a further explanation, not yet understanding fully the meaning of my reply. I then observed that my credentials were in my head, and that I wanted the opportunity of one fortnight as Rector of the academy to give him the satisfaction which he desired. The General seemed diverted with this reply, but still was desirous for further information upon the subject. I then stated to him in order the situation I was under, and the disappointment I had met with on account of not finding Mr. Huntington, with whom I was particularly acquainted.

This account gave entire satisfaction; and I was placed immediately at the head of the academy, where I have flattered myself I have exhibited the promised credentials.

I began my business under such circumstances as would naturally lead me to strong exertions, in order to appear with some degree of reputation at the head of this academy. I spared no pains to effect such a purpose, and soon brought my school into a state of order sufficient to ensure a rapid progress in literary improvement. My prospects for such a purpose were not at first view of the flattering kind. I found the children who frequented my school generally under the care of rich parents, educated without order, system or discipline; accustomed to the most unlimited gratification of their passions and appetites, without any idea of subordination, but on the contrary indulged in the constant exercise of authority over the blacks. Notwithstanding these discouraging circumstances, I succeeded in my undertaking beyond my most sanguine expectations. My school increased apace, and fortune for one moment was willing to smile on my endeavors. I received the co-operation of the leading characters of the place in the establishment of my academic discipline, together with the decided approbation of the board of commissioners, who held the funds of the academy, and superintended its general concerns.

In order to give you some general idea of the state of literature, customs and manners through this state, I will describe the several characters who composed the board of commissioners, as a specimen, which will answer for a tolerable description of the people through the state.

General Williamson was their president, a man by nature endowed with strong mental powers, bold, enterprising and ambitious. His education was small, his mind was uncultivated, and his opportunities for information in the circles of refinement were very much circumscribed; notwithstanding, from a very low beginning he made his way merely by the strength of native genius, to opulence and respectability among his countrymen. He had been a famous partisan leader during the revolutionary war, where the contest had been managed between the Whigs and Tories, much after the manner of the Indians, in whose neighborhood the chief scenes of slaughter and bloodshed were exhibited. From these circumstances the General had imbibed the temper of the natives in many respects. Strong in friendship, even to seek the life of his friend's enemy; implacable in his resentments; patient, persevering and enterprising. Fond of his own family to extravagance, and very desirous to fit them for public service and usefulness. His family did not disappoint the warm expectations of their fond parent. His oldest son, Charles, was fast following his father in the career of military fame, and now held the commission of colonel, with much reputation; his second, Micajah, was a major; and his third, Peter, was a practising attorney. His oldest daughter was married to General John Clerk; his second to John Griffin. Esq. an attorney, concerning whom more will soon be said; his third, to Doctor Bird; all these daughters were characters of very amiable manners, who would have done honor to a drawing room, in the politest circles.

John Griffin, Esq. was the second commissioner of this board. He was a man of handsome, though not great abilities. His education had been barely sufficient for his practice at the bar. He was master of but a very partial share of knowledge in the liberal arts and sciences. He was endowed with industry and enterprise; fond of insinuating himself into the affections of people by flattery, for effecting which, he had considerable abilities, and in return he lent a very willing ear to the flatterer. He was hospitable, humane, and benevolent, and very attentive to measures of public benefit. He had begun his career at the lowest state of poverty and obscurity, and by the mere dint of perseverance, had surmounted all obstacles, and raised himself to notice and esteem. Colonel Willis held the third place among the commissioners. He formerly represented the state of Georgia in the federal Congress. He was a man of an amiable heart, of the most friendly and benevolent disposition, but somewhat versatile in his pursuits, and not the most accurate economical calculator. Doctor Rustin was an automaton in this and every other society. Mr. Terondet, a Frenchman by birth, who bore the character of a good honest thriving man, without any other recommendations or disqualifications which were calculated to claim the attention of mankind.

I received an invitation from General Williamson to make my abode with him, having three of his children under my care.

I had not long resided in this town before I began to learn the leading objects of the principal characters inhabiting this state. I found a rage for land speculation, which absorbed the attention of all classes. This in the first instance had been a business conducted upon a fair scale, and attended with vast profit: at that stage it was managed by a few; but at length the business, from which such great profit being derived, becoming known, all were seized with the mania of rushing suddenly into immense wealth, and the most nefarious schemes were put in practice to defraud a credulous world with the idea of becoming interested in the excellent soil of Georgia lands. Corruption had proceeded so far as to produce an open and notorious violation of all the public offices established for the regulation of the sale of ungranted lands. Hence, millions of acres, which never had existence, were sold in the other states, and to foreigners; and millions more were sold many times over by the same person. Such iniquity could not remain long undiscovered; strangers in some measure became acquainted with the frauds of Georgia, and of course the profits of these speculations ceased.

The greatest part of the state of Georgia remained yet uninhabited, and under the Indian claims. This tract of land extended the distance of four hundred and fifty miles west, to the Mississippi river, and contained the most fertile soil in the southern states. A scheme was concerted by a number, who formed themselves into companies for the purpose, to purchase the pre-emption of the state to the greater part of these lands. General Gunn, Senator in the Federal Congress, was the leading character of these companies. This association produced a counter combination among a number of others, at the head of whom was Mr. Few, former member of Congress from this state, and quondam Governor. The purport of this association was to outbid or otherwise gain the purchase of this land to themselves, from the other companies.

At the sitting of the Legislature in Augusta, the town was crowded with characters who were interested in this business. The spirit of the two parties had become warm and animated, and all the arts of intrigue, corruption and venality were put in practice by both parties to carry their favorite point. Gunn and his associates were ultimately successful, to the great mortification and resentment of the others. This was a signal of alarm which aroused the individual inhabitants of the whole state to take an active part in the contest. The triumphant party were not anxious to carry their animosities to any greater length against their opponents. They had gained the prize, and were willing that the disappointed party should console themselves by bitter invectives and murmurs. Gunn and his party obtained grants from the state to the amount of twenty-two millions of acres of a most fertile and pleasant country.

The exertions of the disappointed party produced an effect, perhaps never before known under any government. They bestirred themselves so effectually as to obtain a very decided majority of members of the legislature at the next election, a year after the grant was made to Gunn and others, and to the astonishment of all mankind, they rescinded the act of the former Legislature, erased it from their records, and declared it to be null and void; notwithstanding the grantees had actually paid the purchase money long before into the state treasury, and had disposed of much of their lands to various characters through the union.

This session of the Legislature assumed judiciary powers, examined witnesses concerning the means of obtaining the grant, and proceeded

[344]

to declare, that the grantees had obtained their grants by bribery and corruption, and that of course the grants were null and void.

However, to return from this digression, I found my school increase apace, and some of the best geniuses were discovered in this academy that ever fell under my instruction, particularly a daughter of General Williamson, of the age of fifteen. The brilliancy of her wit, the strength of her mind, and the amiable disposition of her heart, were objects of the most pleasing kind.

I found parents and children equally gratified at the general emulation and rapid advances which were made in literature by the members of this academy; and youth from distant parts were sent to this institution, as offering the fairest prospect of education of any in the Southern states. Thus were my affairs situated at the expiration of eight months from the time of my commencing my school in this town. My time ran smoothly on; and, had it not been for that corroding anxiety which constantly preyed on my mind, about the welfare of my family, I might have enjoyed pleasure here without interruption; but that single circumstance embittered my days, and rendered my nights sleepless and insupportable. There ever has been a weakness in my resolution and manly fortitude, when brought into collision with this object, which has ever failed me. I could not compose my feelings in any manner, so as to make them tolerable, when the misery of my family was the subject of reflection. Being actuated by these impressions, I accepted an offer which exhibited flattering hopes of realizing more speedily a sufficiency of money to send for my family to this place. The land speculation (the rage of the day) offered to my imagination the animating prospect of speedy affluence. I therefore engaged in it. It was necessary, in order to carry this purpose into effect, in the first place to submit to a series of hardships and self denial. In the capacity of surveyor I traversed those parts of Georgia which were yet in the possession of the natives. My business carried me through the different nations of the Creeks, the Choctaw, and the Chickesaw Indians. When arrived among them, I was astonished to find the state of improvement to which they had arrived, particularly the Creek Indians. They dwelt in buildings of a permanent construction; they cultivated extensive fields of corn and rice; they understood the use of the plough equal to the whites, and could draw from the extraordinary luxuriancy of the soil stores of provisions capable of lasting them many years. They exercised a degree of urbanity, hospitality and benevolence towards all strangers who visited them, which ought to make the civilized part of mankind blush at the comparison. In fact, were it not for the name of civilized people, for the prejudices of education, and for the generally received opinion of Indian barbarity, I should have believed that the native savages of this country had, by some means, found the real state of civil happiness, and were not destitute of those enjoyments which the whites were willing, and did abundantly boast, were in their own exclusive possession. Here the weary traveller found rest and refreshment; the unfortunate found protection, and the poor found a ready and willing supply for his wants. From this circumstance, many blacks fled from their slavery among the whites, and found a secure asylum among the Indians. This, together with many other circumstances, caused the white people of the state of Georgia to make encroachments, and commit depredations upon the Indians of their neighborhood. These were revenged by the death of the whites, without discrimination. From circumstances like these, the relative situation of the two countries towards each other was very unhappy. Much danger attended an intercourse with them at that moment. Yet, for the sake of acquiring wealth with certainty and dispatch, I ventured on the hazardous task, and finally proved successful, even beyond my most sanguine expectations. I found the Indians extremely jealous of my designs when I first came among them, and had actually concluded, in a council of the nation, to put me to death, under a full belief of my coming among them as a spy, in order to explore their country, and be in a situation to lead the white people among them to destroy their nation. However, this information I did not obtain until all the danger was over. Their jealousy was soon allayed, and from suspicion they proceeded to the contrary extreme of friendship. They rendered me every assistance in completing my survey, and in forwarding all my designs; so that, to the astonishment and gratification of my friends, I returned much sooner, and effected my survey much more accurately, than was at first expected.

This land business was intimately connected with concerns in which Robert Morris, Esq. of Philadelphia, was particularly interested; and, as the whole proceeds of the survey were to go to him before I could receive my part, it was agreed by his agent in Georgia that I should have an establishment on the island of St. Simons, at the mouth of the river Altamaha, where Morris owned a very extensive property, and was calculating to establish business to a great amount. To this place therefore I bent my course, and reached it without delay. Here I viewed my unstable and fluctuating situation coming to an end. The island on which I was to take up my permanent residence was pleasant in the extreme. My business here was to be lucrative and permanent. I had already acquired a property which would be abundantly sufficient to defray the expenses of removing my family to this country, and support them with a decent competency afterwards. Having made arrangements for their removal, I set about preparing accommodations for their reception, by procuring materials and employing workmen to repair and fit up an elegant large brick building for their abode, making every exertion to forward the business, being animated with the grateful expectation of seeing myself soon provided with a situation to which I could transport my family, and make them happy.

Such was my situation on the island of St. Simons when I received directions from Mr. Morris to repair immediately to Philadelphia, and bring the books with me which related to the concern of the business there. I immediately obeyed this summons, made ready the full description of the business in this place, and hastened to Philadelphia. When I arrived there, I found Mr. Morris, Gen. Nicholson and Mr. Swanwick were closing a concern which had existed for some time between them, and my attendance with the books was necessary for this arrangement. The parties concerned were much pleased with my attention to their business whilst I was at St. Simons, and the accuracy with which I had exhibited my accounts of the concern, considering the short time I had to effect the business. This circumstance opened a new field for my enterprise, by an offer I had from these gentlemen of undertaking a voyage into the Western world, in order to establish an extensive fur trade with the different tribes of Indians. Very extensive views were entertained of establishing a trade, by a mercantile company, which should command the attention of the different tribes of Indians to the Gulf of California. To superintend this establishment, and to carry it into effect, was a station which I was to occupy,

[347]

with the prospect of very flattering emoluments. Strange as it may seem, I undertook this difficult, hazardous and tedious business.

For a term of five years I must now be absent, traversing immeasurable wilds and barbarous nations of savages, exposed to the vicissitudes of different climes, different nations, and different resources for the primary aliments of life, shut out from almost any chance to hear from my family and friends during that time. I declare to you, Sir, these considerations many times cast a gloom of despondency on the prospect before me. It is true I had made arrangements to furnish my family with money to answer all their necessities during my absence. Indeed Mr. Morris was so much engaged in having me undertake this business, that he very generously offered to provide for my family gratuitously during my absence, by removing them to Philadelphia, and providing them with all the necessaries and comforts of life.

I have no doubt but you will be astonished at this calculation of mine. I declare to you, Sir, when I look back and view the circumstance myself, I do not do it without producing a degree of surprise at my own views on that subject. After I had obtained a competency for myself and family, by acquiring so much property as to be able to afford them all the comforts of life at least, if not the luxuries; after experiencing one continued series of the most heartfelt chagrin in consequence of my separation from them; at such a time to enter voluntarily into a contract to exile myself from them for the term of five years, at the least calculation, and perhaps forever, is almost an enigma in nature, and perhaps may indicate to your view a species of mental madness. But, Sir, when I took into consideration that I might raise my family, by this voyage, to such a degree of wealth as to enable them to enjoy all the splendor which is attached to riches, in spite of every exertion of my enemies for their destruction, it was an object so fascinating to my imagination that every other consideration fell before it. Thus, Sir, is the history of the human heart exhibited to our view.

Yet all the prospects which I had anticipated finally failed. Mr. Morris, by a concatenation of the most astonishing incidents, became embarrassed, notwithstanding his immense property and unequalled fiscal abilities. Being at the head of the concern which was to carry my Western expedition into effect, his failure so far affected the business, that it was laid by for the present moment, and I placed in a state of uncertainty as to my future operations. I spent the summer much in this manner, waiting the turn of times, to determine my own route. During this time I opened a land office by the advice of the gentlemen before mentioned, and through their influence, and the unwearied exertions which I made, my business increased beyond any expectations which I ever even indulged a hope for in this department. I negotiated at my office, business to a great amount for the principal and most respectable merchants in that city.

But at a moment in which I thought myself established here in the most stable manner, and rapidly rising to affluence, my flattering prospects were in a moment blasted. The Honorable —— ——, from the state of Massachusetts, became acquainted with the circumstance of my residence and business in this city. From the most *benevolent* motives he exhibited my character to the citizens of Philadelphia in the most dismal colors. He exerted himself to draw a picture calculated to please his own fancy, and this picture did not by any means fall short of Milton's fruitful imagination in painting Satan.

At this time I had property in my office to the amount of four hundred thousand dollars. A week had not elapsed before it was all taken from me by the owners, and I was left a solitary spectator of the depredations made by the cruel tongue of slander. I was diverted, however, to hear the various excuses and plausible pretences made by the owners of this property when they called it out of my possession; yet not one had the openness to give me an account of the real motives which actuated his conduct.

Under this situation I formed a resolution to return again to the island of St. Simons, and take my family with me. It was a long time since I had seen them, and the moment I found it possible to revisit them, my heart palpitated with an anxiety totally inexpressible. I collected together all the money I was master of, and hired it to Mr. Morris, at common interest, taking a mortgage upon property in Philadelphia for security, consulting a lawyer by the name of Thomas, my agent, to act for me in this business; receive the quarterly interest of my money, and remit it to me whenever I might need it. I found myself now in possession of thirty thousand dollars, besides a sufficiency to answer my travelling expenses, etc.

You will naturally conclude, that with some degree of eagerness I now hastened my return to my family. The nearer I approached, the more ungovernable was my impatience to overcome the distance, and enjoy once more the grateful scene of giving them every assurance of being able to meet their wishes, and make them a comfortable provision through life. I had previously learnt that they had left the inhospitable shores of Long Island, and had returned to Charlton. I therefore bent my course to that town with unabating assiduity. Here I must close the scene. It is absolutely beyond the power of language to describe our meeting, so as to give you the faintest resemblance.

When I had leisure to state all my circumstances, prospects and views to my wife and friends, particularly to my wife's father, I found they had a decided wish that I should now tarry in the Northern, and relinquish entirely the idea of removing my family into the Southern states. Their wishes and opinions certainly had a decided influence in forming my calculations. I had every reason to feel the strongest sensations of gratitude towards my wife's father for the benevolent attention which he showed to my family during the whole time of my absence; and, of course, I considered myself under great obligations to gratify his wishes in my domestic arrangements, so far as in my power. My situation was such, however, as to render it dangerous to abide in Massachusetts. My enemies could take advantage of my peculiar situation in consequence of my leaving Worcester gaol in the manner I did; and I always found *virtuous* people enough in this state to pursue the most bitter course of unrelenting persecutions against me. This kind of *virago virtue* had pervaded all classes and denominations among them, even from the ploughman to the upright judge, to the governor or to the senator in Congress.

Under considerations like these, I determined on a visit to my father, in Hanover, in the state of New Hampshire, to see what prospects might present themselves in that part of the world, for an establishment. When I came to relate to him the whole situation of my affairs, and my intentions, he manifested much anxiety that I should now, after so many vicissitudes and fluctuating scenes of life, settle down with him, and spend the rest of my days in superintending and man-

[350]

aging his concerns, inasmuch as he had advanced far into the vale of life, and I was the only son he had to perform this filial office. After consulting with my friends in Charlton, I finally determined to comply with the united importunity and wishes of my parents. I accordingly brought my family to Hanover, and enjoyed, for a term of about three years, a degree of happiness with them, and with my parents and their friends, beyond description. Fortune appeared for a time willing to make me amends for her ungenerous conduct, and the fickle and faithless goddess promised much more than she performed. She now held out to my fond imagination, the final end of my sufferings, and a total close to all my wandering and fluctuating circumstances.

About this time I received a letter from my agent in Philadelphia, informing me that the power of attorney under which he acted was so circumscribed as to render him unable to transact my business to my advantage, and that it was necessary to execute one which he had sent me, and forward it to him immediately by mail. Having the most absolute confidence in the integrity of my agent, I did not hesitate one moment to comply with his desires, executed the power, and sent it on forthwith. However, this was a fatal stroke to my fortune. By virtue of the power he sold my security in Philadelphia, realized the money, and fled to France.

I will now present you with a course of letters which have passed between me and my friends since I left the state of New York.

"*Charlton, Sept.* 10, 1794.

"To Mr. WILLIAM HALSEY, BRIDGHAMPTON.

"SIR,

"According to our arrangements, I embrace the first opportunity of giving you information of my situation, that you may communicate the same to Mr. Burroughs as soon as you can gain intelligence of the place of his residence.

"My father has made comfortable provision for me and my children, in a house adjoining to my brother-in-law, who keeps a store of general assortments, to which I have access without restraint, on my father's account.

[351]

"My friends treat me with attention and pity, without any of that gall of bitterness which is apt to attend on one in dependent circumstances.

"Application has been made by Mr. Burroughs' parents to have my oldest child, Edward, live with them. I expect he will set out from here for such a purpose, next week.

"My mind is filled with constant anxiety on the account of Mr. Burroughs. I have heard nothing from him since I left Long Island upon which I can depend. Many reports are prevailing here of the most disagreeable kind, respecting him. Some say he is in the prison of New York, and some say he is not in prison, but spending his time in rioting and drunkenness, without any attention to me or his family.

"Probably it is thought that these reports may gain a standing in my mind, and cause me much pain. But those who suggest them are not so well acquainted with facts as they ought to be, or else they would never harbor or surmise such disagreeable ideas.

"You won't wonder at my feeling disagreeable when you take into consideration, that our separation was produced by the blackest malice of a few who call themselves the children of God, but to others it appeared that they were the children of the devil, whose ready service they performed.

"You may think my expressions uncharitable, possibly; but, sir, consider I am wounded in a tender point, and consider this is a truth which I have felt with the liveliest sensations. To be separated in such a manner from a kind and tender husband; to see him banished from his family, thrown out again into the open world in a state of the most destitute poverty, exposed to difficulties in every shape. May truth be his guide through every scene. These things present to our view this picture of human nature, viz. feeble in itself, liable to so many casualties; tortured with so many pains; visited by so many maladies; crazed with so many cares; worn down by so many sorrows; so dependent on others for succor, relief and consolation: but truth possesses the power to revive, improve and mature the feelings of humanity. The spirit of truth is a spirit of commiseration and charity, therefore let selfishness be done away; let benevolence be cultivated, let truth, pure and undefiled, be maintained, and we need not fear but ministering angels will be found in every clime, who, under

[352]

the influence of truth, will wipe away tears, assuage pain, and hand the cup of consolation to the broken-hearted. I remain your humble servant in esteem,

"SALLY BURROUGHS."

"To the Rev. EDEN BURROUGHS.

"Charlton, June 16th, 1794.

"DEAR BROTHER,

"I received a letter from Sally, by a messenger from Long Island, dated the 9th inst. by which I understood that the difficulties prevailing at the time of our being there had increased to such a degree as to destroy the prospect of your son's supporting his family in that place, and accordingly he left there about one month since, for Georgia, and does not expect to return to live on the island any more. He had to leave his family destitute of money or provision, and his wife near being confined in childbed illness. She was under the necessity of applying to the overseers of the poor for relief. She is desirous of returning from the island, as she is uncertain when her husband will be able to assist her, or move her away. I shall go next week to fetch her and children to Charlton. I thought it probable you might wish to have one of the little boys live with you; for should your son ever get into such circumstances to the southward as to send for his wife, I think it would be imprudent to move the children into that unhealthy climate. I wish you would write to me on the subject. I remain your affectionate brother,

"EBENEZER DAVIS."

"To Mr. STEPHEN BURROUGHS.

"Bridghampton, June 9th, 1794.

"DEAR SIR,

"You will undoubtedly wish to know my situation by the first opportunity, and therefore I shall not neglect this, although it may be, you may never receive this letter, for I do not altogether depend on the certainty of its conveyance. Our youngest child, which is a daughter, was born on the 4th of May, and is well; the rest of the family

[353]

in usual health, myself excepted, being something out of health through a state of debility. I have heard nothing from our relations in Charlton since you left me. I made application to Esq. Rogers, the overseer of the poor, and he contributed to my relief, but soon the two engines of cruelty, Hurlbut and Pierson, commenced their attacks upon Mr. Elias Halsey, and have demanded security of him for all the costs arising from my maintenance, together with that of the children, on account of his being the first who rented us a house without giving due notice to the overseers of the poor. Mr. Halsey is totally ignorant of what measures to take in this business, and the two justices say that they will positively have him carried to jail to-morrow if he don't comply with their demand. The business has come to that crisis that I see no other way but to return to my friends at Charlton, for nothing will answer the demands of the two justices against Mr. Halsey but my removal. It is like death to me to be under the necessity of returning and to be treated as I shall by my relations. I had rather work like a slave for my own and children's support, therefore I beg you would make the time as short as possible before you come or send after me, and not think of revenging the injuries you have suffered, by that which will bring the calamity on me and the children. My blood runs cold to think what I yet have got to pass through! I cannot rest, by night or day; my trouble almost bereaves me of my senses. My little boys both stand by and ask what mamma cries so much for, and wish daddy would come home. Poor children, they little know the afflictions of their parents. I beg of you not to wait for a state of affluence before you send for me. A state of poverty is much more tolerable, than living without where I am going. Make it your own case, my dear, and often read this that you may not forget, for one day, that you have a wife and children, who long to see you and live with you. My head is in such confusion that I hardly know what I write, but let me once more remind you to make the time as short as possible before you provide me with a home, where we may both live together. Let me entreat you by the ties of love and friendship, by the tender feelings of a parent, to shorten our affliction as much as possible.

"I feel great anxiety on account of your health. The climate to which you have bent your course is so unsalutary, and your constitu-

[354]

tion so broken and worn down with sickness and misfortune, that I tremble for the event.

"22d. Since I wrote the above I have heard from my father. He is coming to move me back to Charlton. On Wednesday next he will be here. What a meeting shall we have! God only knows my feelings on this occasion. I wish you would not delay one moment to write after you have received this. I should rest much easier, could I hear from you but one word. I scarce know how to end my letter. There seems to be a kind of melancholy pleasure in writing to you, although it is uncertain whether you ever receive the letter. I am much more out of health than when I began the letter. A universal debility, accompanied with night sweats, attends me constantly. The rest of the family are well, the infant excepted, which is extremely restless and unquiet. I remain, dear sir, your loving and affectionate wife,

"SALLY BURROUGHS."

"To the Rev. EDEN BURROUGHS.

"*Sept. 28th,* 1794.

"HONORED AND DEAR SIR,

"I have made a number of trials to communicate letters to you, but not receiving any answer, I presume they have failed. This day being in the post office and looking over the books, I there saw Hanover made a post town, therefore am writing this letter to lodge in the office in this place, expecting it will go to you immediately.

"How my leaving the state of New York for Georgia appears to your view, I cannot even conjecture; but when you come to be informed that the cruel persecution, which I suffered when you were in that state, increased to such a degree as to ruin my circumstances and reduce me to poverty; under this situation you will not wonder at my wishing for a peaceable retreat from such a storm, that I might provide for my family a comfortable subsistence.

"During my journey to this country, I met with a variety of incidents as is usual for me, and some of them of a peculiar nature; yet they are now past and gone, and only leave an impression on my mind faint as the dreams of the night. My present situation is easy and agreeable, one circumstance excepted, viz. the separation from my fam-

[355]

ily. I have heard nothing from them since I left Long Island. I shudder with horror to think of their situation. I beg you to afford them what assistance you can, until I can obtain a situation to grant them relief myself, which I hope will not be long.

"Huntington is gone! forever gone! He died in Charleston, South Carolina, of a putrid fever. I was informed that he resigned himself to his approaching fate, of which he was sensible sometime before his dissolution, with fortitude and calmness. 'Death lets down the curtain, and the play is ended.'

"I saw Mr. Niles in Philadelphia, the particulars of which he has undoubtedly stated to you, long before this. I remain with sentiments of duty, your affectionate son,

"STEPHEN BURROUGHS."

"To Mr. STEPHEN BURROUGHS.

"*Hanover* (*New Hampshire*), *Dec.* 31, 1794.

"DEAR CHILD,

"A few days ago I received yours, bearing date on the 28th September, which is the only letter that has come to hand since your departure from the Northern states.

"The care of your family being undoubtedly the object that is uppermost in your mind, I will inform you what I know concerning them, without holding you in suspense by saying any more previous to such information. Your eldest son is at my house, and has resided with me for about three months. He has the privilege of a school, which he constantly attends. He appears to make good proficiency in learning. I find him to be a pleasant and promising child, and should be highly pleased at keeping him with me until he arrives to a state of manhood if such a thing might comport with your pleasure.

"Your spouse now resides with her family in Charlton. Her father, upon hearing of her straitened circumstances on the island, went and moved her, and made comfortable provision for her near by. The last news from thence was, that she and family were well.

"It has ever been a matter of speculation and surprise to us, that Divine Providence has opened such a door among strangers, and in such a distant part, for your being useful to mankind and of advantage

[356]

to yourself. The voice contained in such a providence is, in my view, like the intercession which the dresser of the vineyard made in behalf of the barren fig tree, 'Lord, let it alone this year, till I shall dig about it and dung it.'

"The bowels of a father, and the piercing affections of a mother do yet constrain us to entreat you to keep this ever in view, that after all the trouble and anguish which you have undergone, and which we have suffered on your account, we may in the decline of our days be comforted with the tidings, that you have learned wisdom and obedience to the calls of your Divine Master, who commands you to give up all for his sake. It is our heart's desire and prayer to God, that in the whole of your pursuits you daily remember that one thing is needful, and that this is life eternal to know the only true God. and Jesus Christ whom he has sent.

"I forgot to mention in its proper place, that in due time after you left Long Island, a daughter was born unto you, who is well. Upon your informing that you saw Mr. Niles in Philadelphia, I felt surprised he had not mentioned it to me at Commencement, which is the only time I have had an interview with him in the interval of his being absent from Congress. In your letters from Georgia, it will be acceptable to have you pay particular attention to an account of everything noticeable in the country, as soil, climate, productions, and especially the manners of the people, and whether there be anything that looks like religion among them. It would likewise be highly gratifying to have an account of your own sentiments upon the subject of religion. I am sensible you have been under a temptation to conclude that there is nothing in religion, from the treatment you have received from its professors. You know it has been my established sentiment for these many years, that we ought not to form an estimate of religion from its professors. Let them dishonor this glorious cause ever so much, they cannot diminish the importance of it. We shall one day stand convicted, that if a man should gain the whole world and lose his own soul, it would profit him nothing. We shall wait with much longing desire till we receive another letter from you; meanwhile we rest your affectionate parents,

"E. and A. BURROUGHS."

[357]

MEMOIRS OF STEPHEN BURROUGHS

"To the Rev. EDEN BURROUGHS.

"*Augusta, Feb. 24th,* 1795.

"HONORED AND DEAR PARENTS,

"Yours of the 31st December came safe to hand yesterday, and with the most heartfelt satisfaction I obtained information for the first time, from my unfortunate family. The hard hand of misfortune has compelled me to pass through difficulties unparalleled in the history of man; yet among all my misfortunes, none so intolerable as the separation from my family, and more especially my separation at such a juncture. God of nature, what a prospect!

"When I heard they were comfortable, and settled in an agreeable situation by Mrs. Burroughs' father, the weight of a mountain was removed from my mind, and I felt an ardor of gratitude to my father-in-law beyond description, and if I had the riches of India, I would have poured them into his possession. I have left the academy in Washington, and am bound to a town called Frederica, on the island of St. Simons, to do business for a company of merchants in Philadelphia. The prospect in this line is more flattering, as it offers a more immediate establishment for my family.

"In obedience to your desire, I should write the particulars relating to things worthy of notice in this country, but as I have kept a journal of all the particulars of my travels, incorporated with remarks upon every subject worthy of notice, which came under my view, I have determined to send you the journal as soon as an opportunity for a conveyance offers. This will give a more extensive view of the subject than is possible to do by letter.

"The religion of Georgia consists in every man's doing that which is right in his own eyes. Dissipation and licentiousness reign here triumphant. This is the worst side of the character of the Georgians. They are hospitable, humane and courteous in the extreme. As to my own sentiments of religion, you may find them comprised in the following line from Pope: 'An honest man's the noblest work of God'; and this honesty consists in following the law of our own mind, without depending on the dogmas of others. I remain, with sentiments of filial affection, your dutiful son,

"S. BURROUGHS."

[358]

A SCENE OF FLUCTUATION

"To the Rev. EDEN BURROUGHS.

"*Philadelphia, May 23d, 1795.*

"HONORED AND DEAR PARENTS,

"I have been in this city for the space of six weeks. I have not written to you, owing to the daily uncertainty of the time when I should leave here. It is now determined that I shall spend the summer in this place; I therefore hasten to give you what information relating to my prospects and present situation is in my power to communicate. I shall leave here early in the fall for the province of Louisiana. If possible I shall make a visit to my family before my departure; however, it is yet problematical whether I shall be able to effect such a desirable object.

"I wish that all the information relating to my family, you would communicate to me in the minutest manner. I have not as yet received any intelligence from them, excepting what is conveyed in your letters. I anxiously wish to see my little boy now with you, but God only knows whether I shall ever be gratified. You may think my foolish fondness on this subject, betokens the exercise of little manly reason; however, I console myself under the indulgence of such feelings, with the instance of like conduct in no less a man than Agesilaus, king of Sparta; being caught one day riding a reed with his children, he desired the man to say nothing on the subject until he had become the father of children himself.

"For one moment turn your attention to my present situation. But little more than a year since, I was in this city on my route to Georgia, and under such circumstances as to give the most exquisite pain at taking them into consideration at this time. I have since been at the head of an academy in Georgia with some reputation. I left it to the regret of parents and students. I then entered into business for a company of merchants. This business I performed to their satisfaction, which finally brought me to this city. A new train of events succeeding, I am detained here through the summer, and my course turned to Louisiana. What a scene of fluctuation. My life is, and has been, uniformly irregular. All these things have taken place by unforeseen events, which no human prudence could prevent.

"No man longs more passionately for domestic ease and retirement

[359]

from the bustle of the world, and no man at present appears to be a greater remove from it; for so long as I have a family unprovided for, I must encounter such objects as offer a prospect for such a purpose, and if I at last prove unsuccessful, I shall have this consolation, that I have done all in my power.

"My residence in Louisiana probably will continue a number of years. My first stage will be New Orleans; from thence I shall endeavor to open a channel of communication. With the most unfeigned desire for your felicity, I remain your dutiful son,

"STEPHEN BURROUGHS."

"To Mr. STEPHEN BURROUGHS.

"*Hanover, N. H., June 12th, 1795.*

"DEAR CHILD,

"Yours of the 23d of May is just come to hand; and though an acceptable present, it fills us with concern in relation to your future welfare in life, while it constrains us to view you as a ship tossed on the ocean, with an uncertainty where it will reach the land, or whether it will ever arrive on shore, without being dashed by the surrounding billows, or wrecked on the quicksands. But amidst the pain of our anxiety for you, we are sensible it ever becomes us to leave you to the guidance of the providence of that God, whose kingdom rules over all. If your trust is in him, and your heart is truly waiting on him, you will surely find in the issue, that his name is a strong tower.

"In relation to your family, I believe you have reason to make yourself perfectly easy and quiet respecting their situation. So far as I can learn, their circumstances are as easy as may be expected. We received a letter from your spouse about one month since, intimating comfortable tidings in relation to the health and situation of the family.

"Your little son appears to be of an uncommonly sprightly mind, and makes good progress in learning. It would, beyond all doubt, be exceedingly gratifying to your family to receive a visit from you this summer; it would be peculiarly so to us. But at the same time we cannot refrain to remind you, that your judgment and not your affections ought to govern you in this respect. We ever wish you to

[360]

conduct not only with that integrity, but also with that discretion, economy and prudence, as to render yourself worthy of the confidence of any gentlemen who may have occasion to commit any part of their concerns to your trust and management.

"You will be mindful to improve opportunities to write to us during your continuance in Philadelphia. It will perhaps be the only channel through which your family can gain information from you. When you shall remove into the Spanish dominions, the greater distance will but increase our desires to receive as frequent information from you as you can attend to communicate. Remember that *one* thing is needful: and receive this as a signal of parental regard from your affectionate parents,

"E. and A. BURROUGHS."

"To the Rev. EDEN BURROUGHS.

"Philadelphia, June 23d, 1795.

"HONORED AND DEAR PARENTS,

"Yours of the 12th was handed to me this morning, having been in the city some days, owing to a mistake of its having fallen into the hands of one of the same name living in this city. My situation remains yet permanent, and will probably so continue until October, when I shall again be on the wing of fluctuation. Some things of a public nature have transpired, which, if founded in fact, will have an influence upon my future prospects, viz. Spain, it is said, has entered into a treaty with France, by which they have ceded the province of Lousiana to the French. This information I had from Mr. Adet, the new French ambassador. M. La Count, another diplomatic character, declared that the Mississippi would be laid open to the Americans without restrictions. Should this be the case, a great change in the situation which I shall there occupy will necessarily follow, and the danger to which I should have been subject, in a measure be removed.

"The shafts of malignity are hurled at me with some degree of rancour, by some of my Northern *friends*, who are in this city; yet they have hitherto appeared to prove harmless. How they may operate, is yet in the womb of futurity.

[361]

"Your letter has produced such an effect upon my nervous system, that I can hardly guide a pen, so strange is the effect on my feelings; and this weakness I find daily increasing. I ever fell a sacrifice to too great a degree of sensibility. To hear my family were comfortable; that my little Edward was doing well; to reflect, at the same time, upon my own situation, absent from my family and dearest connections, traversing the immeasurable wilds of my destiny, produced a confused chaos of pleasure, intermixed with the keenest pain, and a something more, that is indescribable. Pray excuse my incoherent method of writing. You will undoubtedly ask why I write at this moment? The only answer I have is, that I am more unhappy in any other situation; it serves to calm the boiling passions of a tumultuated mind. I hear my sister is keeping a school; may she never feel those deathlike stings of remorse, arising from the treatment of an ungrateful world, for whom she has spent her time and strength, as has fallen to the lot of her unhappy brother.

"The probability is, that Congress will be sooner called together, than the time of their adjournment, owing to a treaty between this country and Great Britain. Should such an event take place, I shall undoubtedly see Mr. Niles, by whom I will transmit a more particular detail of my prospects, etc. by going into the Spanish dominions.

"That our times and changes are fixed and unalterable by the everlasting laws of nature, is what I most firmly believe; and therefore to remain quiet under whatever situation we may find ourselves, is a duty no less apparent. To moralize thus is easy, but to reduce it to practice, is truly difficult, when I find the storm of adversity bursting with impending ruin over my head.

"Whether in prosperity or adversity, your welfare lies near my heart, even next to that of my own family. Before I was married, adversity was supportable; but to fill the cup of misery to the brim, that I might drain it to the dregs, I was destined to be connected to a woman worthy of every blessing, and calculated to render me entirely happy; then to be torn from her under the most horrid circumstances of complicated misery; to leave her, together with my darling infants, unprotected in a savage world!!! Adieu.

"S. BURROUGHS."

[362]

A NEW EMPLOYMENT

"To John Griffin, Esq. Washington, Georgia.

"*Hanover, May 20th, 1797.*

"Dear sir,

"I snatch a hasty moment to communicate this one particular, viz. that after tumbling and tumbling, I have tumbled at last into the bosom of my family. I now behold around my fireside, my wife and children, parents and sisters, with pleasure pictured on every countenance. This is a scene at which I tremble when I view it, lest fickle fortune should chance to hear my exultation, from writing long on this subject, and again dash the cup of pleasure, with wormwood and gall. I close, wishing you every degree of happiness.

"Stephen Burroughs."

P. S. The foregoing memoirs were prepared for the press several years ago. It was expected, as they had lain so long on hand, that the author would have made some additions, before the work was published. But as none have been received, and as the public are impatient to see the book, the proprietor of the manuscript thinks it ungenerous to keep them any longer in suspense. And as the reader will naturally inquire, "Where is Burroughs now, and what is he about?" it may be proper in this place to answer that question. Mr. Burroughs has been, for two or three years past, managing a farm, and certain mills, in the town of Stanstead, near the lake Memphremagog, within the bounds of Lower Canada. The mills, etc., belong to his father-in-law, a respectable gentleman of Massachusetts. And it is believed he is entirely satisfied with his son-in-law's conduct in the business. At present, Mr. Burroughs is turning his attention to the study of physic.

The reader is also informed, that the letter in the note, page 273, was written by Judge Havens.

Boston, Jan. 1804.

APPENDIX

IT may be expected that something further should be said of this extraordinary character, who has been the hero of the preceding Memoirs. Little, however, can be learned of his history in this part of the country, unless he himself should take it into his head to publish a third volume, for which undoubtedly he has abundant materials. Of this, however, there is not much prospect at present.

From sometime previous to the date of his last letter, to the spring of 1799, he appears to have lived with his father at Hanover, in great harmony. He had the chief management of the old gentleman's farm, and other temporal concerns. Towards the latter part of this term, they commenced the building of a large house; and like many others who undertake to build, they did not count the cost, and became embarrassed. This caused uneasiness and mutual crimination, which finally ended in an open rupture and separation. During this period of more than three years, the parents seem to have taken great comfort and satisfaction in their son and his rising family. This satisfaction was expressed by his father in various letters to his friends. as well as by his conduct towards his children. He encouraged and assisted his son in the publication of his Memoirs; and maintained that he had a right to justify himself, as far as he was able, before an impartial public. The Reverend Sire had been a member of the Board of Trustees of Dartmouth College, before the son joined that institution; which office he still holds, with credit to himself and the College. He is a man of great benevolence, piety, and zeal; and does honor to his profession. His mother is equally amiable. As a proof of the good understanding between these families, I take the liberty to publish one of the father's letters, received during this period.

"Hanover (N. H.), April 7, 1798.

"MY DEAR SIR,

"The motive of gratitude, under a sense of your kind attention to my son in the matters which he has committed to your care and trust,

[365]

as also your expressions and acts of benevolence to him in scenes through which he has passed in former years, has lain with weight upon my mind; and I have often felt the force of it to such a degree, that to suppress its emotions, I have found to be a work of painful self-denial. Had I felt a confidence that presenting my thanks in this account could have been regarded by you as anything of an adequate return, my warmest professions of gratitude would have waited upon you long before this. In your communications to my son received this day, we are both comforted by the leaven of friendship and benevolence, with which your letters are ever tempered. I am, Sir, especially pleased with your remarks upon the book he has published. I am ever sensible that a *true* friend will be always as *severe* in censuring the failings of his friend, as he would be tender of his character. Your readiness for this is a circumstance that establishes my confidence in you, and cloaths you with a character opposite to the deceitful, unmeaning, vile flatterer. Upon attending to certain queries contained in your letter, I am apprehensive that the laws of delicacy, and perhaps your own satisfaction, would require that an answer to them should be stated by me rather than by him. To give you then a history of my son's present situation, I feel myself in no danger of transgressing the bounds of candor and moderation by informing you, that, during the time he has resided with me (which is about two years and a half) he has conducted to my good acceptance. As an evidence of my confidence in him, I have committed to his care the whole management of my temporal affairs; and have hitherto been well satisfied as to the wisdom, propriety and economy of his management; as also with the dutiful and affectionate temper with which he has attended to and treated his parents. I am confident that in this testimony I speak the established sentiments of our neighborhood and acquaintances as well as my own. I know the benevolence of your heart will constrain you to rejoice with me and on my behalf. I wish, Sir, I might rejoice with that trembling which always becomes a dependant creature. For this purpose, suffer me, my dear Sir, to remind you of a debt we shall ever mutually owe to each other, to ask for that grace which may guard us from every evil, and preserve us in safety to the kingdom of glory. May Mrs. Burroughs' compliments be acceptable to you and your lady, together with those of, Sir, your affectionate friend, and humble servant,

"EDEN BURROUGHS."

About a year after the date of this letter, a sense of propriety and duty obliged the disappointed and dejected father to notify this same friend, that he had lost all confidence in his son; and cautioned him against any further recommendation. This, he says, he is "constrained, though with the utmost grief and sorrow of heart, to do, as an act of justice," etc.

The son soon departed for Canada, as before stated. For several years he gave great encouragement to his friends, that he might still be a useful member of society. But, alas! how have their hopes been blasted! Common fame says, that several of his last years have been assiduously employed in counterfeiting bills of the various banks of the United States; that he has been in prison at Montreal and at Quebec. But it is hazardous to state anything with certainty relative to this extraordinary man. It is not long since, that two of the Cashiers of certain Banks in Boston received each a letter of similar import, signed Stephen Burroughs, stating that he had been a month in that town, engaged with a company of counterfeiters; that several of their own bills had been nicely imitated; but that there was so little *honor* among the concern, he was determined to expose them; and then calls a number of their names, and warns the Banks of their danger. Upon comparing these letters with Burroughs' handwriting, there was no similarity between them!

It is believed that Burroughs resides at present, with his family, at a place called *Shipton*, in Lower Canada.[1] Whether he still continues to labor in the line of his profession, or whether a late law of the Province has checked him in his mad career, is unknown to the writer. [1811.]

---

[1] A correspondent of the publisher informs, that Mr. Burroughs resides at a place called *Three Rivers*, in Lower Canada, and is at present engaged in teaching a school.
[1812.]

[367]

Printed in the United States
98142LV00002B/308/A

9 781417 952908